Saul Kripke

This collection of essays on Saul Kripke and his philosophy is the first and only collection of essays to examine both published and unpublished writings by Kripke. Its essays, written by distinguished philosophers in the field, present a broader picture of Kripke's intellectual life and work than has previously been available to scholars of his thought. New topics covered in these essays include Kripke on vacuous names and names in fiction, Kripke on logicism and *de re* attitudes toward numbers, Kripke on the incoherency of adopting a logic, Kripke on color words and his criticism of the primary versus secondary quality distinction, and Kripke's critique of functionalism. These essays not only present Kripke's basic arguments but also engage with the arguments and controversies engendered by his work, providing the most comprehensive analysis of his philosophy and writings available. This collection will become a classic in contemporary analytic philosophy.

Alan Berger is a professor of philosophy at Brandeis University and a visiting professor at Harvard University. He formerly served as director of the Saul Kripke Center and is the author of *Terms and Truth: Reference Direct and Anaphoric* (2002), *Quine: From a Critical Point of View* (forthcoming), and numerous articles in scholarly journals including the *Journal of Philosophy* and *Nous*.

Saul Kripke

Edited by

ALAN BERGER
Brandeis University

CAMBRIDGE
UNIVERSITY PRESS

CAMBRIDGE UNIVERSITY PRESS

Cambridge, New York, Melbourne, Madrid, Cape Town,
Singapore, São Paulo, Delhi, Tokyo, Mexico City

Cambridge University Press
32 Avenue of the Americas, New York, NY 10013-2473, USA

www.cambridge.org
Information on this title: www.cambridge.org/9780521674980

First published 2011

Printed in the United States of America

A catalog record for this publication is available from the British Library.

Library of Congress Cataloging in Publication data
Saul Kripke / edited by Alan Berger.
p.   cm.
Includes bibliographical references and index.
ISBN 978-0-521-85826-7 (hardback)
1. Kripke, Saul A., 1940–   I. Berger, Alan.   II. Title.
B945.K794S38   2010
191–dc22   2010019542

ISBN 978-0-521-85826-7 Hardback
ISBN 978-0-521-67498-0 Paperback

Contents

List of Contributors

Alan Berger, at Brandeis University, was founding Director of the Saul Kripke Center at CUNY, Visiting Professor at MIT, and is currently Visiting Professor at Harvard University. He is the author of *Terms and Truth: Reference Direct and Anaphoric* (MIT Press) and the forthcoming *Quine: From a Critical Point of View* (Oxford University Press), and the organizer of a conference in honor of Hilary Putnam's 85th birthday, the proceedings of which he will edit for Oxford University Press.

Jeff Buechner is Principal Research Scholar at the Saul Kripke Center (CUNY, The Graduate Center), Director of the Rutgers-Merck Bioethics Institute, and Lecturer in Philosophy at Rutgers University (Newark campus). His book *Gödel, Putnam, and Functionalism: A New Reading of "Representation and Reality"* was published by MIT Press in 2008.

John Burgess has taught at Princeton University since 1975. He has worked mainly in logic and allied areas, and is author or coauthor of the volumes *A Subject with No Object; Computability and Logic; Fixing Frege; Mathematics, Models, and Modality; Philosophical Logic;* and *Truth.*

Mario Gómez-Torrente is a member researcher at the Instituto de Investigaciones Filosóficas of the Universidad Nacional Autónoma de México (UNAM). He has published papers on several topics in the philosophy of logic and the philosophy of language.

Bernard Linsky is Professor of Philosophy at the University of Alberta, Edmonton. He is the author of *Bertrand Russell's Metaphysical Logic* and a book about the second edition of *Principia Mathematica*, forthcoming from Cambridge University Press, and has written on topics in philosophical logic including abstract objects and possibilia. He learned about theories of reference from his father, Leonard Linsky.

Mark Richard is a Professor of Philosophy at Harvard University. He is the author of *Propositional Attitudes* (Cambridge University Press) and *When Truth Gives Out* (Oxford University Press); *Meaning in Context*, a collection of his essays, is forthcoming from Oxford University Press.

Nathan Salmon is Distinguished Professor of Philosophy at the University of California, Santa Barbara. He is the author of *Reference and Essence* (Prometheus) and *Frege's Puzzle* (Ridgeview). Many of his articles are collected in two volumes: *Metaphysics, Mathematics, and Meaning* and *Content, Cognition, and Communication* (both published by Oxford University Press).

Sydney Shoemaker's B.A. is from Reed College and his Ph.D. is from Cornell, where he taught for many years. His books include *Self-Knowledge and Self-Identity*; *Personal Identity* (with Richard Swinburne); *Identity, Cause, and Mind*; *The First-Person Perspective and Other Essays*; and *Physical Realization*. He was John Locke Lecturer at Oxford in 1972, Josiah Royce Lecturer at Brown in 1993, and Whitehead Lecturer at Harvard in 2002.

Scott Soames is Director of the School of Philosophy at the University of Southern California. He is author of *What Is Meaning?*; *Philosophy of Language, Reference and Description*; and *Philosophical Analysis in the 20th Century*, all published by Princeton University Press, and *Beyond Rigidity* and *Understanding Truth*, published by Oxford University Press.

Robert Stalnaker received his Ph.D. in Philosophy at Princeton University in 1965 and is now the Laurance S. Rockefeller Professor of Philosophy at the Massachusetts Institute of Technology. His most recent book, *Our Knowledge of the Internal World* (Oxford University Press, 2008), is based on his John Locke lectures, given at Oxford in 2007.

Mark Steiner received his Ph.D. at Princeton University under Paul Benacerraf. He taught at Columbia University from 1970 to 1977; since 1977, he has taught at the Hebrew University of Jerusalem, where he has been Chair of the Philosophy Department. He is the author of *Mathematical Knowledge* (Cornell University Press, 1974), *The Applicability of Mathematics as a Philosophical Problem* (Harvard University Press, 1998), and articles on the philosophy of mathematics and other topics. He has translated works of philosophy by the self-taught genius Rabbi Reuven Agushewitz from Yiddish to English and is working on a translation of Hume's *Treatise* into Hebrew.

George Wilson is Professor of Philosophy at the University of Southern California. He also taught at the University of California at Davis and Johns Hopkins University. He is the author of a book on film aesthetics (*Narration in Light*, 1986), a book on the theory of action (*The Intentionality of Human Action*, 1989), and articles on various philosophical topics. He has a new book on film, *Seeing Fictions in Film*, forthcoming from Oxford University Press.

Introduction to Kripke

Alan Berger

Kripke's professional career began as a high school student when he published his early pioneering work in logic on the semantics and completeness proofs of the normal and non-normal modal systems. Not much later, his seminal work on "Semantical Analysis of Intuitionistic Logic" appeared. Shortly after that came his founding of transfinite recursion theory with his two classic papers, "Transfinite Recursions on Admissible Ordinals" and "Admissible Ordinals and the Analytic Hierarchy." Had he accomplished nothing else in his intellectual life, Kripke would have already earned his claim to fame.

But his thoughts in what turned out to be his greatest area of accomplishment, philosophy, were just beginning to gel. Already as a college student he had the basic ideas of his classic seminal work, *Naming and Necessity*, which was to revolutionize the field of philosophy. The work revealed what has become a hallmark of Kripke: his conceptual clarity par excellence. While continuing to develop his ideas in mathematical logic, he developed many important thoughts in philosophy. His work on a new theory of truth for dealing with the Epimenides paradox (the semantical paradox of the liar), on a puzzle about belief, and on his novel interpretation of Wittgenstein on rules and private language have dominated discussion and generated an industry on these topics.

Today, Kripke's accomplishments span several areas of philosophy, including epistemology; metaphysics; and philosophy of language, logic, mathematics, and mind; as well as areas of mathematical logic and more recently of linguistics as well. His work has also extended to important scholarship in the history of twentieth-century philosophy and in the history of logic and set theory.

In his first seminal work in philosophy, *Naming and Necessity*, Kripke discusses his historical predecessors, Mill, Frege, and Russell, and continues the debate regarding the meaning of proper names and general names and their relation to determining the reference of these terms. He defends a view of the reference of these terms akin to Mill's over the then-dominant view of Frege and Russell, but adds a new "picture" of how these terms have their reference determined. This so-called new theory of reference (which is now more than forty years old and should more properly be called "the new received view of reference") replaced the Frege and Russell received view of reference. This Kripkean picture has done much to change our thinking about meaning and reference and the connection between these notions.

Kripke makes perhaps an even greater philosophical impact in *Naming and Necessity* with his discussion of modalities. In particular, he clarifies the epistemic notion of apriority and the metaphysical notion of necessity and the distinction between them. Contrary to the once received view, he argues that not all a priori truths are necessary truths and vice versa. His analysis of these notions has unquestionably changed our philosophical thinking about them.

Kripke ends *Naming and Necessity* with an application of his views on reference and necessity to philosophy of mind. He presents a novel treatment of Cartesianism and a critique of naturalism in philosophy of mind. In particular, he offers a critique of the once dominant view in philosophy of mind, known as the identity thesis, a view that identifies mental states, such as pain, with brain states.

In his book *Wittgenstein on Rules and Private Language*, Kripke presents a novel view of the late Wittgenstein's challenge to the traditional picture of language as having truth conditions. He then presents a novel interpretation of the late Wittgenstein's view that language has assertability conditions and of Wittgenstein's defense of this view. Kripke relates this to Humean skepticism. The book reveals a deep understanding of Wittgenstein's picture of the relation among language, mind, and the world.

In his "A Puzzle about Belief," Kripke shows how the ordinary way in which we attribute belief to people leads to certain puzzles, which previously were thought to present a puzzle for anyone holding a view similar to Mill's on names. This important work reveals further connections between mind and language and has changed our philosophical outlook about what are called propositional attitudes.

In what may be called "philosophical logic," there simply isn't a more important and influential figure in the current discipline. His work on the semantics of modal logic and intuitionism and his outline of a theory of truth have been the foundations for all that is contemporary and state-of-the-art in philosophical logic.

There are many gifted logicians, but none that display Kripke's keen judgment regarding the nature of logic and its philosophical implications, especially with regard to the epistemic status of logic. Countering views that are in vogue, Kripke shows the problems of viewing logic as an empirical science and even of the coherency of claiming that we can "adopt a logic," whether for empirical or linguistic reasons.

STRUCTURE OF THE BOOK

Accordingly, this book on the philosophy of Saul Kripke contains the following parts and chapters.

Part I. Naming, Necessity, and Apriority

Part I consists of the first four chapters. Chapter 1, "Kripke on Proper and General Names," by Bernard Linsky, not only offers an original interpretation of what Kripke means by the rigidity of a general term, but also is a review of Kripke's *Naming and Necessity* lectures, summarizing the famous arguments and examples they introduced, with indications of the lines of investigation that they initiated. Accordingly, this is a good chapter for someone who does not have much familiarity with Kripke's views to read first.

Linsky discusses at length Kripke's famous refutation of the "cluster of descriptions theory of proper names" with his well-known examples of 'Jonah', 'Moses', 'Aristotle', and 'Gödel' and 'Schmidt'. The arguments against the descriptions theory have come to be classified as "modal," "epistemic," and "semantic" arguments. Linsky summarizes notions that Kripke's own account of names introduced, such as "rigid designator," "baptism and chain of reference," and "fixing the reference of a name with a description." He also summarizes Kripke's arguments, which arise from considering identity statements, for a priori contingent and a posteriori necessary truths, in particular the necessity of identity and the essentiality of origin. Whereas Kripke himself only claimed to offer a "better picture" of names than the "cluster theory," almost immediately a range of theories were presented to fill out the picture. Linsky distinguishes several of these attempts to fill out what Kripke had introduced, including the "causal-historical theory of reference" and the "theory of direct reference."

Naming and Necessity also introduced the view that natural kind terms and some general terms are also rigid designators, including 'water', 'tiger', and 'lightning'. Linsky's survey of *Naming and Necessity* concludes with a defense of the very notion of a kind or general term being a rigid designator against recent arguments from Soames. The final section addresses Kripke's discussion of definite descriptions, in particular the account of Donnellan's "referential/attributive" distinction in the 1977 paper "Speaker's Reference and Semantic Reference."

As presented here, the wider importance of the *Naming and Necessity* lectures came from their application to issues outside the narrow dialectic of descriptions and Millian names that had bounded the discussion through Russell, Frege, and Strawson, and on to Searle with the cluster theory. With the sharp distinction between the mechanism that determines the referent of a name and what descriptive properties might pick out that referent, Kripke made it possible to consider metaphysical issues separately from the epistemic issues with which they had been so closely associated. Whereas Quine's "jungle of Aristotelian essentialism" was thus opened to exploration, more immediate results came from the clearing away of possible objections to the thesis of the necessity of identity. As will be seen in the following chapters, Kripke's theory of proper and general names also had consequences in many other areas of philosophy.

In Chapter 2, "Fiction, Myth, and Reality," Nathan Salmon argues that Kripke's account of names from fiction illuminates, but exacerbates, the perennial problem of true singular negative existentials: An atomic sentence is true only if its subject term designates; and yet (S) 'Sherlock Holmes is nonexistent' is true only if its subject term does not designate. In his 1973 John Locke lectures, on vacuous names and names in fiction, Kripke argues that natural-language discourse about (not within) fiction posits a realm of abstract entities, *fictional characters*, supposedly created by storytellers. He contends further that a proper name from fiction, such as 'Holmes', is ambiguous between a primary (in a "primordial" sense), typically object-fictional use – 'Holmes$_1$' – on which it is non-designating and therefore without semantic content, and a secondary (in a non-primordial sense), metafictional use – 'Holmes$_2$' – on which it names the character. He says further that in (S), the name has its primary use, which is "quasi-intensional," with the result that (S) typically expresses that there is no true proposition that Holmes$_1$ exists. But this contention is subject to the same difficulty as the original sentence, since the 'that'-clause is a non-designating term on a par with 'Holmes$_1$'. Salmon proposes an alternative account on which 'Holmes' univocally designates the character, and (*S*), although false, is often used to convey correct information that it does not semantically express.

In Chapter 3, "Kripke on Epistemic and Metaphysical Possibility: Two Routes to the Necessary A Posteriori," Scott Soames argues that *Naming and Necessity* and "Identity and Necessity" contain two routes to necessary a posteriori truths. On the first, they are necessary truths that predicate essential properties of objects or kinds that the objects or kinds can be known to possess only a posteriori. This encompasses all putative instances of the Kripkean necessary a posteriori – including necessary a posteriori statements of non-identity (as in 'Saul Kripke ≠ David Kaplan'), and necessary a posteriori identity statements involving a simple name or natural kind term plus a descriptive constituent (as in 'Water is the substance instances of which are made up of molecules with two hydrogen atoms and one oxygen atom'). Simple identities such as 'Hesperus is Phosphorus' and 'woodchucks are groundhogs', Soames claims, are left out of this picture.

The second route, Soames maintains, commits Kripke to an implicit appeal to his strong disquotational principle connecting evidence required to justify accepting a sentence one understands with evidence required to justify belief in the proposition it expresses. Soames contends that the two routes to the necessary a posteriori differ in that (i) the first applies to a proper subset of cases to which the second is meant to apply; (ii) the first, but not the second, leads to the recognition of epistemically possible world-states over and above the metaphysically possible; and (iii) the first takes the empirical evidence required for a posteriori knowledge of p to rule out epistemic possibilities in which p is false, whereas the second does not. Soames argues that the first route is sound, whereas the second is not.

Nevertheless, Soames maintains that an insight is extractable from the failed second route. Its guiding idea is that belief in singular propositions may result either from understanding and accepting sentences that express them, or from thinking of individuals or kinds as bearers of certain descriptive properties – and that because of this, believing the bare proposition that o is F may always involve also believing a related, descriptive or metalinguistic proposition that provides a way of thinking about o. In short, according to Soames, there may be something broadly Fregean about mental states the contents of which include singular propositions.

In Chapter 4, "Possible Worlds Semantics: Philosophical Foundations," Robert Stalnaker discusses Kripke's early formal contributions to the semantics for modal logic and his philosophical application of possible worlds semantics to philosophical problems in *Naming and Necessity*. This raises questions about the metaphysical status of possible worlds that have been much discussed in the philosophical literature. This chapter is about Kripke's views about some of the questions raised in those discussions. Stalnaker's interpretation of Kripke is based entirely on remarks made in *Naming and Necessity*, and in the preface to the edition of those lectures that was published in 1980.

Kripke made it clear that he rejected David Lewis's modal realist interpretation of possible worlds, according to which they are concrete universes spatially and temporally disconnected from ours, but the alternative "actualist" interpretation of possible worlds raises at least these further questions: What exactly are possible worlds (or possible states of the world, which Kripke suggests would be less misleading terminology)? What contribution do they make to the explanation of modal discourse, and of the distinctive facts that modal discourse is used to state? Does the slogan "necessity is truth in all possible worlds" provide, or point to, a reductive analysis of necessity? Are possible worlds, in some sense, prior to modal operators and modal auxiliaries? If not, in what sense are they explanatory? How are possible worlds, or counterfactual situations, specified? How do they contribute to our understanding of specific metaphysical questions about the relations between particular individuals and their qualitative characteristics, the kinds to which they belong, and the matter of which they are constituted? How are we to understand the possible existence of individuals that do not actually exist? Section 2 discusses Kripke's rejection of modal realism and of the idea that the analysis of necessity and possibility in terms of possible worlds provides a reductive analysis of modal concepts, and raises the question of exactly what role the notion of a possible world plays in a philosophical explanation of modality. Section 3 aims to disentangle what Kripke regards as a pseudoproblem about the identification of individuals across possible worlds from the questions about such identifications that Kripke acknowledges are legitimate. Section 4 speculates about Kripke's views about the status of merely possible individuals – the interpretation of individuals that are members of the domains of other possible worlds, but not in the domain of the actual world.

Part II. Formal Semantics, Truth, Philosophy of Mathematics, and Philosophy of Logic

Part II consists of Chapters 5, 6, 7, and 8. They are devoted to Kripke's work in the semantics of various formal systems, his views in philosophy of mathematics and logic, and his resolution of the Liar Paradox via his theory of truth.

John Burgess's first contribution, Chapter 5, "Kripke Models," is primarily an elementary introduction to Kripke's contributions to developing models for modal and intuitionistic logic, intended to prepare the reader to tackle more formal treatments elsewhere. Burgess takes the occasion to warn against some common misunderstandings (notably the impression that the model theory commits one to a metaphysical rather than a logical understanding of modality), to clarify the history of the subject (notably the roles of McKinsey and Jonsson on the one hand, and Kanger and Hintikka on the other, as precursors, and the greater importance of the former pair), and to indicate something of the relationship of the work in model theory to the work on the nature of modality (the latter is in no way implicit in the former, but the philosophical work is needed to clarify the ultimate significance of the earlier mathematical work).

Chapter 6, "Kripke on Truth," Burgess's second contribution, is again primarily an elementary introduction. It includes a comparison of Kripke's theory of truth with Tarski's and discusses the extent to which they need a hierarchy of metalanguages. The last section does, however, go beyond Kripke's "Outline" to say a little about the content of Kripke's unpublished work on related topics.

In Chapter 7, "Kripke on Logicism, Wittgenstein, and *De Re* Beliefs about Numbers," Mark Steiner discusses Kripke's unpublished Whitehead Lectures, in which he sets forth a new view of numbers that has two main features: (a) Numbers are not numerals, so the view is not nominalist; and (b) the properties of the numbers depend upon the properties of the numerals (and thus, for example, the binary and the decimal numerals refer to different sets of numbers), so the view is not platonist. Steiner calls this view "quasi-nominalist," and argues that the view is the closest to that of the later Wittgenstein that Kripke has set forth. He also discusses what he takes to be the evolution of Kripke's thought concerning Wittgenstein, and suggests a slow convergence of Kripke's views to the actual views of Wittgenstein taking place from *Naming and Necessity*, through *Wittgenstein on Rules and Private Language,* to the Whitehead Lectures. Steiner also discusses Kripke's views on *de re* beliefs about numbers, which is based on Kripke's notion of a buckstopper.

In Chapter 8, "Kripke on the Incoherency of Adopting a Logic," I first discuss Kripke's general objections to the notion of adopting a logic. Whether we view logic as a set of statements or as a formal system, Kripke's various applications of the Lewis Carroll infinite regress argument show that we cannot be neutral and adopt one for evaluation or compare one with another. In Section 2, I consider whether we can adopt a "logic" that is not subject to this argument: "quantum logic." In Section 3, I evaluate the claim of adopting intuitionist logic.

Kripke maintains that there are four possible claims of what one means by a change in logic:

1. We could merely be introducing, or recognizing, a new set of connectives. These connectives may not be introduced by definition, but may be introduced as new primitive notions in any system. This is Kripke's view of intuitionist logic, and he adds, "One may always, of course, invent new connectives, which ... satisfy somewhat different laws [from our connectives] because they have a somewhat different interpretation. That should be uncontroversial."

2. We could be introducing new connectives and repudiating our old connectives as meaningless. This has two forms:

   a) syntactic, or "axiomatic," presentation of the new system of logic.

   Here, we just introduce a language purely syntactically, or an uninterpreted axiomatic, or formal, system, and given something called "formation rules" we are to define something we call "grammatical strings" and then we define which strings are going to be called "axioms" and which will be called "inference rules." But Kripke maintains that if you only look at the formal system, then you really can't tell whether these connectives mean the same as the old ones or not because no one has explained or given you the slightest idea of what they mean. Similarly, as Kripke has been urging, "One has to first use reasoning in order to even see what is provable in a formal system."

   b) semantic interpretation of the symbols.

   The symbols have been explained and the old connectives are repudiated as meaningless. Kripke has argued that accepting these new connectives is not an objection to accepting the old connectives as well. Further, this is the view held by Kreisel, probably Gödel, and Kleene, as well as Kripke.

3. We could claim to have discovered a definite fallacy.

We may discover, in an a priori manner, that something thought of for centuries as a sound principle of logic was actually based on a fallacy. This is not because we are "adopting a new logic," but because we look at the old formal system and see that it wasn't really sound with respect to its informal interpretation, and that the "proof" we had that it was sound was fallacious. This is what happened in the case of the Aristotelian syllogism, and for all we know there are other such proofs that we make that contain a fallacy. But this should no more count against the notion of self-evidence or apriority than the fact that something may seem to be supported by experiment and then later turn out not to be so well supported by experiment should undermine our using *being supported by experiment* as a justification for accepting something.

4. We could claim that we mean what we always meant by a certain connective, but we now have discovered that new laws apply to the connective.

The real problem, Kripke states, is not whether the new connectives mean the same as the old ones, but whether there's anything in the new language satisfying the same laws as the old.

But Kripke's main point is this: "There aren't different logics. There is only logic. There are different formal systems." We use logic to reason about them to see if a new formal system has an interesting interpretation that may have sound principles of logic. But we can't adopt it.

Part III. Language and Mind

Chapters 9, 10, 11, and 12 bridge the gap between Kripke's views on these two topics.

In Chapter 9, "Kripke's Puzzle about Belief," Mark Richard considers whether Kripke's puzzle about Pierre (who thinks true both 'Londres est jolie' and 'London is not pretty') might be a puzzle about belief: Does Pierre, or does he not, believe that London is pretty? But if there is no univocal answer to that question, Richard considers whether perhaps it is more a puzzle about belief ascription: In such-and-such a situation would it be right to say that Pierre believes that? Or perhaps it is a puzzle about translation: Can we invariably translate what Pierre says with 'Londres est jolie' into our idiom? Richard's own view is that the puzzle is first and foremost a puzzle about how we talk about beliefs; his essay attempts to defend this view.

In his second contribution, Chapter 10, "A Note on Kripke's Puzzle about Belief," Nathan Salmon contrasts different versions of Kripke's puzzle about belief, drawing different conclusions from each. Arguing that every instance of the disquotational principle schema is analytic, Salmon reconstructs the original puzzle, which employs that schema, as an argument demonstrating that (evidently contrary to Kripke) one can believe contradictions while being completely rational (and even while being a logician who will correct any belief that he/she recognizes is contradictory). More significantly, Salmon reconstructs the puzzle employing the strengthened disquotation principle schema as a disproof, by *reductio ad absurdum*, of that stronger principle – not merely demonstrating (as Kripke appears to favor) that not all instances of strengthened disquotation are true even if none are false, but demonstrating, moreover, that some instances must be altogether false. A perfectly competent speaker who is reflective and non-reticent, and who believes what is expressed by a simple sentence, may nevertheless sincerely dissent to that sentence under normal circumstances. Such, Salmon argues, is the inevitable moral of Kripke's strengthened puzzle. For further details, see Salmon's abstract at the beginning of his contribution.

Chapter 11, "On the Skepticism about Rule-Following in Kripke's Version of Wittgenstein," George Wilson's contribution, is on what is sometimes referred to as "Kripkenstein's" skepticism in rule-following. It is widely supposed that the conclusion of the Skeptical Argument in Kripke's *Wittgenstein on Rules and Private Language* says that there are no facts about someone's meaning or understanding something by a term. It is also supposed that Kripke's Wittgenstein responds to this conclusion by denying in the Skeptical Solution that ascriptions of meaning even *purport* to state or represent facts – say, facts about a speaker's use of an arbitrary term. In the first section of the paper, Wilson outlines his chief reasons for thinking that these related interpretative suppositions are false. The Skeptical Argument does *not* aim at establishing *semantic non-factualism*, and the Skeptical Solution does not presuppose it. Second, Wilson argues that the framework of the Skeptical Solution actually depends upon the idea that meaning ascriptions *are*, in some substantial sense, factual in content, and he attempts to specify the type of facts that are represented by correct meaning ascriptions according to Kripke's Wittgensteinian perspective. Roughly, the meaning of a term in a community is constituted by facts about the assertability conditions of the term and about its role or utility in the relevant "language games" that the community's linguistic practices have established. It is hard to make sense of the main strands of the Skeptical Solution without attributing to it this much positive factualism about the meaning of terms.

Last, Wilson argues in the lengthy third section that the factualist version of Kripke's Skeptical Solution requires, for its minimal coherence, a certain *temporally externalist* perspective on meaning. That is, the Skeptical Solution allows that the instance-by-instance assertability conditions for a term 'Φ' are "open-textured" over time. Thus, the normative warrant for novel applications of 'Φ' will characteristically not have been settled by prior ascriptions of the term up to and including t. Moreover, what the term comes to mean for the community after t may be affected by determinations about assertibility conditions and "language game" functions that come to be established only when t is in the past.

This latter concession may leave the impression that such temporal externalism, incorporated into the Skeptical Solution, undermines one of Wilson's chief earlier contentions. That is, it may appear that these qualifications imply that the Skeptical Solution *is* committed to *some* significant version of semantic nonfactualism after all. Wilson concludes by explaining why this impression rests on an important confusion and why any residual nonfactualism in the Semantic Solution is philosophically innocuous. The confusion that he investigates at this juncture may have tempted Kripke himself into some of his remarks that make it sound as if Wittgenstein endorsed a notable version of semantic nonfactualism. Wilson does not investigate this speculation about Kripke's exegetical conception at any length, but he does insist that such a temptation should be firmly rejected in an adequate interpretation of Wittgenstein. As Wilson explains, some form of temporal semantic externalism does seem to play a critical but murky role in his thought about following a rule.

In the late 1980s, Kripke expanded the opposition to dispositionalism about color briefly expressed in *Naming and Necessity*. This expansion includes an argument that there could be such a thing as "fool's red," analogous to there being "fool's gold," and its implications to the traditional view of the distinction between primary and secondary qualities. Sections 2 to 4 of Mario Gómez-Torrente's contribution, Chapter 12, "Kripke on Color Words and the Primary/Secondary Quality Distinction," summarizes these expanded ideas. Section 5 briefly reviews some recent defenses of dispositionalism, sketching broadly Kripkean objections to them.

Section 2 explains some of Kripke's criticisms of several arguments for dispositionalism and for the Lockean division of the sensible qualities. The criticized arguments include some perceptual variation arguments and arguments based on the physical diversity of the causes of perceived color.

Dispositionalists typically hold the thesis that biconditionals of roughly the form "o is yellow iff o would produce such-and-such sensations in normal humans under normal conditions" (for some non-trivial filling out of "normal humans" and "normal conditions") are true and a priori. Their apriority supposedly distinguishes the traditional secondary qualities from the primary, for which no such biconditionals are both true and a priori. Section 4 presents some Kripkean counterexamples to the dispositionalist thesis. Kripke noted, for example, that intuitively there might be shades of yellow with such a high brightness as to kill a normal human; this suggests that the "only if" direction of dispositionalist biconditionals is not a priori true. Other counterexamples involve faint colors, substances that distort color vision when seen, and cases of color mixture (for example, where an object looks yellow but from close up appears composed of red and green parts).

In *Naming and Necessity* Kripke had said that the reference of 'yellowness' is fixed like that of a natural substance term, by means of a reference-fixing identity such as 'yellowness is the property which produces such-and-such sensations'. Section 3 explains some refinements Kripke introduced into this view, which help explain our intuitions about his counterexamples. He developed the notion of a *prejudice*, a belief firmly held onto by speakers, which need not be analytic or a priori, but which shapes their intuitions about the reference of the terms involved. The preceding identity is a prejudice about 'yellowness', but there are others, like the belief that certain objects are paradigms of yellow, that yellowness is dissective, and so on. The community of speakers attempts to hold onto as many of these reference-shaping prejudices as possible. For example, by color mixture some paradigms of yellow don't intuitively satisfy dissectiveness, but since they are few, they lose their paradigm status and dissectiveness is kept as a prejudice about 'yellow'. On the other hand, dispositionalism contradicts many of our chromatic prejudices.

Section 5 does three things: (1) It rejects as inadequate some weakenings of the dispositionalist biconditionals introduced by Mark Johnston, noting that most of the Kripkean counterexamples continue to work against them. (2) It criticizes the objection that while Kripke's view implies that science might discover that our intuitive judgments of color similarity are incorrect, such judgments are not scientifically refutable; the objection is weak, for intuitive similarity claims, apparently justified purely visually, are also made about traditionally primary qualities. (3) It rejects Crispin Wright's idea that dispositionalist biconditionals (strictly, similar devices he calls "provisoed biconditionals") may be conceptually necessary but not conclusively recognizable as true, just as Church's Thesis supposedly is; despite the popularity of the idea that Church's Thesis cannot be conclusively recognized as true, if it's conceptually necessary then nothing precludes a recognizably conclusive proof of it.

Part IV. Philosophy of Mind and Philosophical Psychology

Sydney Shoemaker, in Chapter 13, "Kripke and Cartesianism," maintains that Kripke supports a rejection of physicalism by arguing that psychophysical identities (for example, 'pain = C-fiber stimulation') could be true only if they were necessarily true, and that the seeming possibility of their falsehood is reason for thinking they are not necessarily true and so are not true. Shoemaker then points out that Kripke argues that the seeming possibility of their falsehood cannot be explained away in the way we can explain away the seeming possibility of heat not being molecular motion, or water not being H_2O. He seems to assume what Yablo calls "textbook Kripkeanism," the view that "The only way for E to be conceptually possible but not 'really' – metaphysically – possible is for something *else* to be really possible, namely E's presentation E^*." Apparent counterexamples to this principle are presented. The counterexamples suggest that the seeming possibility of necessarily true identity statements being false can be due to a confusion of epistemic possibility and metaphysical possibility. If this is so, then, contrary to Kripke, psychophysical identities can hold necessarily despite the seeming possibility of their not holding.

Jeff Buechner observes in Chapter 14, "Not Even Computing Machines Can Follow Rules: Kripke's Critique of Functionalism," that Kripke's refutation of functionalism is a corollary of his work in *Wittgenstein on Rules and Private Language*; in particular, it is a corollary of the arguments against dispositionalist (and extended dispositionalist) solutions to the meaning normativity paradox. For further details, see Buechner's abstract at the beginning of his contribution.

Most of the chapters are intended to be a detailed introduction to Kripke's views and current state of the art on the controversies that they raise. The volume can be used in an advanced undergraduate course to familiarize someone with the details of Kripke's views, as well as in a graduate course (and by scholars) to bring the reader up to speed with state-of-the-art criticism of and controversies of these views.

First, we would like to thank Saul Kripke for his choice of the contributors to this volume. In addition to Kripke's published material, the following sources were among those used in writing this volume: transcription of the John Locke Lectures; transcription of the Whitehead Lectures; transcription of the Lectures ("No Fool's Red?: Some Considerations on the Primary/Secondary Quality Distinction"); transcription of the International Wittgenstein Symposium lecture on functionalism; tape of Kripke's Duke University lecture on functionalism; tapes of Kripke's course at Princeton on color words and the dispositional analysis of the primary/secondary quality distinction; transcriptions of several of Kripke's seminars on truth including three Princeton lectures; Allen Stairs's "Quantum Mechanics, Logic and Reality" (unpublished Ph.D. dissertation, University of Western Ontario, 1978), which contains a summary of Kripke's University of Pittsburgh lecture "The Question of Logic"; Clifton MacIntosh's notes on Kripke's 1974 seminar on rules and adopting a logic; lecture notes from Kripke's 1974 seminar and the CUNY Graduate Center seminar on the epistemology of logic; and transcription of Kripke's three Princeton lectures on truth. The contributors thank Saul Kripke and these sources for providing access to these materials. We also thank Glenn Branch for his expertise and excellent copyediting and indexing of the entire manuscript.

PART I

NAMING, NECESSITY, AND APRIORITY

1

Kripke on Proper and General Names

Bernard Linsky

Saul Kripke's first contributions to philosophy were his papers on modal logic, which quickly made possible worlds semantics a working tool of philosophical logicians and then of philosophers more generally. The papers on quantified modal logic led him, he says, to think further about "rigid designation" and names.[1] It was the resulting *Naming and Necessity* lectures that guaranteed wider interest in the formal logic and established Kripke as one of the leading figures in analytic philosophy of language and what came to be known as "modal" metaphysics. The lectures were presented January 20, 22, and 29, 1970, to the department of philosophy at Princeton University, where they were tape-recorded and then reworked for publication in 1972 in a volume of papers on semantics. They were then published as a separate book in 1980 with a preface that included a discussion of some replies to the original version and nine pages of "Addenda" and footnotes.

The *Naming and Necessity* lectures had a revolutionary effect on philosophical attitudes toward a number of topics, some of which are described in later chapters in this book. The most significant effects outside of semantic theory were a shift in attitude toward the notion of essential properties and a sudden burst of discussion of the doctrines of essentialism about origin and constitution and other topics that had been dismissed by Quine as belonging in the "jungle of Aristotelian essentialism." The lectures introduced the novel categories of a posteriori necessary truths and even a priori contingent truths and so started a discussion of the content of assertions of knowledge and belief that is still developing. To cap the lectures, Kripke presented a new argument for mind/body dualism, which was at first viewed as a curiosity, but has

[1] In the introduction to Kripke 1980 (1972), p. 3.

since worked its way into the fields of philosophy of mind and historical work on Descartes.[2]

The main argument of the first two lectures was directed at the dominant "descriptional" view of names deriving from Frege and Russell, followed by a sketch of the new theory of names that would replace it. In the third lecture Kripke extended his revolution to general terms, offering an alternative view of general terms which challenged the current view of theoretical identities such as 'water = H_2O' and 'pain = C-fiber stimulation' as well as views about the meaning of "natural kind terms" such as 'gold' and 'tiger'. Other philosophers were talking about similar issues around the same time, but the lectures presented them as part of a coherent bundle of ideas.[3] Kripke went on to further develop his views in later papers, in part by distinguishing his own views on names from these related developments. This chapter is an introduction to these ideas about reference, following Kripke's two works, *Naming and Necessity* (Kripke 1980, [1972]) and "Semantic Reference and Speaker's Reference" (Kripke 1979 [1977]).

1. THE CLUSTER OF DESCRIPTIONS THEORY OF PROPER NAMES

The received view of the semantics of proper names around 1970 was that the correct account lay somewhere among the theories descended from classic papers of Gottlob Frege and Bertrand Russell. Frege's theory in his classic "On Sense and Reference" was that proper names have a sense that encapsulates a "mode of presentation" of an object, a way of thinking about it, which is what connects the name with its referent (Frege 1949 [1892]). When we understand a name, we come to associate with it certain properties, and those properties are the ones which determine what the name stands for. Kripke quotes this well-known footnote from Frege's paper in full:

> In the case of genuinely proper names like 'Aristotle' opinions as regards their sense may diverge. As such may, e.g., be suggested: Plato's disciple and the teacher of Alexander the Great. Whoever accepts this sense will interpret the meaning of the statement 'Alexander was born at Stagira', differently from one who interpreted the sense of 'Aristotle' as the Stagirite

---

[2] See Almog 2002 and the papers in Gillette and Loewer 2001.

[3] Hilary Putnam was writing about natural kind terms in his 1970 and 1975; David Kaplan about "direct reference" of names, indexicals, and rigidified descriptions; and Keith Donnellan in his 1966 had written about the *referential* use of definite descriptions.

teacher of Alexander the Great. As long as the nominatum remains the same, these fluctuations in sense are tolerable. But they should be avoided in the system of a demonstrative science and should not appear in a perfect language. (Kripke 1980, p. 30, citing Frege 1949 [1892], p. 86)

According to Frege, then, for the purposes of "a perfect language," a proper name will have a unique sense, which is captured by the content of a definite description.

Russell, on the other hand, held the view that ordinary proper names (as opposed to *logically proper names*) are "abbreviated," or disguised, definite descriptions.[4] The sense of a name, such as 'Aristotle', should in fact be properly represented by a description, as in Frege's examples, 'The student of Plato and teacher of Alexander the Great', or 'The teacher of Alexander the Great who was born at Stagira', and so on. To know the meaning of the name is to grasp those descriptions as picking out the referent. There are fundamental disagreements in both principle and detail between Frege and Russell, but it was assumed that the truth was to be found somewhere in the space indicated by those two possibilities.

There were cracks in the descriptional view, however. It seems that we can still continue to use a name, without changing its meaning, even when we discover that we have made mistakes about the bearer of the name. Kripke cites this passage from Wittgenstein's *Philosophical Investigations*:

> Consider this example. If one says 'Moses did not exist', this may mean various things. It may mean: the Israelites did not have a single leader when they withdrew from Egypt – or: their leader was not called Moses – or: there cannot have been anyone who accomplished all that the Bible relates of Moses – ... But when I make a statement about Moses, – am I always ready to substitute some one of those descriptions for 'Moses'? I shall perhaps say: by 'Moses' I understand the man who did what the Bible relates of Moses, or at any rate, a good deal of it. But how much? Have I decided how much must be proved false for me to give up my proposition as false? Has the name 'Moses' got a fixed and unequivocal use for me in all possible cases? (Wittgenstein 1950, §79)

Inspired in part by these remarks from Wittgenstein, which suggest that names have a use in a language that isn't characterized by the content of a particular description, some have thought that perhaps the requirement that each name be associated with a particular definite description could be relaxed, and that in fact there might be a vaguely weighted

---

[4] See chapter 16 of Russell 1919.

cluster of descriptions, some more central than others, but which would explain the phenomenon of discovering a mistake. John Searle presents such a view and Kripke identifies him as a source for this variant of the description theory (Searle 1958 [1963]).

The stage was set for Kripke, who broke open the space of candidate theories by presenting a string of vivid examples that, between them, show what is wrong with even this modified version of the traditional Frege-Russell theory of names. That modified theory can be seen as a collection of views about the nature and role of the descriptions that constitute the meaning of the proper name:

1) To every name or designating expression 'X', there corresponds a cluster of properties, namely the family of those properties φ such that A believes 'φX'.

2) One of the properties, or some conjointly, are believed by A to pick out some individual uniquely.

3) If most, or a weighted most, of the φ's are satisfied by one unique object y, then y is the referent of 'X'.

4) If the vote yields no unique object, 'X' does not refer.

5) The statement, 'If X exists, then X has most of the φ's' is known a priori by the speaker.

6) The statement, 'If X exists, then X has most of the φ's' expresses a necessary truth (in the idiolect of the speaker). (Kripke 1980 [1972], p.71)

Just providing such a long and seemingly variegated list of features shows that the standard theory holds together a number of distinct intuitions. The standard theory was actually a combination of views about what the speaker believes about the referent of a name, what in fact does determine the referent of that name, what the speaker knows a priori of what any referent must be like, and of what is possible and necessary for the thing that is the referent. One of the revolutionary effects of Kripke's arguments was to show that the features of determining reference, and of explaining the cognitive and epistemic states of speakers, could perhaps not so easily be brought together in one notion of meaning. While Kripke's work led to a fragmenting of the various goals that Frege's notion of *Sinn* or sense was supposed to achieve, some have argued that he did not then complete the job of accounting for names. While Kripke did give an account of the reference of names, he did not give a positive account of the *meaning* of a name. Numerous philosophers have proposed to supplement Kripke by following Frege in postulating

that the meaning or content of a name is, or is determined by, the contribution that the name makes to the standard content expressed by use
of a sentence containing that name.⁵ Some philosophers have proposed
furthermore that the meaning or content of a name is thus its referent.
On Frege's original theory the sense of a name such as 'Aristotle' is only
a part of the thought expressed by the sentence 'Alexander was born at
Stagira'. That entire thought is the meaning (or sense) of the sentence.
It is also what is believed by some *x* when 'believes that Alexander was
born at Stagira' is true of that *x*. In his paper "A Puzzle about Belief"
(1979), Kripke raised problems for any such account of beliefs expressed
by sentences that include proper names.⁶ The problem of constructing
a theory of belief sentences that fits with Kripke's views of reference has
been one of the main problems for the study of propositional attitudes
ever since. It is therefore best to read *Naming and Necessity* as focusing on
the issue of reference, with negative arguments about the role of beliefs
about the referent in determining the reference of names. We may have
beliefs as in (1), but just how they enter into the determination of the
reference of a name is one thing at issue in a series of vivid and now
famous examples that Kripke discusses.

The argument proceeds by counterexamples which together show how
names *do not* function. One of the less prominent examples, the name
'Jonah', serves as a good entry into the argument. This case relies on
pursuing the force of Wittgenstein's "Moses" example to its ultimate conclusion. Consider how we actually use the name 'Jonah'. The only possible contents for a cluster of descriptions associated with Jonah will be
derived from the biblical story, which is the only source for any candidates
for the cluster of descriptions that might represent the name. Jonah was
the prophet who was swallowed by a big fish while traveling to Nineveh,
and so on. But Kripke invites us to consider what those in search of the
historical Jonah could uncover. It will most likely turn out that if there was
any historical Jonah at all, that he was certainly not swallowed by a fish,
traveling to Nineveh, and so on. Indeed all of those descriptions could
turn out to be false, or certainly enough of them to show that they do not
collectively determine the reference of the name. The example Jonah
shows that condition (4), the referent of a name is whatever satisfies the
weighted majority, is just wrong. Instead, as Kripke will argue, the referent

---

⁵ This notion of *content* in semantic theory comes from Kaplan, as in his (1989), and does
   not appear in Kripke's lectures.
⁶ See Chapters 9 and 10 of this volume.

of the name is *determined* in a way suggested by considering how we might *discover* the referent of that name. We follow the use of the name back to an individual, not following a cluster of descriptions believed about the referent by speakers, but by tracing the actual individual they were intending to talk about. No positive theory of how names do work is necessary to show the description theory wrong on this point.

Following the order of presentation in the lectures, we come next to what has come to be known as "the modal argument" against the cluster of descriptions theory of names. Consider our example of Aristotle, and the description, 'the teacher of Alexander'. Now it is certainly true that Aristotle might not have taught Alexander. It is a contingent truth that he did (if indeed it is a truth at all). But if 'teacher of Alexander' expressed part of the meaning of the name, 'Aristotle was a teacher' would be a necessary truth. It is not. Hence 'Aristotle' provides a counterexample to (6). The statement, 'If X exists, then X has most of the φs', expresses a necessary truth, which is not true in general for the sort of beliefs about referents that we actually have.

These intuitions about the necessary truth of 'Aristotle was a teacher' are explained in a different way by Michael Dummett in his "Note on an Attempted Refutation of Frege" (Dummett 1981 [1973], pp. 110–151). Dummett argues that there is an ambiguity in a statement like 'The teacher of Alexander might not have been a teacher', corresponding to two different scopes of the description, following Russell's theory. One reading, the wide scope, is true, and can be paraphrased as:

> It is true of the teacher of Alexander that he might not have been a teacher.

The other reading, with the narrow scope, can be paraphrased as:

> It might have been the case that the teacher of Alexander is not a teacher

which seems false.

Dummett claims that a name might be replaced by a definite description, provided that the description is always taken with wide scope. In the introduction to the 1980 edition of *Naming and Necessity*, Kripke also addresses Dummett's claim, and argues against it, pointing out that the scope distinction can only apply to names or descriptions in the scope of an operator, like 'necessarily', 'possibly', or 'might'. But, says Kripke, the argument that he himself gives relies only on our intuitions about the truth of the simple sentence 'Aristotle is a teacher' in various counterfactual situations, or possible worlds. It would be false in some, where

'The teacher of Alexander is a teacher' would be true, so it doesn't have the same meaning.

2. RIGID DESIGNATORS

Indeed Kripke relies on our intuitions about what a name refers to in a world. Names refer to the same thing in every possible world; they are "rigid designators," in contrast with definite descriptions, which typically pick out different things in different worlds.[7] Kripke says "Let's call something a *rigid designator* if in every possible world it designates the same object, a *nonrigid* or *accidental designator* if that is not the case" (Kripke 1980 [1972], p. 48). But objects need not exist in every world, so there is a notion of a rigid designator for a necessary existent as *strongly rigid*. Otherwise a rigid designator only need designate an object in every world in which it exists.

The thesis that ordinary proper names are rigid designators is certainly the most well-known doctrine of *Naming and Necessity*. That thesis should not be taken to be the whole content of the new theory, however, for the negative arguments against the description theory of names are as important to the Kripkean revolution in the theory of reference as this positive thesis. The initial portions of the first lecture are devoted to preempting certain misunderstandings of this view. One is casually dismissed with the remark that while the name 'Nixon' is a rigid designator, of course he might not have been *called* 'Nixon' (Kripke 1980 [1972], p. 49). Claims about what a term designates in a world, and about whether a sentence is true in a world, of course do not reflect how those words, or at least sounds, could have been meaningfully used. It is a fact about the words with the meaning they actually have, that they designate what they do in different worlds, and that the sentences they make up are true or false in various worlds. This is the sense in which it is not an objection to saying that '2 + 2 = 4' is a necessary truth that '2' might have been the name for 3 (Kripke 1980 [1972], p. 77). It is with the meaning that it has that we can ask of the reference or truth of an expression at another world.

This seemingly innocent point in fact raises deep issues for semantic theory. What, we might ask, is the nature of the designation relation that it can vary from world to world or not? A purely "naturalist" account in terms of a causal connection between a word token and a referent may be modally fragile, that is, not necessarily holding up across possible

---

[7] Some descriptions are rigid, however, such as 'the even prime number', which designates 2 in all worlds.

worlds. Would that relation have to hold necessarily for a name to be
a rigid designator? It would seem not. Is this an essential property of a
name, then, that it designates the same object in different worlds? Not if
we distinguish what a name *would* designate, as some sort of contingent
property of the name, from what it *designates with respect to* a given world.
The latter is a feature of the actual meaning of the name taken as a
bit of linguistic syntax. One might even ask why designation should be
formally represented by a function of two arguments 'Des(t,w)', taking
a term and a world as arguments, and giving a designatum as a value. A
rigid designator will be one for which this is a constant function, which
yields the same value for every world. A constant function of two arguments, a name and a world, should be distinguished from a one-place
function of a name, say, 'Des(t)', which simply yields a designation. The
one-place function, which yields a designation for a name, can enter
into the truth conditions of a sentence at a world, but only by way of
contributing its designation, not some value with respect to that world.
One might characterize this better as the view that names are "directly
referential" rather than "rigid designators."

A second possible misunderstanding of the thesis that names are
rigid designators comes from questions about the nature of objects with
respect to possible worlds. Kripke considers the case of necessary properties of individuals expressed, say with the sentence 'Nixon is necessarily
human'. It might be claimed that there is a problem of *cross-world identification*, that determining the truth of 'Nixon is necessarily human' requires
determining which object in a given world is to be cross-identified with
the Nixon of our world, and then if that object is human. One might
think, then, that the name must somehow embody or include the criteria
for such a cross-identification, to determine which object must be evaluated in each world. Kripke's notion is that once we determine that it is
the individual Nixon that we are talking about, it is Nixon's properties in
different worlds that determine the truth of sentences using 'Nixon' with
respect to those worlds.[8] Issues in the modal metaphysics of semantic
properties and about whether objects occur in more than one possible
world, or whether it is rather world-bound counterparts that determine
the truth conditions of sentences, are thus raised by the simple notion
of a rigid designator, and obscure the content of the thesis that proper
names are rigid designators.[9]

---

[8] See Chapter 4 of this volume.
[9] Lewis 1968 presents his "counterpart theory."

3. NAMING AND KNOWING

Kripke's use of claims about the designation of 'Aristotle' in different possible worlds presented a new sort of argumentation in semantics, one relying on intuition and data about semantic features of language with respect to worlds, rather than relying indirectly on intuitions about the truth conditions of sentences that themselves possibly include modal operators. That so-called *modal argument* against the description theory of names must be distinguished from what might be called *epistemic* arguments, based on considerations of what can be known by knowing the meaning of a name. One of the doctrines of the description theory is thesis (5), 'A knows a priori that this is true: If X exists, then φX'. (5) belongs in the description theories because whatever is the referent of a name can be known to satisfy (the weighted majority of) the associated descriptions. But we are now asked to think of other possible situations differently, not as ways things *might have been*, but as ways things *could turn out to be* (in the actual world). We consult our intuitions about what we would say about situations where certain (contrary to fact) discoveries are made. Think of Jonah again. Historians can search for the historical Jonah and yet discover that he did not do some of the things that are purportedly part of the cluster of descriptions that constitute the meaning of the name 'Jonah'. Historians can discover that Jonah was not swallowed by a whale – *it can turn out* that he wasn't – so we can't know a priori that Jonah was swallowed by a fish. With other historical or mythical figures of this sort, perhaps our intuitions aren't so clear. Consider Aristotle. Could we discover that Aristotle didn't teach Alexander, or that he didn't study with Plato, and still be talking about *Aristotle*? Yes, argues Kripke. If so, we can't know a priori that he did, and so those descriptions can't be part of the *meaning* of the name. The steps in this epistemological argument are reinforced by the examples that argue against the other epistemic or cognitive features of the description theory, those parts of the theory that tell us what speakers know or believe about the referent of a name.

For most people the proper name 'Gödel' is associated with descriptions such as 'the man who proved the incompleteness of arithmetic', or perhaps 'the man who proved the completeness of first order logic, the incompleteness of arithmetic, and the impossibility of a consistency proof for arithmetic within arithmetic'. Kripke asks us to suppose that in fact it was not Gödel, but one Schmidt who proved the theorem, and somehow Gödel just got the credit. Our intuitions now tell us that we would still refer to Gödel with the name 'Gödel', even though we would be having false beliefs about him, beliefs that are in fact true of Schmidt. Kripke gives an even more extreme case (again offering an example involving Princeton). It would certainly be most likely that what a vast majority of English speakers associate with Albert Einstein is not discovering relativity theory, but being the inventor of the atomic bomb. What we associate with Einstein is simply not true of him. These examples clearly show that (3) above is wrong: it's not true that if most, or a weighted most, of the φs are satisfied by one unique object *y*, then *y* is the referent of 'X'.

These examples are of errors, where we may well feel that we do know an identifying description that picks out the reference. But in fact we don't even think we do in some cases. No one, outside of Kripke's Princeton audience, will know anything about one of the physicists Feynman and Gell-Mann that they don't know about the other.[10] One could be quite happy using both names, and so understanding their meaning, while yet having no beliefs about one that one did not have about the other. These facts show that (2) is wrong, that it isn't in general true that A believes some of the φs pick out X uniquely.

4. KRIPKE'S POSITIVE ACCOUNT OF NAMES

If the cluster theory of names, and so the whole Frege-Russell tradition, is wrong, what is the right view that is to replace it? Kripke suggests a revival of John Stuart Mill's theory of names, as expressed in *A System of Logic* (Mill 1843, chapter II, §5). Rather than the notions of sense and reference, Mill worked with the somewhat different notions of *denotation* and *connotation*. (One difference is that the connotation of a name runs together what Frege separated as the *sense* and *ideas* merely associated with a name). On the "Millian" view, names do not connote properties of individuals, they only denote their referents.[11] Frege's notion of the sense

---

[10] This was before Feynman became a public figure with his work on the commission investigating the space shuttle *Challenger* explosion in 1986, and the famous "O-rings" that froze in ice water. 'Feynman' now becomes like the 'Einstein' example, as he is probably identified by the incorrect description 'The person who discovered the reason for the *Challenger* disaster'.

[11] In this they are much like Russell's *logically proper names*, which Russell contrasted with the "ordinary" proper names to which the description theory applies. Russell's logically proper names would directly stand for objects with which we are acquainted, which he thought were primarily sense data, and ultimately suggests that only the demonstratives 'this' and 'that' really qualify. Still, they fit with some features of Kripke's account of ordinary names.

of names can be seen as in response to a view like Mill's. Frege famously introduces the notion of sense to resolve a puzzle about identity. What is expressed by an identity sentence '*a* = *b*', as in 'The Morning Star = the Evening Star'?[12] Russell's alternative theory of descriptions is motivated by three puzzles about definite descriptions that will also apply to ordinary proper names, as they are later identified as disguised descriptions (Russell 1905, then 1919). The first puzzle is how to account for the failure of substitution of descriptions to preserve truth in propositions about belief. (If George IV wished to know whether Scott was the author of *Waverley*, and Scott was the author of *Waverley*, why doesn't it follow that George IV wished to know whether Scott was Scott?) The second was the problem of negative existential propositions; how do we say meaningfully 'The F does not exist'? The third was the famous puzzle about negation and the logical status of 'The king of France is bald' and 'The king of France is not bald'. How Kripke's new theory of names is to resolve these various problems about names and descriptions that motivated the theories of Frege and Russell is not directly addressed in *Naming and Necessity*, and their absence from the lectures was noted in the subsequent literature on propositional attitudes and semantic content.[13]

So far we have considered the possibility of a description, or more likely a cluster of descriptions, "giving the meaning" of a name. But there is another way in which a description could be associated with a name. A description may "fix the reference" of a name. Perhaps descriptions do not give the meaning of names but they do tell us what the reference of a name is, in a particular way. Here we also start from something noticed by Wittgenstein, who points out a peculiarity about the standard meter bar, and says that it is neither one meter nor not (1950, §50).[14] Kripke gives an explanation of what is peculiar about the standard meter bar. We are asked to suppose that the phrase 'one meter' acquires its meaning in a certain hypothetical way. A given stick S is settled upon to be a standard of measurement. It is decided that the length of S at a given time t_0 is to be one meter. In Kripke's terminology, the description 'the length of S at t_0' *fixes the reference* of the expression 'one meter'. It does

---

[12] Frege does not distinguish definite descriptions, including them in his category of names, as both definite descriptions and proper names will express a sense.

[13] See Chapters 9 and 10 of this volume.

[14] "There is one thing of which one can say neither that it is one meter long nor that it is not one meter long, and that is the standard meter in Paris. But this is, of course, not to ascribe an extraordinary property to it, but only to mark its peculiar role in the language game of measuring with a meter rule."

not *give the meaning* of 'one meter'; that is, it does not define 'one meter'. One way to see the difference between fixing the reference and giving the meaning of a name is to consider what 'one meter' would refer to in different counterfactual situations, or possible worlds. If 'the length of S at t_0' gave the meaning of 'one meter', then if things had been different, that is, in different counterfactual situations, it would pick out different lengths. That stick might have been produced differently, or at a different temperature, and so on. But Kripke says, 'one meter' is a rigid designator, and so given that it is introduced as naming the length of S at t, it picks out that same length in every possible world. Of one of those other worlds we would say that S would not have been one meter in that world, not that one meter would have been a different length. The notion of *fixing the reference* helps to explain this phenomenon. A description may fix the reference of a term by being used to introduce that term. The description identifies the referent as the thing that satisfies it in the actual world. The term then refers to that same thing in all other worlds, whether or not the description used to fix the reference is true of that thing in those worlds. Kripke gives the example of Neptune as perhaps an actual case where this has occurred. 'Neptune' may well have had its reference fixed by a description like 'the one planet perturbing the orbit of such and such other planets [which] exists in such and such a position' (Kripke 1980 [1972], p. 79, fn. 33).

The difference between a description fixing the reference of a name and giving the meaning, as the description theory would have it, also comes out in terms of the status of how we know certain truths about the referent. Condition (5) of the description theory of names holds that A knows a priori that if X exists, then φX. Consider 'one meter' as a name for a length, and suppose that 'the length of S at t_0' is the description used to fix the reference. If that description is thought, on the other hand, to give part of the meaning of 'one meter' then 'The length of S at t_0 is one meter' will express a necessary truth. That this is not so is another example of the problem raised by 'Aristotle' earlier. But it will be also true that whoever fixed the description can know that S (at t_0) is one meter long a priori, as a simple result of knowing the meaning of 'one meter'. This argument relies on a distinction between a priori truths and those that are necessary, which is independent of Kripke's theory of names and which he in fact introduces as a preliminary to understanding the arguments about naming. This will be discussed in Chapter 3, but here it will be introduced through its connection with names.

5. A PRIORI CONTINGENT AND A POSTERIORI NECESSARY TRUTHS

Philosophers have long made out a difference between two distinctions and, since Kant at least, have expressed them with the same terminology. One is the distinction between a posteriori and a priori truths, between those propositions that can be known without recourse to experience and those knowledge of which is justified by experience. There has been a standard association between a priori and necessary truths, and between a posteriori and contingent truths. While Kant did not simply identify the first two, he did hold that necessity was a mark of the a priori, so what is a priori will certainly be necessary since its truth does not depend on contingent experience. It would seem then that if a truth is known a posteriori, and so on the basis of empirical evidence, since that empirical evidence could have come out differently, such a truth will be contingent. Kripke challenges this common assumption, first distinguishing between what has come to be called *epistemic* possibility, what could be the case for all we know, and so-called *metaphysical* possibility, what might have been the case, independently of our knowledge. It would seem that mathematical truths are metaphysically necessary, and not dependent on any contingent facts. But not all mathematical truths are known. Take a famous open problem, such as Goldbach's conjecture that an even number greater than 2 must be the sum of two prime numbers. This has not been proved (or proved false), and so is "possible" in the epistemic sense. Yet we are convinced that this, like all truths of arithmetic, and even mathematics, are necessarily true, if true at all. If Goldbach's conjecture is true, it is necessarily true; if not true (that is, if there is some even number that is not the sum of two primes), it is necessarily false. Now, isn't it possible that we could come to know the truth in an a posteriori fashion, say from seeing the result of a computer calculation, and not by working through a proof? This would be an example of a truth that is necessary, but not known a priori. Might there not be some truth so complex that while still necessary, it could not even possibly be known a priori? Thus we conclude that the categories of necessary and a priori truths are distinct. Kripke argued that the categories are also distinct conversely, that is, that there can also be a priori but contingent truths. These truths are discovered by considering the phenomenon of reference fixing. That the length of S at t_0 is one meter is knowable a priori if the reference of 'one meter' was fixed by the description 'the length of S at t_0'. If we understand the meaning of our words, in this case, how the reference of 'one meter' is fixed, then we know a priori that this proposition is true. Yet it is not a necessary truth, for the bar might have been some other length, just as easily as it might come to be a different length through shrinking or expanding.

That such an example is a genuine case of the a priori knowledge of contingent truths has been disputed. It is claimed, for example, that this example doesn't count as a priori knowledge, as we must have some (contingent, empirical) contact with S to know that it is the standard meter, or to know anything about *it* in particular, and so to know even that it is one meter, also depends on a posteriori knowledge. Keith Donnellan (1979 [1977]) points out that we might know a priori that a certain sentence is true without being said to know what it expresses. Thus, using the Neptune example, we might know a priori that 'Neptune causes the perturbations in the orbit of Uranus' is true, because 'Neptune' has its reference fixed as the thing that causes the perturbations of Uranus. Yet we are in no position to genuinely know the proposition that Neptune causes the perturbations in the orbit of Uranus because we have no knowledge of what thing Neptune is, haven't seen it, etc., and so simply can't in any way be said to have knowledge "of" it (Kripke 1980 [1972], p.50).[15] Despite the disputes about the purported examples of a priori contingent truths, as a result of Kripke's proposal of the idea philosophers generally came to mark the distinction between "metaphysical" and "epistemological" concerns more carefully, to make a clear distinction between a priori and necessary truth, and generally between how a truth is known and the status of the fact it expresses.

One of Kripke's most influential examples of a class of necessary truths which could come to be known in an a posteriori fashion were the very examples of identity sentences that Frege used to introduce the notion of the sense of a name in the first place. If proper names are rigid designators, and hence designate the same individual in each possible world, then if two names 'α' and 'β' designate the same individual rigidly, the proposition asserting the identity '$\alpha = \beta$' will be a necessary truth. Suppose that 'Hesperus' is a name for Venus, perhaps one introduced with the description 'the morning star'. That description might simply fix the reference of the name, or even give its meaning. Suppose that 'Phosphorus' is another name for the same planet, perhaps introduced with the description 'the evening star'. If Hesperus is thus indeed

---

[15] See Chapter 3 of this volume.

the same planet as Phosphorus then 'Hesperus is Phosphorus' will be a necessary truth. Identities involving rigid designators are necessary truths. Behind this application of the view of names in *Naming and Necessity* is another influence from Kripke's earlier work on quantified modal logic. Before 1970 there was some discussion of the notion of purportedly "contingent" identities, both in the philosophy of mind and in discussions of theoretical identifications. It was felt that certain views in the philosophy of mind suggested that while a mental state is identical with some particular state of the brain or central nervous system, that is only a contingent truth, since the physical state might have been some other one.[16]

Kripke insisted, however, that an identity, if true, must be necessarily the case. He offered a simple proof. Suppose that objects x and y are identical, then any property of x is a property of y. But one of those properties of x is being necessarily identical with itself, that is, necessarily identical with x, so y has that property, that is, it is necessarily identical with x. This is not yet a proof that true identities involving names are necessary. There is an important step involved with moving from variables, such as 'x' and 'y', to names, such as 'Hesperus' and 'Phosphorus', and one might in fact speculate that it was thinking about these very issues that led Kripke from his early technical work in quantified modal logic to the theory of names and reference.[17]

Provided that identities involving names, if they obtain, are necessary, then the notion that names are rigid designators gives rise to a whole class of necessary truths, some of which may in fact be discovered a posteriori. With this example in mind, Kripke mentions some other cases, not arguing for the metaphysical assumptions, but in order to show how such truths interact with the use of names. One such doctrine is the "necessity of origin." One might hold that persons have their origin in the meeting of a certain sperm and egg, as a mattter of metaphysical necessity. Thus they will have their parents, in some sense, necessarily. To use Kripke's example, someone could look just like Queen Elizabeth, but be born of other parents, say Mr. (Harry) and Mrs. (Bess) Truman, and so wouldn't *be* Elizabeth Windsor. The logical positivists held that any necessary truth about an individual must in fact be an analytic truth about the individual *under a description*. This doctrine is the source of Quine's example of the bicycling mathematician who, qua mathematician, is rational, but

---

[16] See, for example, Armstrong 1968, p. 91.
[17] See Chapters 4 and 5 of this volume.

qua bicyclist is two-legged, but not in himself one or the other (Quine 1960, p. 199). There can be no such *de re* necessity about individuals in themselves being necessarily one way or the other, he argues, unless one makes invidious distinctions between the accidental and essential properties of individuals. Quine suggested that taking such distinctions seriously led to the "jungle of Aristotelian essentialism" (Quine 1976 [1957], p. 176) and so gave a slogan to the attitude of suspicion towards such metaphysical notions that was only cast off following Kripke's lectures. The new theory of names, which distinguished names so sharply from descriptions, provoked philosophers to abandon the view that *de re* necessity was bound to analyticity "under a description," and so to enter that jungle, and begin to discriminate accidental from essential properties without fear that they were confusing things and their descriptions.

Another intuition about the necessary properties of individuals, also opened up for discussion by the notion of *de re* necessity for objects, independent of their description, is that of the *essentiality of origin* for artifacts. It is an interesting question, and one which perhaps leads inevitably to the "Ship of Theseus" paradox, as to just what material parts a material artifact may lose over time and still remain the same thing. It is a different question to ask to what extent an object could have been made from different material from the start.[18] Kripke's example is of the table before him, which, he claims, since it was made of wood originally, could not have been made from some other material, say, a block of ice. Any table made of ice would not be that very table but some other. The table might perhaps turn into ice over time, without being destroyed, or might turn out to be actually made of ice, in the sense of epistemic possibility that has appeared before, but it is not the case that this table could have originally been made of a different block of ice, or even a different block of wood. The view is just presented without argument in the text of the lectures. A footnote in which Kripke says this view is capable of "something like proof" (Kripke 1980 [1972], p. 114. fn 56) has been the subject of discussion in the literature, and the proof seems to lead to a modal version of the "Ship of Theseus" problem.[19]

---

[18] In the original paradox we are required to figure out what happens when pieces of wood from an original ship are slowly replaced and then reassembled in a new ship. Which ship is the original, the slowly restored ship or the one reconstructed from the salvaged parts? In the modal version, we are asked to figure out what ships would have been which if ships were not changed in time, but had been made from the beginning of various overlapping collections of planks in different possible worlds.

[19] See Salmon (1981, appendix I, pp. 219–52), who picks up the original example from Hugh Chandler 1975.

Kripke says that he thinks he had no ambition to derive these metaphysical conclusions from his account of names, and indeed only the conclusion about the necessity of identity follows from semantics alone. Nevertheless, the impression might be given that these results do follow from semantics alone. Nathan Salmon's book *Reference and Essence* (1981) tries to disentangle the semantic and metaphysical assumptions at play in these doctrines. Even the simple extension of the necessity of identity from cases like 'Hesperus = Phosphorus' to 'water = H_2O', argues Salmon, requires the introduction of substantive metaphysical assumptions that enter into the analogue for kind terms of the "baptism" of individuals. It is not clear, however, to what extent people were taken in by these confusions, at least regarding singular terms. It seems that, while now aware of such possible confusions, discussions of essential properties of individuals have continued within the context of Kripke's account of names as non-descriptional rigid designators.

6. NAMING KRIPKE'S "THEORY" OF NAMES

If the "cluster of descriptions" theory of names is wrong, what should replace it? Kripke hesitates to present a rigorous theory that might give necessary and sufficient conditions for saying that a name has a particular reference. He jokingly suggests that he is too lazy to do so, but the explanation that "philosophical theories are in danger of being false," hints at a view about the possibility of philosophical theories that propose definitions. Instead he proposes a "better picture," a story about a central case of naming, which has suggested to many a replacement for the cluster of descriptions theory. The picture focuses on how names for persons are introduced. In a paradigm case there is an initial "baptism" or other event, by which people intend to associate a given name with a given individual. At a Christian baptism, a baby is present when its name is announced. It may be that some names, for things other than people, are associated with descriptions, which "fix" the reference of the name. Then, although the name is often used in the presence of the reference, it is passed on from speaker to speaker without any further connection with the original source being involved in the process. A name is passed down a chain of speakers who use it with the intention of preserving its reference, so that eventually the name can still be used to refer to that individual after the individual, and even perhaps all knowledge of the properties of that individual, is long gone. Kripke describes the transmission of the name 'Jonah' in just this way.

Despite Kripke's own reluctance to give a "theory" of reference, soon after the publication of the lectures numerous proposals for a wholly new theory of reference appeared, some identifying the new theory as Kripke's own, others as an extension of it and a filling out of the details that he declined to give. A look at the terminology used reveals that different aspects of Kripke's picture were picked up and found to be the essence of the new theory. From early on Kripke was associated with the thesis that "proper names are rigid designators." Others picked up on the fact that the chain which passes along the references of names involves causal contact between speakers. They dubbed the new theory "the causal theory of reference" to mark a similarity with the earlier "causal theory of perception" of Grice (1961), and some other uses of the notion in the field of epistemology.[20] The causal theory of perception held that what makes a visual experience be of one thing rather than another is not the match between an experience and the object, but rather the causal origin of the experience. The object of perception can be found by tracing back the right sort of causal process to its origin in some perceived object. Causal theories of semantic relations such as reference were to fit into a large project of "naturalizing" semantics, of reducing semantic notions to those of natural science, as in Devitt (1981), for example. Donnellan (1974) addressed the question of how the theory could be adapted to names with no denotation, such as 'Santa Claus'. Donnellan proposed that the key point of the new theory was that a name could be followed back from user to user, much as the search for the historical Jonah might be carried out. The search for Santa Claus might end in an individual with very different properties from those associated with Santa, say a bishop Nicholas in the fourth century, or one might judge that at some point no attempt was being made to refer to a real individual and that the name was just made up. Tracing the name back would then end in a "block."[21] This sort of theory goes by the names "historical theory of reference" or "causal-historical theory of reference," emphasizing the role of the historical source of a name as crucial to determining its reference over the causal nature of the links in the chain.

Gareth Evans (1973) concentrated on the nature of the connection between speakers needed to preserve reference. His example was of 'Madagascar', perhaps originally used for a spot on the coast of Africa, and so historically traceable to the mainland, but which

---

[20] Gareth Evans talks of the "the Causal Theory of Reference" and "the Historical Explanation Theory of Reference" (Evans 1989, p. 79).

[21] See Chapter 2 of this volume.

eventually became associated with information from the island that is currently the denotation of the name.[22] Others saw the essence of the theory as the view that names are directly connected with their referents in the way that a Fregean theory of sense would not. Thus on a Fregean theory a reference is seen as "mediated" by a sense. The name is associated with a sense, and the sense denotes an individual. The Kripkean theory was then like that of Russell on logically proper names, a "direct" theory of reference.[23] On this view, Kripke's account of proper names was very much like Donnellan's notion of the referential use of definite descriptions. Kripke did address this related work on reference, arguing that his notion of reference-fixing descriptions is distinct from the notion of the referential use of descriptions. He argues that Donnellan's notion was one of speaker meaning rather than his of word meaning, as will be described later. Even the seemingly neutral name "New Theory of Reference" that some use may mislead. Hilary Putnam was writing around the same time about the meaning of general terms and "natural kind terms" with some ideas similar to Kripke's.[24] So the term "New Theory of Reference" is generally used more broadly, to include Kripke and Putnam and various other authors.[25] This lack of a simple name for Kripke's views is thus no accident. They do not present a single, distinct theory, but rather a bundle of connected views. To top this off, even the simple expedient of identifying the proposals as "Kripke's *theory* of proper names" fails to observe the remarks about this only providing a "picture" of naming and not a philosophical theory.

7. GENERAL NAMES

In the third lecture of *Naming and Necessity*, Kripke extended his ideas about singular terms to general terms.

---

[22] Kripke 1980 p. 173 discusses Evans's example.

[23] Kaplan 1989 describes what he calls the "Semantics of Direct Reference": "By this I mean theories of meaning according to which certain singular terms refer directly without the mediation of a Fregean *Sinn* as meaning" (Kaplan 1989, p. 483). Kaplan goes on to distinguish the way that reference is determined, which in the case of indexicals, might involve something like a sense, from the contribution that a term makes to the propositions to which it belongs, in the case of directly referential terms, simply the referent itself. Kripke's interest in *Naming and Necessity* is in the first issue, and he is silent about the notion of content.

[24] Putnam 1975, "The Meaning of 'Meaning'" and 1970, "Is Semantics Possible?"

[25] Salmon says that the theory was spoken of as the "'new' or 'causal' theory of reference" (Salmon 1981, p. 3).

... my argument implicitly concludes that certain general terms, those for natural kinds, have a greater kinship with proper names than is generally realized. This conclusion holds for certain for various species names, whether they are count nouns, such as 'cat', 'tiger', 'chunk of gold', or mass terms such as 'gold', 'water', 'iron pyrites'. It also applies to certain terms for natural phenomena, such as 'heat', 'light', 'sound', 'lightening', and presumably, suitably elaborated, to corresponding adjectives – 'hot', 'loud', 'red'. (Kripke 1980 [1972], p. 134)

Again returning to Mill's *System of Logic*, Kripke says that while Mill may have been right in holding that proper names have only denotation and no connotation, he was wrong in not saying the same of general terms.[26] Mill was just one in a long line of philosophers who have held that a general term picks out the objects that satisfy it by expressing properties of those objects, what Kant called "marks" of the concept.[27] It was these properties that were related in analytic general truths. Kant's example 'Gold is a yellow metal' was to be counted as an analytic truth, on the grounds that the term 'Gold' has as part of its meaning the property of being a yellow metal.[28] Mill held that a general term has both an "intension," consisting of properties "implied" by the term, and an extension, consisting of the objects of which it is true. What was crucial to Mill's view, and what Kripke rejected, was that this extension is determined by the properties that are part of the meaning of the general term. Kripke suggested that this new view of general terms might be correct for a number of cases, such as names for stuff, 'water' or 'gold', names for species, 'tiger', and more generally, "natural kind terms." The various arguments against a cluster theory of descriptions for proper names would show that kind terms work like names. Thus his examples of 'tigers', 'water', and 'lightning'.

As was the case with proper names, one must now distinguish between a priori truths and necessary truths about kinds. Following the model of the necessity of origin of individuals, there can be similar necessary truths about kinds, such as the truth that cats are necessarily animals.[29] While necessary, such a truth would be known a posteriori, however. The results of the theory extended beyond the possibility of expressing necessary but not analytic truths about kinds. There is also a version of the

[26] Kripke 1980 (1972), p. 134.

[27] Although soon precedents for Kripke's views started turning up, as in Mackie 1974, "Locke's Anticipation of Kripke."

[28] Kripke cites Kant's *Prolegomena to Any Future Metaphysics*, Preamble, section 2.b. (Prussian Academy edition, p. 267) at (Kripke 1980 [1972], p. 177).

[29] Hilary Putnam's example in "It Ain't Necessarily So" (Putnam 1962), and discussed by Kripke at p. 122.

doctrine of the necessity of identity for general terms that is applicable to various philosophical issues, such as the "theoretical identifications" of the sciences, and the mind/body problem in the philosophy of mind. If one views the theoretical identification of lightning with electricity or of water with H_2O, we come up with surprising necessities. Kripke discusses the examples 'Light is a stream of photons', 'Heat is the motion of molecules' (p. 129), and 'Lightning is an electrical discharge' (p. 132). If lightning is the same phenomenon as a certain sort of electrical discharge, then it is so necessarily. If water is H_2O, that is also a necessary truth. These would seem to be the very model of empirically discovered truths, so like necessary identities involving names, they are examples of the necessary a posteriori. There is just no such thing as "contingent identity", even for kind terms.

One purported example of a contingent identity that was prominent in philosophical discussions at the time of the lectures was provided by the identity of mind and body proposed by "materialist" accounts of mind. Kripke discusses the example of the identity of pain with the stimulation of C-fibers. As is the case with proper names, if the general names 'pain' and 'C-fiber stimulation' are both rigid designators, then if 'pain = C-fiber stimulation' is true, it is necessarily true. But surely these seem like contingent truths. Water might not have been H_2O, we think. But that is because there might have been something which looks just like water, but which isn't water. Putnam's example was that it might be some compound "XYZ".[30] This is a case of epistemic possibility like the case of Hesperus and Phosphorus. But Kripke argued, in the case of pain there could not be something that feels just like pain but isn't really since it isn't the stimulation of C-fibers. Anything that feels like pain *is* pain, whatever physical process it might be. Thus the apparent contingency of the identity can't be explained away. Thus, Kripke argued, it must be false, and so was born an argument for dualism in the philosophy of mind, one that has spawned a long discussion in the literature.[31]

It was not only the applications of the theory to general terms that gave rise to a literature, but even the very notion of extending the theory to general terms. It was pointed out that there is a difference between a general term like 'yellow' or 'bachelor' and an abstract *singular* term for a kind or property like 'yellowness' or 'bachelorhood'. While Kripke's

---

[30] In his 1975. XYZ was primarily a hypothetical substance on another world that would have the phenomenal appearance of water, rather than a structure that water might turn out to have.

[31] See Chapter 13 in this volume.

theory might make sense as an account of the meaning of such abstract singular terms, it doesn't make sense as an account of general terms. If a general term designates anything, it is its extension, it was thought, and so a rigid general term will simply be one with the same extension in every world, and so none of the examples Kripke mentions qualify as rigid. On the other hand, if to be rigid is instead to have the same intension with respect to every world, this does not distinguish kind terms from their supposed contrast in terms like 'yellow' or 'bachelor', or indeed any primitive general term.[32] As a result, there has been a dispute about how to generalize Kripke's views about singular terms to general terms, whether they are seen as abstract singular terms or as real, predicative, general terms.

In his book *Beyond Rigidity* (2002), Scott Soames considers and rejects one possible account of what it might mean to treat a general term as rigid that can, at least with some adjustments and added complications, be made to work.[33] The rejected proposal goes like this. We are first to think of general terms as represented by abstract singular terms. The predicate 'blue' becomes 'the property blue' and the kind predicate 'tiger' becomes 'the kind tiger'. The proposal is that if the resulting abstract singular term is rigid, then we would speak of the originating general term as rigid.

As an example, Soames (following Salmon and me) considers the use of the general term 'the color of a cloudless sky at noon', which seems to serve as a nonrigid predicate in this example (p. 261):

7) Her eyes are the color of a cloudless sky at noon.

However, Soames argues that the verb phrase, or predicate, of (7) should be analyzed as composed of two constituents, an abstract singular term, and a use of 'is' (or 'are') that attributes membership in a kind or possession of a property. Accordingly, there will be two different abstract singular terms that can be taken as corresponding to that apparent general term:

8) the color that cloudless skies at noon are instances of

and

9) the property of being the same in color as a cloudless sky at noon

---

[32] See Soames 2002, chapter 9, particularly p. 249 and following, for this point.

[33] Crediting this possible interpretation of the example to Nathan Salmon (p. 366, n.19). Salmon's actual proposal is presented in Salmon 2003 and 2005. Salmon treats both 'blue' and 'the color of a cloudless sky at noon' as general terms rather than singular, and both designating the color blue (rather than the set of blue things).

(8) is a nonrigid abstract singular term, picking out blue in this world, and perhaps a different color, such as red, in a different world. (9) seems to rigidly designate the relational property of having whatever color the sky has.

Soames sees the fact that both (8) and (9) correspond with the predicate of (7) as a refutation of the proposed test. Which analysis of (7) are we to use? To defend this substitution test for distinguishing rigid from nonrigid general terms, one must find a principled distinction between the various singular terms that one might pick and say that a term is rigid just in case the correctly selected abstract singular term is rigid.

The claim that general terms can be either rigid or nonrigid thus requires that there are two ways of reading (7).[34] On the first reading, since (8) contingently designates the property of being blue, the proposition expressed by (7) attributes the property of being blue to her eyes. As represented by (8), however, (7) can be seen as attributing a *different* property to her eyes, namely the relational property of having whatever color the sky has. Consider a world *w* where there is more dust in the sky than in actuality and so the sky is red at noon and not only sometimes in the evening or morning. According to both readings of the predicate, (7) is true at *w* if her eyes are red at *w*. The reading using (8) produces that result because the property (8) (nonrigidly) designates at *w* is that of being red. However, read using (9), (7) gives that result because being the same color as the sky in *w* requires a thing to be red. (9) rigidly designates that relational property.

In his (2003) and (2005), Nathan Salmon argues that it is important to distinguish general terms, which may or may not be rigid, from predicates, for which the distinction cuts differently. He holds that a predicate designates its extension, so a rigid predicate can only be a predicate with a constant extension across possible worlds. (See his 1981, chapter 2c). If a predicate were taken to designate its intension, all predicates would be equally rigid. The alternative view suggested here holds that a predicate 'is F' or 'is an F' inherits the rigid/nonrigid character of the general term 'F' from which it is constructed. Soames, as a third alternative, prefers to analyze 'is F' in these cases as involving an abstract singular term and a relation of possession or kind membership, as 'possesses F-ness' or 'is a member of the kind F'.

This view, that predicates as well as general terms can be rigid or nonrigid designators, can be formally expressed in two ways. One of these

---

[34] I present this account in my 1984 and 2006. See also Martí and Martínez-Fernández (2010) for an elaboration of the view.

ways is to treat at least some predicates as disguised (second-order) definite descriptions. The nonrigid predicates will be represented as nonrigid descriptions, denoting different properties in different worlds. The predicates F from which those descriptions are constructed have conventional semantic values, namely an intension that determines an extension with respect to each possible world. A simple predicate F will be said to designate a property P if F has an intension such that in each world w the extension of F at w contains the individuals that have the property P in w. Such an F will be said to be rigid in the same sense in which a singular term that directly designates a referent (and not as a function of worlds) is rigid. On this account, second-order definite descriptions, however, which can serve as predicates, can be nonrigid designators of properties.

The other way of cashing out this way of reading predicates is to represent the intension of any predicate as a function that takes possible worlds as arguments and yields properties as values. A rigid predicate is then one for which that function is constant, yielding the same property with respect to each world. A nonrigid predicate will instead pick out distinct properties at some different worlds. Let us call this second approach the "double indexing" account, because of the double way in which worlds enter into determining the extension of a predicate, first to determine the property it expresses at a world, and then to determine the extension of that property at a given world. Suppose that a singular term n designates an object o with respect to a world w. Then the atomic sentence 'n is F' will be true at w just in case o has, at w, the property P that F designates with respect to w. The same world index w enters twice over into the computation of the semantic value of the predication. Only in the presence of certain world-sensitive operators, such as actuality operators that fix one of the indices as the actual world, will this double indexing not be redundant by taking the same argument twice over. This is just a sketch of the formal mechanism, but it should be enough to suggest how predicates might be distinguished as rigid or nonrigid.

The defender of the view that predicates can be nonrigid designators will say that predicates need to be distinguished into sorts. On both the double-indexing and descriptional accounts, a sentence like (7) is ambiguous. On one use it says, with respect to the actual world, that her eyes are blue, since the value of the meaning of 'are the color of a cloudless sky at noon' at the actual world is the property blue, but in another world, as described, they would be red. Soames's candidate, (8), 'The color that cloudless skies at noon are instances of', is the abstract singular term that represents this reading. On a somewhat more unusual reading, (7) can be used to say that her eyes take on whatever color the sky may have at noon. On this reading the intension of 'are the color of a cloudless sky at noon' is a function that at each world yields the property of being the same color as a cloudless sky at noon, making it a rigid predicate. Soames's (9), 'the property of being the same in color as a cloudless sky at noon' is the abstract singular term that corresponds with this use. Both interpretations yield the same truth conditions for (7), since whatever has the property that is the color of the sky at a world w will also be a thing that has the same color as the sky at w, yet the semantic mechanisms determining those truth conditions differ. When embedded in a context involving modal or other intensional operators, those two mechanisms will differ enough to yield different truth values, however. This establishes that they are genuinely different meanings.

In discussions of the mind/body problem in the years before *Naming and Necessity,* there was some discussion of the notion of contingent identity between mental states and physical states. It was also proposed that certain mental predicates be seen on the model of definite descriptions. Thus around the time Kripke gave his lectures, David Lewis was developing a view on which psychological terms like 'pain' apply to whatever brain state causes certain behavior when caused by certain stimuli. Indeed one might represent the meaning of 'pain' as a definite description 'the physical type instances of which play such and such functional role in our psychology."[35] Somewhat later D. M. Armstrong, writing about dispositions, suggested that a term like 'brittle' might mean something like "possessing that property (or range of properties) in virtue of which objects (generally) shatter when hit sharply."[36] This analysis could also be seen as representing such terms as (second-order) definite descriptions. It would then treat the identities considered earlier, such as 'pain = C-fiber stimulation', as literally identity sentences involving at least one definite description, and hence only contingently true, if true at all.

David Lewis suggests a double indexing account of such terms in his paper "How to Define Theoretical Terms." There he finds an ambiguity in the expression 'the property of having τ_1'.[37] τ_1 can be thought of as a

[35] Lewis, D 1966, 17–25.
[36] Armstrong 1978, p. 57.
[37] Lewis 1983, p. 87.

definite description, 'the property that plays such and such a theoretical role'. On the first reading, 'the property of having τ_1,' just picks out the same property as τ_1. On the second it names what he, and now others, call the "diagonalized" sense of τ_1:

> The sense of τ_1 may be represented by a function $\| \tau_1 \|$ which assigns to any world w a property $\| \tau_1 \|_w$. A property in turn may be represented by a function P which assigns to any world w the set P_w of things which, in the world w, have the property. Then the diagonalized sense of τ_1 is the property whose representing function assigns to any world w the set of things $(\| \tau_1 \|_w)_w$.

On both readings of 'the property of having τ_1,', it will be both necessary and knowable a priori: $\forall x$ (x is τ_1 iff x is an instance of the property of having τ_1). Indeed, it is the suggestion of such a priori knowledge that seems behind some recent discussion of "two-dimensional" semantics.[38] But there is still a difference between the two readings.

The ambiguity that Lewis finds is represented by the different patterns of double indexing needed to represent the extension of the term with respect to a world. The two world indices are relevant in different ways, one to figure out what property is expressed by a term at each world, the second to determine the relevant world with which to determine the extension of the property. Using Lewis's apparatus, a rigid term will be one that designates the same property with respect to each world: that is, $\| \tau_1 \|_w$ is the same property for every w. A nonrigid term designates different properties in different worlds. Lewis treats most theoretical terms as nonrigid, since they are defined by the sort of construction now referred to as the so-called Ramsey-Lewis method as "the" property that plays such and such a role in a given theory. While Kripke's discussion is of natural kind terms rather than theoretical terms, Kripke's thesis about the terms he considers nonetheless can be seen as opposed to a Lewis-style account of those same terms.

Kripke's slogan that natural kind terms are rigid designators can be interpreted as claiming that kind terms are in fact not to be analyzed as second-order definite descriptions, either in the way I have sketched or in the "double indexing" way that Lewis suggests. For Kripke, 'pain' does not have the sort of meaning suggested by Lewis, as 'the property playing such and such functional role …'. Nor is it a term that designates C-fibers' firing in this world and some other brain property in other

---

[38] Frank Jackson presents such a semantic view as the basis for a program in metaphysics in his 1998.

worlds. There are still options open to Kripke for general terms that are not natural kind terms. He does not mention 'brittle' or other dispositional terms on his list of kind terms 'water', 'tiger', and 'pain'. He could have agreed with Armstrong about 'brittle' as precisely like a definite description, or he could have said rather that 'brittle' rigidly designates the property that in fact underlies or "realizes" the dispositional feature of being brittle. So there is a real issue about which way to analyze various theoretical and kind terms, whether as rigid terms or as definite descriptions. There is some content to the claim that a general term behaves like a description that is not rigid.

Now even on the alternative account of rigid designation for general names which has been described here, the most common sort of general terms such as 'bachelor(hood)' and 'red(ness)' come out as rigid. They directly designate a property that has an extension with respect to each world, what is a bachelor or red in that world.[39] Rigidity, on this account, does not distinguish kind terms like 'gold' from those general terms like 'yellow metal', or from any purported "definition" of 'gold' such as 'the yellow, malleable, ... metal'. Even on this novel account of predicates as designators, most general terms turn out to be rigid, and natural kind terms are not distinctive in this regard. Still, saying that natural kind terms are rigid does make a substantive claim, even if it is one that is denied.

8. SPEAKER'S REFERENCE AND SEMANTIC REFERENCE

In the *Naming and Necessity* lectures, Kripke made use of the distinction between speaker's reference and semantic reference to explain some of our intuitions about the use of names. A speaker's reference is what the speaker intends to refer to and to get her audience to identify as her referent. These notions are implicit in Grice's 1957 theory of meaning, according to which meaning is the result of making an utterance with a certain complex intention, including for the audience to realize that the speaker has that intention. While Grice does not do so, there is a natural way of extending his notion of meaning to the realm of reference. On the Gricean account, a speaker *refers* to an object with a name by using that name with the intention of getting an audience to identify some individual by means of recognizing that very intention, and so

---

[39] There might still be a contrary, minority, opinion even on some of these cases. For one might take 'red' to be a description on the order of 'the microphysical property which makes things look red', where 'looks red' directly refers to a phenomenal, secondary, quality, while 'red' itself turns out to name a physical cause for that secondary quality.

on, following the details and complications of Grice's theory of utterance meaning. For *sentence meaning* the intentions relate to getting the audience to have a certain belief, or at least entertain a certain thought, while with *reference* they involve identifying what object the speaker has in mind. The *semantic reference* of a name will be that which is associated with it conventionally as part of a language, which it can be expected to be used to refer to on the basis of the meaning of the language alone. This distinction helps to explain the heterogeneous look of the list of theses of the "cluster theory" given earlier. Conditions (1) and (2) have to do with what a speaker believes about the referent of a name. Perhaps such beliefs are needed for speaker's reference, but it is less likely that they are needed for semantic reference. Indeed, Kripke's alternative "picture" suggests how a name could get its semantic reference in a language quite independently of what descriptions a speaker believes apply to the referent.

Kripke's 1977 paper "Speaker's Reference and Semantic Reference" is a detailed presentation of this distinction, organized around the refutation of a number of incorrect views about the "referential/attributive" distinction of Keith Donnellan (1966). Donnellan had argued that there are two distinctive uses of definite descriptions, which he called "referential" and "attributive" *uses*. In the 1966 paper it is not clear that these are intended to be different meanings, rather than different uses of an expression with a fixed meaning, though that has come to be openly discussed in later papers by Donnellan and others. Donnellan's chief example is of the description 'Smith's murderer' (which can be represented literally as a definite description by 'the murderer of Smith'). Suppose that we come across Smith foully murdered, and say, based on the state of the corpse, "Smith's murderer is insane" with the appropriate general intention. This is a case of the attributive use of the description. Now someone, Jones, is arrested and put on trial for the murder of Smith. In the courtroom, noticing the demeanor of Jones on the stand, I say "Smith's murderer is insane" again, with the intention of referring to that particular person. This time the use is *referential*. I clearly have a particular individual "in mind." If it turns out that Jones did not kill Smith, I can still be taken to have *said of* Jones that he was insane. Whether these intuitive features of the uses can be turned into sure tests is one of the issues about Donnellan's distinction.

Kripke argues that the referential/attributive distinction should not be confused with other distinctions, some of which he makes in the *Naming and Necessity* lectures. For one thing, the referential/attributive distinction should not be confused with the distinction between *de re* and *de dicto* beliefs. We may talk of two forms of sentences about belief and other propositional attitudes, which would be represented with different scopes of a definite description and sentential operator. We can say "X believes that Smith's murderer is insane" with the *de dicto* sense of 'Smith's murderer', believing that the proposition "Whoever is Smith's murderer is insane" is true. We may also have a belief *of* some individual y, who is in fact the murderer, that y is insane, as in "Of Smith's murderer, X believes that he or she is insane." This is represented with the other scope analysis, with the description having wider scope than the "belief" operator. Kripke rejects identifying the two distinctions, arguing that the referential/attributive distinction is binary while scope distinctions arise for every operator and quantifier or description in a proposition, allowing for so-called intermediate scopes. It's not the same phenomenon.

Nor should the referential/attributive distinction be identified with rigidified definite descriptions. One might think of an operator that could be applied to a description 'the F', such as 'actual' so as to produce 'the actual F'. With respect to any world, this would designate the thing that is F in the actual world.[40] This has been proposed as a variant to Dummett's view of names as being like descriptions with wide scope. One might suppose that names are thus *rigidified descriptions*. To this assimilation Kripke replies that even treated as rigidified, a description such as 'the F' must refer to something that is F, but for the referential use of a description this is not required.

Kripke's own account of the referential/attributive distinction makes use of Gricean notions to distinguish speaker's reference and semantic reference. In what Kripke calls the "simple case," the speaker simply intends to refer to the semantic referent of a name. In the "complex case," the speaker's intentions can differ. The attributive use of definite descriptions is a simple case and the referential use is complex. Part of Kripke's argument that this is not a distinctive semantic feature of definite descriptions is that it arises for other expressions, including names. We may see Smith raking leaves but both we, and our audience, all think that we see Jones. If we say "Jones is raking leaves," it is clear to whom the speaker is referring (Kripke 1979 [1977], p. 14). This is a case where the speaker's referent and the semantic referent can differ for a *name*.

---

[40] Citing Kaplan as making a connection between rigidity and Donnellan's referential use of descriptions. Kaplan presents an account of direct reference and its relation to these other notions in his 1989.

The generality of the phenomenon suggests that it is not a case of an ambiguity for a particular part of speech.

In fact Kripke offers a test for identifying such pragmatic rather than semantic phenomena in general. We are asked to consider a language in which a given phenomenon is stipulated to occur. Suppose we say that there is a language that does have a referential/attributive distinction in the semantics. It will still happen that speakers using the clearly marked attributive description will still have someone in mind and use it referentially. This, Kripke argues, shows that this language is not ours. The referential/attributive distinction is thus a result of the distinction between speaker's reference and semantic reference and not a case of semantic ambiguity. Incidentally, then, it is not possible to see proper names as synonymous with definite descriptions used referentially, and the central argument of *Naming and Necessity* is supported.

9. CONCLUSION

Kripke's *Naming and Necessity* ushered in a new theory of reference, marking a distinct epoch in the twentieth-century development of the subject as great as Strawson's "On Referring" had in 1950. The wider importance of the lectures, however, comes from their application to issues outside the narrow dialectic of descriptions and Millian names that had bounded the discussion through Russell, Frege, and Strawson, and on to Searle with the cluster theory. With the sharp distinction between the mechanism determining the referent of a name and what descriptive properties might pick out that referent, Kripke made it possible to consider metaphysical issues separately from the epistemic issues with which they had been so closely associated. It became easier to discuss issues of *de re* necessity without thinking that such necessity applies to an individual "under a description." While the jungle of Aristotelian essentialism was thus opened to exploration, a more immediate result came from the clearing away of possible objections to the simply proved necessity of identity. As will be seen in the following chapters, Kripke's theory of proper and general names had consequences in many other areas of philosophy.

References

Almog, J. (2002) *What Am I? Descartes and the Mind-Body Problem.* Oxford: Oxford University Press.

Armstrong, D. M. (1968) *A Materialist Theory of the Mind.* London: Routledge & Kegan Paul.

(1978) *A Theory of Universals, Universals and Scientific Realism, Vol. II.* Cambridge: Cambridge University Press.

Caton, C. E. (1963) *Philosophy and Ordinary Language.* Urbana: University of Illinois Press.

Chandler, H. (1975) Rigid Designation. *The Journal of Philosophy*, 72, 363–9.

Devitt, M. (1981) *Designation.* New York: Columbia University Press.

Donnellan, K. S. (1966) Reference and Definite Descriptions. *The Philosophical Review*, 75, 281–304.

(1974) Speaking of Nothing. *Philosophical Review*, 83, 3–31.

(1979 [1977]) The Contingent A Priori and Rigid Designators. In French, P. A., Uehling, T. E. Jr., and Wettstein, H. K. (Eds.) *Contemporary Perspectives in the Philosophy of Language*, 45–60. Minneapolis: University of Minnesota Press. Original publication (1977): *Midwest Studies in Philosophy*, 2, 12–27, Minneapolis: University of Minnesota Press.

Dummett, M. (1973) *Frege: Philosophy of Language*, 2nd ed. 1981. London: Duckworth.

Evans, G. (1973) The Causal Theory of Names. *Aristotelian Society, Supplementary Volume 47*, 187–208.

(1982) *The Varieties of Reference.* Oxford: Clarendon Press.

Frege, G. (1949 [1892]) Über Sinn und Bedeutung. *Zeitschrift für Philosophie und philosophische Kritik*, 100, 25–50. Trans. by H. Feigl as : On Sense and Nominatum, in Feigl, H., and Sellars, W. *Readings in Philosophical Analysis.* New York: Appleton-Century-Crofts.

Gillett, C., and Loewer, B. (Eds.) (2001) *Physicalism and Its Discontents.* Cambridge: Cambridge University Press.

Grice, H. P. (1957) Meaning. *Philosophical Review*, 66, 377–88.

(1961) The Causal Theory of Perception. *Proceedings of the Aristotelian Society, Supplementary Volume 35*, 121–52.

Jackson, F. (1998) *From Metaphysics to Ethics: A Defence of Conceptual Analysis.* Oxford: Clarendon Press.

Kaplan, D. (1989) Demonstratives. In Almog, J., Perry, J., and Wettstein, H. (Eds.) *Themes from Kaplan*, 481–563. New York: Oxford University Press.

Kripke, S. (1980 [1972]) *Naming and Necessity.* Cambridge: Harvard University Press. Original publication (1972): In Davidson, D., and Harman, G. (Eds.) *Semantics of Natural Language*, 253–355. Dordrecht: D. Reidel.

(1979 [1977]) Speaker's Reference and Semantic Reference. In French, P., Uehling, T., and Wettstein, H. (Eds.) *Contemporary Perspectives in the Philosophy of Language*, 6–27. Minneapolis: University of Minnesota Press. Original publication (1977): In French, P., Uehling, T., and Wettstein, H. (Eds.) *Midwest Studies in Philosophy II*, 255–76. Minneapolis: University of Minnesota Press.

(1979) A Puzzle about Belief. In Margalit, A. (Ed.) *Meaning and Use*, 239–75. Dordrecht: D. Reidel.

Lewis, D. (1966) An Argument for the Identity Theory. *Journal of Philosophy*, 63, 17–25.

(1968) Counterpart Theory and Quantified Modal Logic. *Journal of Philosophy*, 65, 113–26.

(1983). How to Define Theoretical Terms. In *Philosophical Papers I*, 78–95. Oxford: Oxford University Press, 1983.

Linsky, B. (1984) General Terms as Designators. *Pacific Philosophical Quarterly*, 65, 259–76.

(2006) General Terms as Rigid Designators. *Philosophical Studies*, 128, 655–67.

Linsky, L. (1963) Reference and Referents. In Caton, C. (Ed.) *Philosophy and Ordinary Language*, 74–89. Urbana: University of Illinois Press.

Mackie, J. (1974) Locke's Anticipation of Kripke. *Analysis*, 34, 177–80.

Martí, G., and Martínez-Fernández, J. (2010) General Terms as Designators: A Defence of the View. In Beebe, H., and Sabbarton-Leary, N. (Eds.) *The Semantics and Metaphysics* of Natural Kinds. New York and London: Routledge.

Mill, J. S. (1843) *A System of Logic*. London: Parker.

Putnam, H. (1962) It Ain't Necessarily So. *The Journal of Philosophy*, 59(22), 658–71.

(1975) The Meaning of "Meaning". In *Mind, Language and Reality: Philosophical Papers, Volume 2*, 215–71. Cambridge: Cambridge University Press.

(1970) Is Semantics Possible? In *Mind, Language and Reality: Philosophical Papers, Volume 2*, 139–52. Cambridge: Cambridge University Press.

Quine, W. V. O. (1963 [1951]) Two Dogmas of Empiricism. In *From a Logical Point of View*, 20–46. Cambridge: Harvard University Press. Original publication (1951) *Philosophical Review*, 60, 20–43.

(1976 [1953]) Three Grades of Modal Involvement. In *The Ways of Paradox*, 158–76. Cambridge: Harvard University Press. Original publication (1953): In *Proceedings of the XIth International Congress of Philosophy, Volume 14*, Amsterdam: North-Holland.

Russell, B. (1905) On Denoting. *Mind*, 14, 479–93.

(1919) *Introduction to Mathematical Philosophy*. London: George Allen & Unwin.

Salmon, N. (1981) *Reference and Essence*. Princeton: Princeton University Press.

(2003) Naming, Necessity, and Beyond. *Mind*, 112, 447–92.

(2005) Are General Terms Rigid? *Linguistics and Philosophy*, 28(1), 117–34.

Schwartz, S. P. (Ed.) (1977) *Naming, Necessity, and Natural Kinds*. Ithaca: Cornell University Press.

Searle, J. R. (1958) Proper Names. *Mind*, 67, 166–73.

Soames, S. (2002) *Beyond Rigidity: The Unfinished Semantic Agenda of Naming and Necessity*. Oxford: Oxford University Press.

Strawson, P. F. (1950) On Referring. *Mind*, 49, 320–44.

Wittgenstein, L. (1950) *Philosophical Investigations*. Trans. by G. E. M. Anscombe. London: Macmillan.

2

Fiction, Myth, and Reality

Nathan Salmon

I

Among the most difficult, and perennial, of philosophical problems are those arising from sentences involving nondesignating names. Chief among these problems is that of true singular negative existentials. Negative existentials naturally arise in separating fact from fiction and in debunking mistaken theories. Consider, for example,

(~1) Sherlock Holmes is nonexistent

interpreted not as an assertion within the Sherlock Holmes canon but as an assertion about reality. So interpreted, the sentence is evidently true. It seems as if (~1) designates someone (by its subject term) in order to say (by its predicate) that he does not exist. But it also entails that there is no such thing to be designated. How can any sentence with a nondesignating term in subject position be true? I call a mistaken theory that has been believed a *myth*. Myth-smashing sentences like 'Santa Claus isn't real' and 'There's no such intra-Mercurial planet as Vulcan' give rise to the same philosophical conundrum as (~1). G. E. Moore put the problem as follows:

> [I]t seems as if purely imaginary things, even though they be absolutely contradictory like a round square, must still have some kind of *being* – must still be in a sense – simply because we can think and talk about them.... And now in saying that there is no such thing as a round square, I seem to imply that there *is* such a thing. It seems as if there must be such a thing, merely

I thank Blackwell Publishing Company for permission to incorporate portions of my 1998 *Noûs* article "Nonexistence." I am grateful to the participants in the Santa Barbarians Discussion Group's ruminations on fictional objects during fall 1996, especially C. Anthony Anderson. I also thank Alan Berger, Kevin Falvey, Steven Humphrey, David Kaplan, Teresa Robertson, and Scott Soames for discussion or comments. Portions of the paper were also presented at numerous venues. I am grateful to those audiences for their comments.

in order that it may have the property of not-being. It seems, therefore, that to say of anything whatever that we can mention that it absolutely *is not*, were to contradict ourselves: as if everything we can mention must be, must have some kind of being. (*Some Main Problems of Philosophy*, London: George Allen & Unwin, 1953, at p. 289)

Saul Kripke's insightful and penetrating work on names from fiction and myth, though unpublished, has generated a great deal of discussion. Kripke's account illuminates and yet exacerbates the chestnut of negative existentials. However, the consistency of Kripke's account is questionable.

Russell's celebrated theory of descriptions provides an account of such sentences involving names from fiction and myth as the following:

(2)   Sherlock Holmes used cocaine
(~2)   Sherlock Holmes did not use cocaine.

Russell held that a proper name generally abbreviates some definite description. In the case of 'Sherlock Holmes' the abbreviated description might be something along the lines of: 'the brilliant but eccentric late-19th-century British detective who, inter alia, solved such-and-such mysteries'. Let us abbreviate this characterization by the artificial adjective 'Holmesesque'. Russell analyzes (2) as equivalent to:

(2′)   Something that is uniquely Holmesesque used cocaine.

Russell analyzes (~2) as ambiguous between the following two readings:

(~2′$_1$)   Something that is uniquely Holmesesque didn't use cocaine
(~2′$_2$)   Nothing that is uniquely Holmesesque used cocaine.

The former is the wide-scope (or *primary occurrence*) reading of (~2). This is false for the same reason as (2′). In reality, there has never been a Holmesesque individual. The latter is the narrow-scope (*secondary occurrence*) reading of (~2). This genuinely contradicts (2′) and is therefore true. In *Principia Mathematica*, instead of analyzing

(1)   Sherlock Holmes exists

by replacing 'used cocaine' in (2′) with 'exists', Russell and Whitehead analyze it more simply as

(1′)   Something is uniquely Holmesesque.

This is equivalent to its analysis in the style of (2′), since the formal symbolization of '*x* exists' is a theorem of *Principia Mathematica*. Although Russell did not distinguish two readings for (~1), he might well have. The narrow-scope reading is equivalent to the following:

($\sim 1'_2$)   Nothing is uniquely Holmesesque.

This does not designate anyone in order to say of him that he does not exist. It is not merely consistent; it is true. By contrast, the wide-scope reading, ($\sim 1'_1$) 'There exists something that both is uniquely Holmesesque and doesn't exist', is inconsistent, and hence, presumably, cannot be what would normally be intended by (~ 1).

Frege's celebrated theory of sense (*Sinn*) and designation (*Bedeutung*, reference, denotation) provides an alternative explanation of how sentences like (2) can semantically express propositions (*Gedanken*, thoughts). While Frege's principle of extensionality requires that such sentences lack truth value, the same principle creates a problem for Frege in connection with existential sentences like (1). It would have been natural for Frege to take (1) and (~ 1) to be analyzable respectively as:

(1″)   Something is the Holmesesque individual
($\sim 1''_2$) Nothing is the Holmesesque individual.

The intended truth conditions for (1″) and ($\sim 1''_2$) are given by (1′) and ($\sim 1'_2$). But since the definite description 'the Holmesesque individual' is improper, (1″) and ($\sim 1''_2$) must instead for Frege be neither true nor false (assuming the standard interpretation for existential quantification, identity, and negation, as Frege gave them in connection with his own notation).

By way of a solution to this difficulty, Frege suggested that (1) is properly interpreted not by (1″) but as covertly quotational. He wrote:

> We must here keep well apart two wholly different cases that are easily confused, because we speak of existence in both cases. In one case the question is whether a proper name designates, names, something; in the other whether a concept takes objects under itself. If we use the words 'there is a ———' we have the latter case. Now a proper name that designates nothing has no logical justification, since in logic we are concerned with truth in the strictest sense of the word; it may on the other hand still be used in fiction and fable. ("A Critical Elucidation of Some Points in E. Schroeder's *Algebra der Logik*," published 1895, translated by Peter Geach in P. Geach and M. Black, eds., *Translations from the Philosophical Writings of Gottlob Frege*, Oxford: Basil Blackwell, 1970, at p. 104)

Elsewhere Frege made similar remarks about singular existentials and their negations: "People certainly say that Odysseus is not an historical person, and mean by this contradictory expression that the name 'Odysseus' designates nothing, has no designatum" (from the section on "Sense and Designation" of Frege's 1906 diary notes, "Introduction to Logic," in H. Hermes, F. Kambartel, and F. Kaulbach, eds., *Posthumous Writings*, translated by P. Long and R. White,[1] Chicago: University of Chicago Press, 1979, at p. 191). Earlier in his "Dialogue with Pünjer on Existence" (pre-1884, also in Hermes, Kambartel, and Kaulbach), Frege observed: "If 'Sachse exists' is supposed to mean 'The word "Sachse" is not an empty sound, but designates something', then it is true that the condition 'Sachse exists' must be satisfied [in order for 'There are men' to be inferred from 'Sachse is a man']. But this is not a new premise, but the presupposition of all our words – a presupposition that goes without saying" (p. 60).[2]

The suggestion is that (1) and (~1), at least on one reading (on which the latter is true), are correctly analyzed as:

(1↑)   'Sherlock Holmes' designates$_{\text{English}}$ something
(~1↑$_2$) 'Sherlock Holmes' designates$_{\text{English}}$ nothing.

Assuming (as Frege evidently did) both that 'Sherlock Holmes' is synonymous with 'the Holmesesque individual' and that each instance of the following metalinguistic schema is true

(*F*)   'the'+NP designates$_{\text{English}}$ something iff that thing is uniquely φ,

where φ is a formalization in first-order-logic notation of the English NP, then (1↑) is true if and only if (1′) is, and (~1↑$_2$) is true if and only if (~1′$_2$) is. Frege's semantic ascent strategy thus attains the same truth conditions for (1) and (~1) as Russell.[3]

Frege's semantic ascent succeeds in capturing information that is indeed conveyed in the uttering of (1) or (~1). But to invoke a distinction I have emphasized in previous work, this concerns what is *pragmatically imparted* in (1) and (2), and not necessarily what is *semantically encoded* or *contained*.[4] Frege does not attain the same semantic content as Russell or even the same modal intension, that is, the same corresponding function from possible worlds to truth values. Indeed, that the semantic-ascent interpretation of (1) by (1↑) is incorrect is demonstrated by a variety of considerations. The semantic-ascent theory of existence is analogous to Frege's account of identity in *Begriffsschrift* (1879). Curiously, Frege evidently failed to see that his objection in "*Über Sinn und Bedeutung*" to the semantic-ascent theory of identity applies with equal force against

---

[1] Except that I here render '*Bedeutung*' as 'designatum'.
[2] Frege also suggests here that there may be an alternative reading for 'Sachse exists', on which it is tantamount to 'Sachse = Sachse', which Frege says is self-evident. He might well have said the same about '(∃x)[Sachse = x]'.
[3] The term 'semantic ascent' is due to W. V. O. Quine. See his *Word and Object* (Cambridge: MIT Press, 1960), §56.
[4] *Cf.* my *Frege's Puzzle* (Atascadero, CA: Ridgeview, 1986,), pp. 58–60 and especially 78–9, 84–5, 100, 114–15, 127–8.

the semantic-ascent theory of existence. Another objection to semantic-ascent analyses has been raised by Frege's most effective apologist and defender, Alonzo Church.[5] Translating 'The present king of France does not exist' into French, one obtains:

Le roi présent de France n'existe pas.

Translating its proposed analysis into French, one obtains:

'The present king of France' ne fait référence à rien en anglais.

These two translations, while both true, clearly mean different things in French. So too, therefore, do what they translate.

A theory of singular existence statements that is equally Fregean in spirit but superior to the semantic-ascent account takes the verb 'exist' as used in singular existentials to be an *ungerade* device, so that both (1) and (2) concern not the name 'Sherlock Holmes' but its English sense.[6] This is analogous to the semantic-ascent theory of existence except that one climbs further up to the level of intension. On an intensional-ascent theory of existence, (1) and (~1) may be analyzed respectively thus:

$(1^\wedge)$ ^Sherlock Holmes^ is a concept of something

$(\sim1^\wedge_2)$ ^Sherlock Holmes^ is not a concept of anything,

where 'is a concept of' is a dyadic predicate for the relation between a Fregean sense and the object that it determines and the caret '^' is a device for *indirect quotation*, that is, quotation not of the expression but of its semantic content (in the home language, in this case standard English with 'concept of').[7] Like the semantic-ascent theory, this intensional-ascent account of existence is not disproved by substitution

5 See Church's "On Carnap's Analysis of Statements of Assertion and Belief," *Analysis*, 10, 5 (1950), pp. 97–9. For a defense of the Church-Langford translation argument, see my "The Very Possibility of Language: A Sermon on the Consequences of Missing Church," in C. A. Anderson and M. Zeleney, eds., *Logic, Meaning and Computation: Essays in Honor of Alonzo Church* (Boston: Kluwer, 2001), pp. 573–95.

6 Church cites 'The present king of France does not exist' as an example of a true sentence containing an *ungerade* occurrence of a singular term ("name"), in *Introduction to Mathematical Logic I* (Princeton: Princeton University Press, 1956), at p. 27 n.

7 Cf. my "Reference and Information Content: Names and Descriptions," in D. Gabbay and F. Guenthner, eds., *Handbook of Philosophical Logic*, 2nd ed. (Dordrecht: Kluwer, 2003), pp. 39–85, at 69 on Fregean indirect quotation. The idea comes from David Kaplan's "Quantifying In," in D. Davidson and J. Hintikka, eds., *Words and Objections: Essays on the Work of W. V. O. Quine* (Dordrecht: D. Reidel, 1969), pp. 178–214; reprinted in L. Linsky, ed., *Reference and Modality* (Oxford: Oxford University Press, 1971), pp. 112–44, at 120–1. In English, the word 'that' attached to a subordinate clause (as in ⌈Jones believes that φ⌉ or ⌈It is necessary that φ⌉) typically functions in the manner of indirect-quotation marks.

of co-designative terms in existential contexts. On a Fregean philosophy of semantics, indirect-quotation marks create an *ungerade* context – one might even say that they create the paradigm *ungerade* context as Frege understood the concept – so that any expression occurring within them designates in that position its own customary sense. The intensional-ascent theory is not as easily refuted as the semantic-ascent approach by the Church translation argument.[8] In place of schema (*F*), we invoke the following:

(*C*)   ^the NP^ is a concept of something iff that thing, and nothing else, is a NP.

Assuming 'Sherlock Holmes' is synonymous with 'the Holmesesque individual', one thereby attains the same Russellian truth and falsehood conditions for (1) and (~1). Unlike (*F*), every instance of (*C*) expresses a necessary truth. The intensional-ascent theory of existence thus obtains the correct modal intensions for (1) and (~1).

Let us say that a singular term is *nondesignating* if there does not exist anything that the term designates. A term may be nondesignating by not designating anything at all. But a term may also be nondesignating by designating a nonexistent object, as with names of the dead. Either way, on Millianism, a nondesignating proper name is devoid of existing semantic content. Furthermore, a Millian like myself, and even a less committal direct-reference theorist like Kripke, may not avail him/herself of Russell's theory of descriptions to solve the problems of sentences with nondesignating names.[9] If α is a proper name, designating or not, it is not a definite

---

[8] On this application of the translation argument, see my "A Problem in the Frege-Church Theory of Sense and Denotation," *Noûs*, 27, 2 (June 1993), pp. 158–66, and "The Very Possibility of Language: A Sermon on the Consequence of Missing Church."

[9] Kripke does not officially endorse or reject Millianism. Informal discussions lead me to believe he is deeply skeptical. (See his repeated insistence in "A Puzzle about Belief" that Pierre does not have inconsistent beliefs – in A. Margalit, ed., *Meaning and Use*, Dordrecht: D. Reidel, 1979, pp. 239–83; reprinted in N. Salmon and S. Soames, eds., *Propositions and Attitudes*, Oxford: Oxford University Press, 1988, pp. 102–48.) Nevertheless, Kripke believes that a sentence using a proper name in an ordinary context (not within quotation marks, and so on) expresses a proposition only if the name refers. Similarly, Keith Donnellan, in "Speaking of Nothing," *The Philosophical Review*, 83 (January 1974), pp. 3–32 (reprinted in S. Schwartz, ed., *Naming, Necessity, and Natural Kinds*, Ithaca, NY: Cornell University Press, 1977, pp. 216–44), says, "when a name is used and there is a failure of designation, then no proposition has been expressed – certainly no true proposition. If a child says, 'Santa Claus will come tonight,' he cannot have spoken the truth, although, for various reasons, I think it better to say that he has not even expressed a proposition. [He adds in a footnote:] Given that this is a statement about reality and that proper names have no descriptive content, then how are we to represent the proposition expressed?" (pp. 20–1).

description, nor by the direct-reference theory's lights does it abbreviate any definite description. For similar reasons, the direct-reference theorist is also barred from using Frege's sense/designation distinction to solve the difficulties. How, then, can the theorist ascribe content to (1), (2), or their negations? In particular, how can (~1) express anything at all, let alone something true? The semantic-ascent theory of existence is refuted on the direct-reference theory no less than on Fregean theory by the Church translation argument as well as by modal considerations (among other things). The *ungerade*, intensional-ascent theory hardly fares much better on direct-reference theory in connection with (1) and (~1). On the Millian theory, it fares no better at all. According to Millianism, if α is a proper name, then its indirect quotation designates α's bearer. If 'Sherlock Holmes' is a nondesignating name, '^Sherlock Holmes^' is equally nondesignating.

It is a traditional view in philosophy, and indeed it is plain common sense, that (1) is false and (~1) true, when taken as statements about reality. For 'Sherlock Holmes', as a name for the celebrated detective, is evidently a *very strongly* or *thoroughly nondesignating* name, one that does not in reality have any designatum at all – past, present, future, or forever merely possible (or even forever impossible). Bertrand Russell lent an eloquent voice to this common-sense view:

> [M]any logicians have been driven to the conclusion that there are unreal objects.... In such theories, it seems to me, there is a failure of that feeling for reality which ought to be preserved even in the most abstract studies. Logic, I should maintain, must no more admit a unicorn than zoology can; for logic is concerned with the real world just as truly as zoology, though with its more abstract and general features. To say that unicorns have an existence in heraldry, or in literature, or in imagination, is a most pitiful and paltry evasion. What exists in heraldry is not an animal, made of flesh and blood, moving and breathing of its own initiative. What exists is a picture, or a description in words. Similarly, to maintain that Hamlet, for example, exists in his own world, namely in the world of Shakespeare's imagination, just as truly as (say) Napoleon existed in the ordinary world, is to say something deliberately confusing, or else confused to a degree which is scarcely credible. There is only one world, the "real" world: Shakespeare's imagination is part of it, and the thoughts that he had in writing *Hamlet* are real. So are the thoughts that we have in reading the play. But it is of the very essence of fiction that only the thoughts, feelings, etc., in Shakespeare and his readers are real, and that there is not, in addition to them, an objective Hamlet. When you have taken account of all the feelings roused by Napoleon in writers and readers of history, you have not touched the actual man; but in the case of Hamlet you have come to the end of him. If no one thought about Hamlet, there would be nothing left of him; if no one had thought about Napoleon, he would have soon seen to it that some one did.

The sense of reality is vital in logic, and whoever juggles with it by pretending that Hamlet has another kind of reality is doing a disservice to thought. A robust sense of reality is very necessary in framing a correct analysis of propositions about unicorns, golden mountains, round squares, and other such pseudo-objects.[10]

Contemporary philosophy has uncovered that (unlike my example of 'Noman') a name from fiction does not even designate a merely possible object. Thus Kripke writes:

> The mere discovery that there was indeed a detective with exploits like those of Sherlock Holmes would not show that Conan Doyle was writing *about* this man; it is theoretically possible, though in practice fantastically unlikely, that Conan Doyle was writing pure fiction with only a coincidental resemblance to the actual man.... Similarly, I hold the metaphysical view that, granted that there is no Sherlock Holmes, one cannot say of any possible person, that he *would have been* Sherlock Holmes, had he existed. Several distinct possible people, and even actual ones such as Darwin or Jack the Ripper, might have performed the exploits of Holmes, but there is none of whom we can say that he would have *been* Holmes had he performed these exploits. For if so, which one?
>
> I thus could no longer write, as I once did, that 'Holmes does not exist, but in other states of affairs, he would have existed.' (*Naming and Necessity*, Cambridge: Harvard University Press, 1980, pp. 157–8)

It is not merely true that Sherlock Holmes does not exist; it is necessarily true. On Kripke's view, the name 'Sherlock Holmes' is a rigid *non*designator, designating nothing – not even a merely possible thing – with respect to every possible world. In a similar vein, Kaplan says:

> The myth [of Pegasus] is possible in the sense that there is a possible world in which it is truthfully *told*. Furthermore, there are such worlds in which the language, with the exception of the proper names in question, is semantically and syntactically identical with our own. Let us call such possible worlds of the myth, '*M* worlds'. In each *M* world, the name 'Pegasus' will have originated in a dubbing of a winged horse. The Friend of Fiction, who would not have anyone believe the myth..., but yet talks of Pegasus, pretends to be in an *M* world and speaks its language.
>
> But beware the confusion of our language with theirs! If w is an M world, then *their* name 'Pegasus' will denote something with respect to w, and *our* description 'the x such that x is called 'Pegasus'' will denote the same thing with respect to w, but *our* name 'Pegasus' will still denote nothing with respect to w....

[10] *Introduction to Mathematical Philosophy* (London: Allen and Unwin, 1919), at pp. 169–70. Cf. Russell's *The Philosophy of Logical Atomism*, D. Pears, ed. (La Salle, IL: Open Court, 1918, 1972, 1985), at pp. 87–8.

To summarize. It has been thought that proper names like 'Pegasus' and 'Hamlet' were like 'Aristotle' and 'Newman-1', except that the individuals denoted by the former were more remote. But regarded as names of *our* language – introduced by successful or unsuccessful dubbings, or just made up – the latter denote and the former do not.[11]

II

Kripke and Peter van Inwagen have argued independently, and persuasively, that wholly fictional characters should be regarded as real things.[12] Theirs is not a Meinongian view – one of Russell's targets in the passage quoted earlier – on which any manner of proper name or definite description, including such terms as 'the golden mountain' and 'the round square', designates some Object, though the Object may not exist in any robust sense and may instead have only a lower-class ontological status (and, as in the case of the round square, may even have inconsistent properties).[13] To be sure, wholly fictional characters like Sherlock Holmes, though real, are not real people. Neither physical objects nor mental objects, instead they are, in this sense, abstract entities. They are not eternal entities, like numbers; they are human-made artifacts created by fiction writers. But they exist just as robustly as the fictions themselves, the novels, stories, and so on in which they occur. Indeed, fictional characters have the same ontological status as the fictions, which are also abstract entities created by their authors. And certain things are true

[11] From appendix XI, "Names from Fiction," of "Bob and Carol and Ted and Alice," in K. J. J. Hintikka, J. M. E. Moravcsik, and P. Suppes, eds, *Approaches to Natural Language* (Dordrecht: D. Reidel, 1973), pp. 490–518, at pp. 505–8. Kaplan credits John Bennett in connection with this passage. The same general argument occurs in Donnellan, "Speaking of Nothing," at pp. 24–5, and in Alvin Plantinga, *The Nature of Necessity* (Oxford: Oxford University Press, 1974), section VIII.4, "Names: Their Function in Fiction," at pp. 159–63.

[12] Kripke, *Reference and Existence: The John Locke Lectures for 1973* (unpublished); van Inwagen, "Creatures of Fiction," *American Philosophical Quarterly*, 14, 4 (October 1977), pp. 299–308, and "Fiction and Metaphysics," *Philosophy and Literature*, 7, 1 (Spring 1983), pp. 67–77. One possible difference between them is that van Inwagen accepts an ontology of fictional characters whereas Kripke is instead merely unveiling an ontology that he argues is assumed in the way we speak about fiction while remaining neutral on the question of whether this manner of speaking accurately reflects reality. My interpretation of Kripke is based primarily on the manuscript of his 1973 Locke Lectures as well as his seminars, which I attended, on the topic of designation, existence, and fiction at Princeton University during the spring of 1981 and at the University of California, Riverside, in January 1983.

[13] Cf. Terence Parsons, "A Meinongian Analysis of Fictional Objects," *Grazer Philosophische Studien*, 1 (1975), pp. 73–86, and *Nonexistent Objects* (New Haven: Yale University Press, 1980).

of these fictional characters – for example, that the protagonist of the Sherlock Holmes stories was inspired in part by an uncannily perceptive person of Sir Arthur Conan Doyle's acquaintance.

On this theory, a negative existential like (~1), taken as making an assertion about the fictional character and taken literally, denies real existence of a real fictional character, and is therefore false. In fact, Holmes may well be the most famous of all fictional characters in existence. The same sentence, understood as making an assertion about the fictional character, may be open to a more charitable and plausible interpretation, albeit a nonliteral one. Perhaps one may reinterpret the predicate 'exists', for example, to mean *real*, in something like the sense: *not merely a character in the story, but an entity of just the sort depicted*. Then (~1) may be understood, quite plausibly, as making an assertion that the character of Sherlock Holmes is a wholly fictional man, not a real one. That is to say, there is a fiction in which Holmes is a man of flesh and blood, but in reality Holmes is merely a fictional character. On this Pickwickian reading, the sentence is indeed true. But it is then not an authentic negative existential, and thus generates no special problem for Millianism, let alone for direct-reference theory.[14]

How can this talk about the fictional character of Sherlock Holmes as a real entity be reconciled with the passage from Kripke quoted earlier, in which he appears to agree with Kaplan and Russell that 'Sherlock Holmes' is nondesignating?

On Kripke's account, use of the name 'Sherlock Holmes' to refer to the fictional character is in a certain sense parasitic on a prior, more fundamental use not as a name for the fictional character. Kripke and van Inwagen emphasize that the author of a fiction does not assert anything in writing the fiction. Instead, Kripke, like Kaplan, says that Conan Doyle merely *pretended* to be designating someone in using the name 'Sherlock Holmes' and to be asserting things, expressing propositions, about him. A fiction purports to be an accurate historical recounting of real events involving real people. Of course, the author typically does not attempt to deceive the audience that the pretense is anything but a pretense; instead the fiction merely goes through the motions (hoaxes like Orson Welles's radio broadcast of H. G. Wells's *The War of the Worlds* and the

---

[14] Cf. van Inwagen, "Creatures of Fiction," at p. 308 n. 11. Kripke argues against any interpretation of (~1) on which the name is used as a name of the fictional character but 'exist' receives a Pickwickian interpretation on which the sentence is true. I am less skeptical. See below, especially note 29. (Van Inwagen's suggestion is neutral between this sort of account and the one proposed there.)

legend of Santa Claus being the "exceptions that prove the rule"). Frege expressed the basic idea as follows:

> Assertions in fiction are not to be taken seriously: they are only mock assertions. Even the thoughts are not to be taken seriously as in the sciences: they are only mock thoughts. If Schiller's *Don Carlos* were to be regarded as a piece of history, then to a large extent the drama would be false. But a work of fiction is not meant to be taken seriously in this way at all: it's all play.[15]

According to Kripke, as the name 'Sherlock Holmes' was originally introduced and used by Conan Doyle, it has no designatum whatsoever. It is a name in the make-believe world of storytelling, part of an elaborate pretense. By Kripke's lights, our language licenses a certain kind of metaphysical move. It postulates an abstract artifact, the fictional character, as a product of this pretense. But the name 'Sherlock Holmes' does not thereby refer to the character thereby postulated, nor for that matter to anything else, and the sentences involving the name 'Sherlock Holmes' that were written in creating the fiction express no propositions, about the fictional character or anything else. They are all part of the pretense, like the actors' lines in the performance of a play. Names from fiction occurring within the fiction are thoroughly nondesignating. It is only at a later stage when discussing the fictional character from a metastandpoint, speaking about the pretense and not within it, that the language makes a second move, this one semantical rather than metaphysical, giving the name a new, nonpretend use as a name for the fictional character. The language allows a linguistic transformation, says Kripke, of a fictional name for a person into a name of a fictional person. Similarly, van Inwagen writes, "we have embodied in our rules for talking about fiction a convention that says that a creature of fiction *may* be referred to by what is (loosely speaking) 'the name it has in the story'" ("Creatures of Fiction," p. 307 n.). On this account, the name 'Sherlock Holmes' is ambiguous. In its original use as a name for a human being – its object-fictional use by Conan Doyle in writing the fiction, and presumably by the reader reading the fiction – it merely pretends to name someone and actually names nothing at all. But in its metafictional, nonpretend use as a name for the fictional character thereby created by Conan Doyle, it genuinely designates that particular artifactual entity. In effect, there are two names. Though spelled the same, they would be better spelled

---

[15] "Logic," in Frege's *Posthumous Writings*, at p. 130. See also Kendall L. Walton, "On Fearing Fictions," *Journal of Philosophy*, 75 (1978), pp. 5–27; and *Mimesis as Make-Believe: On the Foundations of the Representational Arts* (Cambridge: Harvard University Press, 1990).

differently, as 'Holmes$_1$,' for the man and 'Holmes$_2$,' for the fictional character. Neither names a real man. The latter names an abstract artifact,
the former nothing at all. It is the original, thoroughly nondesignating
use of 'Sherlock Holmes' – its use in the same way as 'Holmes$_1$,' – that
Kaplan, Kripke, and Russell emphasize in the passages quoted.

Kripke's theory involves a complex account of object-fictional sentences like 'Sherlock Holmes plays the violin', 'Odysseus was set ashore
at Ithaca while sound asleep', 'Pegasus has wings', and (2). By contrast,
'According to the stories, Sherlock Holmes used cocaine' is metafictional, and literally true. On Kripke's view, object-fictional sentences are
multiply ambiguous, as a result of the two uses of the names and of differing perspectives from within and without the fiction or myth. Using
the name in (2) in the manner of 'Holmes$_1$,' as the pretend name of a
pretend man, and using the sentence to make a statement not within the
pretense and instead about the real world outside the fiction, the sentence expresses nothing and is therefore not literally true. (See note 9.)
But object-fictional sentences may also be used from within the fiction,
as part of the general pretense of an accurate, factual recounting of real
events, not to be mistaken as a "time out" reality check. Interpreted thus,
sentence (2) is a correct depiction, part of the storytelling language-
game. So used, the sentence may be counted "true" in an extended
sense – *truth in the fiction*, as we might call it – conforming to a convention of counting an object-fictional sentence "true" or "false" according
as the sentence is true or false with respect (or according) to the fiction.
This is the sense in which the sentence should be marked "true" on a
true-false test in English Lit 101.[16] Alternatively, the name may be used in
the manner of 'Holmes$_2$,' as a name for the fictional character. With the
name so used, and the sentence used as a statement not about the fiction
but about reality, it is false; no abstract entity uses cocaine or even can.
On the other hand, according to Kripke, we also have an extended use of
predicates, on which 'uses cocaine' correctly applies to an abstract entity
when it is a character from a fiction according to which the corresponding fictional person uses cocaine. Giving the name its use as a name of

---

[16] Kripke recognizes that this is generally equivalent, in some sense, to treating an
object-fictional sentence φ as implicitly shorthand for the metafictional ⌜According
to the fiction, φ⌝, and evaluating it as true or false accordingly. But he says that he
regards it as applying 'true' and 'false' in conventionally extended senses directly to
object-fictional sentences themselves in their original senses. Cf. David Lewis, "Truth
in Fiction," *American Philosophical Quarterly*, 15 (1978), pp. 37–46; reprinted with post-
scripts in Lewis's *Philosophical Papers: Volume I* (Oxford: Oxford University Press, 1983),
pp. 261–80.

the fictional character, and understanding the predicate 'used cocaine' in this extended sense, sentence (2) is true. According to the stories, Holmes$_1$ used cocaine. In virtue of that fact we may say that Holmes$_2$ "used cocaine." The truth conditions of sentence (2) on this reading are exactly the same as the conventional truth-in-the-fiction conditions of the sentence interpreted as 'Holmes$_1$ used cocaine'. But they differ in meaning. The former invokes a new interpretation for both subject and predicate.[17]

Viewing the negative existential (~1) on this same model, it has various interpretations on which it is false. Interpreted in the sense of 'Holmes$_1$ does not exist', it is like 'Holmes$_1$ did not use cocaine' in pretending to express a proposition, one that is false in the fiction. The sentence should be marked "false" on a true-false quiz about the Sherlock Holmes stories. Interpreted in the sense of 'Holmes$_2$ does not exist', the predicate 'exist' may be given its literal sense, or alternatively it may be given its extended sense on which it applies to a fictional character if and only if according to the relevant fiction the corresponding person exists. Either way the sentence is false. The fictional character exists, and moreover the corresponding person existed according to the stories. But suppose (1) is read again in the sense of 'Holmes$_1$ does not exist', this time not as a statement within the fiction but as a statement about the real world. Then it is significantly unlike 'Holmes$_1$ did not use cocaine', which expresses nothing about the real world outside the fiction. For according to Kripke, 'Holmes$_1$ does not exist' is in reality quite true. On this interpretation, the sentence is regarded by Kripke, as by traditional philosophy, as an authentic true negative existential with a thoroughly nondesignating subject term.

This was our primary concern. We have attempted to deal with the problem of negative existentials by concentrating on 'Holmes$_2$ does not exist'. But it is Holmes$_1$, not Holmes$_2$, who literally does not exist. The

[17] Kripke cautions that when one is merely pretending to refer to a human being in using a name from fiction, that pretense does not in and of itself involve naming a fictional character. On the contrary, such a pretense was involved in the very creation of the as-yet-unnamed fictional character. He also remarks that an object-fictional sentence like (2) would be counted true in the conventionally extended "according to the fiction" sense even if the name had only its 'Holmes$_1$' use and the language had not postulated fictional characters as objects. Van Inwagen ("Creatures of Fiction," pp. 305–6) invokes a notion of a fiction "ascribing" a property to a character, but admits that his terminology is misleading. He does not explain his notion of *ascription* in terms of what sentences within the fiction express, since such sentences on his view (as on Kripke's) do not express anything. Instead this kind of ascription is an undefined primitive of the theory.

problem requires more work. Kripke says that it is "perhaps the worst problem in the area."

By way of a possible solution, Kripke proposes that (1) should not be viewed on the model of 'Holmes₁ used cocaine', understood as a statement about the real world – and which thereby expresses nothing – but instead as a special kind of speech act. Consider first the object-fictional sentence (~2), in the sense of 'Holmes₁ did not use cocaine', construed as a statement about reality. One may utter this sentence even if one is uncertain whether Holmes₁ is a real person, in order to make the cautious claim that either there is no such person as Holmes₁ or there is but he did not use cocaine. In that case, the assertion is tantamount to saying that either there is no proposition that Holmes₁ uses cocaine, or there is such a proposition but it is not true. In short, the sentence is interpreted as meaning *there is no true proposition that Holmes₁ uses cocaine.* A similar cautious interpretation is available whenever negation is employed.

Kripke extends this same interpretation to singular negative existentials. He proposes that in uttering a sentence of the form ⌜α does not exist⌝ from the standpoint of the real world, what one really means is better expressed by ⌜There is no true proposition that α exists⌝. What is meant may be true on either of two entirely different grounds: (*i*) the mentioned proposition is not true; alternatively (*ii*) there is no such proposition. If α is 'the present king of France', then one's assertion is true for the former reason. If α is 'Sherlock Holmes' in its 'Holmes₁' use, then one's assertion is true for the latter reason. Kripke's is not a theory that takes (~1) to express that (1) is not true$_{English}$. Semantic-ascent theories are notoriously vulnerable to refutation (as by the Church translation argument). Instead, Kripke takes (~1) to express that there is no true proposition of a certain sort even if only because there is no proposition of that sort at all. This is closer to the intensional-ascent theory of existence – with a wink and a nod in the direction of Millianism.

Kripke extends this account to mistaken theories that have been believed – what I call *myths*. He explicitly mentions the case of the fictitious intra-Mercurial planet Vulcan, hypothesized and named by Jacques Babinet in 1846 and later thought by Urbain Le Verrier to explain an irregularity in the orbit of Mercury. The irregularity was eventually explained by the general theory of relativity.[18] Though the Vulcan

---

[18] Babinet hypothesized Vulcan for reasons different from Le Verrier's. See Warren Zachary Watson, *An Historical Analysis of the Theoretical Solutions to the Problem of the Perihelion of Mercury* (doctoral dissertation, Ann Arbor, MI: University Microfilms, 1969), pp. viii, 92–4; and N. T. Roseveare, *Mercury's Perihelion: From Le Verrier to Einstein* (Oxford: Oxford

hypothesis turned out to be a myth, it nevertheless bore fruit – not a massive physical object, but in the form of a mythical object, an artifactual abstract entity of the same ontological status as Holmes$_2$. Vulcan even has explanatory value. It accounts not for Mercury's perihelion, but for the truth in English of 'A hypothetical planet was postulated to explain Mercury's irregular orbit'. In introducing the name 'Vulcan', Babinet meant to introduce a name for a planet, not an abstract artifact. His intentions were thwarted on both counts. Kripke holds that the dubbing ultimately resulted in two distinct uses of the name – in effect two names, 'Vulcan$_1$,' and 'Vulcan$_2$,' – the first as a name for an intra-Mercurial planet (and consequently thoroughly nondesignating), the second as a name of a mythical object, Babinet's accidental creation. (Presumably these two uses are supposed to be different from two other pairs of uses, corresponding to the fire god of Roman mythology and Mr. Spock's native planet in *Star Trek*.) When it is said that Vulcan$_1$ does not influence Mercury's orbit, and that Vulcan$_1$ does not exist, what is meant is that there are no true propositions that Vulcan$_1$ influences Mercury or that Vulcan$_1$ exists.

III

Kripke's intensional ascent fails to solve the problem. The 'that' clauses 'that Holmes$_1$ uses cocaine' and 'that Holmes$_1$ exists' are no less problematic than 'Holmes$_1$,' itself. Kripke concedes, in effect, that if α is a thoroughly nondesignating name, then propositional terms like ⌜the proposition that α used cocaine⌝ are also thoroughly nondesignating. The account thus analyzes a negative existential by means of another negative existential, generating an infinite regress with the same problem arising at each stage: If α is a thoroughly nondesignating name, how can ⌜There is no proposition that α used cocaine⌝ express anything at all, let alone something true (let alone a necessary truth)? To give an analogy, a proposal to analyze ⌜α does not exist⌝ as ⌜Either {α} is the empty set or it does not exist⌝ yields no solution to the problem of how (~ 1) can express anything true. Even if the analysans has the right truth conditions, it also invokes a disjunct that is itself a negative existential, and it

University Press, 1982), at pp. 24–7. (Thanks to Alan Berger and the late Sidney Morgenbesser for bibliographical assistance. I also researched the Vulcan hypothesis on the Internet. When I moved to save material to a new file to be named 'Vulcan', the program responded as usual, only this time signaling a momentous occasion: **Vulcan doesn't exist. Create? Y or N**.)

leaves unsolved the mystery of how either disjunct can express anything if α is a thoroughly nondesignating name.[19]

There is more. On the accounts proposed by Kaplan, Kripke, and van Inwagen, object-fictional sentences, like 'Sherlock Holmes uses cocaine', have no genuine semantic content in their original use. This renders the meaningfulness of true metafictional sentences like 'According to the Sherlock Holmes stories, Holmes used cocaine' problematic and mysterious. (See note 16.) On Kripke's account, it is true that according to the stories Holmes$_1$ used cocaine, and that on Le Verrier's theory Vulcan$_1$ influences Mercury's orbit. How can these things be true if there is no proposition that Holmes$_1$ used cocaine and no proposition that Vulcan$_1$ influences Mercury? What is it that is the case according to the stories or the theory? How can Le Verrier have believed something that is nothing at all? If object-fictional sentences like 'Holmes$_1$ used cocaine' express nothing, and we merely pretend that they express things, how can they be true with respect (according) to the fiction, and how can metafictional sentences involving object-fictional subordinate clauses express something, let alone something true?

More puzzling still are such cross-realm statements as 'Sherlock Holmes was cleverer than Bertrand Russell', and even worse, 'Sherlock Holmes was cleverer than Hercule Poirot'. The account as it stands seems to invoke some sort of intensional use of 'Sherlock Holmes', whereby not only is the name ambiguous between 'Holmes$_1$' and 'Holmes$_2$', but also accompanying the former use is something like an *ungerade* use, arising in constructions like 'According to the stories, Holmes$_1$ used cocaine', on which the name designates a particular concept – presumably something of the form *the brilliant detective who performed such and such exploits*. Kripke acknowledges this, calling it a "special sort of quasi-intensional use." The account thus ultimately involves an intensional apparatus.

---

[19] As Kripke intends the construction ⌜There is no such thing as α⌝, it seems close in meaning to ⌜$^\wedge\alpha^\wedge$ is not a concept of anything⌝. In our problem case, α is 'the proposition that Holmes$_1$ exists'. Since the 'that' prefix is itself a device for indirect quotation (see n. 7), 'Holmes,' would thus occur in a doubly *ungerade* context. It may be, therefore, that Kripke's intensional-ascent theory presupposes (or otherwise requires) a thesis that proper names have a Fregean *ungerade Sinn*, or indirect sense, which typically determines the name's designatum, the latter functioning as both customary content and customary designatum, but which in the case of a thoroughly nondesignating name determines nothing. This would provide a reason for intensional ascent; one hits pay dirt by climbing above customary content. Kripke's theory would then involve Fregean intensional machinery that direct designation scrupulously avoids and Millianism altogether prohibits.

Indeed, it appears to involve industrial-strength intensional machinery of a sort that is spurned by direct-reference theory, and worse yet, by the very account itself. Further, the intensionality seems to get matters wrong. First, it seems to give us after all a proposition that Holmes$_1$ used cocaine, a proposition that Vulcan$_1$ influences Mercury, etc. – those things that are the case (or not) according to stories or believed by the theorist. Furthermore, depending on how the *ungerade* use of 'Holmes$_1$,' is explained, it could turn out that if there were someone with many of the attributes described in the Sherlock Holmes stories, including various exploits much like those recounted, then there would be *true* propositions that Holmes$_1$ existed, that he used cocaine, and so on. It could even turn out that if by an extraordinary coincidence there was *in fact* some detective who was very Holmesesque, then even though Holmes$_2$ was purely fictional and not based in any way on this real person, there *are* nevertheless true propositions that Holmes$_1$ existed, used cocaine, and so on. The theory threatens to entail that the question of Holmes's authenticity (in the intended sense) would be settled affirmatively by the discovery of someone who was significantly Holmesesque, even if this person was otherwise unconnected to Conan Doyle. If the theory has consequences like these, then it directly contradicts the compelling passage of Kripke's quoted earlier, if not also itself. Kripke expresses misgivings about the theory, acknowledging that the required "quasi-intensional" use of a name from fiction needs explanation.[20]

[20] Cf. Gareth Evans, *The Varieties of Designation,* J. McDowell, ed. (Oxford: Oxford University Press, 1982), at pp. 349–52. The kind of intensionality required on Kripke's account is not merely pragmatic in nature. Taking account of the preceding note, the account may be steeped in intensionality. The danger of entailing such consequences as those noted is very real. The theory of fiction in Lewis, "Truth in Fiction," is similar to Kripke's in requiring something like an *ungerade* use for thoroughly nondesignating names from fiction. Lewis embraces the conclusion that "the sense of 'Sherlock Holmes' as we use it is such that, for any world *w* where the Holmes stories are told as known fact rather than fiction, the name denotes at *w* whichever inhabitant of *w* it is who there plays the role of Holmes" (p. 267 of the version in his *Philosophical Papers: Volume I*). A similar conclusion is also reached in Robert Stalnaker, "Assertion," P. Cole, ed., *Syntax and Semantics, 9: Semantics* (New York: Academic Press, 1978), pp. 315–32, at 329–31. These conclusions directly contradict Kripke's account of proper names as rigid designators. In the first of the Locke Lectures, Kripke argues that uniquely being Holmesesque is not sufficient to be Holmes. Further, Kripke also argues there that the phenomenon of fiction cannot yield considerations against this or that particular philosophico-semantic theory of names, since it is part of the fiction's pretense, for the theorist, that the theory's "criteria for naming, whatever they are, are satisfied." Why should this not extend to the thesis, from direct-reference theory, that names lack Kripke's hypothesized "quasi-intensional use"? Donnellan, "Speaking of Nothing," regards negative existentials as unlike other object-fictional sentences, though his solution differs significantly from Kripke's and

IV

Kripke's contention that names like 'Sherlock Holmes' are ambiguous is almost certainly mistaken. In particular, there is no obvious necessity to posit a use of the name by Conan Doyle and his readers that is nondesignating (in any sense) and somehow prior to its use as a name for the fictional character and upon which the latter use is parasitic.[21]

The alleged use of 'Sherlock Holmes' on which it is thoroughly nondesignating was supposed to be a pretend use, not a real one. In writing the Sherlock Holmes stories, Conan Doyle did not genuinely use the name at all, at least not as a name for a man. He merely pretended to. Of course, Conan Doyle wrote the name down as part of sentences

is designed to avoid intensionality. Donnellan provides a criterion whereby if α and β are distinct names from fiction, then (in effect) the corresponding true negative existentials, taken in the sense of $\ulcorner\alpha_1$ does not exist$\urcorner$ and $\ulcorner\beta_1$ does not exist$\urcorner$ as literally true statements about reality, express the same proposition if and only if α_2 and β_2 name the same fictional character. (I have taken enormous liberties in formulating Donnellan's criterion in terms of Kripke's apparatus, but I believe I do not do it any serious injustice.) This proposal fails to provide the proposition expressed. In fact, Donnellan concedes that "we cannot.... preserve a clear notion of what proposition is expressed for existence statements involving proper names" (p. 29; see note 9 above). This fails to solve the original problem, which is even more pressing for Donnellan. How can such sentences be said to "express the same proposition" when by his lights neither sentence clearly expresses any proposition at all? Cf. my "Nonexistence," *Noûs*, 32, 3 (1998), pp. 277–319, at 313–14 n. 29.

[21] I first presented my alternative account of negative existentials, fiction, and myth in "Nonexistence." Amie Thomasson, in *Fiction and Metaphysics* (Cambridge: Cambridge University Press, 1999), defends an account similar to mine on broadly similar grounds. See also F. Adams, G. Fuller, and R. Stecker, "The Semantics of Fictional Names," *Pacific Philosophical Quarterly*, 78 (1997), pp. 128–48; David Braun, "Empty Names," *Noûs*, 27 (1993), pp. 449–69, and "Empty Names, Fictional Names, Mythical Names," *Noûs* (forthcoming); Ben Caplan, "Empty Names: An Essay on the Semantics, Pragmatics, Metaphysics, and Epistemology of Empty Names and Other Directly Referential Expressions," UCLA doctoral dissertation (2000), and "Creatures of Fiction, Myth, and Imagination," *American Philosophical Quarterly*, 41, 4 (October 2004), pp. 331–7; Gregory Currie, *The Nature of Fiction* (Cambridge: Cambridge University Press, 1990); Anthony Everett, "Empty Names and 'Gappy' Propositions," *Philosophical Studies*, 116 (October 2003), pp. 1–36; Kit Fine, "The Problem of Non-Existence: I. Internalism," *Topoi*, 1 (1982), pp. 97–140; Stacie Friend, review of Amie Thomasson, *Fiction and Metaphysics*, in *Mind*, 2000, pp. 997–1000; Thomas G. Pavel, *Fictional Worlds* (Cambridge: Harvard University Press, 1986); Amie Thomasson, "Fiction, Modality and Dependent Abstracta," *Philosophical Studies*, 84 (1996), pp. 295–320; Nicholas Wolterstorff, *Works and Worlds of Art* (Oxford: Oxford University Press, 1980). Three collections of articles on the philosophy and logic of fiction are: *Poetics*, 8, 1/2 (April 1979); A. Everett and T. Hofweber, eds., *Empty Names, Fiction and the Puzzles of Non-Existence* (Stanford, CA: CSLI Publications, 2000); and P. McCormick, ed., *Reasons of Art* (Ottawa: University of Ottawa Press, 1985).

in the course of writing the Holmes stories. In that sense he used the name. This is like the use that stage or film actors make of sentences when reciting their lines during the performance of a play or the filming of a movie. It is not a use whereby the one speaking commits him/herself to the propositions expressed. Even when writing 'London' or 'Scotland Yard' in a Holmes story, Conan Doyle was not in any robust sense using these names to designate. As J. O. Urmson notes, when Jane Austen, in writing a novel, writes a sentence beginning with a fictional character's name,

> it is not that there is a reference to a fictional object, nor is there the use of a referring expression which fails to secure reference (as when one says "That man over there is tall" when there is no man over there). Jane Austen writes a sentence which has the form of an assertion beginning with a reference, but is in fact neither asserting nor referring; therefore she is not referring to any character, fictional or otherwise, nor does she fail to secure reference, except in the jejune sense in which if I sneeze or open a door I fail to secure reference. Nothing would have counted on this occasion as securing reference, and to suppose it could is to be under the impression that Miss Austen was writing history.... I do not say that one cannot refer to a fictional character, but that Miss Austen did not on the occasion under discussion.
>
> What I am saying is that making up fiction is not a case of stating, or asserting, or propounding a proposition and includes no acts such as referring ("Fiction," *American Philosophical Quarterly*, 13, 2 (April 1976), pp. 153–57 at p. 155).

The pretend use of 'Sherlock Holmes' by Conan Doyle does not have to be regarded as generating a use of the name on which it is nondesignating. *Pace* Kaplan, Kripke, Russell, and traditional philosophy, it *should* not be so regarded. A name semantically designates this or that individual only relative to a particular kind of use, a particular purpose for which the name was introduced. One might go so far as to say that a pretend use by itself does not even give rise to a real name at all, any more than it gives birth to a real detective. This may be somewhat overstated, but its spirit and flavor are not.[22] Even if one regards a name as something that exists independently of its introduction into language (as is my inclination), it is confused to think of a name as designating, or not designating, other than as doing so *on* a particular use. On this view, a common

---

[22] C. J. F. Williams, in *What Is Existence?* (Oxford: Oxford University Press, 1981), argues that 'Sherlock Holmes' is not a proper name (pp. 251–5). This is what Kaplan ought to have said, but he did not. See his "Words," *Proceedings of the Aristotelian Society*, 64 (1990), pp. 93–119, especially section II, "What are Names?" at pp. 110–19.

name like 'Adam Smith' designates different individuals on different uses. The problem with saying that 'Sherlock Holmes' is nondesignating on Conan Doyle's use is that in merely pretending that the name had a particular use, Conan Doyle did not yet attach a real use to the name on which it may be said to designate or not.

I heartily applaud Russell's eloquent plea for philosophical sobriety. But his attitude toward "unreal" objects is fundamentally confused. On the other hand, Kripke's account of fiction and myth is implausibly baroque and of dubious consistency.

The matter should be viewed instead as follows: Arthur Conan Doyle one fine day set about to tell a story. In the process he created a fictional character as the protagonist and other fictional characters, each playing a certain role in the story. These characters are not flesh-and-blood human beings. Rather they, like the story itself, are abstract artifacts, born of Conan Doyle's fertile imagination. The name 'Sherlock Holmes' was originally coined by Conan Doyle in writing the story (and subsequently understood by those who have read the Holmes stories) as the fictional name for the protagonist. That thing – in fact merely an abstract artifact – is, *according to the story*, a man by the name of 'Sherlock Holmes'. In telling the story, Conan Doyle pretends to use the name to designate its fictional designatum (and to use 'Scotland Yard' to designate Scotland Yard) – or rather, he pretends to be Dr. Watson using 'Sherlock Holmes', much like an actor portraying Dr. Watson on stage. But he does not really so use the name; 'Sherlock Holmes' so far does not really have any such use, or even any related use (ignoring unrelated uses it coincidentally might have had). At a later stage, use of the name is imported from the fiction into reality, to name *the very same thing* that it is the name of according to the story. That thing – now the real as well as the fictional bearer of the name – is according to the story a human being who is a brilliant detective, but in reality an artifactual abstract entity.

The use of 'Sherlock Holmes' represented by 'Holmes$_2$', as the name for what is in reality an abstract artifact, is the same use it has according to the Holmes stories, except that according to the stories, that use is one on which it designates a man. The alleged thoroughly nondesignating use of 'Sherlock Holmes' by Conan Doyle, as a pretend name for a man, is a myth. Contrary to Kaplan, Kripke, and the rest, there is no literal use of 'Sherlock Holmes' that corresponds to 'Holmes$_1$'. One might say (in the spirit of the Kripke–van Inwagen theory) that there is a mythical use represented by 'Holmes$_1$', an allegedly thoroughly nondesignating use that pretends to name a brilliant detective who performed such-and-such exploits. This kind of use is fictitious in the same way that Sherlock Holmes himself is, no more a genuine use than a fictional detective is a genuine detective. Instead there is at first only the pretense of a use, including the pretense that the name designates a brilliant detective, a human being, on that use. Later the name is given a genuine use, on which it names the very same entity that it named according to the pretense, though the pretense that this entity is a human being has been dropped.

Literary scholars discussing the Holmes stories with all seriousness may utter the name 'Sherlock Holmes' as if to import its pretend use as the name of a man into genuine discourse – as when a Holmes "biographer" says, "Based on the evidence, Holmes was not completely asexual." Even then, the scholars are merely pretending to use the name as a name for a man. There is no flesh-and-blood man for the name to name, and the scholars know that.[23] If they are genuinely using the name, they are using it as a name for the fictional character. The only genuine, non-pretend use that we ever give the name – of which I feel confident – is as a name for the character. And that use, as a name for that very thing, is the very use it has in the story – though according to the story, that very thing is a human being and not an abstract entity. Conan Doyle may have used the name for a period even before the character was fully developed. Even so, this would not clearly be a genuine use of the name on which it was altogether nondesignating. There would soon exist a fictional character that *that* use of the name already designated.[24] Once the anticipated designatum arrived, to use the name exactly as before was to use it to designate that thing. At that point, to use the name in a way that it fails to designate would have been to give it a new use.

[23] What about a foggy-headed literary theorist who maintains, as a sophomoric antirealist or Meinongian philosophical view (or quasi-philosophical view), that Sherlock Holmes is in some sense no less flesh-and-blood than Conan Doyle? The more bizarre someone's philosophical perspective is, the more difficult it is to interpret his/her discourse correctly. Such a case might be assimilated to that of myths.

[24] On the view I am proposing, there is a sense in which a fictional character is prior to the fiction in which the character occurs. By contrast, Kripke believes that a fictional character does not come into existence until the final draft of the fiction is published. This severe restriction almost certainly does not accord with the way fiction writers see themselves or their characters. Even if it is correct, it does not follow that while writing a fiction, the author is using the name in such a way that it is thoroughly nondesignating. It is arguable that the name already designates the fledgling abstract artifact that does not yet exist. There is not already, nor will there ever be, any genuine use of the specific name as the name of a human being; that kind of use is make-believe.

Once the name 'Sherlock Holmes' has been imported into genuine discourse, Conan Doyle's sentences involving the name express singular propositions about his character. One might even identify the fiction with a sequence of propositions, about both fictional and nonfictional things (for example, London's Baker Street). To say this is not to say that Conan Doyle asserted those propositions. He did not – at least not in any sense of 'assert' that involves a commitment to one's assertions. He merely pretended to be Dr. Watson asserting those propositions. In so doing, Conan Doyle pretended (and his readers pretend) that the propositions are true propositions about a real man, not untrue propositions about an abstract artifact. That is exactly what it *is* to pretend to assert those propositions. To assert a proposition, in this sense, is in part to commit oneself to its truth; so to pretend to assert a proposition is to pretend to commit oneself to its truth. And the propositions in question entail that Holmes was not an abstract entity but a flesh-and-blood detective. Taken literally, they are untrue.[25]

Many have reacted to this proposal with a vague feeling – or a definite feeling – that I have conscripted fictional characters to perform a service for which they were not postulated and are not suited. Do I mean to say that *The Hound of the Baskervilles* consists entirely of a sequence of mostly false propositions about mostly abstract entities? Is it of the very essence of fiction to pretend that abstract entities are living, breathing people?

These misgivings stem from a misunderstanding of the nature of fiction and its population. The characters that populate fiction are created precisely to perform the service of being depicted as people by the fictions in which they occur. Do not fixate on the fact that fictional characters are abstract entities. Think instead of the various *roles* that a director might cast in a stage or screen production of a particular piece of fiction. Now think of the corresponding characters as the components of the fiction that *play* or *occupy* those roles in the fiction. It is no accident that one says of an actor in a dramatic production that he/she is playing a "part." The characters of a fiction – the occupants of roles in the fiction – are in some real sense *parts* of the fiction itself. Sometimes, as in historical fiction, what fictionally plays a particular role is a real person or thing. In other cases, what plays a particular role is the brainchild of the storyteller. In such cases, the role player is a *wholly* fictional character, or what

---

[25] See note 17. If my view is correct, then van Inwagen's use of the word 'ascribe' in saying that a fiction ascribes a particular property to a particular fictional character may be understood (apparently contrary to van Inwagen's intent) quite literally, in its standard English meaning.

I (following Kripke) have been calling simply a "fictional character." Whether a real person or wholly fictional, the character is that which according to the fiction takes part in certain events, performs certain actions, undergoes certain changes, says certain things, thinks certain thoughts. An actor performing in the role of Sherlock Holmes portrays Holmes$_2$; it is incorrect, indeed it is literally nonsense, to say that he portrays Holmes$_1$, if 'Holmes$_1$' is thoroughly nondesignating.

It is of the very essence of a fictional character to be depicted in the fiction as the person who takes part in such-and-such events, performs such-and-such actions, thinks such-and-such thoughts. Being so depicted is the character's raison d'etre. As Clark Gable was born to play Rhett Butler in Margaret Mitchell's *Gone with the Wind*, that character was born to be the romantic leading man of that fiction. Mario Puzo's character of Don Corleone is as well suited to be the charismatic patriarch of *The Godfather* as Marlon Brando was to portray the character on film. Except even more so. The character was also portrayed completely convincingly by Robert De Niro. But only that character, and no other, is appropriate to the patriarch role in Puzo's crime saga. Likewise, the butler in Kazuo Ishiguro's *The Remains of the Day* would have been completely inappropriate, in more ways than one, as the protagonist of Ian Fleming's James Bond novels. It is of the essence of Fleming's character precisely to be the character depicted in the dashing and debonair 007 role in the James Bond stories – and not merely in the sense that being depicted thus is both a necessary and a sufficient condition for being the character of Bond in any metaphysically possible world. Rather, this is the condition that defines the character; being the thing so depicted in those stories characterizes exactly *what* the character of James Bond *is*.

In a sense, my view is the exact opposite of the traditional view expressed in Russell's pronouncement that "it is of the very essence of fiction that only the thoughts, feelings, etc., in Shakespeare and his readers are real, and that there is not, in addition to them, an objective Hamlet." To Russell's pronouncement there is Hamlet's own fictional retort: "There are more things in heaven and earth, Horatio, Than are dreamt of in your philosophy." It is of the very essence of Shakespeare's *Hamlet* that there is indeed an object that is Hamlet. I am not urging that we countenance a person who is Hamlet$_1$ and who contemplated suicide according to the classic play but who does not exist. There is no sense in which there is any such person. The objective Hamlet is Hamlet$_2$ – what plays the title role in the Bard's drama – and hence not a human being at all but a part of fiction, merely depicted there as

anguished and suicidal. It is with the most robust sense of reality pre-
scribed by the philosopher/lord that I should urge recognition of this
fictionally troubled soul.[26]

It is an offer one shouldn't refuse lightly. Unlike Kripke's theory, a
treatment of the sentences of the Sherlock Holmes stories on which they
literally designate (although their author may not) the fictional character, and literally express things (mostly false) about that character, yields
a straightforward account – what I believe is the correct account – of the
meaningfulness and apparent truth of object-fictional sentences like
'Sherlock Holmes uses cocaine', and thereby also of the meaning and
truth of metafictional sentences like 'According to the Holmes stories,
Holmes used cocaine'. Following Kripke's lead in the possible-world
semantics for modality, we say that 'Sherlock Holmes' is a rigid designator, designating the fictional character both *with respect to the real world*
and *with respect to the fiction*. The object-fictional sentence is not true with
respect to the real world, since abstract entities do not use hard drugs.
But it is true with respect to the fiction – or true "in the world of the
fiction" – by virtue of being entailed by the propositions, themselves
about fictional characters, that comprise the fiction, taken together with
supplementary propositions concerning such things as the ordinary
physical-causal structure of the world, usual societal customs, and so on,
that are assumed as the background against which the fiction unfolds.[27]
When we speak within the fiction, we pretend that truth with respect
to the fiction is truth simpliciter, hence that Holmes (= Holmes$_2$) was a
human being, a brilliant detective who played the violin, and so on. Or
what is virtually functionally equivalent, we use object-fictional sentences
as shorthand for metafictional variants. The metafictional ⌜According
to fiction *f*, ϕ⌝ is true with respect to the real world if and only if ϕ is

---

[26] In reading a piece of fiction, do we pretend that an abstract entity is a prince of Denmark
(or a brilliant detective, and so on)? The question is legitimate. But it plays on the distinction between *de dicto* and *de re*. Taken *de dicto*, of course not; taken *de re*, exactly. That
abstract entities are human beings is not something we pretend, but there are abstract
entities that we pretend are human beings. Seen in the proper light, this is no stranger
than pretending that Marlon Brando is Don Corleone. (It is not nearly as strange as
Brando portraying a character in *The Freshman* who, in the story, is the real person on
whom the character Marlon Brando portrayed in *The Godfather* was modelled.)

[27] Cf. John Heintz, "Reference and Inference in Fiction," *Poetics*, 8, 1/2 (April 1979),
pp. 85–99. Where the fiction is inconsistent, the relevant notion of entailment may have
to be nonstandard. Also, the notion may have to be restricted to a *trivial* sort of entailment – on pain of counting arcane and even as yet unproved mathematical theorems
true with respect to fiction. Cf. Lewis, "Truth in Fiction," at pp. 274–8 of his *Philosophical
Papers, I.*

true with respect to the mentioned fiction. In effect, the metafictional receives a Fregean treatment on which the object-fictional subordinate clause φ is in *ungerade* mode, designating a (typically false) proposition about a fictional character. In all our genuine discourse about Holmes, we use the name in the 'Holmes$_2$' way. One may feign using 'Sherlock Holmes' as the name of a man, but this is only a pretend use. To say that according to the stories, Holmes$_1$ used cocaine is to say nothing; what is true according to the stories is that Holmes$_2$ used cocaine.[28]

Consider again sentence (~1), or better yet,

(3)   Sherlock Holmes does not really exist; he is only a fictional character.

Taken literally, (3) expresses the near contradiction that Holmes$_2$ is a fictional character that does not exist. It was suggested earlier that the existence predicate may be given a Pickwickian interpretation on which it means something like: *an entity of the very sort depicted*. In many cases, however, Russell's analysis by means of (~1$'_2$) seems closer to the facts. In uttering (~1) or (3), the speaker may intend not merely to characterize Holmes, but to deny the *existence* of Holmes *as the eccentric detective*. It may have been this sort of consideration that led Kripke to posit an ambiguity, and in particular a use of the name in the alleged manner of 'Holmes$_1$', a pretend-designating nondesignating use on which the 'Holmes$_2$' use is parasitic (and which generates an intensional *ungerade* use). Kripke's posit is also off target. There is a reasonable alternative. We sometimes use

---

[28] Very capable philosophers have sometimes neglected to distinguish among different possible readings of an object-fictional sentence – or equivalently, between literal and extended (fictional) senses of 'true'. See, for example, Richard L. Cartwright in "Negative Existentials," *Journal of Philosophy*, 57 (1960), pp. 629–39; and Jaakko Hintikka, "*Cogito Ergo Sum*: Inference or Performance," *The Philosophical Review*, 71 (January 1962), pp. 3–32.

When we use an object-fictional sentence φ as shorthand for something metafictional, what is the longhand form? Perhaps ⌜There is a fiction according to which φ⌝, perhaps ⌜According to *that* fiction, φ⌝ with designation of a particular fiction, perhaps something else. Recognizing that we speak of fictional characters in these ways may to some extent obviate the need to posit a nonliteral, extended sense for all predicates. On the other hand, something like Kripke's theory of extended senses may lie behind the use of gendered pronouns ('he') to designate fictional people even in discourse about reality.

Perhaps the most difficult sentences to accommodate are those that assert cross-realm relations. Following Russell's analysis of thinking someone's yacht larger than it is, 'Bertrand Russell was cleverer than Sherlock Holmes' may be taken to mean that the cleverness that Russell had is such that according to the stories the cleverness that Holmes$_2$ had was greater. Cf. my *Reference and Essence* (Princeton: Princeton University Press, 1981; Amherst, NY: Prometheus Books, 2005), at pp. 116–35, and especially 147 n.

ordinary names, especially names of famous people, in various descriptive ways, as when it is said that so-and-so is a Napoleon, or another Nixon, a Hitler, no Jack Kennedy, or even (to segue into the fictional realm) a Romeo, an Uncle Tom, quixotic, Pickwickian, and so on. I submit that, especially in singular existential statements, we sometimes use the name of a fictional character in a similar way. We may use 'Sherlock Holmes', for example, to mean something like: *Holmes more or less as he is actually depicted in the stories,* or *Holmes replete with these attributes* (the principally salient attributes ascribed to Holmes in the stories), or best, *the person who is both Holmes and Holmesesque.* In uttering (~1), one means that the Holmes of fiction, Holmes as depicted, does not exist in reality, that there is in reality no such person – no *such* person, no person who is both Holmes and sufficiently like *that*, sufficiently as he is depicted.

Since this interpretation requires a reinterpretation of the name, it might be more correct to say that the speaker expresses this proposition than to say that (~1) or (3) itself does. This is not a use of 'Holmes' as a thoroughly nondesignating name, but as a kind of description that invokes the name of the fictional character. In short, the name is used à la Russell as a disguised improper definite description. It is very probably a nonliteral, Pickwickian use of the name. It is certainly a nonstandard use, one that is parasitic on the name's more fundamental use as a name for the fictional character, not the other way around. It need not trouble the direct-reference theorist. The disguised-description use is directly based upon, and makes its first appearance in the language only after, the standard use in the manner of 'Holmes$_2$,' as (in Russell's words) a "genuine name in the strict logical sense." If an artificial expression is wanted as a synonym for this descriptive use, something clearly distinguished from both 'Holmes$_2$,' (which I claim represents the standard, literal use of the name) and 'Holmes$_1$,' (which represents a mythical use, no genuine use at all) is needed. Let us say that someone is a *Holmesesque-Holmes* if he is Holmes and sufficiently like he is depicted, in the sense that he has relevantly many of the noteworthy attributes that Holmes has according to the stories. Perhaps the most significant of these is the attribute of being a person (or at least person-like) and not an abstract artifact. Following Russell, to say that *the* Holmesesque-Holmes does not exist is to say that nothing is uniquely both Holmes and Holmesesque – equivalently (not synonymously), that Holmes is not Holmesesque. It is an empirical question whether Holmes – the character of which Conan Doyle wrote – was in reality like *that*, such-and-such a person, to any degree. The question of Holmes's existence *in this sense* is answered not by seeking whether someone or other was Holmesesque but by investigating the literary activities of Conan Doyle.[29]

These considerations, and related ones, weigh heavily in favor of an account of names from fiction as unambiguous names for artifactual entities.[30] In its fundamental use that arises in connection with the fiction – its only literal use – 'Sherlock Holmes' univocally names a man-made artifact, the handiwork of Conan Doyle. Contra Russell and his sympathizers, names from fiction do not have a prior, more fundamental use. They do not yield true negative existentials with thoroughly nondesignating names.

The account suggested here is extendable to the debunking of myths. A mythical object is a hypothetical entity erroneously postulated by a theory. Like a fictional object, a mythical object is an abstract (nonphysical, nonmental) entity created by the theory's inventor. The principal difference between myth and fiction is that a myth is believed whereas with fiction there is typically only a pretense.[31] An accidental storyteller,

---

[29] The notion of something being sufficiently as Holmes is depicted may be to some extent interest-relative. Consequently, in some cases the truth value of an assertion made using ⌜α exists⌝, with α a name from fiction, may vary with operative interests. Some scholars tell us, without believing in vampires, that Bram Stoker's character of Count Dracula really existed. (This aspect of the theory I am suggesting raises a complex hornets' nest of difficult issues. Far from disproving the theory, however, some of these issues may tend to provide confirmation of sorts.)

Kripke argues that (3), properly interpreted, involves an equivocation whereby the name has its original nondesignating use and 'he' is a "pronoun of laziness" (Peter Geach) designating the fictional character – so that (3) means that the man Holmes$_1$ does not exist whereas the fictional character Holmes$_2$ is just that. Kripke also says that one should be able to assert what is meant in the first clause of (3) without mentioning Holmes$_2$ at all. This is precisely what I believe cannot be done. The original may even be paraphrased into the nearly inconsistent 'Sherlock Holmes does not really exist and is only a fictional character'. On my alternative hypothesis, the speaker may mean something like: *The Holmesesque-Holmes does not really exist; Holmes is only a fictional character.* This is equivalent to: Holmes is not really Holmesesque, but a fictional character. Besides avoiding the putative 'Holmes$_1$,' use, my hypothesis preserves an anaphoric-like relation between the pronoun and antecedent. (Other possibilities arise if Kripke's theory of extended senses for predicates is applied to 'Holmesesque'.)

[30] In later work, and even in the same work cited in note 12, Kripke argued persuasively against positing ambiguities when an univocality hypothesis that equally well explains the phenomena is available. Cf. his "Speaker's Reference and Semantic Reference," in P. French, T. Uehling, and H. Wettstein, eds., *Contemporary Perspectives in the Philosophy of Language* (Minneapolis: University of Minnesota Press, 1979), pp. 6–27, especially 19.

[31] Donnellan, "Speaking of Nothing" at pp. 6–8, says that myth is not analogous to fiction. I am convinced that he is mistaken, and that this myth about myths has led many other philosophers astray. When storytellers tell stories and theorists hypothesize, fictional and mythical creatures abound. (An interesting possibility: Perhaps the myth invented by Babinet no longer exists, now that no one believes it. Can a myth, once it is disproved,

Le Verrier attempted in all sincerity to use 'Vulcan' to designate a real planet. The attempt failed, but not for lack of a designatum. Here as before, there is ample reason to doubt that 'Vulcan₁' represents a genuine use of the original name. Le Verrier held a theory according to which there is such a use, and he intended and believed himself to be so using the name. Had the theory been correct, there would have been such a use for the name. However, the theory is false; it was all a mistake. Kripke says that in attempting to use the name, 19th-century astronomers failed to designate anything. But this verdict seems to ignore their unintended relationship to the mythical planet. One might just as well judge that the ancients who introduced 'Hesperus' as a name for the first star visible in the dusk sky, unaware that the "star" was in fact a planet, failed to name that planet. Nor had they inadvertently introduced two names, one for the planet and one thoroughly nondesignating. Plausibly, as the ancients unwittingly referred to a planet believing it to be a star, so Le Verrier may have unknowingly referred to Babinet's mythical planet, saying and believing so many false things about it (that it is a real planet,

---

continue to exist as merely an unbelieved theory? If not, then perhaps 'Vulcan' is non-designating after all – though only by designating a nonexistent.)

Kripke extends his account in the natural way also to terms for objects in the world of appearance (for example, a distant speck or dot), and to species names and other bio-logical-kind terms from fiction and myth, like 'unicorn' and 'dragon'. The theory should be extended also to general terms like 'witch', 'wizard', and so on. There is a mythical species designated by 'dragon', an abstract artifact, not a real species. Presumably, if K is the mythical species (or higher-level taxonomic kind) of dragons, then there is a corresponding concept or property of being a beast of kind K, thus providing semantic content for the predicate 'is a dragon'. Kripke believes there is a prior use of the term, in the sense of 'dragon₁', which has no semantic content. But as before, on this point I find no persuasive reason to follow his lead.

Are there dragons? There are myths and fictions according to which there are dragons, for example the legend of Puff. Puff is a fictional character – an abstract artifact and not a beast. Fictional dragons like Puff are not real dragons – though they may be said to be "dragons," if by saying that we mean that they are dragons in the story. (Cf. Kripke's hypothesized extended sense of 'plays the violin'.) Is it metaphysically possible for there to have been dragons in the literal (unextended) sense of the word? No; the mythical species K is not a real species, any more than Puff is a real beast, and the mythical species could not have been a species any more than Puff could have been a beast. It is essential to K that it not be a species. A fortiori there could not have been such beasts. The reasoning here is very different from that of Kripke's *Naming and Necessity*, at pp. 156–7, which emphasizes the alleged 'dragon₁' use (disputed here), on which 'There are dragons' allegedly expresses nothing (hence nothing that is possibly true). In "Mythical Objects," in J. Campbell, M. O'Rourke, and D. Shier, eds., *Meaning and Truth* (New York: Seven Bridges Press, 2002), pp. 105–23, I apply my account to Peter Geach's famous problem about Hob's and Nob's hypothesized witch, from "Intentional Identity," *Journal of Philosophy*, 74, 20 (1967).

that it affects Mercury's orbit, and so on). There may have been a period during which 'Vulcan' was misapplied to the mythical planet before such application became enshrined as the official, correct use. It does not follow that there is a prior, genuine use of the name on which it is thoroughly nondesignating. I know of no compelling reason to deny that Babinet introduced a single name 'Vulcan' ultimately with a univocal use as a name for his mythical planet.[32] One might say that 'Vulcan,' represents a mythical use of the name. As with 'Holmes,', this kind of use is no more a genuine use than a mythical planet is a genuine planet.

It is unclear whether there are significant limitations here, and if so, what they might be. Even Meinong's golden mountain and round square should probably be seen as real mythical objects. Meinong's golden mountain is an abstract entity that is neither golden nor a mountain but as real as Babinet's Vulcan. Real but neither round nor square, Meinong's round square is both round and square according to Meinong's erroneous theory. Perhaps we should also recognize such things as fabrications, figments of one's imagination, and flights of fancy as real abstract entities.

[32] In introducing 'Vulcan', Babinet presumably presupposed the existence of an intra-Mercurial planet to be so named, while making no provisions concerning what the name would designate if there is no such planet. In that case, he failed to endow the name 'Vulcan' with a new type of use on which it designates anything (or even nothing at all). Believing himself to refer by the name 'Vulcan' to a planet, he began referring instead to the mythical planet. Le Verrier thereby inadvertently established a new type of use for the name on which it designates Vulcan. (Thanks to David Braun for pressuring me to clarify this point.) In some cases of "reference fixing," the description employed may have what I call a *bad mock referential*, or *ugly*, use – that is, designation is fixed by an implicit description not codesignative with the description explicitly used. See my "The Good, the Bad, and the Ugly," in M. Reimer and A. Bezuidenhout, eds., *Descriptions and Beyond* (Oxford: Oxford University Press, 2004), pp. 230–60. Cf. Kripke on 'Hesperus', in *Naming and Necessity*, at p. 80 n. 34.

3

Kripke on Epistemic and Metaphysical Possibility

Two Routes to the Necessary A Posteriori

Scott Soames

Saul Kripke's discussion of the necessary a posteriori in *Naming and Necessity* and "Identity and Necessity" – in which he lays the foundation for distinguishing epistemic from metaphysical possibility and explaining the relationship between the two – is, in my opinion, one of the outstanding achievements of twentieth-century philosophy.[1] My aim in this essay is to extract the enduring lessons of his discussion, and disentangle them from certain difficulties that, alas, can also be found there. I will argue that there are, in fact, two Kripkean routes to the necessary a posteriori – one correct and philosophically far-reaching, the other incorrect and philosophically misleading.[2]

PROPOSITIONS

Although Kripke avoids the word "proposition" in *Naming and Necessity*, and tries to keep his theoretical commitments to a minimum, he speaks repeatedly of the necessary or contingent "statements," and "truths," knowable a priori or a posteriori, that sentences express. Evidently, then, he thinks that there are things expressed by sentences that are both bearers of truth value and objects of attitudes like knowledge. Since this is what propositions are supposed to be, his discussion can be understood as implicitly involving propositions, while avoiding, as far as possible, substantive theoretical commitments about what they are. Thus, it should be

---

[1] Saul Kripke, *Naming and Necessity* (Cambridge: Harvard University Press, 1980); "Identity and Necessity," in Milton Munitz, ed., *Identity and Individuation* (New York: NYU Press, 1971).

[2] For a discussion of the philosophical significance of a correct understanding of this matter, see my "The Philosophical Significance of the Kripkean Necessary *Aposteriori*," *Philosophical Issues*, 16, 2006, 287–390; reprinted in Soames, *Philosophical Essays*, vol. 2 (Princeton: Princeton University Press, 2009).

safe to introduce the word into our discussion, so long as we limit our assumptions about propositions to those that are least objectionable and most in tune with Kripke's implicit presuppositions.

A1. Some things are asserted, believed, and known. For an agent to assert, believe, or know something is for the agent to stand in a relation to that thing.

A2. The things asserted, believed, and known are bearers of (contingent or necessary) truth and falsity. These things, which we may call "propositions," are expressed by sentences. The proposition expressed by S is designated by expressions such as ⌈the proposition that S⌉, ⌈the statement/claim/assertion/belief that S⌉ or simply ⌈that S⌉ – for example, the proposition expressed by 'Hesperus is Phosphorus' is the proposition that Hesperus is Phosphorus.

A3. Since different sentences may be used to assert the same thing, or express the same belief, and different beliefs or assertions may result from accepting, or uttering, the same sentence, propositions are not identical with sentences used to express them. Intuitively, they are what different sentences, or utterances, that say the same thing have in common, whatever that may turn out to be.

A4. Attitude ascriptions – ⌈x asserts, believes, knows (a priori or a posteriori) that S⌉ – report that an agent bears a certain attitude to the proposition expressed by S (in the context).

Kripke's central thesis about the necessary a posteriori is that for some propositions p, p is both necessarily true and knowable only on the basis of empirical evidence.

ESSENTIALISM AND THE DISTINCTION BETWEEN EPISTEMIC AND METAPHYSICAL POSSIBILITY

Kripke's first and most compelling route to the necessary a posteriori is illustrated by (1)–(4).

1. Greg Soames ≠ Brian Soames.
2. If Saul Kripke exists, then Saul Kripke is a human being.
3. This desk (pointing at the one in my office) was not made out of metal.
4. If this desk exists, then it is made up of molecules.

Since these propositions are true, they are, according to Kripke, necessarily true. However, it is obvious that they are knowable only a posteriori.
How can this be? How can a proposition that is necessary, and known to
be so, also be knowable only a posteriori? Kripke's answer appeals to our
knowledge of essential properties and relations.[3] We know a priori that
being human, being a desk that was not (originally) made out of metal,
and being a desk made of molecules are essential properties of anything
that has them. We also know a priori that being nonidentical is a relation
that holds essentially of any pair it relates. So, we know a priori that if any
objects have these properties, or stand in this relation, then they have,
or stand in, them in any genuinely possible circumstance in which they
exist. Hence, we know a priori that propositions (1)–(4) are necessary,
if true.[4] Still, discovering that they are true requires empirical investigation. This means that in order to discover whether certain things are
true in all states that the world could, genuinely, have been in, and other
things are true in no such states, we sometimes must first discover what is
true in the state the world actually is in. Sometimes in order to discover
what could and could not be, one first must discover what is.

Implicit in this route to the necessary a posteriori is a sharp distinction
between epistemic and metaphysical possibility – between ways things
could *conceivably* be versus ways things could *really* be (or have been). It is
natural to draw this distinction in terms of the notion of a *possible world*,
or better, a *possible world-state*. For Kripke, possible states of the world
are *not* alternate concrete universes, but abstract objects. Metaphysically
possible world-states are maximally complete ways the real concrete universe could have been – maximally complete properties that the universe could have instantiated. Epistemically possible world-states are
maximally complete ways the universe can coherently be conceived to
be – maximally complete properties that the universe can be conceived
of as instantiating, and that one cannot know a priori that it doesn't
instantiate. These two sets of properties are different. Just as there are
properties that ordinary objects could possibly have had and other properties they couldn't have had, so there are certain maximally complete
properties the universe could have had – metaphysically possible world-
states – and other maximally complete properties the universe couldn't

---

[3] When speaking of (Kripkean) "essential" properties and relations, I mean simply *properties and relations that hold necessarily of objects (in all genuinely possible world-states in which the
objects exist).*

[4] More properly, in the case of (2) and (4) we know a priori that they are necessary, if their
consequents are true. Thanks to Teresa Robertson for pointing this out.

have had – metaphysically impossible world-states. Just as some of the properties that objects couldn't have had are properties that one can conceive them as having, and that one cannot know a priori that they don't have, so some maximally complete properties that the universe couldn't have had – some metaphysically impossible world-states – are properties that one can conceive it as having, and that one cannot know a priori that it doesn't have. These states of the world are epistemically possible. On this picture – which Kripke didn't make explicit, but could have – empirical evidence required for knowledge of necessary truths like (1)–(4) is needed to rule out metaphysically impossible, but epistemically possible, world-states in which they are false.

According to Kripke, then, some things that are coherently conceivable are not genuinely possible. How, then, are conceivability and possibility related? Here, in effect, is his answer.

> If the essentialist view is correct, it can only be correct if we sharply distinguish between the notions of a posteriori and a priori truth on the one hand, and contingent and necessary truth on the other hand, for although the statement that this table, if it exists at all, was not made of ice, is necessary, it certainly is not something that we know a priori.... This looks like wood. It does not feel cold and it probably would if it were made of ice. Therefore, I conclude, probably this is not made of ice. Here my entire judgment is a posteriori... given that it is in fact not made of ice, in fact is made of wood, one cannot imagine that under certain circumstances it could have been made of ice. So we have to say that though we cannot know a priori whether the table was made of ice or not, given that it is not made of ice, it is *necessarily* not made of ice. In other words, if P is the statement that the lectern is not made of ice, one knows by a priori philosophical analysis, some conditional of the form "if P, then necessarily P." If the table is not made of ice, it is necessarily not made of ice. On the other hand, then, we know by empirical investigation that P, the antecedent of the conditional is true – that this table is not made of ice. We can conclude by *modus ponens*:
>
> P ⊃ Necessarily P
>
> P
>
> Necessarily P
>
> The conclusion – 'Necessarily P' – is that it is necessary that the table not be made of ice, and this conclusion is known a posteriori, since one of the premises on which it is based is a posteriori. ("Identity and Necessity," 152–3)

Though not put in terms of the distinction between conceivability and genuine possibility, or between two different, but related, types of world-states, the lesson of the passage can easily be so stated. In Kripke's argument, the fact one cannot know that P a priori means that one cannot know a priori that a world-state in which it is false that P is not instantiated. Such states are coherently conceivable, and so epistemically possible. The fact that one knows a priori that if P, then necessarily P means that one knows a priori that if a world-state in which it is true that P is instantiated, then no world-state in which it is false that P could have been instantiated. Thus, when one finds, empirically, that it is true that P, one learns a posteriori that epistemically possible world-states in which it is false that P are metaphysically impossible.

On this picture, the objects of conceivability – the things we conceive when trying to determine what is metaphysically possible – include not only individual world-states, but entire *systems* of metaphysical possibility, each with a designated "actual" world-state and a space of related states. Someone seeing my desk for the first time who doesn't know what it was (originally) made of can conceive of a world-state in which it was made of mahogany, a world-state in which it was made of oak, and perhaps even a world-state in which it was made of metal. One can conceive of each of these states being instantiated. Accompanying each state, one can conceive of related states that will be genuine metaphysical possibilities, if the initial, designated state, is instantiated. So, accompanying the designated (actual) state in which the desk was made of reddish-brown mahogany, one can conceive of related world-states in which it was made of mahogany stained another color. But given the supposition that the original state is instantiated, one can conceive of *no* state possible relative to it in which that very desk was made of some other material – for example, oak or metal. A similar point holds for other epistemically possible world-states in which the desk *was* made of those things. When they play the role of the designated "actual" world-state – that is, when one considers them as instantiated and asks which states are possible relative to them – one regards world-states in which the desk was made of mahogany as impossible *relative to those states.*

So we have a set of epistemically possible world-states, each of which can coherently be conceived as being instantiated. Along with each such state w_1, we have (epistemically possible) world-states w_2 which we recognize to be metaphysically possible, if the initial, designated "actual" state w_1 is instantiated – that is, we recognize that if w_1 were instantiated, then w_2 would be a property that the universe could have had. Moreover, for each such state w_2 there are (epistemically possible) world-states w_3 which we recognize to be metaphysically possible, if w_2 is instantiated – that is, we recognize that if w_1 were instantiated, then w_3 would be (metaphysically) possibly possible. Repeating this process indefinitely, we generate a coherently conceivable system of metaphysical possibility. Collecting all such systems together, we have a set of epistemically possible systems of metaphysical possibility. Roughly, for a world-state to be metaphysically possible (or possibly possible) is for it to be a metaphysically possible (or possibly possible) member of some epistemically possible system of metaphysical possibility *the designated world-state of which is the state that the world really is in.*

Obviously, this is not a definition of metaphysical possibility in nonmodal terms (something Kripke would never countenance). Rather, it is a way of thinking about the relationship between conceivability and possibility using the primitive notion of a property that the universe could instantiate. On this picture, conceivability is a fallible, but useful, guide to metaphysical possibility. It is fallible because before we know much about what is actual, there are many epistemically possible world-states that appear to be genuinely possible, and so remain candidates for being metaphysically possible. The more we learn about the world, the more we whittle down this field of candidates, and the better able we are to identify the scope of genuine metaphysical possibility. In short, our guide to metaphysical possibility is conceivability plus knowledge of actuality. Whether or not this is a *complete* guide is a further question. If, somehow, we could discover all actual, nonmodal facts, would we know precisely which world-states were metaphysically possible, possibly possible, and so on? Once ignorance of actuality is factored out, are facts about which world-states are metaphysically possible relative to others always knowable a priori? Neither anything I have said, nor any doctrine of Kripke's that I know of, settles the issue.

THE SCOPE OF KRIPKE'S ESSENTIALIST ROUTE TO THE NECESSARY A POSTERIORI

The Essentialist Route to the Necessary A Posteriori (ERNA)

Let p be a true proposition that attributes a property (or relation) F to an actually existing object o (or series of objects), conditional on the object (or objects) existing (while not attributing any further properties or relations to anything). Then, p will be an instance of the necessary a posteriori if (a) it is knowable a priori that F is an essential property of o, if F is a property of o at all (or a relation that holds essentially of the objects, if F holds of them at all); (b) knowledge of o that it has F, if it exists (or of the objects that they are related by F, if they exist) can only be had a posteriori; and (c) knowing p involves knowing of o (or of the objects) that it (they) have F, if it (they) exist at all. (o can be an individual or a kind.)[5]

Instances of ERNA like (2) and (4) are basic cases from which other instances can be derived. For example, since nonidentity essentially relates any pair it actually relates, an argument of this pattern establishes the necessary a posteriority of the proposition that Greg Soames is nonidentical with Brian Soames, if Greg and Brian exist. But since this proposition is trivially equivalent to the proposition expressed by (1), that proposition is also necessary and a posteriori. Similar remarks apply to (3).

Although Kripke's essentialist paradigm explains many putative instances of the necessary a posteriority, certain simple identities raise problems. Although such sentences are standardly taken to be paradigmatic instances of the Kripkean necessary a posteriori, in fact, their status is doubtful. Let o and o* be objects to which the identity relation actually applies, and p be a proposition that (merely) attributes identity to the pair. Then, although conditions (a) and (c) of ERNA are satisfied, condition (b) is not, since knowledge of the pair – that is, of <o,o> – that identity truly applies to it can surely be had a priori. Thus, p is an example of the necessary a priori, not the necessary a posteriori. This point is illustrated by (5).

5. $(\exists x\colon x = \text{Hesperus}) (\exists y\colon y = \text{Phosphorus})$ it is a necessary truth that $x = y$.

Since (5) is true, the proposition expressed by '$x = y$', relative to an assignment of Venus to 'x' and 'y', is a necessary truth. However, since this proposition (merely) predicates identity of Venus and itself, it is knowable a priori, if anything is.

Of course, not all identities pose this problem. For example, let 'a' and 'b' name the sperm and egg from which Saul Kripke actually developed. The possibility of identical twins aside, his doctrine of the essentiality of origin will then characterize (6a) and (6b) as instances of the necessary a posteriori.

6a. Saul Kripke = the individual who developed from a and b (if Kripke exists).

---

[5] If one wishes to generate instances of the necessary a posteriori, like 'Noman is human, if he exists' about a merely possible man, while avoiding a similar characterization of 'Noman is an elephant, if he exists', clause (b) needs to be changed. One way of doing this is to have it read: knowledge of o that it would have F, if it were to exist, can be had, but only a posteriori. In what follows I will ignore such niceties. Thanks again to Teresa Robertson for the underlying observation.

6b. $\lambda x\ [\forall y\ (y\ \text{developed from a and b} \leftrightarrow y = x]$ Saul Kripke (if Kripke exists).

If Kripke is right about the essentiality of origin, then the proposition p expressed by (6b) fits his essentialist account – since (a) it is knowable a priori that the property expressed by the lambda predicate is essential to any individual that has it, (b) knowledge of Kripke that he has this property (if he exists) can only be had a posteriori, and (c) knowing p involves knowing of Kripke that he has the property (if he exists). Hence p is an instance of the Kripkean necessary a posteriori. Since proposition (6a) is trivially equivalent to p, it is, too.

Similar explanations cover (7) and (8).

7. gold = the element with atomic number 79 (if gold exists).
8. water = the substance molecules of which consist of two hydrogen atoms and one oxygen atom (if water exists).

Here, 'gold' and 'water' are treated as designating (abstract) natural kinds k_g and k_w (rather than their concrete instances). Thus, the proposition expressed by (7) is trivially equivalent to the proposition p_g that predicates of k_g the property of being a unique element instances of which have a certain atomic structure (if k_g exists), and the proposition expressed by (8) is trivially equivalent to the proposition p_w that predicates of k_w the property of being a unique substance instances of which are made up of molecules consisting of two hydrogen atoms and one oxygen atom (if k_w exists). Supposing, with Kripke, that these properties are knowable a priori to be essential properties of any kind that has them, even though empirical evidence is needed to justify their attribution to any particular kind, we conclude that p_g and p_w are examples of the necessary a posteriori. Since the propositions expressed by (7) and (8) are equivalent to them, they too fall under this heading.

Examples (9a)–(9c) also fit the essentialist paradigm, even though they are not strictly *identities*.

9a. Cats are animals.
9b. Lightning is electricity.
9c. Light is a stream of photons.

Kripke calls these *theoretical identification statements*, and gives a clue to their correct analysis when he suggests (10b) as the analysis of (10a).[6]

---

[6] *Naming and Necessity*, p. 138.

10a. Heat is mean molecular kinetic energy.

10b. $\forall x \forall y$ (x is hotter than y $\leftrightarrow$ the mean molecular kinetic energy of x is greater than that of y).

Applying this idea to (9) yields (11).

11a. $\forall x$ (x is a cat $\supset$ x is an animal).

11b. $\forall x$ (x is (an instance of) lightning $\supset$ x is (an instance of) electricity).

11c. $\forall x$ (x is (an instance of) light $\supset$ x is a stream of photons).

Proposition (11a) is equivalent to one that predicates of the species cat the property of having only instances that are also instances of genus animal. If this property can be known a priori to be an essential property of any species that has it (even though knowing that a species has it requires empirical investigation), then (11a) falls under Kripke's essentialist paradigm. Analogous remarks hold for (11b), (11c), and (10b).[7]

In sum, Kripke's essentialist paradigm explains a great many genuine instances of the necessary a posteriori. It may even seem that all his putative examples of the necessary a posteriori fall into this category. However, they don't. Sentences of the form (12a), where *m* and *n* are simple coreferential names, do *not* fit the paradigm; nor do sentences of the form (13a), where K and K* are simple natural kind terms (rigidly) designating the same kind k, and ⌈is a K⌉ and ⌈is a K*⌉ are predicates applying to all and only instances of k.

12a. n = m.

12b. Hesperus is Phosphorus.

13a. $\forall x$ [x is a K $\leftrightarrow$ x is a K*].

13b. Woodchucks are groundhogs (and conversely).

Since, according to Kripke, names don't have descriptive senses, it is natural to take a sentence consisting of names plus a relational predicate R to semantically express a proposition that predicates the relation expressed by R of the referents of the names, without any further predication. On this model, the proposition expressed by (12b) merely predicates identity of Venus and itself. Although this proposition is

---

[7] See chapters 9–11 of my *Beyond Rigidity* (New York: Oxford University Press, 2002); "Knowledge of Manifest Kinds," *Facta Philosophica*, 6, 2004, 159–81; and chapter 4 of *Reference and Description* (Princeton: Princeton University Press, 2005). Also, Nathan Salmon, "Naming, Necessity, and Beyond," *Mind*, 112, 2003, 475–92; Bernard Linsky, "General Terms as Rigid Designators," and my reply to Linsky, in a symposium on *Beyond Rigidity*, in *Philosophical Studies*, forthcoming.

necessary, it seems to be knowable a priori. One could, of course, avoid this conclusion by adopting the assumption (foreign to Kripke) that – in addition to predicating identity of Venus and itself – the proposition expressed by (12b) predicates the properties of being visible in the evening and being visible in the morning of Venus. However, then the proposition will be *contingent*.[8] Thus, although Kripke gives (12b), and other instances of (12a), as paradigmatic examples of the necessary a posteriori, one cannot arrive at this result by his standard essentialist route. Analogous remarks apply to instances of (13).

Kripke's Second (Attempted) Route to the Necessary A Posteriori: Hesperus and Phosphorus

The argument for the aposteriority of (12b), given in the last few pages of lecture 2 of *Naming and Necessity*, is based on the observation that the evidence available to a speaker who understands 'Hesperus' and 'Phosphorus' is insufficient to determine that they are coreferential. Kripke illustrates this by noting that there are possible world-states w in which competent users of 'Hesperus' and 'Phosphorus' are in evidentiary situations qualitatively identical to ours (prior to the astronomical discovery), and yet, in w, the names refer to different things.

> The evidence I have before I know that Hesperus is Phosphorus is that I see a certain star or certain heavenly body in the evening and call it 'Hesperus', and in the morning and call it 'Phosphorus'. I know these things. There certainly is a possible world in which a man should have seen a certain star at a certain position in the evening and called it 'Hesperus' and a certain star in the morning and called it 'Phosphorus'; and should have concluded – should have found out by empirical investigation – that he names two different stars, or two different heavenly bodies.... And so it's true that given the evidence that someone has antecedent to his empirical investigation, he can be placed in a sense in exactly the same situation, that is *a qualitatively identical epistemic situation*, and call two heavenly bodies 'Hesperus' and 'Phosphorus', without their being identical. So in that sense we can say that *it might have turned out either way.* (103–4, my emphasis)

This example shows that the evidence available to us, simply by being competent users of the names, doesn't establish (12c) or (12d).

---

[8] Including these properties in the contents of 'Hesperus' and 'Phosphorus', and rigidifying using the actuality operator, would preserve the necessity of (12b) (or near enough). However, such an analysis fails on independent grounds. See chapter 2 of *Beyond Rigidity*.

12c. 'Hesperus' and 'Phosphorus' are coreferential.

12d. 'Hesperus is Phosphorus' expresses a truth.

Thus, these propositions are not knowable a priori.

However, the lesson Kripke explicitly draws is that the proposition expressed by (12b) is not knowable a priori.

> So two things are true: first, that we do not know *a priori* that Hesperus is Phosphorus, and are in no position to find out the answer except empirically. Second, this is so because we could have evidence *qualitatively indistinguishable* from the evidence we have and determine the reference of the two names by the positions of the two planets in the sky, without the planets being the same. (104, my emphasis)

This conclusion is unwarranted. Since the proposition expressed by (12b) is true in all metaphysically possible world-states, it is true in all such states in which agents are in epistemic situations qualitatively identical to ours – even when the proposition *they* use (12b) to express is false. Although both we and they need evidence to rule out the falsity of (12c) and (12d), it has *not* been shown that when (12b) *does* express a true proposition p, evidence is needed to rule out the possible falsity of p. Since it has *not* been shown that evidence is needed to rule out the possible falsity of the proposition actually expressed by *our* use of (12b), it has *not* been shown that we can know that Hesperus is Phosphorus only a posteriori.

In order to derive Kripke's conclusion, one needs a premise that Kripke leaves implicit. In the passage, he exploits a familiar connection between speakers' understanding and acceptance of sentences, and our ability to use those sentences to report what they believe. Before the astronomical discovery, speakers understood but didn't accept sentence (12b); hence, it is natural to conclude, they didn't believe that Hesperus was Phosphorus. Since they wouldn't have been *justified* in accepting (12b), based on the evidence then, it is plausible to suppose that they wouldn't have been justified in believing that Hesperus was Phosphorus. But then, the proposition that Hesperus is Phosphorus must require empirical justification, in which case it must be knowable only a posteriori – exactly as Kripke says.

Here is the argument:

(i) One who understands 'Hesperus is Phosphorus' (a) accepts it and believes it to be true iff one believes that Hesperus is Phosphorus, and (b) would be justified accepting it and believing it to be true iff one would be justified in believing that Hesperus is Phosphorus.

(ii) In order to be justified in accepting 'Hesperus is Phosphorus' and believing it to be true, one needs evidence that the two names refer to the same thing. Given that one knows that 'Hesperus' designates the heavenly body seen in the evening and that 'Phosphorus' designates the heavenly body seen in the morning, one needs evidence that these are one and the same.

(iii) Since one needs empirical evidence in order to be justified in believing that Hesperus is Phosphorus, it is knowable only a posteriori.

When expressed in the framework of propositions, this argument presupposes the following premise.

Strong Disquotation and Justification (SDJ)

If x understands S, uses S to express p, and knows that S expresses p, then (a) x believes p iff x accepts S (and believes it to be true), and (b) x would be justified in believing p on the basis of evidence e iff x would be justified in accepting S (and believing it to be true) on the basis of e.

One who understands 'Hesperus is Phosphorus', while associating the names with 'the heavenly body visible in the evening', and 'the heavenly body visible in the morning', will justifiably accept the sentence and believe it to be true only if one justifiably believes that the heavenly body visible in the evening is the heavenly body visible in the morning. This descriptive belief doesn't involve any *de re* belief about Venus, and so is the sort that Kripke is looking for in his argument. Since justification for this belief requires empirical evidence, justification for accepting 'Hesperus is Phosphorus' does too. SDJ transfers this requirement to one's belief in the proposition one uses the sentence to express – presumably, in our case, the proposition that Hesperus is Phosphorus. Hence, our knowledge of this proposition can only be a posteriori.

Extension of the Argument to Other Instances of the Necessary A Posteriori

In lecture 3, Kripke generalizes this explanation to all cases of the necessary a posteriori. After summarizing his analysis of natural kind terms, and illustrating their role in expressing instances of the necessary a posteriori, he takes up a challenge. Up to now, when describing these instances, he emphasizes that although they are necessary, for all we knew prior to empirically discovering their truth, *they could have turned out otherwise*. Realizing that this may sound puzzling, he gives voice to the following objection.

Now in spite of the arguments I gave before for the distinction between necessary and *a priori* truth, the notion of *a posteriori* necessary truth may still be somewhat puzzling. Someone may well be inclined to argue as follows: 'You have admitted that heat might have turned out not to have been molecular motion, and that gold might have turned out not to have been the element with the atomic number 79. For that matter, you also have acknowledged that... this table might have turned out to be made from ice from water from the Thames. I gather that Hesperus might have turned out not to be Phosphorus. What then can you mean when you say that such eventualities are impossible? If Hesperus might have *turned out* not to be Phosphorus, then Hesperus might not have *been* Phosphorus. And similarly for the other cases: if the world could have *turned out* otherwise, it could have *been* otherwise. (140–1)

The objection covers all instances p of the necessary a posteriori. Since p is a posteriori, its falsity must be conceivable, and so, it would seem, knowledge of p must require empirical evidence ruling out possibilities in which p is false. Without such evidence, *it could turn out that p is false.* But, the objector maintains, if p is necessary, there are no such possibilities to be ruled out, since no matter what possible state the world is in, it is a state in which p is true. Thus, if p is necessary, we don't require empirical evidence to know p after all, and if p is a posteriori, then p isn't necessary. Either way, the necessary a posteriori is an illusion.

Kripke begins his reply by invoking an idea central to his account of (12b). According to that account, the function of empirical evidence needed for knowledge that Hesperus is Phosphorus is *not* to rule out possible world-states in which the proposition is false. There are no such states. Rather, evidence is needed to rule out possible states in which we use the *sentence* (12b) to express something false. Ruling this out involves putting aside our *de re* beliefs about Venus, and determining whether our justified *descriptive* beliefs are up to the task. If they fail to rule out the possibility of an epistemic state *qualitatively identical* to ours in which the names refer to different things, then we can't rule out the falsity of the sentence we accept, and so, the thought goes, we can't justify the belief we use the sentence to express. Kripke's task is to extend this explanation of (12b) to all instances of the necessary a posteriori.

The objector is correct when he argues that if I hold that this table could not have been made of ice, then I must also hold that it could not have turned out to be made of ice; *it could have turned out that P* entails that P could have been the case. What, then, does the intuition that the table might have turned out to have been made of ice or of anything else, that it might even have turned out not to be made of molecules, amount to? I think that it means simply that there might have been *a table* looking and feeling just like this one and placed in this very position in the room, which was in fact made of ice. In other words, I (or some conscious being) could have been *qualitatively in the same epistemic situation* that in fact obtains, I could have the same sensory experience that I in fact have, about *a table*, which was made of ice. (141–2)

Suppose I encounter a table. I examine it and come to know that it is made of wood, not ice. For all I knew, prior to my investigation, *it could have turned out* that the table was made of ice. Kripke tells us that this intuition – that *it could have turned out* that the table was made of ice – is simply the recognition that it is genuinely possible for an agent to be in a situation qualitatively identical to mine prior to my investigation, and be facing a table that *is* made of ice. He generalizes this point in the next paragraph.

> The general answer to the objector can be stated, then, as follows: Any necessary truth, whether *a priori* or *a posteriori*, could not have turned out otherwise. In the case of some necessary *a posteriori* truths, however, we can say that under appropriate qualitatively identical evidential situations, an appropriate corresponding qualitative statement might have been false. The loose and inaccurate statement that gold might have turned out to be a compound should be replaced (roughly) by the statement that it is logically possible that there should have been a compound with all the properties originally known to hold of gold. The inaccurate statement that Hesperus might have turned out not to be Phosphorus should be replaced by the true contingency mentioned earlier in these lectures: two distinct bodies might have occupied, in the morning and the evening, respectively, the very positions actually occupied by Hesperus-Phosphorus-Venus. (142–3)

Here we have the generalization of (12b). In pointing at the table and saying 'This table is not made of ice', I express a necessary truth – since *this very table* could not have been made of ice. However, I would not accept, and would not be justified in accepting, the sentence uttered, unless I *also* believed, and was justified in believing, the descriptive proposition DP that *a unique table over there is not made of ice*. It is my justified belief in DP (shared by agents in qualitatively identical states) that rules out possible situations in which my utterance fails to express a truth. DP is, of course, contingent rather than necessary, and hence not to be confused with the (singular) proposition expressed by the indexical sentence uttered. Still, since I am justified in believing DP only on the basis of empirical evidence, and, since this evidence is required for my utterance to be justified, my justification for accepting the sentence uttered requires empirical evidence. From SDJ, it follows that although it is a necessary truth that *this table* is not made of ice, my knowledge of this truth requires empirical justification, and so is a posteriori.

This is Kripke's second route to the necessary a posteriori. All his examples contain names, natural kind terms, or demonstratives, and semantically express propositions knowledge of which involves *de re* knowledge of the individuals or kinds those terms designate. The *necessity* of these propositions is explained by their attribution of essential properties and relations to those individuals or kinds. Their aposteriority is explained – in his *first* route to the necessary a posteriori – by the fact that the properties and relations can be known to apply to particular individuals and kinds only a posteriori. This explanation, though general, excludes simple identities. Thus, it applies to (1)–(4) and (6)–(11), but *not* (12) and (13). Kripke's *second* (attempted) explanation is meant to apply not only to these stragglers, but to the other cases as well. In the second route, knowledge of a necessary proposition p is linked to acceptance of a sentence S used to express p – which in turn is linked to knowledge of a descriptive proposition DP for which empirical evidence is required. Since justification for accepting S, and believing DP, requires empirical evidence, this evidence is also required for knowledge of p.

The two routes to the necessary a posteriori differ as follows:

(i) The first route applies to a proper subset of cases to which the second is meant to apply.

(ii) Only the first route leads to the recognition of epistemically possible world-states over and above those that are metaphysically possible.

(iii) Only the first takes the empirical evidence needed for a posteriori knowledge of p to rule out epistemic possibilities in which p is false.

There is also another important difference. The first route is, as I have indicated, sound. The second is not.

The Unsoundness of Kripke's Second Route to the Necessary A Posteriori

The problem with Kripke's second route to the necessary a posteriori is that the principle, SDJ, on which it depends, requires an unrealistic degree of transparency in the relationship between sentences and the propositions they express. S_1 and S_2 may mean the same thing, or express the same proposition p, even though a competent speaker who understands both, and knows of each that it expresses p, does *not* realize that they express the same proposition. Such an agent may accept S_1, and believe it to be true, while refusing to accept S_2, or believe it to be true, thereby falsifying SDJ. One such agent is Kripke's Pierre.[9] Although he understands both 'Londres est jolie' and 'London is pretty', he does not realize that they mean the same thing, and so accepts one while rejecting the other. Since SDJ yields the contradictory result that Pierre both believes and does not believe that London is pretty, it cannot be accepted.

A similar result can be reached using Kripke's example of Peter, who encounters different occurrences of (14), wrongly believing that they are about two different men named 'Paderewski'.

14. Paderewski had remarkable musical talent.

Since neither the name nor the sentence is ambiguous, the proposition semantically expressed doesn't change from one occasion, in which Peter accepts (14) because he takes it to be about a musician, to another occasion, in which he rejects (14) because he takes it to be about a statesman. Since Peter understands (14) without realizing that Paderewski the musician is Paderewski the statesman, his acceptance of (14) in one case, and rejection of it in another, leads, by SDJ, to contradiction. Similar results involving indexicals are easily obtained.[10] For these reasons, both SDJ and Kripke's second route to the necessary a posteriori must be rejected – unless some other principle can be found to take the place of SDJ.

When SDJ is applied to Kripke's examples, belief in singular propositions (about individuals or kinds) is linked to acceptance of specific sentences (containing names, indexicals, or natural kind terms) that express them – which, in turn, is linked to belief in certain descriptive propositions related to the original singular propositions. This suggests the possibility of dropping the problematic SDJ and linking the singular propositions directly to their descriptive counterparts. In the case of (12b) my belief that Hesperus is Phosphorus might be linked to (something like) my belief that the heavenly body visible in the evening is the heavenly body visible in the morning, while in the case of Kripke's example about the table, my belief that it is not made of ice might be linked to (something like) my belief that *a unique table over there* is not made of ice. The idea, in each case, is that the linked beliefs are related in two ways: (i) my coming to have the descriptive belief, in the circumstances

9 Saul Kripke, "A Puzzle about Belief," *Meaning and Use*, A. Margalit, ed. (Dordrecht: Reidel, 1979).
10 See chapter 1 of *Beyond Rigidity*, and chapter 15 of my *Philosophical Analysis in the Twentieth Century*, vol. 2 (Princeton: Princeton University Press, 2003).

in question, is necessary and sufficient for me to come to believe the singular proposition, and (ii) my justification for believing the singular proposition rests on my justification for the descriptive belief. Since in each case, justification of the descriptive belief requires empirical evidence, my belief in the putative instance of the necessary a posteriori is taken to require the same evidence.

The resulting nonmetalinguistic substitute for SDJ that emerges from this line of thought is, roughly, the following.

The Strong Descriptive Origin and Justification of *De Re* Belief (SDOJ)

If an agent x in a circumstance C is capable of believing a singular proposition p by virtue of believing a certain related descriptive proposition DP, then (a) x believes p in C iff x believes DP in C, and (b) x would be justified in believing p in C on the basis of e iff x would be justified in believing DP in C on the basis of e.

SDOJ can be used in Kripke's second route to the necessary a posteriori in essentially the same way that SDJ was. Thus, if one accepts the idea that belief in singular propositions about individuals or kinds always results from (or is accompanied by) believing certain related descriptive propositions, one can substitute SDOJ for SDJ, while preserving the structure of Kripke's second route to the necessary a posteriori.

However, one cannot *save* the route in this way, since the same counterexamples that falsify SDJ also falsify SDOJ. In the case of Pierre, a proponent of the idea that belief in singular propositions always arises from belief in associated descriptive propositions must admit that there are several ways that Pierre can come to believe singular propositions about London. He may, for example, come to believe that London is pretty either by believing that the city he lives in is pretty or by believing that the city on the picture postcards brought from Paris is pretty. SDOJ will then give the results that he believes that London is pretty (i) iff he believes that the city he lives in is pretty and (ii) iff he believes that the city on the picture postcards brought from Paris is pretty. Since in fact he believes that the city in the pictures is pretty while failing to believe that the city he lives in is pretty, SDOJ leads to the contradictory conclusion that Pierre both believes and does not believe that London is pretty. The case of Peter and Paderewski yields a similar, unacceptable conclusion. For this reason, SDJ, SDOJ, and Kripke's second route to the necessary a posteriori must all be rejected. Fortunately, this rejection does not diminish the correctness of his first route to the necessary a posteriori. The only thing cast into doubt is the aposteriority of (12) and (13).

ORIGINS OF SDJ AND SDOJ

Although SDJ and SDOJ are false, each may be seen as an incorrect generalization of a defensible idea. The guiding idea behind SDJ is that many of our beliefs (including those in singular propositions) are the result of understanding and accepting sentences (or other representations) that express them. The guiding idea behind SDOJ is the view (i) that thinking of an individual or kind always involves thinking of it *in a certain way* – as the bearer of a certain descriptive property – and (ii) that because of this, believing the bare singular proposition that o is F, always involves also believing a related, descriptive proposition in which some further property is used to think about o.[11] These ideas – behind SDJ and SDOJ – have considerable plausibility, and nothing said here shows them to be false.

The two ideas may be formulated roughly as follows.

The Metalinguistic Origin and Justification of (Some) Belief (MOJB)

Let A be a certain class of agents (including us), C a certain class of contexts, and P a certain class of propositions (including singular propositions about individuals or kinds). For any member x of A, c of C, and p of P, (i) x believes p in c iff there is a sentence (or representation) s such that x understands s, x knows that s expresses p in c, and x accepts s in c (thereby believing p), and (ii) x would be justified in believing p in c on the basis of evidence e iff there is some sentence (or representation) that x understands and knows to express p in c that x would be justified in accepting in c on the basis of e.

The Descriptive Origin and Justification of *De Re* Belief (DOJB)

Let A be a certain class of agents (including us), C a certain class of circumstances, and P the class of singular propositions about individuals or kinds. For any member x of A, c of C, and p of P, (i) x believes p in c iff there is a descriptive proposition DP – related, in c, to x and to p in a certain way – that is such that x believes p in c by virtue of believing DP in c, and (ii) x would be justified in believing p in c on the basis of evidence e iff there is a descriptive proposition DP related, in c, to x and to p as in (i), and x would be justified in believing DP in c on the basis of e.[12]

---

[11] Two illuminating sources of this amalgam of Fregean and Russellian ideas are David Kaplan, "Quantifying In," in D. Davidson and J. Hintikka, eds., *Words and Objections* (Dordrecht: Reidel, 1969), and Nathan Salmon, "Three Perspectives on Quantifying In," in R. Jeshion, ed., *New Essays on Singular Thought* (Oxford: Oxford University Press, 2010).

[12] It is natural to take the relation between x, p, and DP in (i) to involve some sort of (perceptual, causal, or historical) acquaintance relation connecting x's epistemic attitudes toward DP with the objects or kinds that are constituents of p.

We need not here try to determine the truth or falsity of either of these principles (for specified classes of agents, contexts, and propositions). There are, however, two important points to notice. First, the reason they are *not* falsified by Pierre-type examples is that they allow an agent x to believe a singular proposition p by virtue of accepting a sentence S, or believing a descriptive proposition DP, of a certain type – even if x fails to accept other sentences S*, or believe other descriptive propositions DP*, of the very same type (acceptance of, or belief in, which would also be sufficient for believing p). Thus, Pierre believes that London is pretty because he understands and accepts 'Londres est jolie', and believes that the city in the picture postcards is pretty, even though he understands but *doesn't* accept 'London is pretty', and *doesn't* believe that the city he lives in is pretty. The second point to notice is that the very feature of the principles that renders them compatible with Pierre-type examples also renders them *incapable* of playing the roles of SDJ and SDOJ in Kripke's second route to the necessary a posteriori. It does, of course, follow from MOJB and DOJB that any knowledge of the proposition p expressed by 'Hesperus is Phosphorus', that arises *solely* from understanding and accepting that very sentence, or believing that the heavenly body visible in the evening is the heavenly body visible in the morning, is justified by the empirical evidence needed for one's accepting the sentence, or believing the descriptive proposition, to be justified. However, this is not enough to show that p is knowable *only* a posteriori. Unless it can be shown that belief in p can *never* arise from acceptance of some other sentence S* or from belief in some other descriptive proposition DP* – the justification of which does *not* require empirical evidence – the possibility that p is knowable a priori cannot be ruled out. Nothing in Kripke's discussion does this.[13]

Moreover, the prospect of achieving this result by supplementing Kripke's discussion is not promising. Suppose, for example, that Pierre is accompanied in his odyssey from Paris to London by a band of similar unfortunates who share his epistemic fate. One can easily imagine them learning a dialect of English in which the name 'Londres' is imported from French, and in which (15a) semantically expresses the same proposition as (15b).

15a. Londres is London.
15b. London is London.

---

[13] Kripke seems to show an implicit awareness of essentially this point in footnote 44 of "A Puzzle about Belief."

In this scenario, one way for Pierre to know the proposition p expressed by both sentences would be by understanding and justifiably accepting (15a), while knowing that the city in the picture postcards is the city he lives in. Another way of knowing the same thing would be by understanding and justifiably accepting (15b), while knowing that the city he lives in is the city he lives in. Although the first way of knowing p might properly be regarded as a posteriori, the second way of knowing p is a priori.[14] Thus, the proper answer to the question of whether p is an instance of the necessary a posteriori – and the answer supported by MOJB and DOJB – seems to be 'no', since although p is necessary, it is *possible* to know p a priori. Given the clear parallel between this example and the Hesperus/Phosphorus example, as well as other instances of (12a) and (13), we can accept neither Kripke's characterization of these examples nor his second route to the necessary a posteriori.[15]

A FINAL WORD ABOUT STRONG DISQUOTATION AND JUSTIFICATION

Although the original principle, SDJ, cannot bear the weight placed on it by Kripke's second route to the necessary a posteriori, it does have intuitive appeal, and versions of it play a role in our belief-reporting practices. Thus, it is worth separating what is correct about it from what isn't. The key to doing this is, as I have argued elsewhere, to recognize that

---

[14] For purposes of simplicity, here and throughout, I ignore questions concerning the existential commitments of identity statements. Depending on which view of this matter one takes, the necessary complications can easily be added.

[15] Example (15) is similar to a number of less artificial examples in the literature. One involves Nathan Salmon's character Sasha, who learns the words 'catsup' and 'ketchup' from independent ostensive definitions, in which bottles so labeled are given to him to season his foods at different times. The words are, of course, synonymous, though no one ever tells Sasha that. As a result, he does not accept 'Catsup is ketchup' – because he suspects that there may be some, to him indiscernible, difference between the things the two words refer to. Nevertheless he understands both words. As Salmon emphasizes, nearly all of us learn one of the words ostensively, the order in which they are learned doesn't matter, and if either term may be learned ostensively, then someone like Sasha could learn both in that way. But then there will be synonymous sentences S_1 and S_2 which differ only in the substitution of one word for the other, which Sasha understands while being disposed to accept only one – just as with Pierre. Nathan Salmon, "A Millian Heir Rejects the Wages of *Sinn*," in C. A. Anderson and J. Owens, eds., *Propositional Attitudes: The Role of Content in Logic, Language, and Mind* (Stanford, CA: CSLI, 1990). See also Kripke on 'furze' and 'gorse', p. 134 of "A Puzzle about Belief," and Stephen Rieber, "Understanding Synonyms without Knowing that They Are Synonymous," *Analysis* 52 (1992), 224–8.

an utterance often results in the assertion and communication of more than the proposition semantically expressed by the sentence uttered.[16] For example, (14) might be used in a context in which musicians are being discussed to assert or communicate the proposition p_M – *that the musician, Paderewski, had remarkable musical talent* – while being used in a context in which politicians are the topic of conversation to assert or communicate the proposition p_S – *that the statesman, Paderewski, had remarkable musical talent.* The same is true of other attitudes. Sometimes Peter uses (14) to entertain p_M, and sometimes he uses it to entertain p_S (in addition to the bare proposition that simply attributes the property of having remarkable musical talent to Paderewski). This one-many relationship between sentences and propositions affects the application of SDJ. When we apply it to an agent like Peter who uses (14) first to entertain p_M and later to entertain p_S, no contradiction results from Peter's acceptance of (14) in the first case and rejection of it in the second – provided we let p_M play the role of 'p' in the first case, and p_S play this role in the second. However, if we let the bare semantic content of (14) play the role of 'p' in both cases, we do get a contradiction. Hence, particular applications of SDJ can be either unproblematic or clearly incorrect, depending on how, precisely, it is formulated, and whether on not contextual enrichment is involved.[17]

With this in mind, suppose we take Kripke's implicit reliance on SDJ in his discussion of (12b) to involve a modestly *enriched* proposition that speakers might naturally use that sentence to assert or entertain – for example, the proposition that the heavenly body, Hesperus, that is visible in the evening, is the heavenly body, Phosphorus, that is visible in the morning. *This proposition* is, of course, knowable only a posteriori, and the relevant application of SDJ is unproblematic. However, this way of taking the case does not advance Kripke's argument, since the *enriched* proposition is *not* necessary. If, on the other hand, we are asked to focus on the necessary proposition that (12b) *semantically* expresses, then we need a clear account – which Kripke doesn't provide – of precisely which proposition that is.

---

[16] See chapter 3 of *Beyond Rigidity*, "Naming and Asserting," in Z. Szabo, ed., *Semantics vs. Pragmatics* (Oxford: Oxford University Press, 2004), "Beyond Rigidity, Reply to McKinsey," *Canadian Journal of Philosophy*, 35, 2005, 169–78, and "The Gap between Meaning and Assertion: Why What We Literally Say Often Differs from What Our Words Literally Mean" in Soames, *Philosophical Essays*, vol. 1 (Princeton: Princeton University Press, 2009).

[17] This idea is used to illuminate and resolve issues raised by Kripke's puzzle about belief in Mike McGlone, *Assertion, Belief, and Semantic Content* (unpublished Princeton dissertation, 2007), from which my own views have profited.

The semantic theory most in harmony with Kripke's thoroughgoing antidescriptivism – contemporary Millian-Russellianism – won't save his argument, since, according to it, the proposition semantically expressed by (12b) is the a priori proposition also expressed by (12e).

12e. Hesperus is Hesperus.

On this theory, neither (12b) nor instances of (13) are examples of the necessary a posteriori. Of course, Millian-Russellianism cannot be attributed to Kripke. However, if it isn't, then it is mysterious what his positive view is. Being in the dark about this, we are in no position to accept either his argument for the necessary aposteriority of (12b), or his second route to the necessary a posteriori. Fortunately for us, and for the practice of philosophy in the post-Kripkean era, one sound route to the necessary a posteriori remains.[18]

[18] Thanks to Ali Kazmi and Jeff Speaks for their useful comments on an earlier draft.

4

Possible Worlds Semantics

Philosophical Foundations

Robert Stalnaker

1. INTRODUCTION

Saul Kripke did more than anyone else to bring possible worlds into the contemporary philosophical discourse, first with his more formal work on the model theory for modal logic in the 1960s, and then with his more philosophical lectures on reference and modality, delivered in January 1970, that used the possible worlds apparatus informally to clarify the relations between semantic issues about names and metaphysical issues about individuals and kinds.[1] Possible worlds semantics have been widely applied since then, both in philosophy and in other fields such as linguistic semantics and pragmatics, theoretical computer science, and game theory. Kripke's work, along with that of David Lewis, stimulated an ongoing debate about the nature and metaphysical status of possible worlds. Kripke himself has had little to say about the issues raised in this debate, in print, beyond what he said in *Naming and Necessity* and in brief remarks in a preface to a later edition of the lectures, published in 1980. But there is a clear view of the nature of possible worlds, and of the status of an explanation of modality in terms of possible worlds, implicit in the lectures and the preface.

The central focus of the post–*Naming and Necessity* debate about possible worlds has been a contrast between David Lewis's modal realism and various versions of actualism. On this general issue, it is clear enough where Kripke stands: His criticisms of what he describes as the "other countries" picture of possible worlds are an explicit rejection of Lewis's realism about possible worlds.[2] But the rejection of modal realism raises a

---

[1] Kripke (1980). Parenthetical page references in the text of this chapter are all to this edition of these lectures.

[2] Lewis's full articulation and defense of modal realism, in his book (1986), appeared long after *Naming and Necessity*, but the view had already been sketched in a more formal paper, Lewis (1968), to which Kripke refers.

range of further questions: What exactly are possible worlds (or possible states of the world, which Kripke suggests would be less misleading terminology)? What contribution do they make to the explanation of modal discourse, and of the distinctive facts that modal discourse is used to state? Does the slogan "necessity is truth in all possible worlds" provide, or point to, a reductive analysis of necessity? Are possible worlds, in some sense, prior to modal operators and modal auxiliaries? If not, in what sense are they explanatory? How are possible worlds, or counterfactual situations, specified? How do they contribute to our understanding of specific metaphysical questions about the relations between particular individuals and their qualitative characteristics, the kinds to which they belong, and the matter of which they are constituted? How are we to understand the possible existence of individuals that do not actually exist? What is the status of the domains of individuals in merely possible worlds?

My aim in this chapter is to spell out the views about some of these foundational questions that are expressed or at least implicit in Kripke's lectures. In Section 2, I discuss the general contrast between modal realism and actualism and questions about the kind of explanation that possible worlds provide for modal discourse and modal facts. In Section 3, I look at Kripke's views about how possible worlds are specified, in particular at the role of individuals in specifying possible worlds. In Section 4, I consider the problems about merely possible individuals.

2. MODAL REALISM AND REDUCTIVE ANALYSIS

Kripke suggests in a number of places that the overly picturesque phrase "possible worlds" is partly responsible for the misleading picture that he thinks motivated a pseudoproblem about the identity of individuals across possible worlds. The misleading picture is the conception of possible worlds as foreign countries or "distant planets, like our own surroundings, but somehow existing in a different dimension" (p. 15). He suggests that this picture is encouraged by the "terminological accident" (p. 20) of calling these entities "possible worlds"; if we had begun with more sober terminology – "'possible states (or histories) of the world', or 'possible situations'," we might have avoided the "*weltangst* and philosophical confusion that many philosophers have associated with the 'worlds' terminology" (p. 15). But to blame the terminology underestimates the power of the picture. Whatever one calls these entities, it is natural to take their role in the explanation of modality to be something like this: One should understand possibilities and potentialities in terms of the ways that they are realized or actualized, and it is tempting to believe that this idea will be explanatory only if the "worlds" are understood as realizations or actualizations of the possibilities. While some, such as David Kaplan, used the "distant planet" image only playfully as a heuristic,[3] David Lewis took it seriously, and argued that this conception of possible worlds provided the best explanation for modal discourse and modal facts. While few have followed Lewis in accepting a metaphysics of parallel universes, many have thought that this is what is required if one takes the possible worlds framework seriously as more than a useful fiction or a formal device.

A large part of the attraction of modal realism is that it purports to provide a genuine eliminative reduction of modality. Ironically, it was skepticism about primitive modality, and a kind of nominalism that Lewis took over from Quine and Goodman, that motivated his modal realism. Lewis argued that we can understand the idea of the actual universe independently of modal concepts, and that no new conceptual resources are needed to understand the hypothesis that there are many more things like that – a multiplicity of spatiotemporally isolated parallel universes. Modal concepts are to be analyzed in terms of quantification over entities of this kind. Lewis could agree with Kripke that we can think of possibilities as possible states or properties of the world – as ways a world might be – but argued that this does not help to avoid commitment to other universes, since his nominalism committed him to an identification of properties with the sets that are their extensions. There will be a multiplicity of ways a world might be, according to this account of properties, only if there is a multiplicity of total worlds that instantiate or exemplify these properties by being their (unit) members.

Kripke disclaimed any reductionist aim, and would reject the identification of properties with the sets that are their extensions. He expressed at many places a general skepticism about reductive philosophical analysis (for example, "I'm always sympathetic to Bishop Butler's 'Everything is what it is and not another thing' – in the non-trivial sense that philosophical analysis of some concept like reference, in completely different terms which make no mention of reference, are very apt to fail," p. 95), and he specifically denies that possible worlds give us this kind of explanation of modal operators and auxiliaries: "I do not think of 'possible worlds' as providing a *reductive* analysis in any philosophically

3 See Kaplan (1979).

significant sense, that is, as uncovering the ultimate nature from either an epistemological or a metaphysical point of view, of modal operators, propositions, etc., or as 'explicating' them" (p. 19, n.). On the explanatory role of possible worlds, Kripke walks a thin line between the view that they provide some kind of explication and the view that they are merely a convenient heuristic device. "One should even remind oneself," he says, "that the 'worlds' terminology can often be replaced by modal talk – 'It is possible that ...'" But on the other hand, he says "I do not wish to leave any exaggerated impression that I repudiate possible worlds altogether, or even that I regard them as a mere formal device" (p. 16). This raises the question, just what contribution do possible worlds make to our understanding of modality? "The main and original motivation for the 'possible worlds analysis' – and the way it clarified modal logic – was that it enabled modal logic to be treated by the same set-theoretic techniques of model theory that proved so successful when applied to extensional logic. It is also useful in making certain concepts clear." This last remark is not very helpful. How do possible worlds contribute to making concepts clear?

To answer this question, it is useful to compare the role of first-order extensional semantics in the clarification of quantification with the role of modal semantics, with its possible worlds, in the clarification of modal concepts. Quantification in natural language is complicated and (at least before the advent of Tarskian semantics) not well understood. Natural language pronouns play a variety of roles; there are different kinds of devices for making scope distinctions, and there are quantificational terms ('some', the indefinite 'a', 'all', 'every', 'any') that work in different ways. It is helpful to have a formal language with a simple and straightforward syntax and uniform procedures for the kind of cross-reference that quantification involves, and for marking scope. Extensional first-order semantics obviously does not provide a reduction of quantificational concepts to something more basic. As Quine emphasized in explaining the opportunistic "bootstrap" procedure that he called "regimentation," we use natural language, and our intuitive understanding of simple quantification, to explain the resources of the formal semantics that we then use to clarify problematic quantificational constructions, and ultimately, to provide a systematic semantics for natural language. The procedure works because, even when the full range of resources that natural language uses to make quantificational claims are controversial and ill-understood, we can find parts of it that are unproblematic, and that can be used to paraphrase and clarify the rest.

Modal discourse is equally complex. There is a range of modal auxiliaries that work in somewhat different ways, and tense, mood, and aspect
are used in complicated ways, still poorly understood, to make modal
distinctions. Modal expressions interact with quantifiers, singular terms,
and with each other. Basic logical principles concerning identity and
quantification that are unproblematic outside of modal contexts seem
to break down when they interact with modality. Modal semantics, even
if its basic resources are explained in ordinary modal terms, can help to
bring order to this domain by providing a language, and a semantics for
it, that allows paraphrases for problematic modal claims that are reveal-
ing in that they make clear the logical structure of the claim, and the
relations between different modal concepts. As Kripke says, "no one who
cannot understand the idea of possibility is likely to understand that of
'possible world' either," but the paraphrase of claims about what might
or could be true into what is true in some appropriate possible world
may still help to make clearer just what such claims say.

But why, more specifically, does the possible worlds paraphrase help?
One key idea behind the use of possible worlds to clarify modal concepts is this: It seems to be a basic assumption about possibility that some
(indefinite) state of affairs is possible only if there is a specific way that
that state of affairs might be realized. If it is true that Humphrey might
have won the 1968 presidential election, then there must be one or
more specific scenarios in which he wins that might have been realized –
certain specific states that he might have carried, certain specific voters
who might have voted for him. This assumption allows us to think of a
possibility as the set of more specific ways that this possibility could have
been realized, and doing so provides us with a representation that makes
manifest the relation between possibilities, and as Kripke says, makes relevant the set-theoretic apparatus that has been so useful in extensional
model theory: Two possibilities are compossible, or compatible, if the
sets that represent them overlap. And the representation of a possibility
as a set of its more specific realizations also gives us a way to think about
puzzling or controversial possibility claims. If it is unclear or disputed
whether something is possible, one considers, in more detail, what a situation in which it is realized would be like.

The point is not that this procedure provides a decisive way to settle
disputed modal claims. If, for example, some say that Queen Elizabeth
might have been born a swan, and others deny this, it may not help
very much for the defender of the claim to tell a detailed counterfactual
story in which an ordinary swan is born in certain specific circumstances,

and which is stipulated to be identical to the actual queen. But in many cases, modal intuitions become clearer when an allegedly possible scenario is described in more detail. Implicit contradictions in putative possibilities may be revealed when one tries to fill in the details, and this gives us at least some handle on modal epistemology. The procedure is also helpful in clarifying the relation between semantic and metaphysical questions. Suppose someone claims that it is a contingent fact that Hesperus is identical to Phosphorus – that Hesperus might not have been Phosphorus. When she considers, in detail, what the world would be like in the situation envisaged, it comes out that it is a situation in which the referent of at least one of the names 'Hesperus' and 'Phosphorus' would have been, in the counterfactual situation, a different celestial body. Whether that kind of situation would really be one in which it is false that Hesperus is Phosphorus depends on the semantics for that claim – in Kripke's terminology, on whether the names are rigid designators.

The "worlds" terminology is misleading in that it invites confusion of a certain kind of property of the world with something that exemplifies the property, but Kripke notes that the terminology is misleading in a second way as well: There is a kind of metaphysical completeness implicit in the idea of a possible world, even when one is clear that one means by this a possible (total) *state* of the world. Kripke suggests that this kind of completeness is not essential to the use of the possible worlds framework to clarify modal concepts. "The notion of *all* states of the entire world that are possible in the broadest (metaphysical) sense involves a certain amount of idealization, as well as philosophical questions I have not discussed. If we restrict the worlds to a narrower class of miniworlds, essentially all the issues regarding, say, rigid designators, remain the same. So do the questions of modal semantics" (p. 19, n.). This conception of metaphysical completeness has two dimensions: First, there is the idea that the set of *all* possible worlds is the totality of logical space, excluding no part of it; second, there is the idea that each of the individual possible states of the world is maximally specific. A set of miniworlds may be incomplete in both ways, partitioning what may be only a relevant part of logical space, and ignoring differences between possibilities that are irrelevant to the subject matter under discussion. I discuss, in Section 4, some of the metaphysical questions that I think Kripke is alluding to in this remark.

In the retrospective introduction to *Naming and Necessity*, Kripke illustrates the metaphysically deflationary way that he is understanding possible worlds with a simple example of a "grammar school" probability exercise in which one considers the thirty-six ways in which a pair of dice might land. He uses the example both to make vivid the contrast between a possible state of the world and a world that is in that state, and to "allay any [metaphysical] anxieties" about possible worlds by using miniworlds that obviously make no claims to completeness of either of the two kinds. "'Possible worlds' are little more than the miniworlds of school probability blown large" (p. 18).

3. IDENTIFYING INDIVIDUALS

Kripke thinks that the "distant planets" picture of possible worlds contributes to the illusion that there is a problem about the identification of individuals across possible worlds, and that is one of his main reasons for thinking that the modal realist doctrine is a pernicious one. But what exactly is the alleged problem of the identification of individuals across possible worlds, and how is it dissolved? There are, in fact, a number of different problems, as Kripke acknowledges, some to be dismissed, but others that need to be recognized and addressed. And while it is true that the imagery associated with the idea of possible worlds as distant planets, and the "Jules-Verne-o-scope" metaphor that David Kaplan used[4] to try to make vivid a problem of cross-world identification, contributed to the temptation to see the question of identifying individuals in other possible worlds as like the empirical problem of identifying individuals that one meets at different times and places in the actual world, this is a temptation that the modal realist will resist as vigorously as Kripke does. The parallel universes that David Lewis took possible worlds to be are not, according to his theory, things to which we have empirical access, and so there cannot be a question whether an individual, given ostensively, in another possible world, is or is not the same individual (or a counterpart) of one that was observed in the actual world. David Lewis agreed with the point that Kripke repeatedly makes that "'possible worlds' are *stipulated*, not discovered by powerful telescopes" (p. 44). But stipulation (Lewis and Kripke would agree) is selection, and the point that one is free to select whichever counterfactual world one wants to consider is independent of the nature of the domain of counterfactual worlds from which one is selecting. (Even with other countries, one can stipulate that it is Kazakstan, rather than

---

[4] See Kaplan (1979), a paper (unpublished at the time) that Kripke refers to as a locus classicus of the view he is criticizing.

Uzbekistan, that one wants to talk about.) Kripke and Lewis would have disagreed about what is possible, and so about what kinds of possible worlds are available to be selected, but they were both realists about possibility in the sense that they held that there is a fact of the matter about what possibilities there are.

Kripke's primary point was a simple observation that is independent of any substantive metaphysical views either about what possible worlds are, or about how individuals are related to their qualitative characteristics. "A possible world is *given by the descriptive conditions we associate with it*," and nothing prevents us from using any of the resources that are available for describing the actual world to characterize a counterfactual situation. We can characterize a possible situation as one that meets certain qualitative conditions (we may choose to consider a world in which there is a golden mountain), or we may, if we like, characterize a possible world as one containing a certain actual individual (we may choose to consider a possible situation in which Richard Nixon lost the 1968 U.S. presidential election). In general, we select possible worlds by referring to properties, relations, and individuals that we find in the actual world and stipulating that the world in question shall be one in which those properties and relations are exemplified in some particular way, and those individuals exist and exemplify certain properties and relations. There may be questions about how we are able to refer to individuals, or to their characteristics, but if we can do this, there are no further problems about how we are able to use those resources to characterize a counterfactual situation. As Kripke notes, we don't recognize a problem about identifying properties across possible worlds. (How do we know that, in a world in which my hands are painted green, they are the same color as green things are in our world?) Why should it be any different with individuals? "When I ask [about a table that I have in my hands] whether *it* might have been in another room,... I am talking about *it*, in the same way as when I say that our hands might have been painted green, I have stipulated that I am talking about greenness" (p. 53).

This simple observation is metaphysically neutral, but stipulation has its limits. One cannot select what is not there, and what possibilities one takes there to be to select from will depend on substantive metaphysical views. The nonillusory problems about transworld identity come out when one considers what stipulations are successful in selecting possibilities, and what consequences follow from a stipulation one has made. Kripke would deny, for example, that one could stipulate that an aardvark in a possible situation one is imagining is Nixon since the man was essentially human, and so not an aardvark in any possible world. For the same kind of reason, one cannot stipulate that, in a possible situation it is *Nixon* who lost the election unless there is a possible world in which Nixon lost that election. The counterpart theorist, while granting Kripke's general point that possible worlds are stipulated, not discovered, will deny that any individual in another possible world is Nixon.[5]

Kripke emphasized that nothing prevents one from specifying a possible situation by reference to a particular individual, but of course there is also nothing preventing one from specifying a possible situation with a purely qualitative description, and then asking what follows from those descriptive conditions about the identity of the individuals in the possible situation one has described. ("Consider a possible situation containing an individual meeting such and such detailed, but purely qualitative conditions. Is that individual Nixon?") Kripke acknowledges that this kind of question about transworld identity makes perfectly good sense, but observes that one cannot assume, independently of substantive metaphysical doctrines about the relation between individuals and their properties, that this question will always have an answer. Specifically, the assumption that a sufficiently detailed qualitative description would always yield an answer to the question will be justified only if one accepts the doctrine that the identity of an individual is determined by its qualitative character.[6] Kripke rejects this doctrine, holding that while a qualitative description will sometimes entail a negative answer to the question (if the qualitative description includes properties that are incompatible with Nixon's essential properties), it will never suffice to entail a positive answer. But this substantive metaphysical doctrine is independent of Kripke's general observation about the way that possible states of the world are specified. He remarks that "even if there were a purely qualitative set of necessary and sufficient conditions for being Nixon, the view I advocate would not demand that we find these conditions *before* we can ask whether Nixon might have won the election, nor does it demand that we restate the question in terms of such conditions" (p. 47).

---

[5] He will grant that Nixon had counterparts in other possible worlds, and will also grant that, given a counterpart relation, one can use reference to the actual Nixon to stipulate the kind of possible world one is considering.

[6] This doctrine is only as clear as the distinction between purely qualitative properties and properties that depend in some way on individuals – a distinction that might be drawn in different ways. There may also be properties (perhaps natural kind properties) that are neither purely qualitative nor ontologically dependent on particular individuals.

More generally, if one assumes that the identity of an individual will always be *supervenient* on a sufficiently detailed description of kind X (for some X), then one can raise a nonillusory question about transworld identity – whether a possible world containing an individual meeting a certain description of that kind would or would not be identical to a certain actual individual. While Kripke rejects the doctrine that the identity of an individual is supervenient on its qualitative character, he is more sympathetic to the idea that an ordinary individual physical object is supervenient on its history and material constitution. So we might describe a possible world as one including a table whose history is similar in such and such respects to a certain actual table, and that was constituted by molecules most, but not all, of which were strictly identical to the molecules that actually constitute that table. We can then ask whether the counterfactual table we have described is the very same one as the actual table, and if we accept the supervenience thesis, we should expect that a sufficiently detailed description of this kind will yield an answer. Or if it does not, that will be a sign that there is some vagueness in our reference to the individual in question.[7]

The general point is that possible worlds can be specified in a range of different ways, and that there may be substantive metaphysical, or even empirical, questions about the relation between different ways of specifying them. This fact points to significant exceptions to Kripke's observation that "generally, things are not 'found out' about a counterfactual situation" (p. 49), exceptions that are central to Kripke's overall picture (in particular, to the explanation of necessary a posteriori truths). Since possible situations are stipulated by reference to actual things, kinds, properties, and relations, empirical information about those actual things, kinds, properties, and relations will be relevant to the character of the kind of situation one has stipulated. One can, for example, stipulate that there is water in the lake or Hesperus in the sky in a counterfactual situation one chooses to consider, but one then has no choice about whether, in the situation one has stipulated, there is H_2O in the lake or the planet Venus in the sky. Chemical or astronomical evidence may be required to find out these facts about the counterfactual world. Even if the range of our telescopes is limited to the actual world, they may still help us to see what is true about a counterfactual world that we are considering.

---

[7] Kripke recognizes that there are unresolved problems in this area. See the suggestive but inconclusive footnote 18 (p. 51).

To summarize the main points I have tried to make in this section: First, Kripke's observation that possible worlds are stipulated, not discovered, is independent of the difference between modal realism and actualism. Stipulation is selection from a given domain, and the stipulation point remains the same whether the domain from which one selects is a set of "distant planets" or a set of properties that a world might have had. Second, there are two independent points implicit in Kripke's rejection of the problem of transworld identity as a pseudo-problem. The metaphysically neutral point that any of the descriptive resources available to describe the actual world, including reference to particular individuals, may be used to specify a counterfactual situation should be distinguished from the more substantive and controversial point that the identity of a particular person or thing is not supervenient on its qualitative characteristics. Third, Kripke acknowledges that there is "something to be said" for the problem of transworld identity. Questions about whether an individual meeting certain conditions in a counterfactual situation is or is not identical to some actual individual, if carefully formulated, can raise genuine and difficult metaphysical issues. Fourth, we can make empirical discoveries about counterfactual situations, not by observing the nonactual situations themselves, but by investigating the actual world.

4. MERELY POSSIBLE INDIVIDUALS

It is the central idea of the possible worlds representation, I suggested earlier, that a possibility is to be understood in terms of the specific ways that it might be realized. And it is a central idea of the actualist understanding of possible worlds that the specific ways that possibilities might be realized are entities that actually exist – things that are constituted by, and specified in terms of, individuals, properties, and relations that exist in the actual world. There is some tension between these two ideas. The tension is somewhat alleviated by the recognition that there is no need to assume that there are possibilities that are absolutely specific or complete, in some metaphysical sense. Both the formal model-theoretic apparatus of possible worlds semantics and the philosophical uses of the apparatus to clarify concepts remain essentially the same, even if the "worlds" in question are miniworlds that partition logical space only as finely as is needed for the purposes at hand. But even a metaphysically deflationary use of possible worlds semantics faces a problem when the purposes at hand require that logical space be partitioned more finely than can be done with the resources provided by the actual world. Specifically, the problem arises (both in the interpretation of the model theory and in the philosophical applications) when one tries to represent the possibility that there exist individuals that do not in fact exist. It seems reasonable to assume, for example, that George W. Bush might have had a son. So there is an existential proposition (that there exists a person who is a son of GWB) that is possibly true. But an existential proposition can be true only if a more specific proposition is true – a proposition that says, of some specific individual, that he is a son of GWB. But it also seems reasonable to assume that there is no actual person who might have been George W. Bush's son. So if propositions about particular individuals require the existence of the individual, as the actualist picture suggests, there will be no specific way for that existential proposition to be true.

A formal possible worlds model used to represent such a situation would postulate a domain for each possible world; the domain of the possible situation in which the existential proposition about GWB's son is true would have to contain a member to witness that proposition – a particular individual that does not in fact exist. But there are no individuals that do not in fact exist. So how are such domains to be understood?[8]

There are four strategies for solving this problem without giving up the idea that for every existential possibility, there is a specific possibility to witness it. First, there is the modal realist solution that gives up the idea that something must be actual to exist. According to the modal realist, there is a particular (nonactual) person who is (in another place) the son of (a counterpart of) GWB. Second, one may hypothesize that particular individuals are analyzable in terms of purely qualitative properties and relations. On this response, even if there is no actual individual in terms of which we might specify the relevant possible world, there will exist a purely qualitative characterization of a possible state of the world that will determine a unique specific, but merely possible, individual. Third, one may hypothesize that individuals have individual essences – haecceities – that are irreducible to qualitative properties, but that are still a kind of property that may exist even when they are uninstantiated.

---

[8] Kripke does not explicitly address this problem in *Naming and Necessity*. He discussed related problems concerning fictional names and singular negative existential statements in his still unpublished John Locke lectures, but these problems are different, since nonreferring names and kind terms are (as Kripke emphasizes) not names for merely possible individuals and kinds.

The domains of other possible worlds are essential domains – domains of haecceities. The possibility that GWB had a son is witnessed by a possible state of the world that contains, in its domain, an actually uninstantiated essence that would, if instantiated, determine a specific individual son of GWB.[9] The fourth strategy is to give up the assumption that there might be anything that does not actually exist, hypothesizing that if it is really possible for GWB to have had a son, then there must be an actual thing (not necessarily a person, or even a concrete object with an actual spatiotemporal location) that might have been that son.[10] According to this approach, everything that exists exists necessarily, and there could not have existed anything other than what actually exists.

As we have seen, Kripke explicitly rejects the first two strategies, and since he assumes, in both his formal work and philosophical remarks, that there are contingent objects, and he countenances the possibility of things that do not actually exist, we can assume that he would reject the fourth. Kripke has not, to my knowledge, commented in print on the third strategy, but it does seem to involve an implausible metaphysical commitment. Is it really reasonable to assume that there exist properties that are as specific as referential properties, defined in terms of particular individuals (for example, the property of being identical to GWB), but exist independently of the individuals that would instantiate them? Is it plausible to think that there actually exists a perhaps infinite set of individual essences irreducible to any qualitative characterization, representing all the specific individuals that might have been a particular son of GWB?

For those who find this commitment, along with those of the other three strategies, unpalatable, there is a further option, one that I think fits better with the metaphysically deflationary remarks that Kripke made in the lectures and preface. This is to give up the assumption that for every generic existential possibility (such as the possibility that GWB had a son), there exists a specific possibility (one in which a singular proposition of the form '*x* is a son of GWB' is true). If GWB had had a son, then there would have existed singular propositions about him, and a property of being identical to that particular person, but according to this response to the problem, since GWB did not in fact have a son, there are no such propositions, and no such identity property. Propositions,

---

[9] This solution is developed and defended by Alvin Plantinga. See the papers collected in Plantinga (2003).

[10] This strategy is defended in Williamson (2002).

properties, and even possible states of the world, like particular individuals, may exist merely contingently.[11]

This response to the problem involves a qualification to what I have described as the central idea of the possible worlds representation – that for every possibility, there exists a specific way that it might be realized. One must grant that the specific ways that a possibility might be realized are sometimes themselves merely possible ways. It is not just worlds, but states of the world, that sometimes are merely possible.

This response may require a reinterpretation of some of the formal apparatus of possible worlds semantics, but it does not require any modification of the formal theory itself. In a formal semantic model, each "possible world" comes with a domain of "possible individuals." These individuals – at least those of them that do not actually exist – should be thought of, not as specific individuals, nor as individual essences, but as something like roles that an individual might play. The reality behind the member of the domain of an element of a model that represents a possible (state of the) world in which GWB has a son will be a characterization of a generic individual in terms of its qualitative characteristics and relationships to actual individuals, a characterization that is as complete as the resources of the actual world permit.

But just as no purely qualitative description of an individual in a counterfactual world will be sufficient to entail that it is the actual Richard Nixon, so we should not suppose that any purely qualitative description of a possible son of GWB, no matter how detailed, will suffice to determine the specific identity of a particular individual. Suppose we call some particular possible state of the world in which GWB had exactly one son 'w'. We want at least to allow for the possibility that if w had been realized, then there would have been another possible situation, w^*, qualitatively like w, but in which some different individual was the unique son of GWB. But w^* is a merely possible possible state of the world. If possible worlds are properties that a world might have had, then w^* is a merely possible property – a possible state of the world that would have existed (but been uninstantiated) if w had been realized.

Let me use a minor variation on Kripke's example of a pair of dice to illustrate the idea. There are thirty-six possible ways that the dice might

---

[11] The thesis that there are properties and propositions that exist only contingently is defended in Fine (1977). A theory of this kind is developed and defended in Adams (1981), though Adams suggests, I think mistakenly, that this metaphysical view requires major revisions in modal logic and semantics.

have landed – thirty-six "possible worlds." In the original example, which Kripke used to illustrate the dissolution of the problem of identifying individuals across possible worlds, it is assumed that one of these states of the world is the actual one – the way they actually land. This implies that we are assuming (perhaps fictively) that we are talking about an actual pair of dice, which Kripke labeled die A and die B. His main point was that it would be silly to ask, about the possibility in which A lands 6 and B 5, "how we know that it is A, rather than B, that was the 6?" But suppose our dice are a merely possible, generic pair of dice. There is a possible state of the world in which two dice are thrown, one lands 6 and the other 5. There is not a different state or property in which they are thrown, one lands 5 and the other 6. Of course we might add some detail to distinguish the two dice: we might stipulate that one has a scratch on the face with one spot, while the other does not. Then we could distinguish the possible state in which the one with the scratch lands 6 (the other 5) from the situation where the one with the scratch lands 5 (the other 6). But suppose there is no such detail. How do we distinguish the 6–5 situation from the different 5–6 situation? What do we mean when we call one of the dice 'A' and the other 'B'? (That one is A and the other B is not a fact about the possible states that can be used to distinguish them.) Perhaps, strictly speaking, there are just twenty-one, not thirty-six possible states of the world, in the simple generic case. But a full characterization of the state in which one lands 6 and the other 5 will attribute to the one that lands 6 the complex model property of possibly landing 5 while the other lands 6. This requires that, if the (6,5) possibility had been realized, there would have been a different possible situation in which the one that landed 6 landed 5, and the one that landed 5 landed 6. (That is, the following purely general proposition will be true in the (6,5) possible situation, with the predicate 'F' meaning 'lands 5' and the predicate 'S' meaning 'lands 6': $\exists x \exists y (Fx \& Sy \& \Diamond (Fy \& Sx))$.) To represent the truth of this proposition in the (6,5) world, we need a different (6,5) world – one that would be possible if the first were realized. If the set of possible worlds in our model of the situation includes all the possibilities there might be, we will need thirty-six, and not just twenty-one.

I conjecture that when Kripke noted that "the notion of *all* states of the entire world that are possible in the broadest (metaphysical) sense involves a certain amount of idealization, as well as philosophical questions I have not discussed" (p. 19, n. 18), this was one of the problems he had in mind.

References

Adams, R. (1981). "Actuality and Thisness," *Synthese* 49, 3–41.

Fine, K. (1977). Postscript, in A. Prior and K. Fine, *Worlds, Times and Selves*, London: Duckworth: 116–51.

Kaplan, D. (1979). "Transworld Heir Lines," in M. Loux (ed.), *The Possible and the Actual: Readings in the Metaphysics of Modality*, Ithaca, NY: Cornell University Press, 88–109.

Kripke, S. (1980). *Naming and Necessity*, Cambridge: Harvard University Press.

Lewis, D. (1968). "Counterpart theory and quantified modal logic," *Journal of Philosophy* 65: 113–26.

(1986). *On the Plurality of Worlds*, Oxford: Basil Blackwell.

Plantinga, A. (2003). *Essays in the Metaphysics of Modality*, Oxford: Oxford University Press.

Williamson, T. (2002). "Necessary Existents," in A. O'Hear (ed.), *Logic, Thought and Language*, Cambridge: Cambridge University Press, 233–51.

PART II

FORMAL SEMANTICS, TRUTH, PHILOSOPHY OF MATHEMATICS, AND PHILOSOPHY OF LOGIC

5

Kripke Models

John Burgess

1. INTRODUCTION

Saul Kripke has made fundamental contributions to a variety of areas of logic, and his name is attached to a corresponding variety of objects and results.[1] For philosophers, by far the most important examples are "Kripke models," which have been adopted as the standard type of models for modal and related non-classical logics. What follows is an elementary introduction to Kripke's contributions in this area, intended to prepare the reader to tackle more formal treatments elsewhere.[2]

2. WHAT IS A MODEL THEORY?

Traditionally, a statement is regarded as logically valid if it is an instance of a logically valid form, where a form is regarded as logically valid if every instance is true. In modern logic, forms are represented by formulas involving letters and special symbols, and logicians seek therefore to define a notion of *model* and a notion of a formula's *truth in a model* in such a way that every instance of a form will be true if and only if a formula representing that form is true in every model. Thus the unsurveyably vast range of instances can be replaced for purposes of logical evaluation by the range of models, which may be more tractable theoretically and perhaps practically.

---

[1] We may remind the cognoscenti of the *Kripke-Platek axioms* in higher recursion theory, the *Brouwer-Kripke scheme* in intuitionistic analysis, and the *Kripke decision procedure* for the implicational fragment of relevance logic.

[2] Especially Bull and Segerberg (1984), Garson (1984).

Consideration of the familiar case of classical sentential logic should make these ideas clear. Here a formula, say $(p \& q) \lor \neg p \lor \neg q$, will be valid if for all statements P and Q the statement '$(P$ and $Q)$ or not P or not Q' is true. The central observation about classical sentential logic is that the truth value of a compound statement like '$(P$ and $Q)$ or not P or not Q' depends only on the truth values of its components P and Q. Thus rather than consider the vast range of all instances, of all statements P and Q that might be used to instantiate p and q, one need only consider all combinations of assignments of truth values to the letters p and q, of which there are only four. If (as is in fact the case) for each of these four $(p \& q) \lor \neg p \lor \neg q$ works out to be true when the assignment of values is extended to compound formulas according to the rules familiar from elementary logic textbooks, then the formula counts as valid. (The method of truth tables expounded in elementary logic texts is one way of exhibiting all the combinations and testing for validity.)

In general, at the level of classical sentential logic, a model M is simply a *valuation* V or function assigning a truth value T or F to each of the *atoms*, as the letters p, q, r, and so on, may be called. This assignment is then extended to compound formulas by the familiar rules just alluded to. To state these explicitly, for any formulas A and B one has the following (wherein "iff" abbreviates "if and only if"):

(0)	for atomic A, A is true in M	iff	$V(A) = T$
(1)	$\neg A$ is true in M	iff	A is not true in M
(2)	$A \& B$ is true in M	iff	A is true in M and B is true in M
(3)	$A \lor B$ is true in M	iff	A is true in M or B is true in M
(4)	$A \to B$ is true in M	iff	if A is true in M, then B is true in M

A formula is *valid* if it is true in all models, and *satisfiable* if it is true in some model. Note that A is valid if and only if $\neg A$ is not satisfiable. The truth value of any given formula A in a given M will depend only on the values V assigns to those of the atoms that appear in A, and as there are only finitely many of these, there will be only finitely many combinations of values to consider. The result is that in principle one could, in a finite amount of time, by considering each of these combinations in turn, decide whether or not the formula A is valid: validity for classical sentential logic is *decidable*.

Prior to the development of this model theory, several *proof procedures* for classical sentential logic had been introduced. In such a procedure there are generally a certain smallish finite number of *axiom schemes* or rules to the effect that all formulas of certain types (for instance, all formulas of type $\neg\neg A \to A$, where A may be any formula) are to count as axioms, and a certain small finite number of *rules of inference*, often just the single rule of *modus ponens*, permitting inference from $A \to B$ and A to B. A *demonstration* is a sequence of formulas each of which is either an axiom or follows from earlier ones by a rule. A demonstration is called a demonstration of its last formula, and a formula is *demonstrable* or a *theorem* if there is a demonstration of it. A is *consistent* if $\neg A$ is not demonstrable.

The model theory provides a criterion for the acceptability of proof procedures. A procedure is called *sound* if every demonstrable formula is valid, and *complete* if every valid formula is demonstrable. The preexisting proof procedures, and many alternatives introduced since, are in fact all sound and complete.

3. WHAT IS A MODAL LOGIC?

At the simplest, sentential level, modal logic adds to classical logic a further symbol □ for "necessarily." The symbol ◇ for "possibly" may be understood as an abbreviation for $\neg\Box\neg$. Originally necessity and possibility were understood in a logical sense with □ understood as demonstrability (or validity) and ◇ correlatively as consistency (or satisfiability). Later other types of modalities were at least briefly noted in the literature: causal, deontic, epistemic, and – by far the most intensively investigated – temporal.

At the level of sentential logic, proof procedures were introduced by C. I. Lewis, the founder of modern modal logic.[3] But even for the primary, logical notion of modality, there was no general agreement among Lewis's disciples as to which formulas ought to be demonstrable, and a variety of systems had been recognized. All the more important systems agreed as to formulas without iterated or nested modalities, but they differed as to more complex formulas.

The original presentation of these systems was rather clumsy, but an improved approach was suggested by remarks of Kurt Gödel.[4] In

---

[3] See Lewis (1918) and Lewis and Langford (1932).
[4] See his (1932). Gödel left the proofs of the equivalence of his simplified versions to Lewis's clumsy original versions to be worked out by others.

the improved version, the systems are introduced by adding to any sufficient set of axiom schemes and rules for classical sentential logic further specifically modal axiom schemes and rules. All the more important systems have in fact but a single additional rule of *necessitation*, permitting inference from A to $\Box A$. (The intuitive justification of the rule is that if A has been derived as a law of logic, then it is necessary in the logical sense and presumably in any other that may be at issue as well.)

The most important of the additional axiom schemes considered were those that admitted as axioms formulas of the following types:

(A0) $\Box (A \to B) \to (\Box A \to \Box B)$
(A1) $\Box A \to A$
(A2) $\Box A \to \Box\Box A$
(A3) $A \to \Box\neg\Box\neg A$

The most important systems all include, in addition to the rule of necessitation, the axiom scheme (A0). The system with just these and no more axioms and rules has come to be called **K** for Kripke, since it first came into prominence in connection with Kripke's work on model theory. Prior to that work, the systems that had emerged as most important were those obtained by adding certain of (A1)–(A3) to **K**. Specifically, these were the following systems:

T: (A1)
S4: (A1), (A2)
B: (A1), (A3)
S5: (A1), (A2), (A3)

The following discussion will be largely confined to those systems.

The task of devising a model theory for modal logic was thus really a series of tasks, of devising a model theory for each of the various systems. Or rather, it was to devise a general *type* of model theory which, by varying certain conditions, could produce specific model theories for which the various systems would be sound and complete. Were that accomplished, it might then be hoped that by comparing and contrasting the conditions required for different systems, one might be enabled to determine which system was the most appropriate for a given kind of modality.

One thing that should be immediately apparent is that one cannot get a suitable model theory for modal sentential logic simply by extending the model theory for classical sentential logic by adding the clauses for □ and ◇ analogous to those for ¬:

□A is true in M	iff	necessarily A is true in M
◇A is true in M	iff	possibly A is true in M

For the formulas and the models, after all, are mathematical objects (sequences of letters and special symbols, functions assigning one of the values T or F to each of the atoms), and whether a given formula A is true in M is a mathematical fact about those objects. And mathematical facts are all necessary. Thus if A is true in M, it automatically is necessarily so; whereas we certainly do not want to have □A true in M whenever A is true in M, for that would make $A \rightarrow$ □A valid, which it ought not to be. Some more complicated approach will be needed.

4. KRIPKE MODELS FOR MODAL SENTENTIAL LOGIC

A Kripke model for sentential logic will consist of something more than a single valuation. It will, rather, amount to an indexed set of valuations. One of these will represent actuality, the actual combination of truth values of the atoms; others will represent actual possibilities, which is to say, possible combinations of truth values of the atoms; yet others will represent actually possible possibilities, which is to say, possibly possible combinations of truth values of the atoms; and so on.[5]

More formally, a model $M = (X, a, R, V)$ will consist of four components. There will be a set X of indices, a distinguished index a, a binary relation R on the indices, and a function V assigning a valuation $V(x)$ to each index x, and therewith a truth value $V(x)(A)$ to each index x and atom A. The distinguished index a may be thought of as representing *actuality*. The relation R may be thought of as representing *relative possibility*. Then the x such that aRx represent the actual possibilities; the y such that for some x we have aRx and xRy represents the actually possible possibilities; the z such that for some x and y we have aRx and xRy and yRz represent actually possibly possible possibilities,

---

[5] There may also be extraneous indices representing not actuality, nor actual possibilities, nor actually possible possibilities, since one gets a simpler definition if one allows them; but their presence or absence will turn out to make no difference to the truth value assigned any formula.

and so on. The indices in X thus represent "possibilities" in a very broad sense.

The definition of truth at an index in a model then proceeds as follows:

(0)	for atomic A, A is true at x in M	iff	$V(x)(A) = \text{T}$
(1)	$\neg A$ is true at x in M	iff	A is not true at x in M
(2)	$A \,\&\, B$ is true at x in M	iff	A is true at x in M and B is true at x in M
(3)	$A \vee B$ is true at x in M	iff	A is true at x in M or B is true at x in M
(4)	$A \rightarrow B$ is true at x in M	iff	if A is true at x in M, then B is true at x in M
(5)	$\Box A$ is true at x in M	iff	for all y with xRy, A is true at y in M
(6)	$\Diamond A$ is true at x in M	iff	for some y with xRy, A is true at y in M

Here (6) is redundant, since it follows from (5) and the understanding of $\Diamond$ and $\neg\Box\neg$.[6] By the truth value of A in M one may understand the truth value of A at a in M. A formula is *valid* if it is true in all models, and satisfiable if it is true in some model.[7]

The description of the general notion of Kripke model – or as is often said, of *Kripke semantics* – for modal sentential logic is now complete. Or rather, it is complete except for one piece of picturesque terminology. In probability theory and decision theory one often considers a range of "possibilities" in the sense of "possible outcomes" or "possible events," often spoken of simply as "outcomes" or "events." In physics one often considers a range of "possibilities" in the sense of "possible states of a system," often spoken of simply as "states of the system." What the indices

---

[6] In place of V one could use a two-place function, assigning to each pair consisting of an index x and an atom A a truth value T or F. We could also use a function assigning to each atom A a function assigning to each index x a truth value T or F. We could also use, in place of the function assigning each index x an assignment of values to atoms, a function assigning each index x a set of atoms, namely, those that are true at x. Finally, we could also use, in place of a function assigning each atom A an assignment of values to indices, a function assigning to each atom A a set of indices, namely, those at which A is true. Each of these variant versions of the model theory can be met with somewhere in the literature, different ones being convenient for different purposes.

[7] Alternatively, one could equivalently take a model simply to consist of a triple (X, R, V) and call a formula valid if it is true at all indices in all models, and satisfiable if it is true at some index in some models. This option can also be met with in the literature.

in a Kripke model represent may often be illuminatingly thought of as "possibilities" in the sense of "possible states of the world," or simply "states of the world" for short.

These are often spoken of as "possible worlds," or simply "worlds" for short. Kripke himself, echoing Leibniz, originally engaged in this way of speaking, though later he concluded that the more pedestrian language of "states of the world" was less misleading than the more picturesque language of "worlds." Despite Kripke's later reservations about the usage, the indices in Kripke models are still generally called "worlds" in the literature. (To go with the talk of worlds, various expressions such as "accessibility" or "alternativeness" are used for the relative possibility relation R.)

5. SOUNDNESS AND COMPLETENESS

Kripke proved that the system **K** described in Section 3 is sound and complete for the class of all Kripke models. Thus we have: (soundness) if a formula is demonstrable in **K**, then it is true in all Kripke models; and (completeness) if a formula is true in all Kripke models, it is demonstrable in **K**. Each of the other systems mentioned in Section 3 he showed to be sound and complete for some special class of Kripke models.

For instance, the theorems or demonstrable formulas of **T** correspond to the class of Kripke models in which the relation R is *reflexive*, meaning that xRx for all x. That is to say, we have: (soundness) if a formula is demonstrable in **T**, then it is true in all reflexive Kripke models; and (completeness) if a formula is true in all reflexive Kripke models, then it is demonstrable in **T**. The relation between axiom scheme (A1) of **T** and the condition of reflexivity is intuitively fairly clear. The truth of $\Box A$ at a amounts to the truth of A at all x such that aRx, and reflexivity guarantees that a itself will be among these, so that A will be true at a. Thus, if $\Box A$ is true at a, so is A, which is precisely the condition for $\Box A \rightarrow A$ to be true at a. (This is the key observation in the proof of soundness.)

Other axiom schemes correspond to other conditions on R. Thus axiom (A2) corresponds to *transitivity*, the condition that for all x and y and z, if xRy and yRz, then xRz. Assuming the truth of $\Box A$ at a amounts to assuming the truth of A at all x such that aRx, and transitivity guarantees that for any x such that aRx and any y such that xRy, we have aRy, so that A is true at y. It follows that $\Box A$ is true at x for any x such that aRx, and hence $\Box\Box A$ is true at a, assuming $\Box A$ is true at a. This is precisely the condition for $\Box A \rightarrow \Box\Box A$ to be true at a.

Similarly, axiom (A3) corresponds to *symmetry*, the condition that for all x and y, if xRy then yRx. Assuming A is true at a, symmetry guarantees that for any x with aRx there is at least one y with xRy, namely a itself, such that A is true at y. This means $\neg\Box\neg A$ is true at any x with aRx, and $\Box\neg\Box\neg A$ is true at a, assuming A is true at a. This is precisely the condition for $A \rightarrow \Box\neg\Box\neg A$ to be true at a.

Kripke showed that **S4** is sound and complete for reflexive, transitive Kripke models and that **B** is sound and complete for reflexive, symmetric Kripke models. (What has been given in the preceding two paragraphs are the key steps in the soundness proofs. The completeness proofs are substantially more difficult, and cannot be gone into here.) As for **S5**, it is sound and complete for the class of Kripke models where the relation R is reflexive and transitive and symmetric (a combination of conditions called being an *equivalence relation*).[8] Kripke actually obtained a number of other soundness and completeness theorems beyond the scope of the present chapter, and his successors have found yet others.

6. WARNINGS

At this point, the reader may need to be warned against a misunderstanding that is fairly commonly met with, not only among beginning students of the subject, but even among otherwise distinguished logicians who ought to know better. It is a feature of the definition of Kripke model that nothing in it requires that every valuation of the atoms be assigned to some index or other. The confused thought is fairly often met with, even in the published literature, that while Kripke models as just described may be appropriate for various nonlogical modalities, still owing to the feature just indicated they cannot be appropriate for logical modalities:

> What is needed for logical necessity of a sentence p in a world w_0 is more than its truth in each one of some arbitrarily selected set of alternatives to w_0. What is needed is its truth in each *logically possible* world. However, in Kripke semantics it is not required that all such worlds are among the alternatives to a given one.[9]

---

[8] Since in general no indices distinct from those identical with a, those R-related to a, those R-related to something R-related to a, and so on, make a difference to the truth value of any formula in the model, for R an equivalence relation only those indices equivalent to a make a difference, and we may discard all others. But then all undiscarded indices are equivalent, and we may drop mention of the relation R altogether. The condition for the truth of $\Box A$ simply becomes truth at all indices.

[9] Hintikka (1982).

Now it is certainly true, as the complaint alleges, that the valuations to be represented in the model may be "arbitrarily selected." For any set of valuations, there is a Kripke model $M = (X, a, R, V)$ where just those valuations and no others turn up as the valuations $V(x)$ attached to indices x in X by the function V. For instance, there are Kripke models where no index is assigned a valuation that assigns the atom p the value T, and there are Kripke models where no index is assigned a valuation that assigns the atom p the value F.

But contrary to what the preceding complaint suggests, this is just as it should be, regardless of what notion of necessity, logical or otherwise, is at issue. Truth in all models is supposed to correspond to truth in all instances, and as there are certainly logically impossible statements P that might be used to instantiate the atom p, to represent such instantiations there must be models where no index is assigned a valuation that would assign the atom p the value T. Likewise, there must be models where every index is assigned a valuation that assigns the atom p the value T, since there are logically necessary statements P that might be used to instantiate the atom p.[10] And since, of course, there are also many entirely contingent statements P that might be used to instantiate the atom p, there must also be models where the valuations assigned to some indices assign p the value T, while the valuations assigned to other indices assign p the value F.

A further warning may be in order about the picturesque use of "worlds" in connection with Kripke's model theory. This usage has fired the imaginations of contemporary metaphysicians, the most distinguished of whom, the late David Lewis, took the notion of a plurality of possible worlds with maximal seriousness. But the model theory in itself is simply a piece of mathematical apparatus susceptible to many and varied technical applications and philosophical interpretations, and its use (and even the casual use of "worlds" talk as a convenient abbreviation) does not seriously commit one to Ludovician polycosmology.

In this connection a further remark about the dangerously ambiguous word "semantics" may be in order. This word is sometimes used as a synonym for "model theory," but it also has a use as a label for

---

[10] At any rate, this is how things must be if the atoms are to be used in the usual way – the way they are used in classical logic, in the various systems **T**, **S4**, **B**, **S5** of modal logic, in intuitionistic logic, and elsewhere – as capable of representing arbitrary statements. If one adopted some special convention – for instance, that distinct atoms are to represent independent atomic statements, as is in effect done in the rational reconstruction of early twentieth-century "logical atomism" in Cocchiarella (1984) – then, of course, a different model theory might be appropriate.

the theory of meaning. A serious danger of ambiguity lurks in this double usage, for formal models need not have anything very directly to do with intuitive meaning. It would, for instance, be a fallacy of equivocation of the grossest sort to infer from the fact that "possible worlds" figure in Kripke models the conclusion that ordinary talk of what would or might have been has really meant all along something about "possible worlds" in the sense of Lewis (or for that matter, in any other sense).[11] To avoid confusion, a distinguishing adjective is sometimes added, so that one contrasts "formal semantics" with "material semantics" (or "linguistic semantics"). But even this usage can be faulted for suggesting that we have to do with two different varieties, formal and material, of one and the same thing, semantics, rather than two things whose relation or irrelevance to each other remains to be investigated.

7. HISTORICAL NOTE

No major discovery or advance in science or philosophy is without precursors. Kripke obtained his results on models for modal logic while still in high school, but there were results in the literature when he was in elementary school that, if combined in the right way, would have yielded his soundness and completeness theorems for **S4** and a number of other important systems. This is not the place for a detailed, technical account of these matters, but the following may be remarked. First, the work of McKinsey and Tarski (1948) connected systems of modal logic with certain "algebraic"'models – for the cognoscenti, Boolean algebras with operators – with different axiom schemes corresponding to different algebraic conditions, while work of Jónsson and Tarski (1951) connected the algebraic structures involved structures consisting of a set X with a binary relation R – now generally called *frames* – with different algebraic conditions corresponding to conditions of reflexivity, transitivity, and symmetry on the frames.

McKinsey and Tarski made no mention of frames, and Jónsson and Tarski no mention of modal logic, but between them the two teams had done all that was necessary to obtain the kind of soundness and completeness theorems reported in the preceding section. But no one – not

---

[11] Neither Kripke nor Lewis is guilty of this confusion, but some nominalists seem to have thought that they must avoid ordinary modal locutions because of their unacceptable "ontological commitments."

even Tarski – put two and two together. Still, the existence of this work by Tarski and students would seem to make other priority questions more or less moot. Nonetheless, following the example of Kripke, who has been scrupulous in citing precursors, one may make mention here of a couple of rough contemporaries of his who were also working to develop model theories for modal logics, and who conjectured – *but did not publish proofs of* – a connection between systems like **T**, **S4**, and **S5** and conditions like reflexivity, transitivity, and symmetry.[12]

One of these was Stig Kanger, who presented a model theory for modal logic in his dissertation. In their standard survey article, Bull and Segerberg ascribe the comparative lack of influence of his work to two factors, the "unassuming mode of publication" and the fact that his work is "difficult to decipher." In fact, though the dissertation was printed, as all Swedish dissertations of the period were required to be, it was never published in a journal and was largely unknown outside Scandinavia.[13] It is very difficult to read owing to an accumulation of non-standard notations and terminology – even for conditions like reflexivity, transitivity, and symmetry. The two factors are related, since going through the refereeing and editorial process involved in journal publication would surely have resulted in a more reader-friendly presentation. A measure of the reader-unfriendliness of the work is the fact that it was only more than two decades after its appearance that it was realized that the model theory differs in a fundamental way from Kripke's: it involves the "misunderstanding" warned against at the beginning of the preceding section.[14]

Much closer to Kripke's approach was that of Jaakko Hintikka,[15] who is often mentioned as Wallace to Kripke's Darwin. Compared with Kripke's approach, Hintikka's is less clearly, cleanly model-theoretic or "semantic": it is proof-theoretic or "syntactic" to the extent that what the relation R relates are not indices but sets of formulas. As a result there is nothing directly corresponding to the feature of Kripke's approach that allows *duplication*, meaning that it allows two indices to have the same valuation assigned to them. But this latter feature is only likely to be appreciated by one who goes into the technicalities

---

[12] For Kripke's own comments on these figures, and for other names, see the long first footnote to Kripke (1963a).

[13] Kanger (1957) has only recently been made available in Kanger (2001).

[14] A more sympathetic description of this difference from Kripke models is given in Lindström (1998); but the fact of the difference is not denied: rather, it is emphasized.

[15] See Hintikka (1963).

of the subject.[16] A more immediate reason for the lesser influence of Hintikka's work is cited by Bull and Segerberg, namely, the absence of proofs, which gives his main paper the aspect of an extended abstract or research announcement.[17]

Differences between Kripke's approach and those of others such as Kanger and Hintikka are more conspicuous at the level of predicate logic (which was not considered at all by the Tarski school). But the main reason why the models with which we are concerned have been called "Kripke models" is perhaps not so much that Kripke was in fact the first to present models of the precise kind that have been most convenient in later technical work, or even that he was the first to make generally available in print complete proofs of soundness and completeness results for systems like **T** and **S4** and **B** and **S5**, but rather that he was the first to demonstrate the immense utility and versatility of model-theoretic methods as they apply not only to sentential but to predicate logic, not only to extensions of **K** but to significantly weaker systems as well, not only to questions of soundness and completeness but to questions of decidability, and not only to modal but to intuitionistic and other logics. There can be no question of describing here all the large body of work to be found in Kripke (1959, 1962, 1963a, 1963b, 1963c, 1965), but something must be said at least about intuitionistic logic and about modal predicate logic.

8. KRIPKE MODELS FOR INTUITIONISTIC LOGIC

Mathematical intuitionists, followers of the Dutch topologist L. E. J. Brouwer, object to *nonconstructive existence proofs*, purported proofs of the existence of a mathematical object with some mathematical property that do not provide any means of identifying any particular object with

[16] Such a reader will, however, recognize its importance, and may have difficulty crediting the claim in Hintikka (1963) to have soundness and completeness theorems for tense logic, since allowing duplication is crucial to such results. One hypothesis is that Hintikka had in mind some non-standard approach to tense logic, in which the temporal modalities are not "has always been" and "is always going to be" but "*is* and has always been" and "*is* and is always going to be."

[17] Surprisingly, Hintikka is the most distinguished of the logicians who has fallen into the confusion warned against in Section 5. The *locus classicus* for the confusion is indeed a curious paper of Hintikka (1982), where he in effect simultaneously argues both that he has priority in developing the kind of models used by Kripke, and that the kind of models used by Kripke are inferior to Kanger's. A comical feature of the paper is that Hintikka carefully avoids the term "Kripke models" (except in scare quotes) when arguing over priority, but freely uses it whenever the models in question are being criticized.

the property. This objection ultimately leads intuitionists to reject basic laws of classical logic, and led to the development of an alternative logic for which a proof procedure was provided by Arend Heyting (1956).

Consider, for instance, the statement *P* that there are seven sevens in a row somewhere in the decimal expansion of π. A classical mathematician would accept a derivation of a contradiction from the assumption that ¬*P* as a demonstration that *P*; an intuitionist would not, unless there were at least implicit in the proof a method for actually finding out where the seven sevens appear. Thus the intuitionist cannot accept ¬¬*P* → *P* as an instance of a law of logic, and it is not a theorem of Heyting's system.

The intuitionist position is most readily made intelligible by explaining that intuitionists attach a nonclassical meaning to such logical connectives as ¬ and →. For the intuitionist, every mathematical assertion is the assertion of the constructive provability of something. The denial of the constructive provability of something is not itself the assertion of the constructive provability of anything, and so the intuitionist cannot understand negation as simple denial, but must understand it as something stronger. For the intuitionist ¬*P* asserts the constructive provability of a contradiction from the assumption that *P*.

Such explanations suggest a kind of translation of formulas *A* of intuitionistic sentential into formulas *A** of classical modal logic, with necessity □ thought of as constructive provability. If *A* is one of the atoms, the translation *A** is □*A*, reflecting the fact that the only statements considered by intuitionists are assertions of constructive provability. The translation (¬*A*)* of the negation of a formula *A* is □¬*A**, the necessity of the negation of the translation of *A*. The translation (*A* → *B*)* of a conditional is □ (*A** → *B**), and similarly for other connectives. It turns out that one can get away with taking as (*A* & *B*)* simply *A** & *B** rather than □ (*A** & *B**), mainly because □ (□*p* & □*q*) is equivalent to □*p* & □*q* in the relevant modal systems. Similarly for disjunction. Such a translation was first proposed by Gödel (1932), who asserted without proof that *A* will be demonstrable intuitionistically if and only if *A** is demonstrable in **S4**.

This fact suggests a notion of Kripke model for intuitionistic logic. Such a model *M* = (*X*, *a*, *R*, *V*) consists of a set *X* of indices, a distinguished index *a*, a reflexive and transitive binary relation *R*, and a valuation *V* with the special property called being *hereditary*, meaning that if *A* is an atom and if *V* (*x*) (*A*) = T and if *xRy*, then *V* (*y*) (*A*) = T. (Reflexivity and transitivity are the distinguishing conditions for models of **S4**, the modal system Gödel claimed to have a special relation to intuitionistic logic. The hereditary property that if $V(x)(A) = T$ and if xRy, then $V(y)(A) = T$, is one possessed in **S4** models by formulas that are – or that are equivalent to formulas that are – of the form $\Box A$, as the modal translations of intuitionistic formulas are.)

One then defines truth at an index in the model as follows:

(0)	for atomic A, A is true at x in M	iff	$V(x)(A) = T$
(1)	$\neg A$ is true at x in M	iff	for any y with xRy, A is not true at y in M
(2)	$A \& B$ is true at x in M	iff	A is true at x in M and B is true at x in M
(3)	$A \vee B$ is true at x in M	iff	A is true at x in M or B is true at x in M
(4)	$A \rightarrow B$ is true at x in M	iff	for any y with xRy, if A is true at y in M, then B is true at y in M

The clauses (1) and (4) of the definition correspond to the translation of intuitionistic $\neg$ as $\Box\neg$ and intuitionistic $\rightarrow$ and $\Box\rightarrow$.

Every **S4** model $N = (X, a, R, U)$ gives rise to an intuitionistic model $M = (X, a, R, V)$ by replacing the original function U by the function V obtained by setting, for each index x and each atom A, the value $V(x)(A)$ to be T or F according as $\Box A$ is true or false at x in N. It can be checked that whatever the old function U, this new function V is hereditary. It can also be checked that for any intuitionistic formula A and any index x, A is true at x in M if and only if its modal translation A^* is true at x in N. A proof of soundness and completeness for Heyting's system of intuitionistic logic relative to this notion of model can be obtained by combining the fact just stated with the soundness and completeness of **S4** for reflexive and transitive Kripke models and Gödel's translation result stated previously. Alternatively, a soundness and completeness proof can also be given directly, as was done by Kripke, and Gödel's translation theorem can then be proved in a new way as a corollary. Various other facts about intuitionistic logic that had previously been established by rather difficult arguments follow directly as corollaries to the soundness and completeness theorem.[18]

---

[18] One of these is the disjunction property, that if $A \vee B$ is a theorem of intuitionistic logic, then either A is or B is. In particular, $p \vee \neg p$ cannot be a theorem, since certainly neither p nor $\neg p$ is!

Kripke's model theory for modal predicate logic (which will be discussed later) also can be adapted to provide a model theory for intuitionistic predicate logic, which Kripke used to obtain further important results. Notably, whereas the classical logic of one-place predicates is decidable, like classical sentential logic, and undecidability sets in only with the classical logic of two- or many-place predicates, with intuitionistic logic the logic of one-place predicates is already undecidable.

9. KRIPKE MODELS FOR MODAL PREDICATE LOGIC

Modal predicate logic, combining modal operators $\Box$ and $\Diamond$ with quantifiers $\forall$ and $\exists$, was introduced by Ruth Barcan (later Marcus) (1946), and by Rudolf Carnap (1946). From the beginning the problem of interpretation for formulas combining modalities with quanitifiers was acute. Carnap's interpretations did not satisfy other philosophical logicians, and Barcan's work was purely formal and did not broach the question of interpretation at all.

One, though not the only, source of difficulty was that the earliest proof-procedures for modal predicate logic involved the following *mixing* laws:

(B1) $\Box \forall v Fv \to \forall v \Box Fv$ (B2) $\exists v \Diamond Fv \to \Diamond \exists v Fv$

(B3) $\forall v \Box Fv \to \Box \forall v Fv$ (B4) $\Diamond \exists v Fv \to \exists v \Diamond Fv$

Here (B1) and (B2) are commonly called the *converse Barcan* and (B3) and (B4) the *Barcan* formulas. A proof procedure simply combining the usual sorts of axioms and rules for modal sentential and for nonmodal quantificational logic will automatically yield the former. Following a suggestion of Frederic Fitch, his student Barcan took the latter as additional axioms.

But none of the four is plausible: (B1) seems to imply that since necessarily whatever exists exists, whatever exists necessarily exists. (B4) seems to imply that if it is possible that there should exist unicorns, then there exists something such that it is possible that *it* should be a unicorn. Kripke devised a less simplistic proof procedure in which none of (B1)–(B4) is automatically forthcoming, and none is assumed as axiomatic. Moreover, he devised a model theory to go with the proof procedure, thus liberating the subject from the counterintuitive mixing laws.

Kripke's model theory for modal predicate logic is related to his model theory for modal sentential logic rather as the standard model theory for nonmodal predicate logic is related to the standard model theory for nonmodal sentential logic. Though there can be no question of a full review here, some of the key features of the model theory for nonmodal predicate logic may be briefly recalled. A model M consists of two components, a nonempty set D, called the *domain* of the model, and an *interpretation* function I assigning to each one-, two-, or many-place predicate F, a one-, two-, or many-place relation F^I on the domain D.

In order to define what it is for a closed formula A to be *true* in M, we need to define more generally what it is for an open formula $A(v_1, \ldots, v_n)$ with n free variables to be *satisfied* by an n–tuple of elements $d_1, \ldots, d_n$ of the domain D. The interpretation function essentially gives the definition of satisfaction for atomic formulas. For instance, if F is a three-place predicate, the formula $A(u, v, w) = Fuvw$ will be satisfied by the triple of domain elements c, d, e if and only if the relation F^I holds of that triple c, d, e; the formula $B(u, v) = Fuvu$ will be satisfied by the pair of domain elements c, d if and only if the elation F^I holds of the triple c, d, c; and analogously in other cases. The notion of satisfaction is extended from atomic to more complex formulas by a series of clauses, consisting of the analogues of (1)–(4) of Section 2 for ¬, &, ∨, →, and two more clauses to handle the quantifiers.

The quantifier clauses read as follows:

(5)	$\forall u\, A(v, u)$ is satisfied by d in M	iff	for every c in D, $A(u, v)$ is satisfied by c, d in M
(6)	$\forall u\, A(v, u)$ is satisfied by d in M	iff	for some c in D, $A(u, v)$ is satisfied by c, d in M

It is to be understood that in either (5) or (6) we may have n variables $v_1, \ldots, v_n$ in place of v, and n domain elements $d_1, \ldots, d_n$ in place of d.

Now a Kripke model for modal predicate logic will consist of five components, $M = (X, a, R, D, I)$. Here, as with modal sentential logic, X will be a set of indices, a a designated index, and R a relation on indices. As for D and I, the former will be a function assigning each x in X and set D_x, the *domain* at index x, while the latter will be a function assigning to each x in X and each predicate F a relation F_x^I, the *interpretation* of F at x, of the appropriate number of places. The one genuine subtlety in the whole business is that F_x^I is to be a relation not merely on Dx but rather on the union D^* of the D_y for *all* indices y in x. Thus even when d and e are *not* both in the domain D_x and in this sense at least one of them does not exist at x, we may ask whether d and e satisfy Fvw at x. (They will do so if F_x^I holds of them.)

The definition of satisfaction at an index x then proceeds much as in the case of definition of truth at an index x in modal sentential logic, so far as ¬, &, ∨, and → are concerned. The clauses for quantifiers read as follows (wherein as in (5) and (6) v and d may be n–tuples):

(5*)	$\forall u\, A(v, u)$ is satisfied by d at x in M	iff	for every c in D_x, $A(u, v)$ is satisfied by c, d in M
(6*)	$\forall u\, A(v, u)$ is satisfied by d at x in M	iff	for some c in D_x, $A(u, v)$ is satisfied by c, d in M

Note that only c in the domain D_x, only c that exist at x, count in evaluating the quantifiers.

The Barcan formula (2a) fails in a very simple model, with just two indices a and a', both R-related to each other, where the domain D_a has a single element d, and the domain $D_{a'}$ has the two elements d and d', where F_a^I holds of d and of d', and $F_{a'}^I$ holds of d but not of d'. In fact, the Barcan formula (B3), or equivalently (B4), corresponds to the special assumption that when xRy the domain gains no elements as we pass from Dx to any Dy. The converse Barcan formula (B1), or equivalently (B2), corresponds to the converse assumption that the domain loses no elements.

There is not space here to discuss soundness and completeness (which are harder to prove in the predicate than in the sentential case), nor to describe the corresponding notion of Kripke model for intuitionistic predicate logic.[19] Nor is there space to survey the numerous variant versions that have been developed for special purposes.[20]

10. THE PROBLEM OF INTERPRETATION

We have already warned of the danger of confusing model theory or so-called formal semantics with a substantive theory of linguistic meaning.

[19] It may just be said that in the latter one assumes a kind of hereditary property for domains: if xRy, then D_x must be a subset of D_y.

[20] Garson (1984) surveys many of the options.

Before closing we will look a little more closely at the relationship between the two in three cases, those of temporal "modalities" or tense operators, of intuitionistic logic, and of plain "alethic" modalities.

In *temporal* or *tense* logic, □ is understood as "it is always going to be the case that" and ◇ as "it is sometimes going to be the case that." With such a reading, the connection between Kripke models and intuitive meaning is quite clear. The "possibilities" or "possible states of the world" are *instants* or *instantaneous* states of the world, the "relative possibility" relation is the "relative futurity" relation, which is to say the *earlier-later* relation. The clause according to which □A is true at x in M if and only if A is true at y in M for every y with xRy is simply the formal counterpart of the trivial truism that it is always going to be the case that A if and only if at every future instant it will be the case that A. Various axioms correspond to conditions on the earlier-later relation, and the question which of the many systems of modal logic is the right one for this notion of modality becomes the question which of these various conditions the earlier-later relation fulfills. That is presumably a question for the physicist, not the logician, to answer; but the theory of Kripke models for temporal modalities indicates clearly just what is at stake with each proposed axiom scheme. The source of clarity in this case is the fact that different physical theories of the structure of time do more or less directly present themselves as theories about what conditions the earlier-later relation among instants fulfills.

There is more of a gap between Kripke's formal models for intuitionistic logic, and Brouwer's and Heyting's explanations of the intended meaning of intuitionistic negation and other logical operators. In particular, Kripke's theorem on the "formal" soundness and completeness of Heyting's system for his model theory does not in and of itself show that Heyting's system is "materially" sound and complete in the sense of giving as theorems all and only those laws that are correct when the logical operators are taken in their intended intuitionistic senses. As it happens, in this case the formal soundness and completeness proof can serve as an important *first step* in a proof of material soundness and completeness, but substantial additional steps – beyond the scope of the present article – are needed to make the connection.[21]

---

[21] The needed additional ideas were in effect supplied by George Kreisel. For an exposition, see Burgess (1981). A similar situation obtains in the area known as *provability logic*, where the formal and material semantics are connected by ideas of Robert Solovay. For an exposition of this case, see Boolos (1993).

In the case of "necessity" and "possibility," the primary readings of □ and ◇, the gap between formal models and intuitive meaning is larger still. Different conceptions of modality do not in general directly present themselves as theories about what conditions the "accessibility" relation between "worlds." There is, for instance, a widespread feeling that something like **S5** is appropriate for logical necessity in the sense of validity, and something like **S4** for logical necessity in the sense of demonstrability. The locus classicus for this opinion is Halldèn (1963). But the considerations advanced there in favor of this opinion have nothing to do with the thought that "the accessibility relation between satisfiable worlds is symmetric, but the accessibility relation between consistent worlds is not."

More seriously, the grave objections of W. V. Quine against the very meaningfulness of combinations like $\exists v \,\square\, Fv$ when □ is read as "it is logically necessary that" or "it is analytic that" are not answered by Kripke's model theory, nor in the nature of things *could* they be answered by any purely formal construction. Quine's worry is this: The truth of $\exists v \,\square\, Fv$ would require the existence of some thing such that Fv is analytically true of it, but what can it mean to say that an open formula Fv, or rather, an open sentence such as 'v is rational' or 'v is two-legged' represented by such a formula, is analytically true of a *thing*, independently of how or whether it is named or described?

For instance, 'Hesperus' and 'Phosphorus' denote the same planet, but the open sentence 'v is identical with Hesperus' becomes analytic if one substitutes 'Hesperus' for v, and not so if one substitutes 'Phosphorus'. What on earth – or in the sky – can be meant by saying that the open sentence is or isn't analytically true *of the planet?* The problem is a major one, and led early defenders of modal predicate logic (such as Arthur Smullyan, and following him Fitch [1949], and following the latter his student Marcus) to desperate measures, such as maintaining that if 'Hesperus' and 'Phosphorus' are proper names, denoting the same object, then 'Hesperus is Phosphorus' is analytic after all.[22]

---

[22] Marcus maintained this position in Marcus (1960) with acknowledgments to Fitch, and again in Marcus (1963a) with vaguer acknowledgments that the view is "familiar." In discussion following the latter paper, Marcus added that, at least for names in an ideal sense, there would presumably be a dictionary, and that the process of determining that 'Hesperus is Phosphorus' is true is not the empirical operation of scientific observation but would be like looking something up in a dictionary, the question simply being, does this book tell us these two words have the same meaning? This idea is reiterated in Marcus (1963b): "One does not investigate the planets, but the accompanying lexicon."

Kripke was eventually to cut through confusions in this area by distinguishing "metaphysical" possibility, *what potentially could have been the case*, from logical "possibility," *what it is not self-contradictory to say actually is the case*. He was then able to say, as in Kripke (1971), that Quine was right that such identities are empirical; Marcus was right that there is a sense in which such identities are necessary; but taking necessity in this sense, both were wrong in confusing necessity with epistemological notions. But by his own account the main ideas in Kripke (1971) and Kripke (1972) date from the academic year 1963–64, when he began presenting them in seminars at Harvard. By contrast, his formal work on model theory in large part was a half-decade old by then, and was already (belatedly) in print or at press. The model theory came first, the recognition of the importance of distinguishing different senses of "necessity" came after.

As Kripke has said in another context, "There is no mathematical substitute for philosophy." As regards modal predicate logic, Kripke's early mathematical work in model theory does not settle the disputed issues of interpretation, but rather Kripke's *later* philosophical work on language and metaphysics is needed to clarify his model theory. His model theory cannot in and of itself settle disputed questions about the nature of modality. But if that is its weakness, it has a correlative strength: not being bound to any very particular understanding of the nature of modality, the model theory is adaptable to many. It is a very flexible instrument, still very much in use in the greatest variety of contexts today.

References

Boolos, George (1993) *The Logic of Provability*, Cambridge: Cambridge University Press.

Bull, R. A. and Segerberg, Krister (1984) "Basic Modal Logic," in D. M. Gabbay and F. Guenthner, eds., *Handbook of Philosophical Logic*, vol. 2: *Extensions of Classical Logic*, Dordrecht: D. Reidel, 1–88.

Burgess, John P. (1981) "The Completeness of Intuitionistic Propositional Calculus for Its Intended Interpretation," *Notre Dame Journal of Formal Logic* 22: 17–28.

Carnap, Rudolf (1946) "Modalities and Quantification," *Journal of Symbolic Logic* 11: 33–64.

Cocchiarella, Nino (1984) "Philosophical Perspectives on Quantification in Tense and Modal Logic," in D. M. Gabbay and F. Guenthner, eds., *Handbook of Philosophical Logic*, vol. 2: *Extensions of Classical Logic*, Dordrecht: D. Reidel, 309–54.

Fitch, Frederic (1949) "The Problem of the Morning Star and the Evening Star," *Philosophy of Science* 16: 137–41.

Garson, James W. (1984) "Quantification in Modal Logic," in D. M. Gabbay and F. Guenthner, eds., *Handbook of Philosophical Logic*, vol. 2: *Extensions of Classical Logic*, Dordrecht: D. Reidel, 249–308.

Gödel, Kurt (1932) "Eine Interpretation des intuitionistischen Aussagenkalküls," *Ergebnisse eines mathematischen Kolloquiums* 4: 39–40.

Haldèn, Søren (1963) "A Pragmatic Approach to Modal Theory," *Acta Philosophical Fennica* 16: 53–64.

Heyting, Arend (1956) *Intuitionism: An Introduction*, Amsterdam: North-Holland.

Hintikka, Jaakko (1963) "The Modes of Modality," *Acta Philosophica Fennica* 16: 65–82.

   (1982) "Is Alethic Modal Logic Possible?" *Acta Philosophica Fennica* 35: 89–105.

Jónsson, Bjarni and Tarski, Alfred (1951) "Boolean Algebras with Operators," *American Journal of Mathematics* 73: 891–939.

Kanger, Stig (1957) *Provability in Logic*, Acta Universitatis Stockholmensis, Stockholm: Almqvist and Wiksell.

   (2001) *Collected Papers of Stig Kanger with Essays on His Life and Work*, vol. 1, G. Holmström-Hintikka, S. Lindström, and R. Sliwinski, eds., Synthese Library volume 303, Dordrecht: Kluwer.

Kripke, Saul (1959), "A Completeness Theorem in Modal Logic," *Journal of Symbolic Logic* 24: 1–14.

   (1962) "The Undecidability of Monadic Modal Quantification Theory," *Zeitschrift für mathematische Logik und Grundlagen der Mathematik*, 8: 113–16.

   (1963a) "Semantical Considerations on Modal Logic," *Acta Philosophica Fennica*, 16: 83–94.

   (1963b) "Semantical Analysis of Modal Logic I. Normal Propositional Calculi," *Zeitschrift für mathematische Logik und Grundlagen der Mathematik*, 9: 67–96.

   (1963c) "Semantical Analysis of Intuitionistic Logic I," in J. N. Crossley and M. A. E. Dummett, eds., *Formal Systems and Recursive Functions* (Proceedings of the Eighth Logic Colloquium at Oxford, July, 1963), Amsterdam: North-Holland, 92–129.

   (1965) "Semantical Analysis of Modal Logic II. Non-Normal Modal Propositional Calculi," in J. W. Addison, L. Henkin, and A. Tarski, eds., *The Theory of Models* (Proceedings of the 1963 International Symposium at Berkeley), Amsterdam: North-Holland, 206–20.

   (1971) "Identity and Necessity," in M. K. Munitz, ed. *Identity and Individuation*, New York: New York University Press.

   (1972) "Naming and Necessity," in D. Davidson and G. Harman, eds., *Semantics of Natural Language*, Dordrecht: Reidel, 253–355, 763–9.

Lewis, C. I. (1918) *A Survey of Symbolic Logic*, Berkeley: University of California Press.

Lewis, C. I. and Langford, H. (1932) *Symbolic Logic*, New York: Century Company.

Lindström, Sten (1998) "Kanger's Early Semantics for Modal Logic," in
    P. W. Humphreys and J. H. Fetzer, eds. *The New Theory of Reference: Marcus,
    Kripke, and Its Origins,* Dordrecht: Kluwer, 203–33.
Marcus, Ruth Barcan (1946) "A Functional Calculus of First Order Based on
    Strict Implication," *Journal of Symbolic Logic* 11: 1–16.
    (1947) "Identity and Individuals in a Strict Functional Calculus of First Order,"
    Journal of Symbolic Logic 12: 3–23.
    (1960) "Extensionality," *Mind* 69: 55–62.
    (1963) "Modalities and Intensional Languages," in M. Wartofsky, ed.,
    Proceedings of the Boston Colloquium for the Philosophy of Science 1961/1962,
    Dordrecht: Reidel, 77–96.
    (1963) "Classes and Attributes in Extended Modal Systems," *Acta Philosophica
    Fennica* 16: 123–36.
McKinsey, J. C. C. and Tarski, Alfred (1948) "Some Theorems About the
    Sentential Calculi of Lewis and Heyting," *Journal of Symbolic Logic* 13: 1–15.

6

Kripke on Truth

John Burgess

1. INTRODUCTION

Saul Kripke's "Outline of a Theory of Truth" (1975) has been the most influential publication on truth and paradox since Alfred Tarski's "The Concept of Truth in Formalized Languages" (1935). It is thick with allusions to related unpublished work, and the present account will provide some information on this additional material, but the ubiquitously cited "Outline" must remain the main focus in the limited space available.

2. LIAR SENTENCES

Let us dispose at the outset of the potentially distracting issue of the *bearers* of truth. Suppose Y says, "What X just said is true," and Z asks, "But what *did* X say?" Then Y may answer with either a direct or an indirect quotation of X, perhaps saying, "X said, 'Snow is white,' and that's true," or perhaps saying, "X said that snow is white, and that's true." Since it seems that a direct quotation denotes a sentence while a that-clause denotes a proposition, it seems that Y is attributing truth in one case to the sentence X uttered and in the other to the proposition X thereby asserted.

Kripke applies "true" and "false" to sentences, though he holds that some sentences are neither; but some philosophers apply "true" and "false" only to propositions, and some hold that every proposition is one or the other. Is there more than a merely verbal difference here? Well, nothing Kripke says is incompatible with the view that "true" and "false" apply to sentences only in a sense derivative from their application to propositions (a sentence counting as true or false only insofar as it expresses a true or a false proposition), or with the view that a sentence can fail to have a truth value only by failing to express a proposition (rather than by expressing a proposition that fails to have a truth value). Kripke focuses on sentences rather than propositions because he finds it clear that sentences can refer to themselves and unclear whether propositions can do so.[1]

In the pre-Kripkean literature, at least four kinds of apparently self-referential sentences in natural language can be distinguished, giving rise to four different kinds of liar paradox. On the one hand, it appears that a sentence may refer to itself directly. This may be through demonstratives, as with:

(1a)   This very sentence is false.

Or it may be with proper names, as when we let "Pseudomenon" name the sentence:

(1b)   Pseudomenon is false.

On the other hand, it appears that a sentence may refer to itself indirectly, by describing a certain sentence while being itself the unique sentence fitting that description (or by making a generalization about sentences of some kind while being itself a crucial instance of that kind). This may be so for what may be called structural reasons, as with the Grelling-Quine example:

(1c)   "yields a falsehood when appended to its own quotation" yields a falsehood false when appended to its own quotation.

Or it may be so for what may be called historical reasons, as when the only sentence on the blackboard in room 101 happens to be:

(1d)   The only sentence on the blackboard in room 101 is false.

Another type common in the literature arises when reference numbers for displayed sentences are used in philosophy papers, as with (1a)–(1d) above. We may then get something like this:

(1e)   (1e) is false

It is unclear whether this type is best assimilated to one of the other types or considered sui generis.

---

[1] It is difficult to make out Kripke's exact attitude toward the possibility of propositional self-reference. He seems inclined to reject the possibility of directly self-referential propositions while arguing for the possibility of directly self-referential sentences. But what of indirect propositional self-reference? It may be added that, despite his concessive tone toward propositionalism in his work on truth, toward the end of the preface to the book edition of *Naming and Necessity* (1980), Kripke express suspicion that the whole apparatus of "propositions" may simply break down in certain situations.

In cases (1a), (1b), and (1c) the self-reference is, so to speak, *intrinsic*, but in (1d) it is *extrinsic*. What may be the earliest form of the liar, in which Epimenides the Cretan says that everything said by Cretans is false, which is paradoxical only on the historical assumption that everything *else* said by Cretans is false, is also of the extrinsic kind. Kripke does not deny the possibility of the (1a) kind of self-reference, argues for the possibility of the (1b) kind, recalls the possibility of the (1c) kind, and emphasizes the possibility of the (1d) type, from which he draws the conclusion that it is hopeless to look for any intrinsic test for paradoxicality. He also uses the (1e) type without comment.

As for the possibility of self-reference in formal as contrasted with natural languages, Gödel proves that under fairly modest conditions – or at any rate, under conditions fairly modest for a language in which to discuss *mathematics* – there will always exist a sentence that in effect refers to itself and attributes to itself any desired property expressible by a formula of the language. (The phrase "in effect" here is by way of acknowledgment of the complication that in the Gödel situation as standardly presented one does not literally have reference by linguistic expressions to linguistic expressions, but only to *code numbers* of linguistic expressions.) Moreover, under the same fairly modest conditions, a wide range of syntactic properties (including provability) will be expressible by formulas of the language. Kripke in the "Outline" displays little interest in formal languages so artificially truncated as not to meet Gödel's fairly modest conditions.

While it is self-reference and consequent dependence of the truth or falsehood of a sentence S_0 on the truth or falsehood of S_0 itself that is at the root of the liar examples, it has been recognized since medieval times that paradox can also arise when S_0 depends on S_1 while S_1 depends on S_0, as when Socrates says, "What Plato is about to say will be false," and Plato says, "What Socrates just said was true." Longer circles are also possible, and Kripke recognized also the possibility of problematic examples resulting from infinite sequences where S_0 depends on S_1, which depends on S_2, which depends on S_3, and so on.[2]

In mathematics a dependence relation is called *non-well-founded* if there is a nonempty set having no element not dependent on an element of the set. (This covers all three cases of a_0 depending on itself, circles with a_0 depending on a_1 depending on ... a_n depending on a_0, and infinite sequences with a_0 depending on a_1 depending on a_2 and so on. The 'bad' sets in these different cases are $\{a_0\}$ and $\{a_0, a_1, \ldots, a_n\}$

---

[2] Infinite sequences play a crucial role in some proofs of technical results Kripke mentions in passing, for instance, that reconstructed as Theorem 6.1 in Burgess (1986).

and $\{a_0, a_1, a_2, \dots \}$.) Of course, the rigorous mathematical terminology cannot properly be applied until we have a rigorous mathematical definition of the dependence relation at issue. Kripke picks up from the literature the alternative term "ungroundedness," which prior to his treatment had been used only in an intuitive way, and aims eventually to give it a rigorous definition.

3. TARSKI ON TRUTH

The liar paradox was introduced by Eubulides and much discussed by Chrysippus and others in ancient times, while it and related paradoxes, under the label *insolubilia*, were much discussed by Bradwardine and others in the Middle Ages.[3] Modern discussions began in the period around 1900, when the set-theoretic paradoxes were being discovered, from which period date paradoxes about the notion of definability (Berry's, Richard's, König's) that brought truth-related notions into disrepute among mathematicians. Tarski, envisioning significant mathematical applications of such notions, sought a partial restoration of their reputation in work that is the starting point for all later discussions, Kripke's included.

Tarski's work has both a positive and a negative side. Both start from the assumption that a predicate may be deemed a *truth* predicate for a language just in case we have the following for all sentences of the language:

(2) $T(a)$ if and only if A

where the term a denotes the sentence A as the quotation "Snow is white" denotes the sentence 'Snow is white.' There is no need for a separate *falsehood* predicate if one assumes, as do Tarski and his successors, that the falsehood of an item is equivalent to the truth of its negation and the truth of an item to the falsehood of its negation.

On the negative side, Tarski observes that if, as with natural language, the language for whose sentences the predicate expresses truth itself contains that very predicate, and has means of self-reference, then universal applicability of (2) leads to contradiction. Hence the slogan "A language cannot contain its own truth predicate," or in terminology whose felicity is open to question, "A language cannot be semantically closed." Tarski concludes that the intuitive notion of truth, expressed by the predicate

---

[3] See Spade (2005) for the history.

'is true' of natural language, is contradictory. He therefore seeks to reha-
bilitate not this intuitive notion, but only a restricted version, sufficient
for his envisioned applications, predicated only of sentences of formal
language *not* itself containing the truth predicate.

Kripke emphasizes that it is a gross mistake to say that Tarski bans
self-reference. He could not have done so even if he had wanted to,
owing to Gödel's results. If he bans anything, it is the presence of *semantic* predicates (such as truth) as contrasted with *syntactic* predicates (such
as provability). Even here "ban" is not the right word, since when Tarski
says, "A semantically closed language is impossible," what he means is not
an imperative, "Thou shalt not make unto thee any semantically closed
language," but rather a declarative, "You could not have a semantically
closed language even if you wanted to."

On the positive side, Tarski proposes for a formal language of a certain
kind to give a mathematically rigorous definition of a predicate for which
all instances of (2) admit mathematically rigorous proof. The kind of formal language Tarski considers has predicates and terms, from which may
be formed atomic sentences, from which may be formed other sentences
using negation, conjunction, disjunction, and universal and existential
quantification. There is a universe of discourse, and elements of that
universe are assigned as denotations to the terms while sets of n–tuples
of elements are assigned as extensions to the n–place predicates.

On the simplifying assumption that every element of the universe of
discourse is the denotation of some term, the extension of a one-place
predicate F is completely determined by a total assignment of truth
values, true or false, to all atomic sentences of form $F(a)$, wherein a may
be any term – subject to the proviso that if a and b have the same denotation, then $F(a)$ and $F(b)$ must be both true or both false. Similarly
in the many-place case. From the assignment of truth values to atomic
sentences, the assignment of truth values to other sentences is determined by the rules of classical logic.

The rule for negation has already been mentioned: A negation is true
if and only if what it negates is false, and vice versa. A conjunction is true
if all conjuncts are true, and false if all or some conjuncts are false and
any others true. Disjunctions are treated dually (a disjunction is false
if all disjuncts are false, and true if all or some disjuncts are true and
any others false). On our simplifying assumption, quantifications are
treated analogously (a universal quantification is true if all instances are
true, and false if all or some instances are false and any others true, and
existential quantifications dually). Without the assumption that every

element of the universe of discourse is the denotation of some term, the definition is more complicated, and requires an auxiliary notion of *satisfaction*. The details need not be recalled here, since the definition given in any present-day logic textbook is close to Tarski's.

The connection between the negative and positive sides of Tarski's work is that his truth definition just discussed is given not in the "object language" itself, but in a "metalanguage." On Tarski's approach, if we wanted a notion of truth not just for the original formal language L_0, but for the language L_1 containing of the original language *plus* a predicate T_0 for 'is a true sentence of L_0' we would need another truth predicate T_1; and if we wanted a notion of truth not just for L_1, but for the language L_2 containing L_1 *plus* a predicate T_1 for 'is a true sentence of L_1', we would need yet another truth predicate T_2; and so on. But in practice the applications made by Tarski and by subsequent workers in *model theory*, the branch of logic originating with his paper, hardly ever involve such a hierarchy of languages and truth predicates – indeed, they hardly ever require any truth predicate beyond the initial one.

4. TRUTH-VALUE GAPS

Some subsequent philosophical writers – many of whom seem to have been, unlike Tarski, seeking to vindicate the intuitive notion of truth, seeking to show that it is subject only to apparent paradoxes, not real antinomies – have suggested that, contrary to Tarski's conclusions, a language *can* contain its own truth predicate, if one gives up the classical assumption of bivalence (that every sentence is true or false) and allows *truth-value gaps*. (If there is anything that may properly be called a "ban" in Tarski, it is an unstated prohibition against considering such gaps.) Kripke's main aim in the "Outline" is to produce a rigorous version of the truth-value-gap proposal.

Quite independently of considerations about paradoxes, several circumstances in which truth-value gaps arguably arise have been noted in the philosophical literature. These include *failure of existential presupposition* ("The King of France is bald," said after the abolition of the French monarchy), *vagueness* ("The King of France is bald," said under the French monarchy at a time when the reigning monarch has lost much but not all of his hair), and *nonsense* ("The King of France is a boojum," said at any time).

Suppose then we work with a language that is a modification of the kind considered by Tarski, in that each *n*–place predicate is not just assigned an extension, or set of n–tuples of elements of the universe of discourse of which it is true, but an *extension* and *anti-extension*, a set of n–tuples of which it is true and a set of n–tuples of which it is false, with the two sets nonoverlapping, but with their union perhaps not the whole universe of discourse. On the simplifying assumption that every element of the universe of discourse is the denotation of some term, the extension of a one-place predicate F is completely determined by a *partial* assignment of truth values, true or false, to some atomic sentences of form $F(a)$, wherein a may be any term – subject to the proviso that a and b have the same denotation, then $F(a)$ and $F(b)$ must be both true or both false or both without truth value. Similarly in the many-place case.

But by what rules is the partial assignment of truth values to other sentences to be determined from the partial assignment of truth values to atomic sentences? Different schemes of rules have been proposed for evaluating logical compounds some or all of whose logical components may lack truth value, with some schemes looking more plausible for some types of truth-value gap and others for others, and with all schemes agreeing with the classical rules recalled earlier in cases where all logical components do have truth values.

On the *Frege weak three-valued* scheme, any compound having a component without truth value is without truth value. On the *Kleene strong three-valued* scheme, a conjunction is false if at least one conjunct is false, and without truth value if at least one conjunct is without truth value and no conjunct is false. Disjunction is treated dually (a disjunction is true if at least one disjunct is true, and without truth value if at least one disjunct is without truth value and no disjunct is true). Universal and existential quantification are treated analogously to conjunction and disjunction (a universal quantification is false if any instance is false and without truth value if at least one instance is without truth value and no instance is false, and dually for existential quantification).

On the more elaborate *van Fraassen supervaluational* approach, a partial valuation of atomic sentences determines a set of total valuations, namely, the set of all those that agree with the partial valuation as far as it goes. A nonatomic sentence then counts as true under the original partial valuation if it is true under all these total valuations, and false if false under all, and otherwise without truth value. Thus in contrast to the Kleene scheme, where a conjunction of two sentences without truth value is always itself without truth value, on the van Fraassen scheme a conjunction of two sentences without truth value will be false if one conjunct is the negation of the other, because any total valuation will make such a conjunction false. Disjunction is treated dually and quantification analogously.[4]

Kripke in his "Outline" barely mentions the Frege approach, gives more attention to the van Fraassen approach, but gives most attention to the Kleene approach. (He also briefly mentions that yet other approaches are possible.) As to which approach is the correct one, he is cautious to the point of being cryptic.[5]

A crucial feature, heavily emphasized by Kripke, of all three schemes mentioned is *monotonicity*. Given two partial assignments of truth values to atomic sentences, the second being an extension of the first (agreeing with the first as far as it goes, but assigning truth values to some atomic sentences the first left without truth value), then the assignment of truth values to nonatomic sentences determined by the second will also be an extension of the assignment of truth values to nonatomic sentences determined by the first.

A related feature, less heavily emphasized by Kripke,[6] of all three schemes mentioned is that the biconditional in (2) will or may be without truth value if A and $T(a)$ are. For Tarski, making as he does the classical assumption of bivalence, the universal truth of the biconditional (2) is equivalent to the universal truth-preservingness of these inferences:

(3)

(a)   from A to $T(a)$
(b)   from not-A to not-$T(a)$
(c)   from $T(a)$ to A
(d)   from not-$T(a)$ to not-A

By contrast, if one allows truth-value gaps, and treats them by any of the three schemes mentioned, then the truth of (2) becomes a strictly stronger requirement than the truth-preservingness of (3), and indeed an arguably unreasonably strong requirement. So where Tarski takes (2)

---

[4] See Blamey (1986) for the three-valued approach and van Fraassen (1969) for the super-valuational approach.

[5] See his footnote 30 and the paragraph to which it is attached. He says in the body of the paper that he is somewhat uncertain, not as to how natural language handles truth-value gaps, but rather as to *whether there is a definite factual question* as to how natural language handles truth-value gaps. He then adds in the footnote that he does not intend to *assert* that there is no definite factual question, nor that he does not himself favor one approach over others.

[6] But emphasized in the later commentary of McGee (1989).

(for him equivalent to (3)) as his criterion for calling a predicate a *truth predicate*, Kripke in effect takes (3) (for him strictly weaker than (2)) as his criterion.

5. JUMPS AND FIXED POINTS

Kripke's goal may be described as follows. Suppose we have settled on one or another monotonic scheme of the kind mentioned for extending a partial assignment of truth values to atomic sentences to a partial assignment of truth values to arbitrary sentences. And suppose we start from a language of the kind Tarski considers, with full assignments of truth values to all atomic sentences, and then add a predicate *T*. Then we want to prove that (without changing the assignment of truth values to sentences not involving *T*) there is a partial assignment of truth values to atomic sentences involving *T* such that, when it is extended to assignment of truth values to other sentences involving *T* according to the scheme we have settled on, all instances of (3) are truth-preserving.

Kripke's goal may be described in more detail using two technical notions he introduces, *jump* and *fixed point*. To begin, suppose we have a partial assignment of truth values to atomic sentences of form $T(a)$, determining a partial assignment of truth values to arbitrary sentences according to whatever scheme we have settled on. And suppose that our partial assignment is *sound* in the sense that all instances of (3c) and (3d) are truth-preserving. We can now produce a new partial assignment, to be called the *jump* of the original, as follows: Count an atomic sentence $T(a)$ true or false under the new assignment whenever the sentence A denoted by a counted as true or false as the case may be under the original assignment, and let this new partial assignment of truth values of atomic sentences determine a new partial assignment of truth values to other sentences according to the scheme we have settled on.

By soundness of the original partial valuation, any atomic sentence $T(a)$ that had a truth value under the original assignment will retain it under this new assignment. (If it was true, say, on the original partial valuation, then by the truth-preservingness of (3c), the sentence A denoted by a will have been true on the original partial valuation, hence $T(a)$ will be true under the new partial valuation.) Then by monotonicity of the scheme for handling truth-value gaps, all nonatomic sentences that had truth values under the original assignment will retain them under the new assignment as well: The new assignment will be an extension of the original one. The new assignment will also be sound, all instances of

(3c) and (3d) being truth-preserving by construction. (For $T(a)$ is made true only when A was made true by the original partial assignment, and in that case, by what we have just said, A is made true by the new partial assignment also.) Moreover, all instances of (3a) and (3b) for sentences that had a truth value under the original partial assignment will be truth-preserving under the new partial assignment. (This is not to say that *all* instances of (3a) and (3b) will be truth-preserving, since there in general will be sentences made true by the new partial assignment that did not have truth values under the original partial assignment.) Moreover, the jump operation thus described is itself monotonic, in the sense that if a second sound partial assignment is an extension of a first, then the jump of the second will be an extension of the jump of the first.

If the jump of a given sound partial assignment is not different from the partial assignment itself, then we have a *fixed point*, and then all instances of (3a) and (3b) as well as of (3c) and (3d) will hold. Kripke's goal, in this new terminology, is to show that fixed points exist.

In fact, using various results from the mathematical theory of inductive definitions,[7] he shows there is a minimum fixed point, contained in all others, in which all and only the grounded sentences have truth values – this may be taken as the rigorous definition of "grounded" – as well as various further kinds of fixed points. Thus in the end he presents not a single proposal, but rather a family of proposals, corresponding to different kinds of fixed points under different schemes for handling truth-value gaps. He does not unqualifiedly endorse any one, but the minimal fixed point under the Kleene scheme seems to be his favorite, or at any rate receives the most attention, both in Kripke's paper and in the subsequent literature.

6. THE MINIMUM FIXED POINT

To produce the minimum fixed point, start at stage 0 with V_0, the *null* assignment of truth values to atomic sentences of form $T(a)$, that which leaves them all without truth value. At stage 1 take the jump V_1 of V_0, at stage 2 take the jump V_2 of V_1, at stage 3 take the jump V_3 of V_2, and so on. Note that since the null assignment is trivially sound and the jump preserves soundness, all these partial assignments will be sound. Note also that since any partial valuation extends the null valuation, V_1 extends V_0;

---

[7] Some to be found in the then-just-published compendium Moschovakis (1974), the main technical reference Kripke cites; others original.

since the jump operation is monotonic, the jump of V_1 extends the jump of V_0, which is to say V_2 extends V_1; for the same reason V_3 extends V_2; and so on. Given a sentence '_____' not involving T, on the order of 'Snow is white' that is true at stage 0, '$T($'_____'$)$' will be true at stage 1 though it was not at stage 0, while '$T($'$T($'_____'$)$'$)$' will be true at stage 2 though it was not at stage 1, and so on. Let us call this sequence of sentences the "snow sequence." Because more and more terms of the snow sequence acquire truth values at later and later stages, none of the stages V_n is a fixed point.

Cantor's transfinite ordinals, expounded in any introductory work on set theory, were introduced precisely in order to number the stages of repetition of a process repeated beyond a first, second, third, and so on, time.[8] The first ordinal after all of 0, 1, 2, and so on is called ω. At stage ω we take the union of everything we have so far, the valuation V_ω that makes an atomic sentence of form $T(a)$ true or false if and only if some V_m (and hence every V_n for $n > m$) does so. A little thought shows that V_ω is sound (since there are no new instances of (3c) and (3d) to consider that did not arise already at some finite V_n). But this V_ω will still not be a fixed point if the language contains a sentence amounting to "Every sentence in the snow sequence is true." For this sentence will not become true at any finite stage and therefore will not be true at stage ω; but since every sentence in the snow sequence is true at stage ω, this other sentence should become true at the *next* stage, where we have $V_{\omega+1}$, the jump of V_ω. Similarly, '$T($'Every sentence in the snow sequence is true'$)$' will not be true even at this stage but will become true at the next stage, where we have $V_{\omega+2}$, the jump of $V_{\omega+1}$. Beyond stages ω, $\omega + 1$, $\omega + 2$, and so on comes stage $\omega + \omega = \omega \cdot 2$, and we may not be done even at that stage. And so on.

For each successor ordinal (ordinal next after some ordinal) $\alpha + 1$, $V_{\alpha+1}$ will be the jump of V_α. For each limit ordinal (ordinal *not* the next after any ordinal) β, V_β will be the union of the V_α for $\alpha < \beta$. Since there is a restricted number of sentences (in the usual kind of language, a *countable* infinity of them) and an unrestricted number of ordinals (in particular an *uncountable* infinity of them), we cannot keep getting new sentences true at each stage in the process, and must come to a stage

---

[8] Melvin Fitting (1986) and others have offered accounts of Kripke's theory avoiding discussion of the ordinals, but one cannot avoid them if one wants a full understanding of Kripke's theory, and especially if one wants eventually to go on to compare it to rival theories developed by various writers (Gupta, Herzberger, Belnap) in its wake.

where the jump yields nothing new, in other words, to a fixed point V^*. (At a fixed point $V_\alpha = V_{\alpha+1} = V_\beta$ for all $\beta > \alpha$.) Monotonicity implies that if U is any other fixed point, then U extends each V_α along the way and so in the end extends V^*, which is therefore a *minimum* fixed point.

7. OTHER FIXED POINTS

For any sound W_0, the same construction yields a fixed point W^* extending it, and a minimum among those extending it. There are also other fixed points beyond the minimum ones thus obtained, including various *maximal* fixed points, or fixed points not contained in any properly larger fixed points.[9]

Kripke uses the existence of other fixed points to mark distinctions among various types of ungrounded sentences:

(4a)   (4a) is false.
(4b)   (4b) is true.
(4c)   (4b) is true or not-(4b) is true.
(4d)   (4d) is true or not-(4d) is true.

All of these are ungrounded, (4a), (4b), and (4d) being self-dependent and (4c) dependent on the self-dependent (4b), so none has a truth value in the minimal fixed point.

Now (4a), the liar, is paradoxical in the fullest sense and has no truth value in *any* fixed point. By contrast, if we start with a valuation that differs from the null valuation *just* by giving (4b) a truth value, Kripke's construction produces a fixed point extending this initial valuation, in which (4b) retains that truth value; indeed, (4b) has a truth value in every maximal fixed point, though that value is true in some and false in others. By contrast, (4c) and (4d) have the same truth value, true, in all maximal fixed points.

There is a subtle difference between them, in that to make (4c) true we must give a truth value to a sentence (4b) that could have had the opposite truth value, while to make (4d) true we need not give a truth value to any sentence that could have had the opposite truth value. Examples of type (4d) Kripke calls *intrinsically* true, and he shows there

---

[9] Despite his sometimes severe criticism of earlier writers, Kripke acknowledges a debt to some post-Tarskian writers, among them Robert Martin. As Kripke notes, the existence of maximal fixed points was first proved – with reference to a specific scheme, but by a general method – in Martin and Woodruff (1975). The proof requires the Axiom of Choice or an equivalent (such as Zorn's Lemma).

is a *maximum intrinsic* fixed point (a fixed point making no sentence true that some other fixed point makes false). If the minimum fixed point has any rival for the title of most natural fixed point to consider, it is this maximum intrinsic fixed point.

While it is Kripke's making rigorous the notion of *ungroundedness* that seems to have made the biggest impression on subsequent writers, in his own mind the distinguishing of various kinds of problematic sentences through consideration of their status in various other fixed points is a feature of equal importance. Certainly Kripke's theory of truth cannot simply be *identified* with the construction of the minimal fixed point and consequent rigorous definition of ungroundedness.

8. KRIPKE VERSUS TARSKI

Since, by Gödel's work, all sorts of *syntactic* predicates will be available under fairly modest assumptions, including the predicate S_0 for 'is a sentence not involving T,' we can define on Kripke's approach a predicate equivalent to Tarski's T_0, namely, the conjunction of Kripke's T with S_0. We will then have a predicate S_1 for 'is a sentence involving T only in conjunction with S_0' and a predicate equivalent to Tarski's T_1, namely, the conjunction of T with S_1. And so on. So in some sense the whole Tarski hierarchy is comprehended in Kripke's construction.

The sentences of which T_0 holds will be among the sentences true at stage 0 in Kripke's construction. The sentences of which T_1 holds will be among the sentences true at stage 1 in Kripke's construction, but they will not include *all* such sentences. The sentences of which T_1 holds will be sentences that for *intrinsic* reasons involve the truth predicate only in application to sentences that do *not* involve the truth predicate, but the sentences true at stage 1 in Kripke's construction will include also sentences that for *extrinsic* reasons involve the truth predicate only in application to sentences that do not involve the truth predicate. Such would be the sentence "Most things Nixon said about Watergate are false," if historically it happens to be the case that Nixon said nothing about Watergate that involved the notion of truth. An example like "Most things Nixon said about Watergate are false," is disallowed on the Tarski approach since it does not have an intrinsic level, but is allowed on the Kripke approach where it may "find its own level" on extrinsic grounds, depending on the levels of the things Nixon said about Watergate.

There is nothing on the Tarski approach that corresponds to the transfinite stages in Kripke's construction. One could indeed add to the

Tarski approach a predicate T_ω and extend the Tarski hierarchy one level into the transfinite ordinal numbers, but Kripke hints there are difficulties with proceeding much further. In any case, as we have already seen, Kripke's approach allows sentences to have truth values that do not come in anywhere in the Tarski hierarchy, because they are grounded only for extrinsic, not intrinsic reasons. Also, of course, Kripke's approach allows ungrounded sentences, too, to count as genuine well-formed sentences, albeit ones without truth value. Indeed, allowing an example like "Most things Nixon said about Watergate are false," with no intrinsic level, creates a *risk* of paradox, if what Nixon said about Watergate consists of equal numbers of truths and falsehoods together with "What was said about most things I said about Watergate being false is true." Thus in several respects Kripke's approach is very much more generous and general than Tarski's.

And yet he in the end faces some of the same kinds of limitations. All discussions of the liar eventually come round to discussing the "strengthened liar problem" (or as people have taken recently to calling it, in imitation of the titles of certain movie sequels, the "revenge of the liar"). The exact formulation varies with the theory of truth for which the problem arises. For Kripke's theory, the problem is simply that he has presented his theory as a piece of orthodox mathematics, in a classical metalanguage, and has allowed himself to say, for instance, that if '_____' is a liar sentence, then '_____' is not true. But according to his own theory, if '_____' is a liar sentence, then 'not-T('_____')' is itself not true. So in expounding his theory he seems to be saying things that, according to that very theory, are not true. If one felt while reading Kripke's theory that perhaps his theory *was* true, then one's notion of truth when one thought that can*not* have been the notion of truth Kripke's theory was describing.

On the relation of his theory to the intuitive notion of truth Kripke's position is cautious.[10] He in the end suggests that the theory he states is a theory of language at a stage "before philosophers reflect on its semantics," and the theory itself, being a philosopher's reflection on the semantics of the language at that stage, is not itself part of language at that stage. And thus he concludes that "The necessity to ascend to a metalanguage may be one of the weaknesses of the present theory. The ghost of the Tarski hierarchy is still with us."

---

[10] See his footnote 34 and the paragraph to which it is attached.

9. GLIMPSES BEYOND

The "Outline" is based on a single lecture in December 1975. A transcript of an audiotape (unfortunately marred by gaps) of a series of three lectures at Princeton in June 1975 (and of portions of the question-and-answer sessions that followed them), is also in existence (along with unsigned notes on parts of the lectures that partially fill in at least one of the gaps in the tape). It contains more detail on several points that are mentioned only in passing in the published paper, information briefly summarized in the following supplementary remarks.[11]

Self-referential sentences. In his "Outline" discussion of directly self-referential sentences, Kripke hints at the possibility of proving Gödel's theorem using a Gödel sentence rather like (1b). This would contrast with the usual proof, which uses a Gödel sentence much like (1c) (except for having the syntactic "something unprovable" in place of the semantic "a falsehood"). In this case the supplementary material makes it clear in the first lecture what Kripke was hinting at, and gives a new way of proving Gödel's theorem of possible pedagogical interest.[12]

The impossibility of a semantically closed language. Kripke in the supplementary material emphasizes that what Tarski shows to be impossible is not – despite the language used in this account so far, which has contrasted a "syntactic" property like provability, whose expressibility Gödel shows to be possible, with a "semantic" property like truth, whose expressibility Tarski shows to be impossible – the presence in a language of any predicate that might be called "semantic," but specifically the presence in a language *with a negation connective* of a predicate for which (2) holds *unrestrictedly*. Kripke reminds us that in the language of arithmetic, truth *restricted to sentences of the language only up to a certain degree of logical complexity* (where the "degree" is *not* closed under negation) is expressible in the language (and by a formula of whatever degree of complexity is at issue). It is even possible to construct truth-teller sentences on the order of (4b), of which some will be true and some will be false (though the discussion of this point in the first lecture is one of several marred by a gap in the audiotape). The attempt to construct a liar sentence on the

---

[11] Topics are taken up in the order in which they appear in the preceding account, rather than the order in which they appear in the lectures and discussion, both of which, but especially the latter, jump from topic to topic.

[12] A conjectural reconstruction of Kripke's proposed variant proof of Gödel's theorem was offered in print by Visser (1989).

order of (4a) fails, since the relevant "degrees of logical complexity" are not closed under negation. (One gets either something that says its negation is a true sentence of the given degree of logical complexity, which is unparadoxically and trivially false, since its negation is not a sentence of the right degree of logical complexity at all, or something that says it is not a true sentence of the given degree of logical complexity, which is unparadoxically and trivially true for the same sort of reason.)

Does the Tarski hierarchy eliminate ungroundedness? Kripke discusses briefly in the supplementary material a possibility barely mentioned in the "Outline," namely, that of a sequence of languages L_0, which contains and contains a truth predicate for L_{-1}, which contains and contains a truth predicate for L_{-2}, and so on. The possibility of such a sequence shows that merely insisting on a separation of object language from metalanguage does not prevent the occurrence of problematic sequences in which each sentence depends on the next.[13]

Schemes for handling truth-value gaps. In the "Outline"' Kripke refers only very briefly to additional possibilities beyond the Frege and Kleene three-valued logic and the basic van Fraassen supervaluational scheme. In the second lecture Kripke gives a welcome example of a scheme for handling truth-value gaps that is *not* monotonic and therefore not possible to use in his construction: the famous Lukasiewicz three-valued logic. In the third lecture he enlarges on additional alternatives that *are* possible to use in his construction that take the form of *restricted* supervaluational schemes. In such schemes, given a partial valuation, one does not consider the set of *all* total valuations that agree with it as far as it goes, but rather only those that satisfy some condition: say never making both $T(a)$ and $T(b)$ true, where a and b denote A and B, if B is the negation of A. Because he discusses the options at greater length in the three-lecture series, Kripke's preference for the Kleene strong three-valued logic over the rivals he considers becomes much more conspicuous than in the "Outline."[14]

---

[13] Kripke explicitly considers a sequence in which each item says the next is true. This produces a puzzle comparable to "This very sentence is true," rather than a paradox comparable to "This very sentence is false." Yablo (1993) considers a sequence in which each items says all the later ones are false, which produces a liarlike paradox.

[14] By the time of the seminar a dozen years later, Kripke had given up thinking of the different schemes as *rivals*. For one thing, since it is possible to define the connectives of the Frege weak three-valued logic in terms of those of the Kleene strong three-valued logic, the Frege scheme can be in a sense subsumed by the Kleene scheme. Kripke then also shows that the connectives of the Kleene scheme can be defined, not indeed in terms of the connectives of the van Fraassen scheme alone, but in terms of these plus the

Can the Tarski hierarchy extend to the transfinite? Kripke discusses at greater length in the supplementary material the problem of extending the Tarski hierarchy into the transfinite. Some readers may have guessed that the problem is that we need to fix transfinite numerals for the transfinite numbers, to use as subscripts on the additional truth predicates. Kripke explains how there is a problem here about the lack of a canonical choice of ordinal notations, and reports that in the case one is starting from the language of arithmetic the problem can be solved – or rather, has in effect already been solved in a somewhat different guise in the theory of so-called *hyperarithmetical sets* – though the situation is much less clear with other starting points, especially where the universe of discourse is uncountable.

Intrinsically and extrinsically paradoxical sentences. In the discussion following the third lecture, Kripke briefly notes a way of modeling, using his formalism, the distinction between sentences that are intrinsically paradoxical, like (1a), (1b), and (1c), and those that are extrinsically paradoxical, like (1d). Start with arithmetic, add a one-place predicate P, thought of as representing "empirical" information, and consider various different total assignments of truth values to atomic sentences of form $P(a)$. Then add the predicate T and construct fixed points. Sentences like (4a), (4b), (4c), and (4d) will be ungrounded regardless of the interpretation of P, but a sentence like '$P(0)$ or (4a)' will be true if $P(0)$ is true and ungrounded otherwise. A sentence that is grounded regardless of the interpretation of P Kripke calls *safe*. The sentences of the "inner Tarski hierarchy" (described at the beginning of the preceding section of the present account) are all safe in this sense, but more surprisingly Kripke announces a result to the effect that every safe sentence is equivalent to a sentence of the inner Tarski hierarchy (when the latter is appropriately extended into the transfinite).

"*The ghost of the Tarski hierarchy.*" In the discussion after his second lecture, Kripke is more explicit than in the "Outline" as to his views about the relationship between his theory and the intuitive notion of truth, and the distinction between the "prereflective" stage of the development of the notion of truth, which his theory describes, and the "reflective" stage to which his theory belongs. In this discussion he becomes almost Tarskiesque in expressing pessimism about the prospects for a "universal language."

truth predicate, once we have a fixed point and a truth predicate available. This is the most notable amendment (as opposed to addition) to his earlier views that the present author has found upon cursory examination of as much of the transcript of the seminar as was available.

Monotonicity. The negation ~ in the language to which Kripke's theory applies is false when what it negates is true, true when what it negates is false, and without truth value when what it negates is without truth value. What is missing is a "negation" ¬ that is true when what it negates is false *or without truth value,* and false when what it negates is true. When, expounding his theory, Kripke says that the liar sentence is *not true,* the "not" here is ¬ rather than ~. But ¬ cannot be in the language to which the theory applies, *because its presence would destroy monotonicity.* This important point, implicit from the beginning, only becomes fully explicit in the discussion following the second lecture.

Complexity. Logicians have various ways of measuring the complexity of the definitions of definable sets, and in the "Outline" Kripke just touches on such questions as that of the complexity of the minimum or the maximum intrinsic, fixed point on the Kleene or the van Fraassen scheme, starting from arithmetic or in general. The discussion following the second lecture reveals that six months earlier some results mentioned in passing in the "Outline" had already been obtained, but others had not.[15]

Limitations of time and space preclude fuller discussion here. It should be evident that philosophers and logicians alike would benefit from publication of the parts of Kripke's work on truth at present unavailable in print.[16]

---

[15] Among those that had was the one to appear later as Theorem 6.1 in Burgess (1986). Among those that had not were the results attributed to Leo Harrington in footnote 36 of the "Outline."

[16] Audiotapes exist from a three-semester seminar at Princeton in 1988–89, and those for the first two semesters have been transcribed. (There were twelve lectures each semester, but several of those in the second semester were by guest speakers rather than Kripke himself, and were not recorded.) This later material naturally contains more detail on points mentioned in the "Outline" and the three-lecture series, but also reactions to some of the literature that appeared in their wake, including vigorous responses to certain critics. The present author had available the transcriptions mentioned just in time to speed-read them before the deadline for producing the present account. Consultation of this additional material has been useful in a negative way, in avoiding misinterpretation of various fragmentary asides in the "Outline"; but there was not time to make full positive use of it. Topics taken up in the first semester of the seminar but not the "Outline" or the three-lecture series include: languages whose means of self-reference are pathologically weak, proof procedures for logics of truth-value gaps and theories of truth presented in such logics, comparison of various versions of Kripke's proposal with rival proposals of Herzberger and Gupta and Belnap, and more. Topics taken up in the second semester of the seminar include results on complexity and exposition of background material on higher recursion theory.

References

Blamey, Stephen (1986) "Partial Logic," in D. M. Gabbay and F. Guenthner, eds., *Handbook of Philosophical Logic*, vol. 3: *Non-Classical Logics*, Dordrecht: Reidel, 1–70.

Burgess, John P. (1986) "The Truth Is Never Simple," *Journal of Symbolic Logic* 51: 663–81.

Fitting, Melvin (1986) "Notes on the Mathematical Aspects of Kripke's Theory of Truth," *Notre Dame Journal of Formal Logic* 27: 75–88.

Kripke, Saul (1975) "Outline of a Theory of Truth," *Journal of Philosophy* 72: 690–716.

  (1980) *Naming and Necessity*, 2nd ed., Cambridge: Harvard University Press.

Martin, Robert and Woodruff, Peter (1975) "On Representing 'Truth-in-*L*' in *L*," *Philosophia* 3: 213–17.

McGee, Vann (1989) "Applying Kripke's Theory of Truth," *Journal of Philosophy* 86: 530–9.

Moschovakis, Yannis (1974) *Elementary Induction on Abstract Structures*, Amsterdam: North-Holland.

Spade, Paul (2005) "Insolubles," *The Stanford Encyclopedia of Philosophy*, <http://plato.stanford.edu/archives/fall2005/entries/insolubles/>.

Tarski, Alfred (1935) "Der Wahrheitsbegriff in den formalisierten Sprachen," *Studia Philosophica* 1: 261–405.

van Fraassen, Bas (1969) "Presuppositions, Supervaluations, and Free Logic," in K. Lambert. ed., *The Logical Way of Doing Things*, New Haven: Yale University Press.

Visser, Albert (1989) "Semantics and the Liar Paradox," in D. M. Gabbay and F. Guenthner, eds., *Handbook of Philosophical Logic*, vol. 4: *Topics in the Philosophy of Language*, Dordrecht: Reidel, 617–706.

Yablo, Stephen (1993) "Paradox without Self-Reference," *Analysis* 53: 251–2.

7

Kripke on Logicism, Wittgenstein, and *De Re* Beliefs about Numbers

Mark Steiner

Besides giving an overview of Kripke's rather original proposal concerning these three topics, I intend to discuss the evolution of Kripke's thinking about Wittgenstein. Kripke tells us that his thinking about the topics was "dialectical," meaning that various initial ideas that he had were taken back, though they contributed to the "final synthesis." I find a similar dialectical thinking in Kripke about Wittgenstein himself; Kripke has devoted much thought to Wittgenstein's philosophy over the years, and I detect an evolution in his thoughts on Wittgenstein. In my opinion, in the present work – which is not presented as exegetical – Kripke succeeds best in penetrating Wittgenstein's "mindset," despite (what I see as) deep ideological differences of the kind which tend to impede sympathetic reconstruction.[1]

The work I shall be discussing in this essay has never been published. Nevertheless, the editor of the present volume thought that it would be valuable to give an account of Kripke's ideas concerning the concept of number. My discussion will be based on MS Word transcripts of Kripke's Whitehead Lectures (referred to here as WL I and WL II), which were delivered at Harvard University on May 4 and 5, 1992. As a result my discussion will be doubly tentative: not only may I not have understood Kripke in every point, but the transcript may not fully reflect what Kripke had in mind. The responsibility is great, since the reader will not be able to check what I say against the transcript. Nevertheless, I will make the attempt. I would like to thank Professor Kripke for creating new philosophical worlds in this and all his writings, and for inspiring me to return to Wittgenstein's philosophy of mathematics. This research was supported by the Israel Science Foundation (grant no. 949/02), and I am very grateful for the support.

[1] Kripke, of course, has never published a work in which he claims to give a faithful rendition of Wittgenstein's texts. He usually issues a disclaimer in this regard, in which he denies that he intends such a faithful rendition. (Compare Wittgenstein's own disclaimer, in the preface to *Philosophical Investigations*: "For more than one reason what I publish here will have points of contact with what other people are writing today. – If my remarks do not bear a stamp which marks them as mine, then I do not wish to lay any further claim to them as my property.") Nevertheless, as I will show, there are ideas he expresses

I am not surprised at Wittgenstein's fascination for Kripke, by the way. I have always marveled at the deep similarities in their approaches to philosophy. It is said that Wittgenstein compared philosophy to diving underwater: the deeper you go, the harder it gets.[2] Kripke, too, castigates philosophers who are glib: "Now, I disagree with this attitude because what it means is that he confidently says that because he, Dennett, cannot think of the distinction it doesn't exist. I mean, well that may be true of him, but at any rate in my own case I think I am a bit slower and that philosophy is slow and that if a distinction is used there may be something to be ferreted out there, even though the philosophers have not thought about it."[3]

Philosophy is a struggle for clarity, and both Wittgenstein and Kripke have the power to get to the absolute nub of a problem, taking nothing for granted, especially the orthodoxies of academic philosophy. Both abhor pseudosolutions that rely on dressing up the problem in a technical vocabulary. An important difference between the two, however, is that Kripke is a mathematician as well as a philosopher, and the way Wittgenstein looks at mathematics is anathema to most mathematicians.

My account of Kripke's proposal will go in the opposite direction from his, beginning with the proposal itself, and then moving on to its motivation.

Kripke's view on the identity of numbers is very simple to state: The numbers are finite sequences of the objects 0, 1, 2...., 9 – where the objects can be taken to be "Frege-Russell" (FR) numbers: 3 is the set of all triples, 4 the set of all quadruples, and so on.[4] Kripke takes the FR numbers to represent the basic intuition that we "abstract" the *cardinal* numbers from finite

---

in earlier works that Wittgenstein *could* not have held. In the present work, however, almost everything is compatible with Wittgenstein's actual views, the only discrepancy, if any, being in what Kripke *fails* to say.

[2] I cannot find the source for this quote, yet I find it impossible to believe that I made it up. At any rate, the experts I consulted agree that Wittgenstein *could* have said this.

[3] WL II, p. 11. Norman Malcolm (Malcolm 1984) writes that after his classes, Wittgenstein ran to a movie house, choosing always B movies that would not require him to think. As for Kripke, I have noticed that he does not like to chat casually about philosophy, and I think one of the reasons is that he finds thinking about philosophical questions quite difficult, even painful, despite his success in the field.

[4] To simplify an oral presentation, Kripke suppressed some important details about Frege's definition of number. First, numbers are not actually sets, but extensions of concepts – Frege regarded the latter, but not the former, as a logical notion. For example, 0 is the extension of the concept: "equinumerous to the concept non-self-identical." Second, even if we do regard numbers as sets, they are not for Frege sets of sets, but sets of concepts – in our example, zero is the set of concepts that are equinumerous to the concept "non-self-identical," an equivalence class under the relation equinumerosity. And 4 would turn out to be (though of course is not defined as) the set of all concepts which apply to exactly four objects.

sets of objects, leaving out from our intuition every property of the objects but their number.[5] This account is plausible for numbers less than 10, but not for larger numbers, since we cannot survey large sets to tell how many members they have.[6] In any case, Kripke does not agree with Frege and Russell that the FR numbers are the only ones in which the question "how many" can be fully answered – for example, to say that there are two major parties in the United States. Using the FR numbers, all we need to say is that the set of major U.S. parties is a *member* of the FR number 2. While this is an elegant solution, Kripke, siding with Paul Benacerraf (1965), says that we can say this using any progression of objects, that is, objects of order type ω. Namely, we can say that there is a bijection between the set of major U.S. parties and the set consisting of the elements before the third element of that progression.[7] Thus, Kripke is free to adopt his "mixed" proposal, in which FR numbers are *only* used for the numbers less than 10.

Kripke points out, however, that none of the FR numbers can exist in the usual set theories. This is true because the FR numbers, as sets, are "too big": every number is the "size" of the entire universe, that is, the (illegitimate) set of sets. But it is also true because the FR numbers allow ill-founded sets: for example, take a set X with seven elements. Then X is a *member* of the FR number 7 (which is the set of all unordered septuples). But also 7 is a member of X! Such cycles, Kripke points out, are explicitly disallowed by the Axiom of Foundation.[8]

---

[5] Kripke is aware that this notation of abstraction is anathema to Frege, but I believe his comparison of Frege's view to that of Berkeley (WL I), and his attribution also to Frege of the view that "you can't actually get to any particular concept simply by being or pretending to be forgetful" is incorrect – Frege agrees that *concepts* are formed by abstraction from particulars, but *numerical* concepts, being second-order concepts, similar to quantifiers, are not. Cf. Frege's *Grundlagen* (Frege 1980), sec. 45.

[6] It is said of the Gaon (genius) of Rogatchov, Rabbi Joseph Rosen, that he could glance at a flock of sheep and tell their number.

[7] Since we start with 0, there are *n* numbers before *n*.

[8] As a review of note 4 will show, the actual situation with Frege, with regard to these "cycles," is apparently not so bad: not the septuples, but the concepts that apply to septuples are members of 7; and some of these concepts – for example, "being a number between 6 and 13" – apply to the number 7. As for the concepts themselves, Frege has a hierarchy of concepts that does not allow cycles. Nor does he have the epsilon "membership" relation between sets, and thus avoids the entire problem of set cycles. What *is* allowed by Frege, and what ultimately leads to paradox, is the more subtle kind of cycle in which a second-order concept X can apply to a first-order concept C, which in turn applies to the *extension* of X (an object, according to Frege). This can lead to Russell's Paradox in the following form: let a concept C be "reflexive" if it applies to the *extension* of some concept that also applies to C itself; otherwise C is said to be "nonreflexive." Now let C be the concept: "being identical to the *extension* of the concept 'nonreflexive.'" We

Two solutions to the FR problem are mentioned by Kripke. First, there are nonstandard set theories in which the FR construction can be carried out (the one Kripke mentions is Quine's NF – he remarks also that he worked on the problem himself). The other is to treat the FR construction *intensionally* – meaning that the numbers become *properties* of *n*–tuples (rather than sets of them): for example, 2 is the property all unordered pairs have in common. But note carefully that the FR construction is to be used only for numbers less than 10. For 10 and beyond, the numbers are identified with finite sequences of the numbers from 0 to 9, disallowing sequences that begin with 0.

The sequences are ordered "lexicographically," and under this ordering, form an infinite progression. Canonical names of the sequences are formed in the obvious way, by concatenating occurrences of numerals '1', '2', '3',.... Using the canonical names, it is an effective and trivial procedure to decide of two numbers, as described by canonical names, whether one is the successor of the other, or whether one is smaller than another. Essentially the point is that the numbers are chosen so that their canonical description will turn out to be our decimal positional ("Arabic") notation. Numbers above thousands are sequences with commas in the very place that our decimal positional notation demands: for example, 1,522,756. Kripke seems to say (it's not explicit in the text I used) that the commas are part of the "practice," which is almost to say that they are part of the numbers.

Despite appearances, Kripke's view is not nominalist – for him, numerals are not numbers. Even if they were, the numerals themselves are abstract objects, so nominalism does not rear its head. But Kripke shares with nominalism the idea that the numbers have common properties with the numerals that "refer" to them. In particular, the decimal

---

note that C therefore applies uniquely to the extension of the concept NR. Using the principle later called by Frege Axiom V, but of course presupposed in the *Grundlagen*, namely that $\text{ext}(F) = \text{ext}(G)$ if and only if $\forall x(Fx \leftrightarrow Gx)$, we can show that C is reflexive iff C is nonreflexive. For if C is nonreflexive, then every concept X applying to C is such that C does *not* apply uniquely to $\text{ext}(X)$. By hypothesis, NR applies to C, but C, as above, *applies* uniquely to $\text{ext}(NR)$, which yields a contradiction. If, on the other hand, C is reflexive, then there must be a concept X applying to C where C in turn applies uniquely to $\text{ext}(X)$. But C, again as above, applies uniquely to $\text{ext}(NR)$, so $\text{ext}(NR) = \text{ext}(X)$. Since by hypothesis X applies to C, by Axiom V, then so does NR, so C is nonreflexive, which again yields a contradiction. (This is a "popularization" of the formal proof of this paradox in (Boolos 1987), reprinted in (Demopoulos 1995) and (Boolos 1998). I am happy that I was able to show it to Boolos shortly before his untimely death, and that he enjoyed going through it.)

numerals "reveal the structure" of the decimal numbers. For this reason (and others), the decimal representation of a number is – for us – the ultimate and final answer to the question, "But what number is that?" Conversely, of a number in some other notation, it is always in place to ask "But what number is that?" For this reason, the decimal numerals are called by Kripke "buckstoppers"[9] – a term he uses instead of "canonical notion." The general principle is that the "buckstopping" notation for numbers is the one that reveals their structure.

It is not even correct, he feels, to define the decimal numerals as polynomials in 10, as I did in (Steiner 1975) chapter 2: when we refer to a number as $3 \cdot 10^2 + 2 \cdot 10 + 5$, it still makes sense to ask, "But what number is that?" and to calculate the result as 325. Of course, there is an intimate connection between decimal numerals and polynomials in 10. The "school rules" for addition, for example, correspond transparently to polynomial addition, though the proof of this is not itself necessarily transparent.

Clearly, Kripke's conception of the numbers, though it accepts "mathematical objects," is nevertheless more congenial to Wittgenstein's thinking than most of the usual platonist conceptions of numbers. For Kripke, the relation between numbers and numerals is quite different from the relation between personal names and their bearers. Kripke himself says that his conception mirrors Wittgenstein's remarks at *PI*[10] §8.

More significant: the concept of a "buckstopper" takes account of the Wittgensteinian intuition (*RFM*[11], part III) that mathematical notation must be perspicuous to *be* mathematical. It is internal to the concept of a calculation that the calculation should have the power to persuade us to accept the result. For example, an "unsurveyable" calculation is not, strictly speaking, a calculation at all, since it cannot persuade us to accept the result.[12] And no doubt Wittgenstein would have accepted Kripke's idea that the result of a calculation must be (not only surveyable but)

---

[9] The connection between the concept of a "buckstopper" and that of *de re* belief is simply that some philosophers believe that a sentence expresses a *de re* belief about an object x, only if x is designated in the sentence by a buckstopper, that is, a designator that is a final answer to the question, "But what is that?" But *de re* belief as such plays no other role in Kripke's lectures – it is used only to motivate the notion of a buckstopper.

[10] In this essay, *PI* refers to *Philosophical Investigations* (Wittgenstein 1968).

[11] *RFM* refers to *Remarks on the Foundations of Mathematics* (Wittgenstein 1978).

[12] For Wittgenstein in *RFM*, this is true of all mathematical proofs. Crucial to Wittgenstein's view is a position that presumably Kripke would reject: that mathematical theorems are rules for the use of terms like "plus" which are adopted as a result of proofs, which are nothing but "schematic pictures." (For an explanation of this, see *RFM*, I, and (Steiner 1996).) By hypothesis an unsurveyable proof cannot result in the adoption by human beings of a rule.

canonical, that is, a "buckstopper." For Wittgenstein, this requirement would, like surveyability, follow from the general demand that proofs must be perspicuous. One must know *what* one has proved for there to *be* a proof. Now this requirement is less trivial than it might appear (though Wittgenstein wanted it to appear trivial). For example, in geometry, Wittgenstein would distinguish between the proposition that a given ink blot fits into its background on the page, and the proposition that every square fits into the circle which intersects its four vertices. The former is a pseudoproposition, because we have no independent way of characterizing the geometrical form of the blot, on the one hand, and the background, on the other.[13] For the natural numbers, at least for the smaller ones, it is the decimal notation that is perspicuous – for us – and, working backwards, this forces the numbers to be those objects of which the notation is structurally revelatory, hence finite sequences, ordered lexicographically. For any notation, though, once the numbers get too big, their canonical numerals stop being buckstoppers,[14] a fact we shall have to ponder later.[15]

Kripke notes himself that his proposal implies that the identity of the numbers is culturally dependent. A culture that calculated with the base 7 would perforce be calculating with different numbers – not just different numerals – from ours. Even a culture that recognized decimal numbers, but did not use our system of positional notation for the numbers (examples would be the Roman numerals or the Hebrew system) would be using different numbers, and not just different numerals. Thus, the proposition that there is no one preferred system of numbers, originally put forth by Benacerraf (1965) with reference to the Zermelo and the

[13] Again, to fully understand this point, one must understand Wittgenstein's point that every mathematical theorem is a new rule (Cf. note 12). Rules govern human behavior, and the rule about ink blots, for the reason given, cannot have any impact on human behavior. The rule about the circle and the square can, on the other hand, impact on human behavior: a sketch that violates geometrical theorems is said to be "incorrect" or "rough." As I already wrote, I doubt that Kripke is sympathetic to this particular doctrine.

[14] In his lecture, Kripke did not discuss the implications of this, except to say that the decimal numbers defer the issue for a long time, longer than the other suggestions in the literature (Frege, Russell, Zermelo, von Neumann).

[15] The notion of a "buckstopper" does not generalize easily to the real numbers, either. Here is an example, courtesy of Lawrence Zalcman: Let $B = \sqrt[3]{2 + \sqrt{5}} + \sqrt[3]{2 - \sqrt{5}}$. Is the real number B given by a "buckstopper"? By Cardan's formula, or by direct calculation, B is a root of the cubic equation $f(x) = x^3 + 3x - 4 = 0$. By inspection, 1 is a root of this equation, and indeed its only real root (seeing that $f'(x)$ is positive for $x > 1$). Hence B is 1, a mathematical "accident" if ever there was one. There seems to be no way to verify this by ordinary calculation, so what does it mean to say "But what number is B?"

von Neumann numbers, is given a surprising twist, in the direction of cultural, rather than professional, pluralism.

(The numbers, in Kripke's version, are similar to calendar dates. In Israel, for example, there are two calendars in use by Jews: the Jewish and the civil [a euphemism for Gregorian] calendar. If we ask a modernist, for example, "When is Yom Kippur next year?" he will consult a calendar and tell us: in 2004, Yom Kippur is on October 13 – he may add that Yom Kippur is "late" next year [Jackie Mason quips that the Jewish holidays are never on time: they are either late or early, but never on time]. But if we ask a strictly Orthodox Jew, he'll tell us that Yom Kippur is the same every year: Tishri 10 – it's October that's "early." If we tell him that Yom Kippur is on October 13, he'll ask us, "When is that?")

Another idea of Benacerraf (also in Benacerraf 1965), suitably modified, which finds its way into Kripke's "synthesis" is that, in order to be a candidate for the natural numbers, a sequence must have a primitive recursive "less than" relation. Now, literally, this idea is circular, Kripke points out, because what we mean by a recursive function is precisely a certain type of function on the natural numbers.[16] Nevertheless, Kripke observes, it is possible to define the notion of recursiveness and primitive recursiveness for notational systems. Benacerraf's requirement now becomes transformed into the requirement that the *numeral system* used in referencing the natural numbers must have an effectively calculable "less than" operation. Even this is not enough: Kripke argues that the *successor* relation on the numerals must be transparent – unlike the example, which Kripke gives, of a positional notation based on the prime power expansion of numbers such that 2 is [1], 3 is [10], 4 is [2] = [[1]], 5 is [100], 6 is [11], 7 is [1000], 8 is [3] = [[10]], etc. Here, on the one hand, whether a number is prime or not is trivial: a prime is denoted by a 1 followed by a string of zeroes. What is not trivial (although primitive recursive) is the successor relation, which requires calculation.

In light of the above (and of what I will say next), it is true, but slightly misleading, to say that the numbers and the numerals, in Kripke's view, share properties. That would be like saying that I share properties with my shadow. For the identity of the natural numbers depends upon, and

---

[16] Compatible considerations led Benacerraf himself to recant his original requirement of recursiveness. Cf. his retrospective article in the Festschrift in his honor (Morton and Stich 1996), which Kripke does not seem to be aware of. In any case, we will now see that he accepts the intuition behind Benacerraf's (mistaken) requirement.

is parasitic upon, the notation we use to denote them. In a more bombastic style, we can speak of the "conceptual priority" of the numerals over the numbers. Thus, although Kripke is not a nominalist, I think that he could be called a "quasi-nominalist," since he asserts the conceptual priority of numerals over numbers.

In order to get a better feel for this notion, let us use an analogy that Kripke cites himself: the concept of a recursive function. Many students have a problem with this mathematical concept, because they do not understand the conceptual priority of the notation for the function over the function itself. A favorite textbook example is the function defined as follows:

$$f(x) = 0, \text{ if the Riemann hypothesis is true; otherwise, } f(x) = 1.$$

Most students think that this function cannot be recursive; yet, using the law of the excluded middle, we can see that it is. For the function is either the constant function 0 or the constant function 1, and in either case, it is recursive: the definition of "recursive function" is "one for which an algorithm to compute it exists." The way the function happens to be defined in this problem does not count: we know that there is an algorithm to compute the function; we just don't know which one. A function is picked out, but not by canonical, "buckstopping" notation, which, for a recursive function, would be its recursion equations. The properties of the function derive from the canonical notation – the trick in the example is that the function is specified uniquely, but not by canonical notation.

The classical notion of an "algorithm," due to Gödel, Church, Turing, and others, places no limit on the amount of time it takes to compute the values of the function. Nor is there a limit on the amount of memory a machine that computes the function would need.

A subset of the recursive functions are the functions which are computable in practice, functions that have algorithms allowing values to be calculated in a reasonable amount of time, given the size of the inputs. In recent years, the mathematical theory of computational complexity has developed to study this subset.

Kripke's theory of the numbers draws some inspiration, as he himself points out, from this idea of "computability in practice." For him, the natural numbers are objects for which we have a structural description suitable for calculation in real time. Calculations are defined as operations on the descriptions, but the numbers are not those descriptions. In the case of recursive functions, a concept introduced by mathematicians, the notion of algorithm was clear. In the case of the natural numbers, the descriptions are given by history. We have various base notations, and even when the base is fixed, as in the decimal notations, there are several notations that are used: the letter notation as in Roman and Hebrew numerals, and the Arabic positional notation.

All notations, however, seem to be sequences in a finite alphabet, and these sequences we call "numerals." This suggests that the numbers themselves should be sequences, in order that the notation should be structurally descriptive of the objects denoted. The rules for manipulating the numerals (that is, the sequences) induce the abstract operations on the numbers. The algorithm for finding the next numeral imposes the definition of "successor" on the "denotations" of these numerals. Just as we fix the notion of algorithm and then see what functions are defined, so do we fix the notion of calculation as symbolic manipulation and then see what numbers there are. Small wonder that philosophers and lay people are confused concerning the difference between numerals and numbers.

This is what I mean, then, by "quasi-nominalism." The identity of the numbers is induced by the properties of the notation, and thus their existence is, in some sense, derivative.

Now let's look more carefully at Wittgenstein's views on some of these issues; I have stated that Kripke is close to Wittgenstein, let us now see how close.

It is true that Wittgenstein thought that the idea of "mathematical objects" was nothing short of superstitious. But he explicitly rejected nominalism as well: "So it may look as if what we were doing were Nominalism. Nominalists make the mistake of interpreting all words as *names*, and so of not really describing their use, but only, so to speak, giving a paper draft on such a description" (*PI* §383). In other words, both platonism and nominalism make the *same* mistake – they mistake the grammar of the numerals. To say "There are no numbers" is thus the same mistake as to say "There are numbers."

At the same time, Wittgenstein spends most of his time attacking various forms of mathematical realism and platonism: "Is it already mathematical alchemy," he muses, "that mathematical propositions are regarded as statements about mathematical objects, and mathematics as the exploration of these objects?" (*RFM*, V, 16). These arguments are sometimes borrowed from the nominalist arsenal. That Wittgenstein repudiates the apparent conclusion of these arguments (refusing to adopt an explicit nominalism) is in line with his credo that philosophy is not in the business of putting forward theses or theories.[17] Wittgenstein's neutrality, however, is clearly biased toward nominalism. This bias shows itself in Wittgenstein's refusal to refer to mathematical objects in the metalanguage in which he states the criteria for counting and calculating. (In the case of physical objects, no such bias exists: some of the criteria for using the word "comb" will have to refer to combs.) This sounds like quasi-nominalism.

Similarly, one might characterize Wittgenstein's view of mathematics as "quasi-finitist." Wittgenstein, not surprisingly, held that mathematical realism and finitism both proceed from the same delusion. In *Lectures on the Foundations of Mathematics* (Wittgenstein 1976; *LFM*), Wittgenstein is quoted as saying to a class: "If you say that mathematical propositions are about a mathematical reality – although this is quite vague, it has very definite consequences. And if you deny it, there are also queer consequences – for example, one may be led to finitism. Both would be quite wrong" (*LFM*, p. 141). Wittgenstein had said earlier to the same class: "Hence we want to see the absurdities both of what the finitists say and of what their opponents say – just as we want in philosophy to see the absurdities both of what the behaviourists say and of what their opponents say. Finitism and behaviourism are as alike as two eggs. The same absurdities, and the same kind of answers. Both sides of such disputes are based on a particular kind of misunderstanding which arises from gazing at a form of words and forgetting to ask yourself what's done with it, or from gazing into your own soul to see if two expressions have the same meaning, and such things"[18] (*LFM*, p. 112).

The specific mistake made by finitism (and its opponents) was spelled out by Wittgenstein to his class in *LFM*, lecture XXVII: "If one were to justify a finitist position in mathematics, one should say just that in mathematics 'infinite' does not mean anything huge. To say 'There's nothing infinite' is in a sense nonsensical and ridiculous. But it does make sense to say we are not talking of anything huge here." We see, then, that both

---

[17] *PI* §126: "Philosophy simply puts everything before us, and neither explains nor deduces anything. – Since everything lies open to view there is nothing to explain. For what is hidden, for example, is of no interest to us." *PI* §128: "If one tried to advance theses in philosophy, it would never be possible to debate them, because everyone would agree to them."

[18] And here is what he said (to the class) of another philosophical alternative to mathematical realism: "Intuitionism is all bosh – entirely" (*LFM* 237). One last comment: I am characterizing Wittgenstein's opinions during the period he was working on *PI*, which I believe had changed (or developed) from those he expressed in such earlier works as *Philosophical Grammar*.

finitism and its opponents mistake criteria governing the use of the term "infinite," and, insofar as the meaning of a term can be identified with the criteria for the use of the term, they both mistake the meaning of the term "infinite." On the other hand, Wittgenstein's neutrality is again biased – in favor of finitism – so that it is no wonder that some of his commentators have mistaken him for a finitist, and nobody has mistaken him for a realist with respect to infinity.

Wittgenstein has even been labeled a strict finitist,[19] one who does not "accept" even finite numbers if they are "too" large – one who rejects, not only the actual infinite, but the "potential infinite" as well. And though Wittgenstein was, as we have seen, no kind of finitist (since he would never have expressed his view as "There are no infinite numbers") there is a grain of truth in the "strict finitist" label as well. In practice, after all, we do not, because we cannot, handle very large numbers with the same techniques as we do with the small ones. What this means, for Wittgenstein, is not that "there are no very large numbers," – an absurdity – but that the meaning of the arithmetic terminology cannot be held constant over the entire range of the natural numbers.

Returning now to Kripke, it is interesting that Kripke's thoughts in the Whitehead Lectures on the issue of finitism are much closer to Wittgenstein's real position than in his previous writing, even in his famous book on Wittgenstein and rule-following (Kripke 1982, referred to here as *WRP*). For in the latter work, Kripke sees in Wittgenstein's[20] *PI* an argument that Wittgenstein could never have given.

The argument is one of a number intended to support the conclusion (C) that there is no fact about an individual speaker in virtue of which that speaker means something in particular by a given word.[21] For example, there is no fact about a speaker in virtue of which he means "addition" by the sign '+', rather than some other operation that agrees

---

[19] Cf. (Kielkopf 1970).

[20] One cannot write "attributes to Wittgenstein" with respect to Kripke (1982), because Kripke denies that he is attempting to reconstruct Wittgenstein's actual position; he says only that the book is Wittgenstein's position as it struck Kripke. "Kripkenstein," according to the wags, is the philosopher there characterized. My own students, on the other hand, have taken to calling me "Kripkensteiner."

[21] In order that this doctrine should mean something, we have to make clear what is meant by "fact" for Wittgenstein in his later period. In this period, Wittgenstein warned against distorting the ordinary meaning of words, and particularly against turning ordinary words into quasi-technical terms in order to turn academic philosophy into an explanatory "science." The term "fact" is of course one of these words. I believe that Wittgenstein regarded the ordinary use of fact as empirical and scientific. Facts are verified by observation. Thus, it is not a "fact" in the ordinary sense that somebody does, or does not, follow a rule. The question, then, is whether there are facts about a person's

with addition over the range of the speaker's past behavior but diverges from addition on numbers which the speaker has never calculated.

Before I give the argument, I would like to point out for the record that I agree with Kripke that Wittgenstein did hold conclusion (C). I also agree that the other arguments for (C) that Kripke finds in Wittgenstein are actually there, though I will have to make the case for this elsewhere. My point is that *one* of the arguments Kripke uses could not have been given by Wittgenstein.

The argument is the so-called infinity argument.[22] It goes as follows: addition is a function from (pairs of) the natural numbers to the natural numbers, that is, a binary function on an infinite domain. If we see "meaning addition by '+'" as a disposition[23] to calculate certain results, given certain pairs of numbers, a disposition identical to a certain brain state, then this disposition would have to be an "infinite disposition," a disposition to behave appropriately across the entire domain of (pairs of) natural numbers. The brain, having a finite number of neurons, could not house such an infinite disposition.

Wittgenstein could not give such an argument for a number of reasons, one of which is relevant to our topic. It is simply wrong that the arithmetic operation of addition has the same meaning throughout the entire range of the natural numbers. Once the numbers are not surveyable, the concept of addition actually changes. For example, in the expression '$10^{10^{10}} + 1$', the symbol '+' has a related (recall "family resemblance" from *PI*) but different meaning from the meaning it has in the expression '$10 + 1$'.

Wittgenstein says this in the passages in which he attacks Russell's logicism, part III of *RFM*:

> We extend our ideas from calculations with small numbers to ones with large numbers in the same kind of way as we imagine that, if the distance from here to the sun could be measured with a footrule, then we should get the very result that, as it is, we get in a quite different way. That is to say, we are inclined to take the measurement of length with a footrule as a model even for the measurement of the distance between two stars.

mind, or brain, that underlie rule-following. In this sense of "fact," Kripke is correct (a) that Wittgenstein denies that there is any such fact in virtue of which somebody is following a rule; (b) that such a fact could not be a criterion for rule-following; and (c) that this denial is crucial to Wittgenstein's analysis of rule-following.

[22] Cf. Kripke 1982, pp. 26ff.

[23] Kripke takes the (reasonable) position of many philosophers of science, that dispositions are meaningless unless backed up by facts. Thus, the disposition of salt to dissolve has no meaning, unless there is some fact about the salt, presumably its microstructure, which is responsible for the salt typically dissolving in water. In fact, however, it is

And one says, e.g. at school: "If we imagine rulers stretching from here to the sun..." and seems in this way to explain what we understand by the distance between the sun and the earth. And the use of such a picture is all right, so long as it is clear to us that we can measure the distance from us to the sun, and that we cannot measure it with footrules. (p. 146)

I thought of defending Kripke here by means of a hermeneutical principle I have developed: not every argument that Wittgenstein offers is an argument that he identifies with. To the contrary, many of the arguments he offers, particularly the "skeptical" arguments (and there are surprisingly many in his later writings) are ad hominem, directed against Wittgenstein's philosophical enemies in academia. They are meant to undermine academic philosophy from within. For example, the skeptical argument Kripke identifies in *PI*, which leads to the conclusion that no one ever means anything by any word, is not one that Wittgenstein could have, or intended to have, given. Academic philosophy however, leads to rank skepticism; it "self-destructs" from within.

Thus one could, apparently, defend Kripke by interpreting his infinity argument as ad hominem: not as one that Wittgenstein could identify with, but as one whose premises should be acceptable to the positions Wittgenstein intends to undermine.[24] There is thus no inconsistency if Wittgenstein himself should reject the principle that mathematical rules – as originally stated and, especially, learned – cover infinitely many cases. As soon as the number of cases gets too large to survey, the rule must be reinterpreted to make it surveyable.

Yet Kripke appears to attribute the principle that mathematical rules cover infinitely many cases not just to Wittgenstein's opponents but to Wittgenstein himself. In his discussion of Chomsky's "competence/performance" distinction, Kripke states:

I certainly do not mean, exegetically, to assert that Wittgenstein himself would reject the [competence/performance] distinction. But what *is*

---

doubtful that Wittgenstein himself held this position, and thus, to confuse matters even more, I think it is actually true that Wittgenstein held that rule-following is a kind of disposition. Wittgenstein explicitly compares understanding and other such phenomena to a disposition. I think that Wittgenstein's student, Friedrich Waismann, "betrayed" the master precisely on this point.

[24] This is how I would defend Kripke against the charge – often made against *WRF* – that he must be misunderstanding Wittgenstein if he attributes to Wittgenstein any kind of skepticism. Not Wittgenstein, but his opponents turn out to be committed to the total breakdown of language. Wittgenstein's writings are full of skeptical arguments, and these are meant to show only that academic philosophy self-destructs.

important here is that the notion of 'competence' is itself not a dispositional notion. It is normative, not descriptive, in the sense explained in
the text.[25]

Translating this comment into philosophy of mathematics, Kripke seems
to be saying that it is consistent with Wittgenstein's *actual* view (not just
with his polemics) that meaning addition by the symbol '+' means to
have the competence to add any two numbers, where competence is
meant as a normative notion, even though the performance of the individual calculator can fall short of the ideal competence.

But then "competence" turns out to be at least an infinite *norm*, which
is as objectionable to Wittgenstein as an infinite human disposition. The
reason is very simple. Arithmetic norms (that is, correct calculations or
theorems) are "hardened" regularities, as Wittgenstein himself puts it:

> The justification of the proposition $25 \times 25 = 625$ is, naturally, that if
> anyone has been trained in such-and-such a way, then under normal
> circumstances he gets 625 as the result of multiplying 25 by 25. But the
> arithmetical proposition does not assert that. It is so to speak an empirical
> proposition hardened into a rule. It stipulates that the rule has been fol-
> lowed only when that is the result of the multiplication. It is thus withdrawn
> from being checked by experience, but now serves as a paradigm for judg-
> ing experience.[26]

From this it follows that our norms, so to speak, can go no farther than
our regularities. In doing calculations with very large numbers, where
the regularities peter out on account of "nonsurveyability," our competence to multiply (understood even normatively) peters out with it.

My conclusion is that Kripke has attributed to Wittgenstein a position
that the latter could not have held – not polemically, and not in his own
name. I speculate that Kripke's deep-seated realism about, perhaps even
his respect for, mathematics created between the two great philosophers
a "communication gap."

Here is another example of a "communication gap." In *Naming
and Necessity* (Kripke 1980) (cited henceforth as *NN*), Kripke cited
Wittgenstein's assertion that the only object of which it can't be said that
it is a meter is the standard meter in Paris. To which Kripke objected, you
can at least say that it's 39.37 inches, so why can't you say it's a meter?

In fact, Wittgenstein dedicates a good deal of part VI of *RFM* to just this
example: the relation between the meter and the foot, which Wittgenstein

[25] Kripke 1982, pp. 30–1, n. 22.
[26] *RFM*, VI, 23, p. 325.

regards as exactly analogous to mathematical propositions.[27] In the metric system, what Wittgenstein is saying amounts to this: the conversion of units is, in effect, a rule for "correct" measuring, that is, a norm. This norm is based on a "hardened" regularity concerning what happens when we measure the standard meter with a footrule. The norm dictates that if we do not measure 1 meter as 39.37 inches (to the nearest hundred of an inch), we have made a mistake in measuring. Only once the norm has been laid down can we assert that the standard meter is a meter, on the basis of measuring it with a footrule. In the passage that Kripke cites (*PI* §50), Wittgenstein is speaking of the situation before this postulate. He doesn't go into the intricacies of his view, because in that passage he is using the standard meter as an illustration of another point.

Here the "communication gap" is again caused by Kripke's basic realism – here, realism concerning magnitudes (or, if you like, Wittgenstein's antirealism concerning magnitudes). Kripke simply assumes that "length" is something to be designated – rigidly – on a par with anything else that could be named. Wittgenstein, of course, thinks otherwise.

This insight into Kripke's underlying realism about magnitudes like length provides, incidentally, a solution to a question that has occurred to those who have had access to the Whitehead Lectures. The question is: if Kripke thinks that every change in the use of notation for numbers implies a change in the numbers themselves, does he then think that every change in the unit of length means a change in the magnitude we call length? Is "length in inches" a different magnitude from "length in centimeters"?

---

[27] For example:

Someone tells me: "this stretch is two hundred and forty inches long." I say: "that's twenty foot, so it's roughly seven paces," and now I have got an idea of the length. – The transformation is founded on arithmetical propositions and on the proposition that 12 inches = 1 foot.

No one will ordinarily see this last proposition as an empirical proposition. It is said to express a convention. But measuring would entirely lose its ordinary character if, for example, putting 12 bits each one inch long end to end didn't ordinarily yield a length which can in its turn be preserved in a special way.

Does this mean that I have to say that the proposition "12 inches = 1 foot" asserts all those things which give measuring its present point?

No. The proposition is grounded in a technique. And, if you like, also in the physical and psychological facts that make the technique possible. But it doesn't follow that its sense is to express these conditions. The opposite of that proposition, "twelve inches = one foot" does not say that rulers are not rigid enough or that we don't all count and calculate in the same way.

The proposition has the typical (but that doesn't mean simple) role of a rule. I can use the proposition "12 inches = 1 foot" to make a prediction; namely that twelve inch-long pieces of wood laid end to end will turn out to be of the same length as one piece measured in a different way (*RFM*, VI, §1, p. 355).

We see that the answer to this question is negative. There is only one magnitude called "length," variously measured. Length is real, an objective thing, independent of the notation we use to denote it. Numbers are conceptually dependent upon notation. Kripke is a realist concerning length, a "quasi-nominalist" concerning numbers. Wittgenstein is a realist concerning neither.

True, the concept of a buckstopping reference does exist for both numbers and magnitudes. For example, we can ask "How hot is that?" when we are told that the temperature outside is 36 degrees Fahrenheit and we are used to degrees Celsius. The difference is that, in the case of numbers, the numbers are those objects that share the structure of the buckstopping notation, or at least whose structure is revealed by that of the buckstopping notation. Length need not share the structure of the notation that denotes it. Kripke's remark about the standard meter in *NN*, therefore, is not one which could refute what Wittgenstein says about the standard meter, given Wittgenstein's antirealism about length.

Let us, however, return to the question of a person's "infinite competence" to add. I argued that, in *WPL*, Kripke attributed to Wittgenstein *at least* the view that "meaning addition by the symbol '+'" is a normative notion, and that the norm is an infinite norm. Given Wittgenstein's version of antirealism about norms, this is a serious misattribution. In the Whitehead Lectures presently under discussion, however, Kripke does penetrate the ideological wall separating him from Wittgenstein. It is hard to believe that the Kripke of the Whitehead Lectures could have attributed the views about "infinite dispositions" (or infinite norms) to Wittgenstein – tailoring, as he does in the Lectures, a calculator's competence to his performance.

It is interesting, though, to take note of what Kripke does *not* say in the WL. In the transcript I received, Kripke was asked (by the late Robert Nozick), after the first lecture, what very large numbers would be, taking into account the fact that a huge number in the decimal notation would not be a "buckstopper." Kripke promised to deal with the matter in the second lecture, but in fact all he said was:

> And the case mentioned already by Bob Nozick, you know, of some very long decimal string that we might then choose to express more perspicuously in another way, is a case of this. There is no notation for natural numbers that will be exempt from this. The advantage of the natural numbers is that this problem arises much later than it does arise for the stroke notation, the Frege-Russell numbers, where the problem sets in much quicker.

The Wittgensteinian thing to say here would be that the original concept of natural number is not preserved when we go into huge numbers.

Here we are not simply "expressing a decimal string more perspicuously in another way," but rather altering the very concept of a number as we get higher into the stratosphere. But this would have taken Kripke much further into Planet Wittgenstein than he wanted to go.

Works Cited

Benacerraf, Paul. 1965. What numbers could not be. *Philosophical Review* 74: 47–73.

Boolos, George. 1987. The consistency of Frege's *Foundations of Arithmetic.* In *On Being and Saying: Essays for Richard Cartwright,* edited by J. J. Thomson. Cambridge: MIT Press, 3–20.

    1998. *Logic, Logic, and Logic.* Cambridge: Harvard University Press.

Demopoulos, William, editor. 1995. *Frege's Philosophy of Mathematics.* Cambridge: Harvard University Press.

Frege, Gottlob. 1980. *The Foundations of Arithmetic: A Logico-mathematical Enquiry into the Concept of Number,* translated by J. L. Austin. Evanston, Ill.: Northwestern University Press.

Kielkopf, Charles F. 1970. Strict Finitism: An Examination of Ludwig Wittgenstein's Remarks on the Foundations of Mathematics. The Hague: Mouton.

Kripke, Saul. 1980. *Naming and Necessity.* Cambridge: Harvard University Press.

Kripke, Saul A. 1982. *Wittgenstein on Rules and Private Language.* Cambridge: Harvard University Press.

Malcolm, Norman. 1984. *Ludwig Wittgenstein: A Memoir.* 2nd ed. Oxford: Oxford University Press.

Morton, Adam, and Stephen P. Stich, editors. 1996. *Benacerraf and His Critics.* Oxford: Blackwell.

Steiner, Mark. 1975. *Mathematical Knowledge.* Ithaca and London: Cornell University Press.

    1996. Wittgenstein: Mathematics, regularities, rules. In *Benacerraf and His Critics,* edited by A. Morton and S. P. Stich. Oxford: Blackwell, 190–212.

Wittgenstein, Ludwig. 1968. *Philosophical Investigations,* translated by G. E. M. Anscombe. 3rd ed. Oxford: Basil Blackwell.

    1976. *Wittgenstein's Lectures on the Foundation of Mathematics.* Edited by C. Diamond. Ithaca: Cornell University Press.

    ed. 1978. *Remarks on the Foundations of Mathematics.* Edited by G. H. Von Wright, R. Rhees, and G. E. M. Anscombe. revised ed. Cambridge: MIT Press.

8

Kripke on the Incoherency of Adopting a Logic

Alan Berger

In 1974, Saul Kripke gave a graduate seminar at Princeton purportedly on Wittgenstein's *Philosophical Investigations*, with emphasis on the role of rules in Wittgenstein's private language argument. Before beginning this topic, Kripke said that he would first make a "few remarks" on a topic related to the central point of Wittgenstein's discussion of "rule-following," namely, the topic of "adopting a logic." Kripke chose to address some other related questions. They included his views on whether it is coherent to "have a logic" or for there to be an "alternative logic." He also concentrated on the more restrictive thesis of whether there is a nontrivial, "non–garden variety" way in which one can "revise logic." These "few remarks" took up the entire seminar, with many classes running more than one hour over the three hours allotted to each class.

In Section I, we discuss Kripke's general objections to the notion of adopting a logic. In Section II, we consider a part of logic that may be immune to these objections. In particular, we consider whether it is coherent to adopt "quantum logic." In Section III, we evaluate the claim of adopting intuitionist logic. Last, in Section IV, I suggest some morals to be learned.

Before discussing any specific arguments for or against any theses on the nature of logic, I should say that I, like Kripke, find the notion of "having a logic" or "adopting a logic" incoherent and, hence, having or adopting "an alternative logic" incoherent. But if one could make sense of people "having an alternative logic" to ours, then I believe that neither we nor they would understand each other, and all we could each do is pound our fists on the table and each insist that we are right. I take this to be a conclusion from one of Kripke's central claims that unlike a hypothesis, toward which we can be neutral and chose to adopt, one cannot be neutral toward "logic" and choose to adopt it.

I. LOGIC AS A SET OF STATEMENTS AND
LOGIC AS A FORMAL SYSTEM

Philosophers most associated with claims that we can adopt and revise our logic for empirical reasons are W. V. Quine and the Hilary Putnam of the late sixties and early seventies. Quine's general picture of the epistemic status of logic is that there is no sharp cleavage between logic and other domains of (empirical) scientific inquiry. Logic is just one of a variety of tools in organizing our experience. Logic is simply statements or hypotheses that we accept to account for experience. So far, classical logic, which is the logic that we have originally "adopted" just as we have adopted any statement or hypothesis, has well stood the test of experience. It of course should not be abandoned for trivial reasons, and it has been well confirmed, since by using classical logic we have been able to make a large number of predictions that are well justified. In response to recalcitrant experience, however, we could, in principle, choose to revise our logic rather than to revise something else like physics or geometry or any other statement or hypothesis that we accept, and perhaps someday experience will lead us to do so.

Quine states his general picture of knowledge in metaphoric terms in his classic essay "Two Dogmas of Empiricism" as follows: "total science is like a field of force whose boundary conditions are experience. A conflict with experience at the periphery occasions readjustments in the interior of the field. Truth values have to be redistributed over some of our statements. Re-evaluation of some statements entails re-evaluation of others, because of their logical interconnections – the logical laws being in turn simply certain further statements of the system, certain further elements of the field. Having re-evaluated one statement we must re-evaluate some others, which may be statements of logical connections themselves."[1]

Further, since Quine thinks that all elements of the field have empirical content, he says, "Any statement can be held true come what may, if we make drastic enough adjustments elsewhere in the system. Even a statement very close to the periphery (such as "there is a brick house on Elm Street" or "there are no centaurs") can be held true in the face of recalcitrant experience by pleading hallucination or by amending certain statements of the kind called logical laws."[2]

[1] See W. V. Quine, "Two Dogmas of Empiricism," in *From a Logical Point of View*, Cambridge: Harvard University Press, 1963, pp. 20–46, at p. 42.
[2] "Two Dogmas of Empiricism," p. 43.

The main issue Kripke chose to talk about first is whether logic is a set of statements, and not whether logic is revisable. In fact, Kripke certainly doesn't want to maintain that logic is unrevisable, because there are very trivial and simple senses in which there are "garden variety" ways in which logic can be revised. These two issues are independent. Someone might hold logical laws are revisable (in the nontrivial garden variety way, to be discussed below) even though they're not just "certain statements of the system," but then, Kripke maintains, one has to formulate things somewhat differently from the way they usually are.

Alternatively, someone could agree that logic consists in certain statements of the system, even if one thought they were a priori. Someone could think, for example, that, say, geometry or number theory was something we saw by some kind of intuitive self-evidence, but we just take the axioms of number theory as certain truths that we believe, only for a special kind of reason, and then use them to draw consequences, to organize our experience, and so on, just like an empirical hypothesis. So, regardless of whether the laws of logic are a priori or not, are they simply certain "further statements of the system, further elements of the field"?

In arguing against this view, Kripke cited several quotations from the literature. A typical one (quoted by Kripke) under the influence of Quine is an article by George Berry in the volume *Words and Objections.*

> The logical rule of universal instantiation, the Pythagorean theorem, and Newton's Law of Gravitation, display in ascending order various degrees of dependence on the world of sensory data. Yet these three are similar in that, although none confronts that world directly, each mediates between the so-called observation senses that do; witness the fact that each of the three principles may play its role in the single prediction of one observed position from others. Each such principle provides connective tissue invaluable in passing by inference or computation from observation to observation. Each is justified pragmatically, for each is tied up with observation by being part of the overreaching theory which is science as a whole.[3]

Thus according to Berry, the rules of logic and the laws of geometry, as well as the laws of physics, are all used in making predictions. We use logic in making deductions from hypotheses. For example, given Newton's Law of Universal Gravitation, "Two bodies attract each other

---

[3] See George Berry, "Logic with Platonism", in Donald Davidson and Jaakko Hintikka, eds., *Words and Objections: Essays on the Work of W. V. Quine*, New York: Humanities Press, 1970, pp. 243–77, at p. 246. Kripke also discussed Michael Gardner's paper, "Is Quantum Logic Really Logic?" *Philosophy of Science* 38 (4): 508–29.

with a force proportional to the product of their masses," we can then deduce that the Moon and Earth attract each other with a force proportional to the product of their masses only if we also use the Law of Universal Instantiation (UI, hereafter). So both UI and Newton's Law play, according to Berry, a role in making this prediction. I have to universally instantiate to get this particular conclusion.

Oversimplifying, the prediction turns out to be correct: The Earth and the Moon do turn out to attract each other in this way. Then one might say that both Newton's Law and UI have been well confirmed by this particular observation. Likewise, should the prediction turn out to be incorrect, according to this Quinean picture, we are free to make changes in UI, rather than in Newton's Law. But, of course, "Having re-evaluated one statement we must reevaluate some others, which may be statements logically connected with the first or may be the statements of logical connections themselves" ("Two Dogmas"). This is Berry's basic Quinean idea.

Before discussing anything further about this Quinean thesis, quotes from Quine such as the preceding one should give reason for pause, in my opinion, and one should be wary of them from the start. Where does the *must* come from? Why is it that "re-evaluation of some statements *entails* re-evaluation of others, *because of their logical interconnections*" (emphasis added)? What is the force of the *must* or *entails* here? To paraphrase Kripke, are we to assume a superlogic that transcends normal logic? And is this superlogic immune from revision? If not, then it seems to me that there is no force to the "must" or "entails" and hence no reason to make "suitable adjustments elsewhere."[4]

The central aspect of this picture that Kripke chose to discuss initially is whether we can say that the rule or the law of UI is a well-confirmed hypothesis when it leads to a correct prediction. For example, in order to deduce "this crow is black" from "all crows are black," we make the hypothesis that all crows are black *and* also make the hypothesis (or use the rule) of UI. From these two assumptions or hypotheses, we can then deduce that this particular crow is black. Then both the law that all crows are black *and* the law of UI are well confirmed. For it is part of this picture that the laws of logic are just "certain other statements of the system, like any other," *and* that we cannot deduce that this particular crow is black only from the law that all crows are black. Such an argument is an enthymematic argument, which requires the additional assumption of UI in order to complete it.

---

[4] Jerrold Katz, Saul Kripke, and I each raised this objection to Quine independently.

Along with criticizing the view that logic is a set of statements, Kripke also criticized the view that the notion of "adopting a logic" is a coherent one. It was prevalent in the literature then, and has become standard in the literature now, to talk about "adopting a logic." "If we adopt a certain logic, then we will get such and such a result." Proponents of this view, for example, Putnam of the late sixties, Michael Gardner, Michael Friedman, and others, use this kind of phrase practically as if it were a well-known technical term or a nontechnical term, in either case with a very clear sense. "The adoption of such a propositional logic blocks certain (empirically discovered) measurement paradoxes (in quantum mechanics)." It is part of the picture that we can adopt a logic and then see what paradoxes are or are not blocked. Presumably we have at a very primeval stage already adopted classical logic, but then we could choose to adopt another one. This terminology appears in Putnam's paper, "Is Logic Empirical?" where he states, "If we adopt quantum logic, then we will get this result," and so on.[5] In another paper of his, "The Analytic and the Synthetic," he says, "the adoption of intuitionist logic leads us to forswear certain types of reasoning which are classically valid."[6]

Kripke has never understood what it is to adopt a logic. Accordingly, he states that he can't say whether the adoption of quantum logic would or would not block certain measurement paradoxes because he never has felt there is such a thing as adopting a logic or that this even could ever be done. (We shall see why shortly.)

Three Applications of the Lewis Carroll Argument to Refute Three Related Claims

Accordingly, Kripke chose to discuss the Lewis Carroll article, "What the Tortoise Said to Achilles."[7] It is my view that we can distinguish three claims that Kripke's application of the central argument in this article refutes. First, that the logical laws are just other statements of the system. Kripke said to forget about whether they can be revised to meet recalcitrant experience, and to concentrate on the question of whether they are just statements of the system. Second, that the logical laws have fruitful consequences that

[5] Hilary Putnam, "Is Logic Empirical?" *Boston Studies in the Philosophy of Science*, vol. 5, eds. Robert S. Cohen and Marx W. Wartofsky (Dordrecht: D. Reidel, 1968), pp. 216–41.

[6] Hilary Putnam, "The Analytic and the Synthetic," *Minnesota Studies in the Philosophy of Science*, vol. 3, eds. Herbert Feigl and Grover Maxwell (Minneapolis: University of Minnesota Press, 1962), pp. 358–97.

[7] See Lewis Carroll, "What the Tortoise Said to Achilles," *Mind* 4 (1895): 278–80.

are well confirmed by experience. Third, that we can adopt a logic, and presumably, we have adopted classical logic. Accompanying this last claim is the picture that supposedly the classical logic system is inborn in us and that we could've adopted another system. But implicitly we adopted this one and then we are committed to drawing certain consequences from this adoption as long as we hold to it. Further, if we adopt a different logic, then we will no longer be committed to some of these same consequences and be committed to different ones. Kripke discussed these related claims specifically in connection with the law of UI.

The problem with the first claim was, ironically, well stated by Quine in "Carnap and Logical Truth"[8] when he argued against the linguistic doctrine of logical truth. Quine characterizes this view, held by logical positivists, as the view that logic is derived by some conventions for the use of language which we set up. Logical truths, in turn, are just *consequences* of these conventions. There he says:

> For it is impossible in principle, even in an ideal state, to get even the most elementary part of logic exclusively by the explicit application of conventions stated in advance. The difficulty is the vicious regress familiar from Lewis Carroll which I have elaborated elsewhere. Briefly the point is that the logical truths being infinite in number must be given by general conventions, rather than singly. And logic is needed then to begin with in the meta-theory in order to apply the general conventions to individual cases.

The point is that since the logical truths must be given by general conventions rather than singly, logic is then needed to begin with in advance of setting up these conventions in order to apply these general conventions to particular cases. Hence logic can't be identified with (the infinite class of) logical truths that are just "further statements of the field."

This still leaves open the possibility of the conventions being implicit, and thus avoiding this regress argument. I have argued elsewhere that Quine replies to this possibility by claiming that "in dropping the attributes of deliberateness and explicitness from the notion of linguistic convention, we risk depriving the latter of any explanatory force and reducing it to an idle label," which Quine spells out with his behavioral notion of "obviousness." I then go on to argue that this reply is inadequate in Quine's own terms.[9]

---

[8] W. V. Quine, "Carnap and Logical Truth," in *The Ways of Paradox and Other Essays*, revised edition, Cambridge: Harvard University Press, 1976, pp. 107–32.

[9] See Alan Berger, "A Central Problem in the Dispositional Account of Language and Logic," in Robert B. Barrett and Roger F. Gibson Jr., eds., *Perspectives on Quine*, Oxford: Blackwell, 1990, pp. 17–35.

But in any case, the Lewis Carroll argument shows that the second claim Kripke criticized – that the logical laws have fruitful consequences that are well confirmed by experience – is false. For, if we think of logical principles as systems of hypotheses or explicit conventions, they would be of no help to us in drawing conclusions. The problem is that, as in the objection to the first claim, we would need prior conventions or hypotheses in order to deduce anything from these "adopted hypotheses or conventions," and that leads to an infinite regress. Using an example of Kripke's, suppose we believe that everything is black, that is, $\forall x(Bx)$. According to Berry, this doesn't commit us to Ba (this crow is black.). We also have to believe in UI. This means that if UI were missing from our overall system of laws or conventions that we accept, we couldn't deduce Ba. According to this view, it is because one accepts, believes, or presupposes, in addition to '$\forall x(Bx)$', UI. Thus we can say the law UI is constantly being used, confirmed, and has fruitful consequences. That is, arguments as they stand are really enythememmatic, and they require logical statements to complete the argument and draw fruitful consequences.

Kripke holds that so regarded, UI is completely useless (that is, he denies the second claim). It has never led to any prediction whatsoever. For, so regarded, they lead to the above infinite regress. So it can't be said to be confirmed. Moreover, it cannot be said that we can adopt UI. Hence the third claim is also false. For it would have done us no good in drawing any consequences from its adoption. Kripke argues that logical rules can't rest on presuppositions, assumptions, or whatever else we think. Hence, we cannot "have" or "adopt" a different logic by rejecting these presuppositions or assumptions and "adopting" different ones. To illustrate why both these claims are false, consider the inference:

(1)   All things are black. ($\forall x(Bx)$)
Therefore, (2) The Eiffel Tower is black. (Be)

Does (2) follow from (1)? Kripke has us imagine someone who didn't accept UI, so, according to this Quinean holistic view, he can't conclude (2) from (1) alone. We tell him to adopt the law:

(1′) All universal statements imply all of their instances, so from $\forall x(Fx)$, it is valid to infer Ft, for any term t and any predicate F.

He accepts (1), but must he now acknowledge that (2) follows? It seems not. The person may say, "I accept (1′), but does *this* universal statement imply *this* instance?" This is as dubious as the original. (In fact, we now have to use UI twice, whereas before we only had to use it once.)

Kripke's general point here is that if we didn't already have the habit of inferring instances from universal statements, no amount of accepting or adopting additional laws, rules, or statements would help us. We cannot be neutral with respect to what follows from such a universal statement. Hence the third claim is also false. We cannot simply adopt a logic (viewed as a law, rule, hypothesis, or convention) and then be committed to drawing certain consequences from this adoption and, likewise, be committed to different consequences if we adopt a different logic.

Replies to Various Applications of the Infinite Regress Argument, Rejoinders to These Replies, and Kripke's Novel Application of the Infinite Regress Argument

What we have just seen, then, is that with some laws of logic one cannot draw any consequences unless one already uses the very pattern of inference one is supposed to be adopting. In response to this argument, some people may say that it shows the difference between rules of inference and axioms, and that both are needed. That is, it shows that any inference rule that we cannot "adopt" due to an infinite regress argument must be used as a rule of inference. But if that were so, the preceding argument with regard to UI would be wrong. For, there are formal systems with only modus ponens as a rule of inference. Besides, if a rule is needed, we could try to add it – "From every universal statement infer every instance." But if someone didn't accept that from (1), (2) follows, adding this rule would not help him.

Another reply to this argument might be that if someone doesn't follow this rule correctly, he doesn't understand us. Kripke does not want to commit himself on that, except to point out that if that is true, it also holds for the original inference, that is, he didn't understand (1). So again, if he cannot infer (2) before being given the laws or rules of logic, being given such laws will not help him.

Still another reply to Kripke's use of the infinite regress argument might be to argue that to "adopt a logic" is just to infer in accordance with certain rules. (I will say more about this when discussing Kripke's formulation of the infinite regress argument.) But Kripke rightly points out that this isn't something like adopting a hypothesis. It is true that inferences that accord with UI are made. But to say that this confirms UI (when the conclusions are true) is just to say that it is because we accept UI that these inferences are permissible. The above argument, which shows the futility of "adopting UI" if we didn't already have the habit of inferring in accordance with it, is unanswerable if one thinks that all laws of logic are just statements or elements in the field *required in order to draw any inferences.*

Another way of showing that the idea of "adopting a logic" is nonsense is by showing that, unlike scientific hypotheses, we cannot be neutral toward logic. This also ties in with a central problem with the view that to "adopt a logic" is just to infer in accordance with certain rules.

Kripke dramatically illustrated the problem with these two views by presenting his own version (or application) of Carroll's infinite regress argument. Consider someone who accepts the following inference rule of Perverse Instantiation: from $\forall x(Bx)$, infer $\sim B(t)$. That is, he infers "in accordance" with it. Maybe he doesn't say this, but we find him always reasoning according to this pattern, whether he says this or not. So he says, and you hear him reasoning, "All things are black. Therefore the Eiffel Tower is not black." Then he looks at it and he finds it not to be black. So he thinks that his hypothesis that all things are black is being well confirmed. Now suppose he says that he will be neutral and agree to accept any rule, principle, or statement that we give him. Thus we try to correct him. Accordingly, we tell him to accept the following rule or principle:

All inferences of the following form:
$\forall x(Bx)$
Therefore, $\sim Bt$

are fallacious.

Now you present him with a particular inference that he draws from Perverse Instantiation. Well, what does he conclude? He says, "I agree with the principle or rule you stated, and I always have agreed with you on this principle or rule. Therefore, this particular inference is not fallacious! And of course, the very inference by which I concluded that this inference is not fallacious is itself not fallacious by this principle, because it too is an inference of that pattern, so it too is not fallacious."

The problem is that since he didn't already have the habit of accepting inference patterns that we accept as according with UI, or the habit of accepting what we accept as following from universal statements, no amount of accepting or adopting additional laws, rules, or statements will help him. For we cannot be neutral toward what inference pattern we see accords with a given rule or law. This, in my opinion, illustrates the main objection to the view that to adopt a logic is simply to infer in accordance with certain rules. The point is that logic, even if one tried to reject intuition, cannot be just like any hypothesis because one cannot adopt logical laws as hypotheses and draw their consequences. You need logic in order to draw these consequences. There could be no neutral ground in which to discuss the drawing of consequences independently of logic itself. Now this is the basic point that Kripke wants to make.

Can We Change the Laws of Logic?

Kripke is not saying, however, that the laws of logic can never be changed. I believe that strictly speaking, Kripke should say that he doesn't know what that means because he doesn't know what it means to adopt a logic. We didn't set up the laws of logic that we have by fiat, convention, or experimental evidence to make empirical predictions. We recognize that certain principles of inference helped, but we did not adopt them. If we tried to adopt them, that would have done us no good.

Rather, what Kripke means by recognizing the possibility of changing the laws of logic is something that I describe as one of the two cases below. Kripke discussed four possibilities of what one could mean by a change in logic and rejected several of these "possibilities" as incoherent. In fact, it is my claim that all of Kripke's examples of legitimate "changes in logic" are simply one or both of these two cases, and further, that they are the only ways in which one can coherently make sense of a change in logic. I also maintain that, strictly speaking, it is a misnomer, or at best misleading, to call either of the following two cases a "change in logic."

The first case is a *trivial change of logic based upon our intuitive reasoning to correct a fallacy*. For short, I shall call it a *change in logic to correct a fallacy*. Once logicians have formulated what principles they believe hold in logic, they can sometimes turn out to be wrong. But they see why they were wrong because of an intuitive argument, not because a different formal system was proposed and then adopted, or we discover that the logical principle does not lead to fruitful predictions, or the like. The most famous case of this kind (which Kripke discussed) is the case of traditional Aristotelian logic, which permits the inference from "All As are Bs" to "Some As are Bs." What people initially didn't notice is that this inference is fallacious if one allows empty terms. That is, a "law of logic" was accepted for a number of centuries. Then it was later seen that this fails to be a law of logic, not because a new formal system was developed and someone said, "Let's adopt it," or that the principle did not lead to empirically fruitful consequences, but rather because *a mistake was noticed*, namely, of overlooking the possibility that A is empty. That was a famous case in which something that used to be universally accepted became widely thought to be false or fallacious due to presenting an intuitive a priori argument. Hence we no longer see this principle as expressing a law of logic.

So the first kind of change is based upon our intuitive ordinary reasoning that a mistake, or fallacy, was made in accepting a certain principle as a logical law. My own view is that this should not even be called a "change in logic" but rather a correction in what we believe to be a correct principle of a logical law. Clearly, this kind of "change in logic" neither undermines intuitive a priori reasoning nor constitutes an "alternative logic" and thus shouldn't undermine the notion of self-evidence. The fact that something can seem to be self-evident and later turn out to be wrong shouldn't undermine our using self-evidence as a principle of seeing that things are true any more than the fact that something may seem to be supported by experiment and then later turn out not to be so well supported by experiment should undermine our using support by experiment as a justification for accepting something. On the contrary, instead of undermining the notion of self-evidence, our justification for concluding that we were wrong about a particular principle being self-evident presupposes the very notion of intuitive a priori reasoning and self-evidence, and makes use of it to correct our fallacious mistake.

The second case I call a *trivial semantic change of logic*. Ironically, this view is well expressed and endorsed by Quine in his book *Philosophy of Logic*. In discussing "deviant logics" he states:

> The kind of deviation now to be considered … is a question of outright rejection of part of our logic [a set of truths] as not true at all. It would seem that such an idea of deviation in logic is absurd on the face of it. If sheer logic is not conclusive, what is? What higher tribunal could abrogate the logic of truth functions or of quantification?[10]

Quine's statement is certainly in the spirit of what Kripke (and I) accepts, unless, of course, as in the first case above, we are simply correcting a fallacy based upon our intuitive reasoning. Quine goes on to state a "popular extravaganza":

> what if someone were to reject the law of non-contradiction and so accept an occasional sentence and its negation both as true? An answer one hears is that this would vitiate all science. Any conjunction of the form 'P&~P' logically implies every sentence whatever; therefore acceptance of one sentence and its negation as true would commit us to accepting every sentence as true, and thus forfeiting all distinction between true and false.

[10] See Quine, *Philosophy of Logic*, p. 80–1.

> In answer to this answer, one hears that such a full-width trivialization could perhaps be staved off by making compensatory adjustments to block this indiscriminate deducibility of all sentences from an inconsistency. Perhaps, it is suggested, we can so rig our new logic that it will isolate its contradictions and contain them....
>
> My view of this dialogue is that neither party knows what he is talking about. They think they are talking about negation, '~', 'not'; but surely the notation ceased to be recognizable as negation when they took to regarding some conjunctions of the form 'P&~P' as true, and stopped regarding such sentences as implying all others.

The point that Quine is raising in the quotes above goes against his famous "Two Dogmas" view, where it is coherent to revise anything, even the laws of logic (and presumably, without changing the meaning of the words or the subject matter that the words express).[11] In the quotes, Quine maintains that it is incoherent simply to change the laws of logic and think that these revised laws can still govern the same logical connectives or quantifiers. His view here is that we are no longer talking about the same logical connectives and quantifiers. It shouldn't be either surprising or controversial that different concepts will satisfy different laws, and likewise that different connectives and quantifiers meaning something different from classical truth-functional connectives and classical quantifiers, respectively, will satisfy different laws of logic from these classical notions. Accordingly, these different concepts may well have different inferences as valid.

This mere trivial semantic change of logic, of course, as in the trivial change in logic to correct a fallacy based upon our reasoning, should also not be controversial. To quote Kripke, "One may always, of course, invent new connectives, which are similar in meaning to the old 'or' and 'and' or anyway similar in the laws they satisfy, but satisfy somewhat different laws because they have a somewhat different interpretation. That should be uncontroversial."

Quine concludes from his quotes above:

> Here, evidently, is the deviant logician's predicament: when he tries to deny the doctrine he only changes the subject.

This sums up the case that I am calling *trivial semantic change of logic.*

---

[11] Several people have raised this objection against Quine that what he says in *Philosophy of Logic* regarding "deviant logic" contradicts what he says in his famous "Two Dogmas" thesis. See, for example, Barry Stroud, "Conventionalism and the Indeterminacy of Translation," *Synthèse* 1968: 82–96 and my "Quine on 'Alternative Logics' and Verdict Tables," *Journal of Philosophy* 77 (1980): 259–77.

II. PUTNAM, QUANTUM LOGIC, AND "LOGIC" AS A FORMAL SYSTEM

We next consider whether there is a part of logic that may be immune to the infinite regress argument, and accordingly, may be revised or replaced by alternatives to it, and hence may be "adopted." In particular, we shall consider whether it is coherent to adopt quantum logic.

In his classic paper, "Is Logic Empirical?" Hilary Putnam argues that in quantum mechanics we "empirically discover" a paradox, and that in order to resolve this empirical paradox, and to defend realism in quantum mechanics, we must "adopt" a logic. Hence in solving this paradox, we are "adopting a logic" and doing so for empirical reasons. In particular, Putnam argues that we should "adopt" a logic that rejects the distributive law of logic, where by a logic, he means a formal system. This "logic," due to Birkhoff and von Neumann, is known as quantum logic.[12]

The Analogy of Alternative Logics to Non-Euclidean Geometry

To defend this thesis, Putnam compares adopting "quantum logic" to the adopting of non-Euclidean geometry in the general theory of relativity. He says that it seems to us to be perfectly self-evident that two lines both perpendicular to a common line cannot meet. But now in the general theory of relativity, we are told that this may be false since this theory makes use of Riemannian geometry where the claim, above, about two lines is false. Putnam thus argues that the intuitive feeling of contradiction that arises from contemplating two lines like this intersecting is no less and no greater than other apparent contradictions based upon the meaning of its words.

The analogy is supposed to be that just as we have rejected intuition or commonsense a priori reasoning once formal systems of alternative geometries are under consideration, as in the case of non-Euclidean geometry, once formal systems of alternative logics are under consideration, we may abandon any intuitive or commonsense preference for a particular system of logic. This analogy is supposed to apply to only that part of logic that is immune to the infinite regress argument.

---

[12] Hilary Putnam no longer defends quantum logic. Since this is so, it would be best to read the names "Birkhoff and von Neumann" for the name "Putnam," as they are the founders of this form of quantum logic and, unlike Putnam, they never renounced it.

Speaking for myself, it is not at all clear why according to this view one should trust our intuitions to preserve internal coherence and predictive power. If intuition is "thrown to the wind" then there should be no exception to throwing it to the winds.

Kripke holds to the following general remarks about such a reply to the regress objection to adopting a logic. First, such a reply doesn't really get the basic idea because Kripke doesn't really mean we have some basic ur-logic that we cannot adopt since the infinite regress argument applies to it, but the rest of logic may be adopted. Rather, Kripke's main point here is that you *can't undermine intuitive reasoning* in the case of logic and try to get everything on a much more rigorous basis. One has to just think not in terms of some formal set of postulates or postulates in a formal system, but think intuitively, that is, one has to reason. One can't just adopt a formal system independently of any reasoning about it, because if one tried to do so, one wouldn't understand the directions for setting up and deriving anything from the system itself. As Kripke says, in my opinion rightly, "One cannot reason by setting up a formal system and then deciding to reason within it because if one had no way of reasoning before, and tried to hold back in suspense one could not understand this alleged setting up of a formal system." Kripke called this the *formal system fallacy.* Thus any comparison of logic to geometry that says that in the case of logic, as in the supposed case of geometry, intuition can be given up, that is, reasoning outside the system of postulates can be given up, must be wrong. One can only reason as we always did independently of any special set of rules called logic in setting up a formal system or in doing anything else. And if proof by cases was part of our intuitive apparatus (as indeed it is in the case of the distributive law, as we shall shortly see), there is no analogy to geometry that says that this should not be respected. That is the first and really central point. Kripke is saying that one can't give up intuition and adopt a new way of reasoning. One can only reason intuitively, but that is to say, one can only reason first by reasoning.

The Situation in Quantum Mechanics that Motivates Putnam's Proposal

In classical (Newtonian) physics, if we consider a single particle system, we can represent its state by its position (three coordinates) and its momentum (three coordinates). In quantum mechanics, we require a more complex representation. A quantum mechanical state of a system is represented by a line in an infinite-dimensional Hilbert space. Following Putnam, we shall oversimplify, and instead of thinking of a Hilbert space $H(s)$ as a certain continuous infinite-dimensional vector space, we shall think of the space $H(s)$, as a three-dimensional real Hilbert space (that is, ordinary three-dimensional Cartesian space). We can formulate this in the standard way in which we set up three-dimensional space. Set up three axes and suppose they have a fixed origin. Then we can rotate them. Quantum mechanics postulates that what one knows about the state of a particle can be represented by a line through the origin, o. But even if we know that, we may not be certain what the result of a measurement will be. Suppose there are only three possible values, a, b, and c, that the position (quantity) of the particle may have. Then there are three possible states of the system: if it is in state 1, it has value a; state 2, value b; and state 3, value c. Then those three states are represented by lines perpendicular to each other. They are a possible set of axes for graphing the space. If the state of the system is represented by the x-axis, the value is a, the y-axis, b, and so on, and if we measure for this quantity, the result will be certain that the system will be represented by one of its axes, although we can't always tell in advance which one.

Suppose, now, that the measurement of another quantity of the particle, momentum, say, will also yield three such values, or three axes corresponding to them. This set of axes will be tilted at an angle with respect to the position axes. Now, if we make measurements on the system represented by a space whose axes correspond to the values of, say, position, then the result of measuring another quantity isn't given with certainty, but only with probability.

To keep things simple, let's suppose that two quantities, A and B, can have one of two values, 1 or 2. The principle of complementarity says that though one can be sure in advance that the measurement of quantity A will give the value 1 or 2, or that the measurement of another quantity B will give the value 1 or 2, you cannot measure both. Suppose you were to measure A and find that the value is 1 as a result of the measurement. Then you will be forever precluded by the experimental setup from measuring B. Most people in physics have concluded from this that you can't adopt a completely realistic interpretation of the quantities A and B. The measurement has called one value of A into existence, but the value would not be determined in advance, and if B was the one that was not measured, it never did have one of the values 1 or 2.

Now, one might try and express this formally by saying that you can't measure and get any of the four pairs of possible states (A = 1 and B = 1, or A = 1 and B = 2, and so on) because it is the measurement itself that throws one quantity into one of these states to obtain a value of 1 or 2; but we can't say of the other quantity not being measured whether its value is 1 or 2. It is the measurement of the quantity itself that throws that quantity into a definite state and hence determines its value. This is the standard Copenhagen view that most people in physics accept. Putnam thinks this is too Berkeleyan: values get called into existence by looking. Instead, Putnam wishes to be a realist. He wishes to say that every statement in quantum mechanics is true or false, and also that a definite value always existed in advance (prior to our measurements).

Putnam's Proposal

Accordingly, to be a realist in the sense stated above, Putnam wishes to assert that

1) A = 1 or A = 2, and
2) B = 1 or B = 2

were already true in their usual interpretation before a measurement was made so that the value of B was equal to 1 or the value of B was equal to 2. He also, though, wishes to assert (3), (4), (5), and (6):

3) It is not the case that A = 1 and B = 1.
4) It is not the case that A = 2 and B = 2.
5) It is not the case that A = 1 and B = 2.
6) It is not the case that A = 2 and B = 1.

That is, he wishes to exclude the value of A = 1 and B = 1, the value of A = 1 and B = 2, the value of A = 2 and B = 1, and the value of A = 2 and B = 2.

According to Putnam, then, these two numbers A and B can be such that (1) through (6) definitely hold. But he rightly points out that by normal intuitive reasoning, it is impossible for all six statements to hold. Putnam calls these statements logical truths; at the very least, they are supposed to be laws of physics (for reasons that we shall see later). Now, this set of statements Kripke calls Putnam's Hypothesis, and it is the heart of Putnam's paper to claim that these six statements hold simultaneously.

Kripke says that if one wanted to refute or argue against this hypothesis, one would argue against this by a standard proof by cases. Thus one would say that since A is equal to either 1 or 2, let's first suppose that A = 1. Now, B is equal to either 1 or 2. But, it can't be that B = 1 because of case 3. So we consider the other possibility that B = 2. But that is impossible by case 5. So since B = 1 or B = 2, the only thing that can be wrong is our hypothesis that A = 1. So A = 2. But, here again, you seem to get into the same trouble because if B = 1, that would contradict case 6, and if B = 2, that would contradict case 4. So therefore, this leads to a contradiction too, so A = 2 is ruled out. But that exhausts all the cases, so this hypothesis is refuted. Kripke maintains that this is as conclusive an argument as there could possibly be. But anyone who is attracted to Putnam's Hypothesis will say something like, "you are assuming the distributive law, and this is the very point which is at issue." And Kripke would say in reply, "I was not assuming anything called the distributive law. On the contrary, I deduced the contradiction from these premises alone, not from these premises plus something else called the distributive law."

The central point that Kripke is making is that there cannot be a better or more basic refutation of Putnam than to be able to use proof by cases, that if one says at least one of two things is true, one can see what would be the case if the first one of these things were true and what would be the case if the second one of these things would be true. But that is exactly what is being said when one holds to the first two statements of Putnam's Hypothesis.

Putnam's Formal System and Quantum Logic

Putnam refers to a formal system that he calls "quantum logic" (after the proposal of Birkhoff and von Neumann), which he says can "be read off from Hilbert space." By this he means first, that "Statements of the form $m(s) = r$ – 'magnitude m has the value r in the system S – are the sorts of statements we shall call *basic physical propositions* here."

Second, in *Quantum Mechanics*, "a certain infinite dimensional [Hilbert] vector space $H(s)$ is coordinated to each physical system S, and each basic physical proposition is coordinated to a subspace of the vector space." By a zero-dimensional subspace of a Hilbert space we mean the origin, 0. By a one-dimensional subspace, we mean any line passing through 0. By a two-dimensional subspace, we mean any plane passing through 0. Each basic physical proposition $m(s) = r$, where $m(s)$ is a 'nondegenerate' magnitude, is to be coordinated to, that is, corresponds to, a one-dimensional subspace, V_r, of the Hilbert vector space, and the one-dimensional subspaces V_r 'span' the whole space. As we shall soon see, every physical proposition is coordinated to a subspace of the Hilbert space.

If we assume, along with Putnam, that all physical magnitudes have finitely many values, and thus the space $H(s)$ would be just an ordinary finite dimensional vector space, then "To each number, r, which is a possible value of such a physical magnitude as position.... there corresponds a single *dimension* of the space $H(s)$ – i.e. V_r is simply a *straight line* in the space – and the lines V_r corresponding to all the possible values of, say, position form a possible coordinate system for the space.... If we change from one physical magnitude $m_1(s)$ to a different magnitude $m_2(s)$ (say, from *position* to *momentum*) then the new coordinates V'_r will be inclined at an angle to the old, and will not coincide with the old. But each possible momentum r will correspond to a straight line V'_r, though not to a straight line which coincides with any one of the lines V_r corresponding to a possible *position r*."

Last, the mapping is then extended to compound statements by the following rules. (Let $S(p)$ be the space corresponding to a proposition p.)

$S(p \vee q)$ = the *span* of the spaces $S(p)$ and $S(q)$ (the smallest space formed containing both subspaces, $S(p)$ and $S(q)$,

$S(pq)$ = the intersection of the spaces $S(p)$ and $S(q)$,

$S(\sim p)$ = the orthocomplement of $S(p)$.

In analogy with interpreting truth-functional connectives as set-theoretic operations, Putnam interprets a statement containing the above interpretation of the connectives as expressing a logical truth if the statement corresponds to the entire space $H(s)$. Thus, for example, if $r_1, \ldots, r_n$ are all the possible values of some (non-degenerate) magnitude, n is the number of dimensions of $H(s)$, and thus the statement:

$(m(s) = r_1) \vee (m(s) = r_2) \vee \ldots \vee (m(s) = r_n)$

(where m is the magnitude in question) is interpreted as always true. Putnam shows that given this reading of the connectives as operations on subspaces of a Hilbert space, intersection and union (span), the analogue of truth-functional conjunction and disjunction, fail to distribute.

As Kripke has pointed out, we should first note that there is a problem regarding Putnam's definition for his disjunction (union of two subspaces): it does not guarantee that we get something that is a subspace of a Hilbert space. In general, we get something bigger.

Before stating Kripke's main objection to the above way of introducing quantum logical connectives, let's see what proposition according to Putnam corresponds to 'A = 1 or A = 2'. One might think that it is the state of the system lies anywhere in the x-y plane. There is a justification for this. Quantum mechanics tells us that even if the state-line is on a diagonal, if we measure the system we will get the value 1 or 2. That is the reason for calling this the disjunction of the two statements – 'it lies on the x-axis' and 'it lies on the y-axis'. But Kripke points out that there is something odd about this. The intuitive motivation works (to some extent) for calling this disjunction when we have perpendicular axes, that is, two values of the same quantity. But if we try to extend this to the case of different quantities (m_1 is measurement of position, m_2 of momentum, say), for $m_1(s) = 1 \lor m_2(s) = 4$, where m_2 is represented by another set of three perpendicular axes at an angle to those for m_1, there is no similar motivation for using disjunction.

Even if we were to restrict ourselves to just one quantity, Kripke points out that there is something unnatural about Putnam's interpretation of the quantum logical statement 'A = 1 $\lor$ A = 2'. We would take this to say the state of the quantity A lies on the x-axis (for value = 1) or it lies on the y-axis (for value = 2). Putnam's proposal is, however, to consider any line in the plane to satisfy (A = 1) $\lor$ (A = 2). It is true that if we made a measurement it would give 1 or 2 as a value. Still, Putnam's proposal is counterintuitive, since were we to ask, "is A = 1 or A = 2?" Putnam would reply "yes" simply on the grounds that A is on a slanted line. Kripke maintains that the ideal situation for saying '(A = 1) $\lor$ (A = 2)' is when we've measured it (put it on the corresponding x- or y-axis) but forgotten its value: was it on the x-axis or the y-axis? Accordingly, Kripke accuses Putnam of equating "If a measurement is made it will definitely (that is, with certainty) give value 1 or if a measurement is made it will definitely give value 2" with "If a measurement is made it will definitely give value 1 or value 2."

Since Putnam's proposal is that the proposition corresponding to (A = 1) or (A = 2) is the state of the system lies anywhere in the x-y plane, and since we disagree, let us introduce a new symbol, $\lor$, to mean the span, as opposed to 'v', which we reserve for truth-functional disjunction. Accordingly, for Putnam, the proposition that the state of the system lies anywhere in the x-y plane corresponds to (A = 1) $\lor$ (A = 2), that is, the span of these two (axis) lines. From this it would, however, now follow that (A = 1) $\lor$ (A = 2) $\rightarrow$ (A = 1) $\lor$ (A = 2), but not conversely. (A = 1) $\lor$ (A = 2) can be true but ((A = 1 $\lor$ A = 2) & A = 1) can be false (indeed, even a logical impossibility, for it means the system lies on two different non-perpendicular lines). The lines intersect at one point and no system corresponds to a point. Similarly for $((A = 1 \vee A = 2)\ \&\ A = 2)$. This is the famous failure of the distributive law. This could be taken just as the failure of distribution of & over $\vee$, where $\vee$ is a new connective. This is no mystery and no change of logic. We get a mystery and a change only if Putnam insists that, appearances to the contrary, '$\vee$' is just '$\vee$', i.e., simply truth-functional disjunction. This could mean that $((A = 1) \vee (A = 2)) \leftrightarrow ((A = 1) \vee (A = 2))$. We think that is just false.

Alternatively, we could say that we don't know what 'or' means; we have to get along with '$\vee$' as best we can, wherever we would have used 'or'. But then, what about the case of the physicist who determines that $A = 1$ or $A = 2$, but forgets which? He knows it isn't on a slanted line. How can he say that?

Putnam's idea is to take '$\vee$' as representing 'or'. Then he can say the value of $A = 1$ or $= 2$ *before measurement.* In the old interpretation one had to say it was the measurement that brought a definite value into being. But as we said earlier, Putnam dislikes this as not realistic enough.

Kripke's main problem with Putnam's way of introducing quantum logical connectives is that it fails to be a genuine proposal. The problem with the analogy with truth-functional connectives read set-theoretically is that we have no clear way of interpreting what these connectives mean. For, given that the above interpretation of the connectives presupposes a Hilbert space and is supposed to represent operations on subspaces of a Hilbert space, we do not know how to understand the propositions allegedly expressed with quantum logical connectives. Recall that the whole point of introducing quantum logic is to put quantum mechanics on a sound foundation, making it paradox-free. But in fact, they presuppose a prior understanding of the apparatus used to develop quantum mechanics and Hilbert space – which was based upon fallacious reasoning using our old connectives (or a wrong law to which our connectives allegedly conform) where we reasoned in accordance with the distributive law of & over $\vee$.

But Putnam wants "the logic to be those principles which are valid in Hilbert space," that is, those things that, when we assign subspaces to Hilbert space, and when we adopt the new operations of interpretations of the connective, always come out true if it is the analogue of the set-theoretic interpretation of the classical connectives giving us the whole set. For example, in the classical case, to say that A or not-A holds with the set-theoretic interpretation of the operations is to say that a set union with its complement is always the whole set. Analogously, in the quantum logical case, with its new operations of "orthocomplement" and "span," $S(p \vee \sim p)$ will always come out as the whole Hilbert space. Likewise, the premise implies the conclusion of a quantum logical proposition if the subspace corresponding to the one is always contained in the subspace corresponding to the other. That's the picture.

Now, the main problem is that part of the specification is all based on classical mathematics, which uses classical logic, and that's what's supposed to be given up as false. We're not just supposed to be introducing new connectives. We're supposed to be discovering a mistake in the old classical logic (or a mistake in what laws govern our logical connectives). So, how are we to understand the specification? We first have to know what the Hilbert space based on this new logic is, and given that we understand that, perhaps we then can see what principles hold. But as Kripke rightly says, "it goes in circles because if I don't know what the new logic is, I don't know what will hold in the new kind of Hilbert Space." Kripke argued that if Putnam thinks that mathematics will remain undisturbed if we "adopt a new logic," as we shall now see, this is not so.

Kripke's "Proof" in Quantum Logic that $2 \times 2 \geq 5$

Kripke then went on to "prove" that in quantum logic $2 \times 2 \geq 5$. It should be first noted that Putnam has given only a system of propositional calculus specified in terms of his interpretation of classical Hilbert space (which is not an intuitive one), but he hasn't really gone much further. Consequently, we don't know how this will fit into a system of mathematics and physics. He really needs a much bigger formal system, and as I have tried to argue, Putnam has not given us an interpretation of this formal system that is independent of presupposing classical logic. Instead, we shall assume for the moment that we can just think purely syntactically; take this as a kind of provision to which Putnam appeals. Kripke says that we will play the following kind of game. We will accept the statements (1) through (6), which Putnam says are even logical truths. That is, when you interpret them in a funny Hilbert space interpretation, they all come out to correspond to the whole Hilbert space. Kripke will try never to use the distributive law in his reasoning in his proof of this "theorem." Since the distributive law is really proof by cases, that is, together with the fact that we can use not only A and B, we can say (letting 'B' be 'Q ∨ R'): Q or R is true: if Q were true, something would be true; if R were true, something would be true. We can't say this and use as the reasoning any other premise A. We can use only Q and R alone. That's the rejection of the distributive law. Still it is, even according to Putnam, permissible to use the premise P provided it is the logical law corresponding to the whole space. Otherwise, one can't use it if it is a mere empirical fact, like, say, that A = 1. Then the reasoning will be fallacious. So Kripke wants to accept all the standard stuff except the distributive law. Of course, Kripke doesn't know how this answers Putnam's intentions because Kripke doesn't know his intentions in the rest of mathematics; therefore, Kripke doesn't know which of several other options Putnam can make to avoid this particular "theorem." Nonetheless, Kripke argued that other such options would also be a very big revision of our ordinary mathematics. So we will use the above sense of theorem in proving that $2 \times 2 \geq 5$.

The usual notion that $2 \times 2 = 4$, when arithmetic is reduced to set theory, goes something like this. Suppose you have two sets with two elements. Then the cardinality of their product is the cardinality of the Cartesian product of the two sets, that is, the number of ordered pairs <x,y>, where x comes from the first set and y comes from the second set. We want to consider how many ordered pairs there are. Let's assume that both two-membered sets consist of {1,2}. So the classical arithmetician says there are four, namely, <1,1>, <2,1>, <1,2>, and <2,2>. But according to quantum logic, there is a fallacy in the conclusion that these are the only pairs. For, our reasoning was as follows: since x comes from the first set, either x = 1 or x = 2. Since y comes from the second set (which is the same as the first, in this case), either y = 1 or y = 2. Therefore, it is concluded that either (x = 1 and y = 1) or (x = 1 and y = 2) or (x = 2 and y = 1) or (x = 2 and y = 2). But this of course is a fallacy. That's the distributive law! Now, everyone will agree these are all ordered pairs in the Cartesian product: <1,1>, <1,2>, <2,1>, <2,2>. So we will not contest this. Now, Kripke claims that there is a fifth pair: <a,b> where these are the two quantities mentioned by Putnam. Putnam does not think that these are funny pseudonumbers, but actual numbers. The whole idea is that a was already definitely one of the numbers 1 or 2. And let's remember that when we measure, we find this one. We can't measure both. Since b was definitely one of the numbers 1 or 2 already, a is certainly in the first set, call it S_1 because a is either = 1 or = 2. And b is certainly in the second set because b is either = 1 or = 2. So <a,b> is in the Cartesian product. But certainly we do not say that <a,b> = <1,1> because that would mean that a = 1 and b = 1, and that's false by statement (3). So <a,b> does not = <1,1>. Similarly, <a,b> does not = <1, 2>,

<2, 1>, or <2, 2>, which is false according to statements (4), (5), and (6). So here is the "fifth" ordered pair in the Cartesian product of these two finite sets. So one can see that $2 \times 2 \geq 5$.

As we mentioned earlier, Kripke showed that several other ways in which quantum logic can be developed to avoid the above theorem also lead to very big revisions of our ordinary mathematics. So any claim that we can simply "read the logic off of the Hilbert space" is far from clear once we consider a Hilbert space that is developed by only allowing reasoning in accordance with quantum logic.

I shall end this section by simply remarking that Kripke also showed that if all we were presented with was a formal system, we would not be able to see what theorems, or anything else can be derived from this system. Kripke gave an analogous "proof" of this using a baby formal system. This should be obvious at this point, if one understands the problem of the perverse instantiator and the moral of this section: The Formal System Fallacy – One can't just adopt a formal system independently of any reasoning about it, because if one tried to do so, one wouldn't understand the directions for setting up the system itself.

To this one might reply, "Don't we have machines that can prove theorems in a given formal system without the need to reason? All it has to be is programmed." With this, Kripke (and I) surely agree. The mistake is to think that one has something independent of any reasoning. You just do this. But the problem as I see it, and as I believe Kripke sees it as well, is that it is the programmer who is reasoning to make sure a given machine may or may not be correctly programmed to follow out this formal system.

Further, what is it that gives us confidence that a machine is correctly set up to prove all and only theorems of a given formal system? Kripke has rightly pointed out that our confidence in the machine doing so is based upon: (a) a mathematical proof that any abstract Turing machine or program will do so, which uses both logic and mathematics; (b) a physical argument that this particular object is built up in such a physical way that it will behave like this Turing machine program, which depends on our belief in certain laws of physics; and (c) an engineering belief that in fact the machine is well set up so that it won't blow a fuse at this point. All of these are very special pieces of knowledge. And one cannot think that apart from any knowledge of these things one could have any confidence that this particular machine represents this particular formalism. As Kripke says, "It is a great illusion to think otherwise."

III. INTUITIONIST LOGIC, NEW CONNECTIVES, AND A NEW SUBJECT[13]

Unlike quantum logic, intuitionist logic is commonly given as the most standard example of a change in logic. Intuitionists have supposedly adopted a logic different from "the received one" and have based a whole different system of mathematics upon it, as well as having rejected classical mathematics. According to Kripke, the intuitionists did not really propose to modify the laws of logic for the classical connectives. Rather, they merely proposed to "adopt," or more appropriately *introduce,* new connectives, which satisfy different laws, and are more appropriate according to intuitionists for mathematics.

Regardless of the historical claim of what intuitionists proposed, Kripke maintained that there are four possible claims of what one means by a change in logic.

1. We could merely be introducing, or recognizing, a new set of connectives (which happen to obey laws similar to the connectives of classical logic).
These connectives may not be introduced by definition, but rather by explication. That is, you can define them in terms that we already have, and thus in some sense, these concepts are not really new. Alternatively, you can explicate them without literally defining them. Hence, in that sense, they may be new primitive notions. For example, when the concept of set is introduced in a class on set theory, one certainly can't pretend to define the notion. It would have to be a primitive in any system. Similar remarks apply to the notion of natural number when it is introduced in grammar school. Still, many people get the idea even without prior familiarity with set theory (or number theory). This is Kripke's view of intuitionist logic.

2. We could be introducing new connectives and repudiating our old connectives as meaningless. This has two forms.
A) SYNTACTIC, OR "AXIOMATIC," PRESENTATION OF THE NEW SYSTEM OF LOGIC.
Here, we just introduce a language purely syntactically, or an uninterpreted axiomatic, or formal, system, and given something called "formation rules," we are to define something we call "grammatical strings,"

---

[13] Due to the length of this chapter, and the fact that another chapter in this volume is partially devoted to the semantics of intuitionist logic, this section is brief. At a later time, I hope to develop further my thoughts on this topic.

and then we define which strings are going to be called "axioms" and which will be called "inference rules." We are then told that if we write down a bunch of these marks without saying anything about what they mean (beyond the labels), it is somehow supposed to make sense to us to be told to believe all the axioms and all the conclusions that follow from them by means of these inference rules. It is not at all clear how we can say what this means. Even declaring that the axioms are true has no meaning beyond putting a check mark next to the axiom. Since no one has told us what any of this means, Kripke says that it seems hard for him to say what it means to call these strings true unless one is in some sense given a semantics for this system that has said what all this means, not just what we will call 'axioms' and 'inference rules'.

According to Kripke, this is what Quine has in mind. Quine says[14] that people have tried to explain what the intuitionist connectives mean, but he doesn't understand what they could mean. For him, instead, one should just look at the formal system presented by intuitionists. But Kripke maintains that if you only look at the formal system, then you really can't tell whether these connectives mean the same as the old ones because no one has explained or given you the slightest idea of what they mean or some other kind of explanation, as in the case of sets or natural numbers.

My own view is that this is a bit too narrow a reading of Quine. Rather, what Quine has in mind is that we assume when we are presented with a formal system that we know what is meant by "formation rules," "axioms," "inference rules," and perhaps even "truth." Then, once you change the laws of logic, that is, the axioms of a formal system, whatever connectives these new axioms govern, by fiat or definition, so to speak, gives us all there is to the meaning of these connectives. There is no further explanation relevant for Quine to explain the meaning of the connectives. Recall, his slogan is, "Change in logic [laws or axioms], change in subject." Since the laws or axioms determine the meaning of the new connectives, Quine's holism prevents him from saying which if any of the connectives are the same as the old ones since they were governed by different laws. In fact, they have to be different connectives because they obey different laws. Then he adds that by definition, that means that they are new connectives. We repudiate the old connectives in the sense that allegedly there's nothing satisfying the laws supposedly satisfied by the old connectives.

---

[14] See Quine, *Philosophy of Logic*, pp. 83–5.

Given my reading of Quine, Kripke is right to point out that even restricting ourselves to interpreting the new connectives as being governed by laws expressed in a given axiom system does not guarantee a unique interpretation of the new connectives. There can be several nonstandard connectives that satisfy even classical logic, but intuitively mean something different. Hence, we need more than satisfying a set of axioms as an explanation of the new connectives. Intuitively, we would need the kind of explanation needed for introducing or recognizing a new set of connectives, as discussed above.

In fact, it has been shown, mainly by Gödel, how one can translate all of classical logic into intuitionistic logic and all of classical number theory into intuitionistic number theory. Kripke rightly concludes from this that since some intuitionistic connectives mean something different from classical connectives, merely satisfying the same laws of logic (or the axioms of a formal system) does not guarantee the same logical connectives. By presenting a more complicated translation of the connectives than what Quine calls a homophonic one, that is, saying "'and' means and, 'or' means or," and so on, Gödel was able to define this translation.[15] Gödel, commenting on some of these translations, says that his theorem "shows that the intuitionistic arithmetic and number theory is only apparently narrower than the classical. In fact, it includes the entire classical number theory, merely with a somewhat different interpretation. However, for the intuitionists, this interpretation is the essential thing."

This shows that if we took a purely syntactical view, we wouldn't repudiate anything, at least for all these languages, since there is a purely syntactic translation of classical number theory into intuitionist number theory, and even a classical tautology could be translated as valid in intuitionist logic, that is, into a subsystem of an intuitionistic formal system of the propositional logic. Of course, the intuitionist would say that this mere syntactic translation does not preserve the way we interpret the mathematical statements and our connectives, and that is exactly what is lost by this method. According to the intuitionist, sentences using classical connectives do not express propositions about the domain of mathematical objects, which is what sentences using their connectives

---

[15] See S. C. Kleene, *Introduction to Metamathematics*, New York: van Nostrand, 1952, section 81, "Reductions of Classical to Intuitionistic Systems." See also Kurt Gödel, *Collected Works*, vol. 1: *Publications 1929–1936*, eds. Soloman Feferman, John W. Dawson Jr., Stephen C. Kleene, Gregory H. Moore, and Robert M. Solovay, Oxford: Oxford University Press, 1986, "On Intuitionistic Arithmetic and Number Theory", pp. 287–95.

are about. So the point is that one can have nonstandard interpretations of the classical connectives that preserve some syntactical translation but fail to capture any intended interpretation of the connectives. Hence any slogan along the lines of "same laws, same connectives" or "different laws, different connectives" cannot make sense since we often can have a nonstandard interpretation of connectives that are governed by the same laws. Thus the same laws do not guarantee the same connectives and different laws do not guarantee different connectives.

B) SEMANTIC INTERPRETATION OF THE SYMBOLS. The symbols have been explained and the old connectives are repudiated as meaningless. According to Kripke, it is the fact that intuitionists have an interesting interpretation of their new connectives that leads them to develop a new discipline, such as intuitionistic number theory, and historically the Heyting formal system came later. So despite what Quine says, intuitionism is not merely the introduction of new laws or an axiom system, with the interpretation for the connectives of the new system following afterward.

Kripke has argued that accepting these new connectives is not an objection to accepting the old connectives as well. Further, this is the view held by Kreisel, probably Gödel, and Kleene, as well as Kripke.

3) We could claim to have discovered a definite fallacy.
This view was discussed in Section I of this chapter. My only additional comment regarding this view is that intuitionists claimed the logical paradoxes are due to a certain view of the infinite in set theory. Whether this is true, at best, it can be seen only as an a priori argument, based upon our ordinary garden variety reasoning, and thus cannot be viewed as something undermining our notion of self-evidence.

4) We could claim that we mean what we always meant by a certain connective, but we now have discovered that new laws apply to the connective.
According to Kripke, this is really basically the same view as the view discussed earlier, that we are introducing new connectives and repudiating our old connectives as meaningless, except we are claiming that we still mean what we always meant as long as the new laws differ by only "small enough" changes from the laws that we used to accept. This is Putnam's view discussed in the previous section. The real problem, Kripke states, is not whether the new connectives mean the same as the old ones, but whether there's anything in the new language satisfying the same laws as

the old. I presume that Kripke means that the real problem is not only whether there's anything in the new language satisfying the same laws as in the old language, but also whether it has the same intuitive interpretation as our old connectives did.

Intuitionistic Arithmetic and the Meaning of Intuitionistic Connectives

In classical mathematics, if we want to know if a number exists that has a certain property, we permit the following sort of reasoning: assume that every number fails to have the property, that is, $(x)\sim P(x)$, and then show that this assumption, $(x)\sim P(x)$, is false. From this, classical mathematicians conclude that some number has the given property, that is, $(\exists x)P(x)$. Also, classical mathematicians allow the following form of reasoning: assume A, and then show that A is false; from this, conclude that $\sim A$ is true. Both of these forms of reasoning are not permitted in intuitionistic mathematics. Now, the reason that intuitionists reject this form of reasoning is because they maintain that the proper subject matter of mathematics is mental mathematical construction. Accordingly, Kripke maintains that for the intuitionist mathematician, a mathematical statement 'A' really means something about mental mathematical construction:

'A' *means* I have performed a mental construction (proof) that A.

Since for the intuitionists, the proper study of mathematics is mental construction, simple classical negation of A, that is, $\sim A$, would be an uninteresting statement, namely, that I have not performed such a construction, they treat negation as any other of their operators as a special type of mental construction. Accordingly, Kripke proposed the following interpretations of their negation, conditional, and universal quantifier (Kripke maintains that intuitionists mean the same as classicists for the other connectives):

'$\neg$A' *means* I have performed a mental construction (proof) that A is absurd (that is, leads to a contradiction), (where '$\neg$' is intuitionistic negation).

Although the classical conditional, 'A $\rightarrow$ B' is defined as '$\sim$A $\vee$ B', the intuitionist conditional cannot be so defined. Instead, for the intuitionistic conditional:

'A $\rightarrow$ B' *means* I have effected a hypothetical construction that given a proof of A, I have given a proof of B.

Similarly, for the intuitionistic universal quantifier:

'($\forall$x)P' *means* that a general method of construction can be given such that this construction, applied to any x, yields a proof of the quantified statement. (The method of construction is not allowed to depend on limitations in our ability to consider numbers to which the construction is applied.)

Kripke maintains that the intuitionistic existential quantifier is really the same as the classical one, except the range of objects is restricted to mental entities, so '$\exists$x' means I have an object in mind. On the other hand, '$\exists$x' is allowed when I have a definite method for finding an object but have not actually carried it through. For example, consider:

($\forall$x)($\exists$y)(x < y & P(y)) (There are infinitely many primes.)

The statement asserts that given an x, I can find a y such that.... In any particular case, I may not have found the prime y greater than x, but I have a definite method from Euclid for finding it.

Kripke concludes from this that since the intuitionists mean something different from classicists regarding three of their connectives, and since intuitionists regard the proper subject matter of mathematics to be about mental mathematical construction, their mathematical propositions do not mean the same as classicists. Neither logicians are committing a fallacy. Rather, intuitionists have simply created a new discipline. As such, there is no inconsistency in maintaining both. As I said earlier, this is the view held by Kreisel, probably Gödel, and Kleene, as well as Kripke. It is a true case of Quine's dictum, "Change in logic[al connectives], change of subject."

My own view regarding intuitionistic logic is slightly different from Kripke's. As I said earlier, intuitionistic mathematical propositions don't mean the same as classical mathematical propositions, and their quantifiers don't range over the same kind of entities as that of classical mathematics. We said, for example, that for the intuitionist, a mathematical sentence, 'A' *means* there is a construction (proof) that A, and each connective is about a particular mathematical construction.

Now, my concern is the following. Is the intuitionists' view about the subject matter of mathematics a thesis, that is, a theory that all arithmetical statements just mean something about our mental constructions, or a stipulation that this is how they intend to use mathematical propositions?

If it is the former, then there is, indeed, a disagreement between classical mathematicians and intuitionists since an intuitionist would have to say, 'A' is true iff I have performed a mental construction (that is, formed a proof) of A. Accordingly, the intuitionist would have to say that if there isn't a construction (proof) of A or of 'not A', then neither A nor 'not A' is true (or they can say that they are both false until someone performs a construction of one of these ['A' or 'not A']), whereas classical mathematicians would say that the disjunction is true, but we just don't know which disjunct is true, and hence the intuitionists are committing a fallacy. Also, it would mean that intuitionists have a problem stating, "Either one has constructed a proof of A or one hasn't constructed a proof of A." For intuitionists, although this would not be expressible in the domain of mathematics, it seems that they would still have to acknowledge a need for classical negation as well as intuitionistic negation in order to make such statements.

But the disagreement would then be not over "can I adopt one logic over another?" but whether one of us is making a mistake as to what an arithmetical proposition means and, accordingly, whether one of us is committing a fallacy, in the sense of a fallacy in Aristotelian logic.

If, on the other hand, intuitionists are merely making a proposal, that is, a stipulation, that the subject matter of mathematics *should* be about mental mathematical construction, then, of course, the two can be made compatible. They are merely different disciplines, and it is no surprise that they may require different connectives to express their subject matter. Indeed, in that case, intuitionism would be a paradigm case for Quine's slogan that a change in logic is merely a change of subject.

IV. GENERAL MORALS

One moral is this: Kripke showed that we don't know what adopting an uninterpreted formal system means until we interpret it. Second, and related, if logic is up for grabs, then even what's provable in the given formalism is up for grabs. How can we possibly begin to deliberate about a formal system when we just don't know what its theorems are independently of reasoning about it? For there is no "Archimedean point" in the notion of a formal system, from which we can choose to set up, adopt, or reject at will, and then tailor our logic to it. As Kripke has been urging, "One has to first use reasoning in order to even see what is provable in a formal system." One reasons about them using the same reasoning that one always did. If we give them an interpretation, we can reason about them the way we always reason, and it is Kripke's main point that we have no other reason. Using our ordinary reasoning, we can check whether they are sound and complete. In quantum logic we saw that if we try to interpret the "quantum logical" connectives as 'or', 'and', and 'not', the propositional logic will be incomplete in that it will lack the distributive law, which holds for these connectives. If one tries to say, "You have an opposing logic. You can't use it in thinking about this, try and do without it, and think about these things", one will fail and not even know what formal systems one is comparing.

But Kripke's main point is this: "There aren't different logics. There is only logic. There are different formal systems." We use logic to reason about them to see if a new formal system has an interesting interpretation that may have sound principles of logic. But we can't adopt it. Using our ordinary reasoning, we can try and prove that a formal system has sound principles, and perhaps even complete principles for some domain of connectives. There may be laws, and new connectives that we haven't thought about before, and new laws that apply to them. In some noncontroversial sense we might call this "introducing a new logic," but only in a trivial and uninteresting sense.

We may also discover, in an a priori manner, that something thought of for centuries as a sound principle of logic was actually based on a fallacy. This is not because we are "adopting a new logic," but because we look at the old formal system and see that it wasn't really sound with respect to its informal interpretation, and that the "proof" we had that it was sound was fallacious. This is what happened in the case of the Aristotelian syllogism, and for all we know there are other such proofs that we make that contain a fallacy. But this should no more count against the notion of self-evidence or apriority than the fact that something may seem to be supported by experiment, and then later turn out not to be so well supported by experiment, should undermine our using *support by experiment* as a justification for accepting something.

Clearly a "proof" that we can't adopt a logic or that this notion is incoherent would require a proof by cases, and Kripke can only discuss cases that have been proposed in the literature. I believe that Kripke has succeeded in dealing with these cases. In the absence of any clear and successful sense of what "adopting a logic" could mean, the burden is on those who find the notion coherent.

PART III

LANGUAGE AND MIND

9

Kripke's Puzzle about Belief

Mark Richard

1

You are, of course, familiar with the story of Pierre. Raised in France, he acquires the name 'Londres' as a name of London. He accepts, in French of course, many claims about the city – elle est grande, jolie, dans Angleterre, and so on, and so forth.[1] Spirited away to England, confined to an unpleasant part of London, forced to learn the language by speaking to the natives, he acquires 'London' as a name of London. He accepts, in English of course, many claims about the city – it is large, not at all pretty, in England, and so on, and so forth. He does not recognize that the city he is in is the city, Londres, of which he learned in France. He remembers, and continues to accept in French, all the claims he learned in France about Londres – qu'elle est grande, jolie, dans Angleterre, and so on.

Pierre's experience in France warrants our saying that he believed that London is pretty. That, and the fact that he doesn't seem to have changed his mind about what he learned in France, warrants our saying that he still believes that. Pierre's experience in England warrants our saying that he believes that London is not pretty. This, Kripke claims, leads to

[1] When I say that someone x accepts the claim that p in a particular language, I mean roughly that: there's a sentence S of the language that, used by x, says that p; x is related to S in a way that warrants saying that he understands it; and (because x takes the sentence to be true) he has a belief that he could express by uttering S. Thus, for example, the text tells us that Pierre's relations to his language warrant us in thinking that he understands the French sentence 'Londres est grande, jolie, et dans Angleterre' and, because he accepts this sentence as true, believes what he would say by uttering it.

This usage means that the inference *Pierre accepts the claim that London is pretty; so, Pierre believes that London is pretty* is not trivial. Obviously, the validity of the inference is closely related to the validity of the disquotational principle discussed herein.

a puzzle: "Does Pierre, or does he not believe that London is pretty? It is clear that our normal criteria for the attribution of belief lead, when applied to *this* question, to paradoxes and contradictions."[2]

How so? Why not say that poor Pierre has contradictory beliefs – that he believes that London is pretty and that London is not pretty? The short answer is that Pierre is (to be supposed to be) rational and reflective. So if Pierre has these beliefs, we have a case of a rational and reflective person who has contradictory beliefs. But this is impossible: "surely any-one … is in principle in a position to notice and correct contradictory beliefs if he has them. Precisely for this reason, we regard individuals who contradict themselves as subject to greater censure than those who merely have false beliefs" (122).

It does indeed seem that we cannot imagine a sane person under-standing and sincerely uttering a sentence of the form

(A)   b is such and such, although b (the very same b) is also not such and such.

No sane person would think of the world in this way. And this sug-gests that we cannot imagine a sane person having beliefs that he would ascribe to himself with a sentence such as (A). Call such a situation – in which someone *does* have such beliefs, and has them because he thinks of the world in the way in which someone who would sincerely utter (A) thinks of it – a case of contradictory belief.[3]

Call a use of a sentence of the form

(B)   a believes that b is such and such, and a believes that b is not such and such

in which we do not capitalize on any ambiguity or contextual shiftiness in *b* or *such and such* a case of ascribing inconsistent beliefs.[4] One thinks that to ascribe inconsistent beliefs is to imply that the ascribee has contradictory beliefs. And if this is so – if saying that Pierre believes that London is pretty

---

[2] Saul Kripke, "A Puzzle about Belief," in N. Salmon and S. Soames, eds., *Propositions and Attitudes* (Oxford: Oxford University Press, 1988), p. 124. Subsequent references are indicated parenthetically. Kripke's paper originally appeared in *Meaning and Use*, ed. A. Margalit (Dordrecht: Reidel, 1979), pp. 239–83.

[3] Perhaps you are wondering what exactly is meant by saying that someone thinks of things in *the* way in which someone who would sincerely utter (A) thinks of it. If you are, try to go with the flow until Section 3.

[4] Note that here and in the following, 'a has contradictory beliefs' and '[in uttering (B) we are saying that] a has inconsistent beliefs' are used in the quasi-technical senses just assigned to them.

and he believes that it is not pretty implies that Pierre has contradictory beliefs – then Kripke is right: our normal criteria for ascribing belief lead to trouble in the case of Pierre. For a rational person could be in a situation like Pierre's. Indeed, rational people often *are* in such situations.[5] So there are possible – indeed actual – situations in which our normal criteria for ascribing belief lead us to say (things that imply) that there are cases in which rational people have contradictory beliefs. But we think it's impossible that a rational person should have such beliefs.

2

Why should we care about Pierre? Kripke suggests that the way the puzzle about Pierre arises casts doubt on a standard argument against "Millianism," the view that the semantic role of a proper name is exhausted by its being a name of whatever it names.

Millianism seems to imply that names of one thing have the same semantic role; thus, it seems that (setting aside quotation and other contexts where a name's shape or sound is invoked) if we accept Millianism, we must accept a principle of substitutivity:

> (S) If one sentence comes from another by replacing a proper name with a coreferential one, then (provided the sentences are relativized to the same context, and the names are not being quoted or the like) the sentences don't differ in truth value.

A familiar objection to Millianism seizes on this apparent consequence of the view: Surely, the objection goes, someone rational could believe that, say, Twain wrote *Huck Finn* and that Clemens did not. If so, and (S) is true, a rational person could believe that Twain wrote the book and believe that Twain didn't.[6] So a rational person could have contradictory beliefs. But a rational person can't have such beliefs. So Millianism is false.

---

[5] David Sosa, for example, tells us (in "The Import of Kripke's Puzzle about Belief," *Philosophical Review* 105, 1996, p. 384) that for some time he didn't realize that John Glenn the astronaut was the same person as John Glenn the senator.

   Here and below I assume that (B) ascribes inconsistent beliefs iff the result of replacing the second occurrence of 'b' therein with a pronoun anaphoric on the first 'b' does; I also assume that if (B) implies that someone has contradictory beliefs, such a variant does as well.

[6] Of course the argument here relies on going back and forth, from an ascription of belief to an ascription of truth to such an ascription; such back and forth is taken to be justified by the obviousness of things like *Pierre believes that London is pretty iff 'Pierre believes that London is pretty' is true in English* ('English' here understood as naming the language of the sentence in which it occurs).

What's the connection with the puzzle about Pierre? Kripke's idea is that what justifies us in thinking that someone might believe that Twain wrote the book and that Clemens did not is *au fond* the same set of principles – those which govern our ascriptions of belief and other propositional attitudes – that justify us in thinking that Pierre believes that London is pretty and that London is not pretty. So those principles all by themselves – quite apart from appeal to Millianism or a principle such as (S) – lead to the conclusion that a rational person might have contradictory beliefs. So it seems somewhat precipitate to object to Millianism in the way just rehearsed. For either we must reject the principles that underwrite the claim that someone might think Twain wrote a book but Clemens did not, or we must renounce our conviction that rational people can't have contradictory beliefs.[7] Either way, the objection to Millianism is undermined.

3

As we are using "contradictory beliefs," one has them when one believes of something that it is so and so, believes of it that it is not so and so, and has these beliefs because one thinks of the world in the way in which someone who accepts a sentence of the form *a is F and a (the very same a) is not F* thinks of it. I know that you would like an account of what I mean by "thinks of the world in the way in which someone who accepts sentence S" does. I know that I would like to give you an account. Sadly, I can't find one. At least I can't find one that will be neutral among all the views of belief and its objects which you, gentle readers, hold.

We could, of course, make things somewhat clearer if we adopted one or another of these views. A Fregean can cash out the notion of contradictory belief in terms of the "constituent senses" in the objects of the contradictory beliefs. Russell could have done something similar in terms of "propositional constituents." Someone who thinks that propositional attitudes are realized by "representations," and that such representations can be typed both semantically and in terms of properties that the thinker is sensitive to (so that we can speak of different token representations as being of "computationally identical" types), can cash the notion out in those terms. It is noteworthy that Frege, Russell, and the representationalist would all

---

[7] Or we must say that the truth of a sentence like (B) – that is, the truth of an ascription of inconsistent beliefs – doesn't imply that anyone has contradictory beliefs. See the next section.

say that a thinker is sensitive to the identity and distinctness of the ways of thinking involved in her beliefs. Frege seemed to think that when names have the same sense for a speaker, he accepts an identity involving them; Russell's idea that we are acquainted with propositional constituents of our thoughts is apparently supposed to guarantee something like this; something similar is true of "synonymy in the language of thought."

Probably no particular precisification of the notion of a way of thinking is uniquely determined by our pretheoretic commitments about belief and other attitudes. But there *is* a commonsense notion of contradictory belief; there *is* commonsense talk of people thinking of objects in similar and dissimilar ways. And it is, I think, plausible to think that the first notion is to be explicated, as I have tried to explicate it, in terms of the second. If we take Kripke to have something like this notion in mind when he writes "surely anyone ... is in principle in a position to notice and correct contradictory beliefs if he has them," then I think we must agree with him; and, I think, we must agree that such beliefs are a mark of irrationality. For having contradictory beliefs is a matter of being (relevantly like) someone who is disposed to sincerely think to himself 'this is F and this (very same thing) is not F'. Since we can become aware of and evaluate such occurrent mental states, since a rational person is disposed to retract beliefs when he is aware of their impossibility, and since those who understand something with a meaning like that of the form *a is F and (the very same) a is not F* are aware of its impossibility, someone who has contradictory beliefs is indeed in a position to become aware of them and correct them.

Do all who believe that Paris is pretty and that Paris is not pretty have contradictory beliefs?

One wants to tie belief in language users fairly closely to assent. Suppose that Jones understands the sentences he utters, that he is not given to deceiving others, and that he is not suffering from self-deception or kindred pathology. Then if he or we ask him 'S?', and after reflection he assents, surely he believes what he or we say, when we utter the sentence S. Kripke's version of this principle – one of the above-mentioned principles governing attitude ascription – is the principle of disquotation

(D)   If a normal English speaker, on reflection, sincerely assents to 'p', then he believes that p.

This is a schema, 'p' to be replaced inside and outside of quotes with a sentence which "is to lack indexical or pronominal devices or ambiguities" (113). If we accept (D), we will also accept its analogues in other languages.[8]

Now, tense and the contextual shiftiness of 'pretty' set to the side as irrelevant, neither 'London is not pretty' nor 'Londres est jolie' appears ambiguous or context-sensitive in their languages. So given (D), it would appear that

(C1) Pierre believes that London is not pretty

(C2) Pierre croit que Londres est jolie

are true in their respective languages. The truth of (C1) in English implies that, indeed, Pierre believes that London is not pretty. And even a C+ student in second-semester French can tell you what (C2) means – it means what 'Pierre believes that London is pretty' means – that is, that Pierre believes that London is pretty. But sentences that, in their respective languages, mean the same thing can't differ in truth value in those languages. As Kripke puts it, we accept a principle of translation:

> (T) If a sentence of one language expresses a truth in that language, then any translation of it into any other language also expresses a truth (in that language). (114)

So, by appeal to what every mediocre student of French knows, Pierre believes that Paris is pretty.

So the answer to our question seems to be "no": Someone like Pierre who believes that London is pretty and that London is not pretty need not have contradictory beliefs. Pierre, after all, does *not* have contradictory beliefs. He has, after all, no disposition whatsoever to assent to a sentence of the form *a is F, and a – the very same a – is not F*. He does not think of the world in the way that someone who has such dispositions thinks of it. Though he is French, he is not crazy.

---

[8] Kripke also discusses a strengthened version of (D), in which assent to 'p' is said to imply and be implied by belief that p. Relatively little is made of this principle in Kripke's essay and very little will be made of it here. It will be clear by the end of this discussion that I think that the stronger principle is false. Anyone who thinks that we may believe what a sentence says although our understanding of the sentence is "imperfect" (in the way that, for example, the understanding of the sentence 'I have arthritis' in Tyler Burge's well-known example is imperfect) will be inclined to dismiss Kripke's strengthened principle. (This is because (a) one can believe what is said by sentences one only imperfectly understands, and (b) one could apparently have imperfect understanding of synonymous sentences which led one to reject one but not the other.) The example by Burge appears in "Individualism and the Mental," in P. A. French, T. E. Uehling, Jr., and H. K. Wettstein, eds. *Midwest Studies in Philosophy IV* (Minneapolis: University of Minnesota Press, 1979), pp. 73–121.

4

One feels something has gone seriously awry. If we accept the argument just given, we will conclude that Pierre believes that London is pretty and (that he believes that) London is not pretty. How can we then *not* say that Pierre has contradictory beliefs? Commonsense tells us that someone who believes that London is pretty and (that it) is not pretty is deranged. Surely Pierre's irrationality is implied by saying that he so believes. Since he is not irrational, there must be something wrong with (D) or (T), or our translations from Pierre's idiom into ours, or in some unmentioned bridge principle carrying us from the story of Pierre and these premises to the contrary conclusion.

It will help, in trying to determine whether we have gone off the rails, if we return to speaking of "the way in which someone thinks of the world" when they believe this or that. However we choose to make sense of this notion, we will surely take ways of thinking of the world to be "made up" of ways of thinking of the things that make the world up, as well as ways of thinking of the properties and relations these things have and bear. We will thus be able to talk about constituent relations amongst ways of thinking, as well as saying such things as: When a thinks that b is F and c thinks that b is G, they think of b in the same way, though when d thinks that b is F, he thinks of b in some other way. In particular, we will be able to say things like:

(E1) In thinking that London is pretty (as he does when he says 'Londres est jolie'), Pierre thinks of London in the same way as he does when (saying 'London is not pretty') he thinks that London is not pretty.

(E2) In thinking that London is pretty (as he does when he says 'Londres est jolie'), Pierre thinks of London in a different way than he does when (saying 'London is not pretty') he thinks that London is not pretty.

Presumably, Pierre is irrational only if something along the lines of (E1) is true.

The suggestion is that our notion of contradictory belief as something irrational (irrational, in part, because it is something that a responsible and reflective thinker can be aware of as a matter of course) presupposes that when one has a belief (or other propositional attitude) with a particular content, associated with the belief are "ways of thinking" of the objects and properties the belief is about; these ways of thinking determine, or at least reflect, the thinker's "access to the content of the belief." By this I mean (for example) that if A's beliefs that b is F and that b is G involve the same way of thinking about b, then A takes those beliefs to present a single individual as being F and G. If all this is so, then whether a belief is irrational will be (in large part) determined by the ways of thinking it involves. After all, if (E1) were true, then given what we just said about ways of thinking, Pierre takes those beliefs to present a single individual as both pretty and not pretty. But part of rationality is being disposed to withdraw at least some of any set of beliefs with this property.

The suggestion, then, is that the irrationality of a belief is a matter of relations among the ways of thinking involved in the belief. In particular, the irrationality of a belief one would self-ascribe with a sentence of the form of (A) is a matter of its involving thinking of an individual *with a single way of thinking* as both having and lacking a property. Suppose that the suggestion is correct. And now suppose further that when we ascribe beliefs and use an expression e several times, reoccurrence of e in the ascription implies identity of ways of thinking involved in the attitudes ascribed. Suppose, for example, that if we say *Pierre believes that London is blah blah, and that London is blee blee*, we imply that there is a way of thinking of London such that, thinking of London in that way, Pierre thinks that it is both blah blah and blee blee. Then an ascription of inconsistent beliefs *does* indeed imply that the ascribee has contradictory beliefs.

We began this section wondering how to reconcile our feeling – that to say that Pierre believes that London is pretty and that it is not pretty *is* to imply that he has contradictory beliefs – with the observations that belief ascription seems to be governed by (D) and (T), and that if a practice is so governed then to say that Pierre believes that London is pretty and that it is not pretty *is not* to imply that he has contradictory beliefs. We have in effect offered an explanation of the first mentioned feeling, by linking the notion of contradictory belief to the notion of a way of thinking, and by saying that our practice of ascribing beliefs is governed by a principle along the lines of

(R)   Multiple occurrences of an expression within ascriptions of attitude to a single person indicate that the attitudes involve multiple occurrences of a single way of thinking in the attitudes ascribed.

Given that (D), (T), our ordinary practices of translation, and (R) govern our practices of ascribing attitudes, and given that our notion of contradictory belief reflects the ideas about ways of thinking and irrationality just sketched, we have an explanation of both our feeling that Pierre must have contradictory beliefs, and our feeling that, obviously, he does not.

The explanation is, of course, only as good as our evidence for (R). It seems to me that it is not hard to garner evidence for this principle. Consider, for example, explanations of behavior by ascription of attitudes, such as

(F)   Mary hit Twain because she wanted to humiliate him, and she thought that if she hit him, she would humiliate him.

We take these to be potentially explanatory. Notably, we do not have the same attitude towards ascriptions in which different names of a single individual occur. While, for example, we find (F) or

(F′)   Mary hit Twain because she wanted to humiliate Twain, and she thought that if she hit Twain, she would humiliate Twain

to be explanatory without supplement, we do not feel that way about

(F″)   Mary hit Twain because she wanted to humiliate Twain, and she thought that if she hit Clemens, she would humiliate Clemens.

What, after all, if Mary didn't know that Twain was Clemens? (F″) as an explanation is just bizarre without supplement. (R) provides the basis of an explanation of both why (F′) should be explanatory, as well as why (F″) needs supplementation before it is explanatory.[9]

5

With studied vagueness, I have said that (D), (T), and (R) "govern" our practices of ascribing attitudes. But what does that mean? Are (D) and (T) supposed to be true, full stop, so that it is true, full stop, that Pierre believes that London is pretty and that it is not? Or are they rules which tell us something about when we are, ceteris paribus, warranted in saying that someone has a certain belief? For that matter, what exactly is (R) supposed to mean? Is "indicate" in (R) to be understood as involving some semantical rule, or some defeasible pragmatic signal?

What can be said in favor of the thought that (D) and (T) (with (T) informed by our normal practices of translation) are true, full stop? Well, they *do* have the air of trivialities. One way to come to believe something is by considering its verbal expression and, understanding what one is doing, assenting to it. If Pierre asks himself, having been in England for three years, "Is this place ugly?" and looking around, says with disgust, "Sure is," what good reason can be given for saying that he is not expressing what

⁹ For further discussion of these issues, see my "Propositional Attitude Ascriptions," in M. Devitt and R. Hanley, eds., *The Blackwell Guide to Philosophy of Language* (Malden, Mass: Blackwell, 2006).

he thinks? And how, if he understands what he is saying, can he not be expressing the claim that London is ugly? As for (T), it apparently follows from the absolutely trivial claims that (a) translation preserves meaning, and (b) meaning determines truth (that is, sentences which mean the same thing must have the same truth values).[10]

What can be said against (D)? The most likely objection to (D) is that it combines a relatively benign idea about belief with controversial – some would say obnoxious – ideas about language identity. What, it might be asked, is the import of the phrase "normal English speaker" in (D)? Are we to suppose that there is some one language all of us "English speakers" speak? That is, are we to suppose that there is some one set of syntactic, phonetic, and semantic principles that correctly describe "the" language being spoken by everyone who has (say) received passing grades in American high school English? Chomsky tells us that to think this is to confuse politics and linguistics.[11]

Certainly it is true that the syntactic and phonetic description of my language will be different from the description of the language of others, assuming that such description is supposed to generate the sentences I produce when I am not tired, misspeaking, being linguistically creative, and so on. After all, you say toe-may-toe, and I say toe-ma-toe. Suppose we allow that this shows that language is idiosyncratic, so that strictly speaking no two people speak the same language. Once we allow that when Pierre is "speaking English" he may not be speaking a language with the same semantics as the language in which we speak when we formulate (D), (D) seems either implausible or too weak to yield the conclusions it is supposed to yield. For suppose that Pierre's spoken language – PL, call it – is not the same as my spoken language – call it ML. How are we to understand an instance of (D) such as

(D1)   If Pierre, on reflection, sincerely assents to 'London is not pretty', then he believes that London is not pretty?

---

[10] Of course meaning doesn't determine truth simpliciter. 'I am sad' in English means the same as 'je suis triste' in French, but while the first is false when I use it, the second is true when Pierre uses it. The correct principle is *something* along the lines of *sentences with the same meaning taken relative to the same (or relevantly similar) context(s) have the same truth value*. Since we are supposed to be concerned only with expressions that aren't context-sensitive, such as 'London', Kripke presumably thought it was acceptable to simplify the principle of translation.

I return to the issues raised in this note in the last sections of this discussion.

[11] This claim appears repeatedly in Chomsky's writings. See, for example, *Rules and Representations* (New York: Columbia University Press, 1980), pp. 117–20.

If I utter (D1), my utterance is an utterance of a sentence of my language, ML. But both ML and PL contain a sentence that looks like 'London is not pretty'. Which one does (D1)'s quotation name name? That is, should we understand (D1) as

(D1.1) If Pierre, on reflection, sincerely assents to the PL sentence 'London is not pretty', then he believes that London is not pretty,

or as

(D1.2) If Pierre, on reflection, sincerely assents to the ML sentence 'London is not pretty', then he believes that London is not pretty?

We have, it might be argued, no reason to think that (D1.1) is true. Since ML and PL are different languages, 'London is not pretty' may mean different things in them. When Pierre sincerely assents to 'London is pretty' he is, we may assume, expressing a belief in what this string says in PL. But since the string may mean one thing in PL and another in ML, this fact doesn't give us reason to think that Pierre believes that London is not pretty – that is, it doesn't give us reason to think that the ML predicate 'believes that London is not pretty' is true of Pierre. On the other hand, it is not clear what to make of Pierre's assent to the ML sentence 'London is not pretty'. Presumably he has not made the theoretical judgment that his language and my language are distinct, so it has not even occurred to him that he is assenting to something that is not a sentence of his language. He may, when he assents, be indicating belief, but there is no reason to think that he is indicating belief in what the relevant string says in *my* language. After all, he understands the utterance as he understands his own utterances. So once again, we have no reason to think that the principle is true.

So I imagine someone objecting to (D). Note that someone who so objects to (D) need not be objecting to the idea that assent indicates belief. Indeed, we can imagine someone who objects to (D) in this way allowing that certain "first-person variants" of (D) are perfectly acceptable. What I have in mind is something along the lines of

(D2) Pierre's uses (in the language he speaks in London) of 'If I, Pierre, on reflection, sincerely assent to 'p', where 'p' is a sentence of my language, then I, Pierre, believe that p' are true in the language Pierre speaks in London.

This, like (D), is a schema in which 'p' is to be replaced by a nonambiguous, non-contextually sensitive sentence. Given that Pierre's language has a disquotational truth predicate and a normal logic, it follows that if Pierre assents, on reflection, to 'London is not pretty', then Pierre can, speaking his London language, say truthfully

(P)   I, Pierre, believe that London is not pretty.

French analogues of (D2) establish that Pierre can, speaking his Parisian language, say truthfully

(P')   Je, Pierre, crois que Londres est jolie.

We can use (T) and our normal practices of translation to go on to derive the conclusions that Kripke finds so puzzling.

Whether we accept the Chomskyean objection to (D) or not – I will take that objection up in the next section – the derivation of Kripke's puzzle just sketched is worth contemplating. For instances of schemata like (D2) certainly do seem plausible. What (D2) captures is the idea that *whatever it is that Pierre is saying, when he sincerely assents to a sentence of his language, it is something he believes.* It is hard to see how this idea could fail to be correct. And as just indicated, it seems that we need only it, our usual practices of translation (including our practice of homophonic "translation"), and (T) to generate the conclusion that Pierre believes that London is pretty and that it is not pretty. If we think this conclusion cannot be correct, it seems, we must lay the blame at the feet of (T) or our practices of translation.

6

It is easy to see why someone might be moved to say that phonetics and syntax differ enough to make it implausible that we English speakers all speak a single language. That doesn't imply that our normal practices of translation (including our practice of homophonic translation) don't preserve meaning.

We think we all *mean* the same by 'London is pretty'; we think that the way to *translate* any normal French speaker's use of 'Londres est jolie' is with 'London is pretty'. Why? Well, the fact is that we understand one another, and our translating the French in the conventional way allows us to understand them. By saying that we understand each other, I mean (roughly) that we are able to make sense of each other's verbal behavior (in the context of each other's behavior as a whole), and we do this in a nonaccidental way (that is, if interpreter and interpretee proceed in the ways they have been proceeding, our understanding will continue). It is hard to see this understanding as not based in the presupposition that (ambiguity and context sensitivity to the side, and speaking now schematically and for myself) when you utter 'p', you are saying p. These facts – that we undeniably understand one another, and that our understanding seems to be grounded in the assumption that we say the same things with our sentences – provide one route to the idea that we mean the same thing with these sentences. And of course this idea underwrites the idea that our sentences homophonically translate each other.[12]

One might respond by pointing out – correctly – that we have very different concepts of the things to which we refer. Often, our concepts are different enough that – save for the fact that we label them with the same public language word – we would never think that they were concepts of the same thing or property. And this, the response concludes, shows that we can't really mean the same thing by our words.

It is hard – for me, at least – to take this response seriously. If successful linguistic interpretation can (and often does) proceed despite the fact that very different mental structures are associated with our words, that simply shows that those mental structures do not have to be identical (or even very much the same) in order for us to successfully interpret. And since we understand one another when we successfully (and non-accidently) interpret each other, this shows that the mental structures in question need not be very much the same in order for us to understand each other. As I see it, nonaccidental homophonic interpretation is a sign that interpreter and interpretee mean the same things by their words. What more evidence could we possibly demand?

Now, the argument I have been giving could well be taken as an argument for an analogue of Kripke's disquotational principle (D):

(N)   If a normal English speaker, on reflection, sincerely (and without irony) utters 'p', then he (sincerely) says that p.[13]

The argument is, put simply, that using (N) allows us to make sense of each other; it wouldn't do so if it weren't true. It is noteworthy that a perfectly similar argument seems to be possible for (D). After all, to make sense of one another requires knowing not just what we say, but what we think. And we determine this, in good part, by interpreting one

---

[12] Some of a Davidsonian bent would say that the facts – that we make sense of each other, that we do this by translating homophonically – simply entail that we mean the same thing by our sentences; there is, they would say, nothing more to same-meaning. Others who yet like to visit the museum on a Sunday afternoon see no entailment here. We can sidestep this dispute. For only a jejune skeptic would say, in the face of our ability to make sense of each other, that we do not understand each other.

[13] (N) is, of course, subject to the same sort of caveats concerning substitutends for 'p' as is (D). It requires other caveats for cases in which sincere, nonironic speech is not assertive, which I won't try to formulate.

another's speech and (assuming that the speech is sincere) ascribing belief in what is said. That is, we assume

(O)   If a normal English speaker sincerely says p, he believes that p.

(N) and (O), nearly enough, entail (D).

I will return, at the end of this essay, to the status of principles such as (N), (O), and (D).

7

Let us take stock. We have isolated a sense of "contradictory belief" in which no rational person has contradictory beliefs. We have observed that we have reason to think that our ordinary practices of translation preserve meaning. We have noted that the principle (T) Kripke invokes, to the effect that translation preserves truth, seems absolutely banal. And we have observed that (a) our reasons for thinking that our ordinary practices of translation preserve meaning are in fact reasons for accepting Kripke's disquotation principle (D), and (b) even if we reject (D), far weaker and seemingly undeniable principles are sufficient, once the other things just mentioned are in place, for deriving the conclusion that Pierre believes that London is pretty and that it is not pretty.

It is beginning to look as if what we should do is understand (R) in such a way that while

(G)   Pierre believes that London is pretty and that it is not pretty

implies that Pierre has contradictory beliefs, the implication falls short of entailment. We are familiar enough with the idea that we may imply something without actually saying it. One conclusion to draw from Kripke's essay is that (G) does not entail that Pierre is irrational. If we do draw this conclusion, we may well go on to conclude that the semantics of attitude ascription is Millian through and through.

Some have drawn these conclusions; some have contested them.[14] I don't propose to rehearse past arguments. I will observe that the last conclusion – implying as it does that if Mary believes that Twain wrote *1609*, she believes that Clemens wrote it – is somewhat fantastic.

---

[14] Keith Donnellan is an example of someone who reads Kripke as providing a good argument for Millianism; see "Belief and the Identity of Reference," in P. A. French, T. E. Uehling, and H. K. Wettstein, eds., *Midwest Studies in Philosophy XIV* (Minneapolis: University of Minnesota Press, 1989). Sosa, "The Import of Kripke's Puzzle about Belief," resists the conclusion.

It is fantastic because it is so at variance with our understanding of our talk about our attitudes. We presuppose that the syntax of the content sentences of attitude ascriptions reflects properties of the mental states ascribed. We assume, for example, that if Mary believes that if p, then q, and she wants q, she has some inclination to make it the case that p; it goes without saying that if Marty thinks that if p, then q, but is pretty sure that it's not the case that q, he will be pretty sure that it isn't the case that p, either.[15] We not only assume that the attitudes are (Freudian and such forces set to the side) under rational control and are motivational; we also assume that our way of ascribing them invokes the properties that make the attitudes subject to rational review and motivational. The properties we are invoking in such ascriptions, if the semantics of those ascriptions are Millian through and through, are *not* properties in virtue of which the attitudes are motivational or transparent to reason.[16] What is in my opinion completely fantastic in the thought that attitude ascriptions have a Millian semantics is the idea that the meaning of talk about the attitudes could be this far out of whack with its purpose and use. Only someone in the grip of a philosophical theory could think that what we mean and what we do with our words was *this* disconnected.

This leaves us with the intermediate conclusion, that (R) is to be understood so that (G) does not *entail* that Pierre's beliefs are contradictory. If we accept this conclusion – and by the end of the essay, we shall – we need some explanation of how we can draw this conclusion but avoid drawing a Millian conclusion from the puzzle about Pierre.

8

One reaction to Kripke's essay – a reaction that the last few sections may tend to reinforce – is that Kripke has uncovered a genuine puzzle; but it is really a puzzle about belief *ascription*, not a puzzle about *belief*. The puzzle just posed – how can (G) be true if Pierre doesn't have contradictory beliefs? – is a puzzle about our talk about Pierre. And, in any case, it might be said, it is clear enough what Pierre believes: He believes that London – that is, the city of which he heard in France, called 'Londres' – is pretty, and that London – that is, the city in which he currently finds himself, whose inhabitants call it 'London' – is not pretty. What is puzzling is not what Pierre believes (which is perfectly consistent), but how

---

[15] Kripke emphasizes this in discussing the puzzle at p. 122.
[16] Argument for this claim can be found in my "Propositional Attitude Ascriptions."

to say what he believes in the idiom for belief ascription provided by English, if we limit ourselves to identifying the object of his beliefs with the name 'London'.[17]

Kripke anticipates this reaction towards the end of "A Puzzle about Belief." According to Kripke, one can't get rid of the puzzle simply by saying that Pierre associates different identifying properties with 'London' and 'Londres' (and thus his beliefs are "really" consistent), since "the puzzle can arise even if Pierre associates exactly the same identifying properties with both names" (125). After all, Pierre might "define" 'Londres' as 'la capitale d'Angleterre' and "define" 'London' as 'the capital of England'. If he did, and we individuate his beliefs in terms of the objects, properties, and relations they are about, we will conclude that he expresses exactly the same belief with 'London is pretty' as he does with 'Londres est jolie'.

One way to put Kripke's point is this. If Pierre "associates the same identifying properties" with the names, then the way he thinks of London when he speaks French is *the same* as the way he thinks of it when he speaks English. And this is quite puzzling apart from any issue about how we might ascribe Pierre's beliefs: How can Pierre be rational, if thinking of London in one way (as England's capital) he thinks it pretty, while thinking of it in the *same way* he thinks it not pretty?

It will be objected that if Pierre "defines" the names in this way, he must associate different properties with the English and French names of Britain.[18] But why is this? We come to know individuals "under guises," and can fail to recognize an individual from encounter to encounter because we do not take the guises under which he appears to be guises

---

[17] There is a family of proposals along these lines. The simplest ones insist that all belief (or all belief save that about the self, or save that about the self and the present moment) is descriptive. Others take the modal profile of all beliefs (or all beliefs save those about the self, or save those about the self and the present moment) to be explained in terms of David Lewis's counterpart relations. Natural ways of fleshing *this* out render Pierre's "French beliefs" consistent with his "English beliefs" because different counterpart relations are used to interpret Pierre's "French thought" and his "English thought." (Something like this is suggested in Lewis's "What Puzzling Pierre Does Not Believe," in Lewis, *Papers in Metaphysics and Epistemology* (Cambridge: Cambridge University Press, 1999), 408–17. Lewis's own proposal is complicated by the suggestion that there are two ways to interpret someone, "narrowly" (using a counterpart relation) and "widely".)

What follows is meant to be responsive to all such proposals. (In the case of Lewis's proposal, let me add somewhat cryptically that the primary problem with it is that it is inconsistent with the idea that what motivates us has the semantics of the language in which we report what motivates us – it is, if you like, inconsistent with the idea that what we say is what we think.)

[18] Thus Sosa at p. 397.

of one individual. Why shouldn't this be true of properties and relations as well? One might respond that properties and relations are different: if being F just is being G, one just *can't* know what it is to be F, know what it is to be G, but mistakenly think that being F isn't being G.

This seems desperate. It requires us to find meanings for 'capital of England' and 'capitale d'Angleterre' as used by Pierre that characterize the city in terms of different properties. Are we to suppose that Pierre's utterance of 'Londres est jolie' means something along the lines of *the capital of the country the French call 'Angleterre' is pretty* or *the capital of the country my countymen call 'Angleterre,' is pretty*? Then we are being asked to simply reject all the lessons about the modal profile of a sentence involving names that we learned on reading *Naming and Necessity*. Are we supposed to divorce what our sentences mean from the beliefs we express with them, saying with Russell that (since we must have an intimate epistemic relation to something before we can have a belief about it) there is a judgment about London that we should like to make (one which is expressed by our sentence 'London is pretty'!), but cannot, because when we try to make it, we are "necessarily defeated, since the actual [London] is unknown to us"?[19] As Kripke observes, saying this leads to saying that no two people (or person at different times) mean the same thing – at least, express the same beliefs – with their sentences.[20] As Stephen Schiffer once said, "believe it if you can."

If one thinks of a way of thinking as something to be identified with, or at least individuated in terms of, a collection of objects, properties, and relations, the puzzles Kripke presents us with are indeed difficult to solve. If one thinks of thought in the way that Russell did, it is hard to know how else to think of a way of thinking. A – perhaps the – standard way of thinking of Frege's notion of the sense of a name thinks of senses in this way.[21] The proper conclusion to draw, it seems to me, is that what I have been calling ways of thinking are not to be individuated (simply) in terms of objects, properties, and relations. Whether two expressions

---

[19] "Knowledge by Acquaintance and Knowledge by Description," most easily accessible in Salmon and Soames, *Propositions and Attitudes*, p. 22.

[20] Sosa, who thinks that Pierre's uses of 'Londres' and 'London' must have different meanings, seems prepared to endorse this conclusion in Sosa, "The Import of Kripke's Puzzle about Belief," p. 398.

[21] This understanding arises, I think, because of Frege's habit of using different codesignating descriptions to provide examples of different senses that present the same object, along with the assumption that predicate senses, as public but platonic entities, must be the sort of thing Russell had in mind in speaking of universals. I am frankly uncertain whether this is the proper way to understand Frege.

(as used by a particular individual) are associated with the same way of thinking is not a matter of their semantic properties (where these are individuated in terms of the expressions' conventional potentials for referring or applying to objects). It is a matter of their cognitive properties, properties reflected by such facts as whether (if the expressions are terms) the user accepts or is disposed to accept the relevant identity. This sort of fact is (of course) relevant to whether the person has contradictory beliefs, and to the issues raised by Kripke's puzzle.

9

Kripke's puzzle is a puzzle about belief. But it turns into a puzzle about translation: Can we, or can we not, translate Pierre's use of 'Londres est jolie' with our use (or Pierre's, for that matter) of 'London is pretty'?

There are at least two projects we may undertake which could be called "interpretation" or "translation." One is finding a projectable way of going from someone's utterances (inscriptions and even occurrent linguistic mental events) to (potential) utterances (inscriptions and occurrent mental events) of our own, a way of doing this which allows us to understand the other's language. Armed with such, we would be in a position to say things like "Pierre's utterance of 'London is pretty' means that London is pretty," or "Pierre's use of 'je ne pense pas que Roubaix est au sud de Lille', meant that he doesn't think that Roubaix is south of Lille." A second project is finding a way of getting from the other's utterances (inscriptions, occurrent mental events), behavior, and general position in the world to a characterization of what he thinks, wants, says, and so forth – and thus, to a position in which we can say things like 'Pierre thinks that London is pretty', or 'Pierre wishes that Roubaix were south of Lille'. Call the first project *linguistic interpretation,* the second *individual interpretation.*

These are not completely separate projects, of course. But it is worth insisting that they *are* separate projects, and are typically subject to differing constraints.[22] Linguistic interpretation is, and must be, done at the wholesale (not the retail) level: it is impossible to start anew with each individual and puzzle out what their words mean. What we do – do because we have learned to do it and expect one another to do it – is

---

[22] Davidson's use of the idea of radical interpretation as an account of linguistic interpretation is unfortunate in that it blurs the fact that linguistic interpretation and individual interpretation are quite different projects.

impose a single scheme of interpretation on those around us, tinkering at the edges when it seems advisable. The scheme we impose, of course, is usually the scheme we were *taught* to impose, when we were "taught the ambient language." Wholesale imposition of such a scheme on one another allows us to understand one another in large part because our wholesale mutual imposition of (and acquiescence in) a uniform scheme of interpretation helps make it the case that we all mean the same thing with our words. The *point* of our all behaving as if we speak the same language is that our behaving in this way pretty much guarantees that (niceties about morphophonetic and small syntactic variation to the side) we *do* have a common language. Our so behaving thus helps to ensure that linguistic interpretation can pretty much proceed on automatic pilot.

Linguistic interpretation is not exactly Millian, but it is, or at least is usually, pretty close. How, after all, could it help but be? Our talk is about objects, their properties, and their relations; we care very much what others say and think about them. We care enough about this that we demand that interpretation preserve reference and satisfaction conditions. And beyond reference and satisfaction conditions, there just isn't that much that linguistic interpretation can preserve. It is, as Kripke notes, pretty rare for a word like a name to have a community-wide connotation (108), and so it is for the most part impossible for translation to preserve such. Ways of thinking are so idiosyncratic, for the most part, that requiring translation to preserve them would bring the enterprise to a grinding halt.[23] A (more or less) Millian scheme of linguistic interpretation seems like a good place – pretty much the only place – to start, if we are looking for a way to interpret those in the environs.

But when I want to know what someone thinks, wants, and hopes – when I want to interpret an individual – something more than this is called for. To know the attitudes of another is to be in a position to understand how those attitudes motivate him, to know "how the world seems" to him. If I am to come to know these things by interpreting the other's utterances and behavior in my own idiom, that interpretation needs to reflect more than just what objects, properties, and relations he refers to or thinks about. After all, if only that were reflected in individual interpretation, such interpretation could not distinguish between someone who had contradictory beliefs (believing that, say, Twain is dead and

---

[23] Our ways of thinking are, of course, also typically unknown to others, so that even if they were shared, our ignorance of them would – if we need to preserve them to linguistically interpret –bring linguistic interpretation to a standstill.

Twain – the very same Twain – is not dead), and someone whose beliefs
were inconsistent but not contradictory (as are those of one who thinks
that Twain, but not Clemens, is dead).

Over and above correctly capturing the reference of another's words,
what seems necessary (and in practice seems to be all we can reasonably
be expected to achieve) for individual interpretation is that we capture
the overall structure of the way in which they think about the world – capture the identity and difference of their ways of thinking of things and
properties, as those ways of thinking are deployed in their hopes, knowledge, desires, and dreams. If, for example, the other's use of sentences S
and S′ involve the same (different) way(s) of thinking of an individual,
that is to be reflected in our interpretation of those uses. Of course, the
natural way to achieve this is for our account, of what another believes,
wants, and so on, to satisfy a principle like (R). It is easy enough to see how
one attempts to satisfy such a principle: One surmises when utterances
(or actions expressive of an attitude) involve the same way of thinking of
an individual, and when they involve different ways of thinking thereof;
one tries to preserve such sameness and difference in interpretation,
assigning to each way of thinking its own linguistic representation. Of
course, that may not always be possible, at least not without introduction
of neologisms – as when one says, of a person who thinks that Paderewski
the politician and Paderewski the musician are distinct, that they do not
realize that Paderewski the politician is Paderewski the musician.[24]

[24] David Braun suggested to me that Kripke's example of Peter (who accepts 'Pederewski
was a musician' and 'Pederewski wasn't a musician') casts doubt on the claim at the
beginning of this section that Kripke's puzzle turns on a puzzle about translation. I
disagree. What is puzzling about the man who doesn't realize that Pederewski the musician is Pederewski the politician is – I would say – that the meaning of 'Pederewski was a
musician, but Pederewski wasn't a musician' – the linguistic meaning of the sentence –
as he uses it is the same as the meaning – the linguistic meaning – of the sentence as
we use it. Ditto for 'Peter believes that Paderewski is a pianist, but Paderewski is not a
pianist'. But when the confused man (sincerely) utters the first sentence, he doesn't
express a contradictory belief, while we would do so if we uttered it. And while it is no
big thing for the man to use the second sentence in a way that doesn't imply that Peter
has contradictory beliefs, it is difficult indeed for us to do this. What is puzzling, that is,
is how these sentences could mean the same as Peter and we use them – how one could
translate the other – but have such different properties when it comes to what mental
states they express and what the implications of using them in ascribing such states are.
   The problem here, as in the case of Pierre, is one that arises because identity of linguistic meaning is not a reliable guide to identity of belief expressed, even given that
we are looking at someone who understands the sentences in question (and so "knows
what they mean"). That is, the problem arises because (given the identity of linguistic
meaning) we can translate the other's idiom into ours, but that translation doesn't allow
us to interpret (in the sense of the text) the other.

Linguistic intepretation is something one does (so far as is possible) in advance. Individual interpretation is much more a one-off affair. This is, of course, partly a matter of its being (more nearly) possible to know in advance, and independently of much interaction with another, what her words and gestures mean, than it is to know how those words or gestures express beliefs. But individual interpretation is also one-off simply because there is no one way to do it. This is not (or not just) because (for Quinean reasons) there is semantic indeterminancy. Rather, it is because there will be, when others are confused or ignorant, more than one way to limn the structure of their pictures of the world, which is determined by the ways they think of its objects.

Linguistic intepretation is something we can (almost) always pull off, if only because we work so hard (all of us going to school and "learning the same language") to be in a position to be able to (effortlessly) pull it off. Individual interpretation is something we cannot always do – or cannot always do limited to the resources at hand. In the case of Pierre, for example, we are hamstrung: His way of looking at the world has a structure not reflected in the vocabulary we have to describe it. He has two ways of thinking of a thing for which we have but one name.

This section began with a question about translation: Can we, or can we not, translate Pierre's use of 'Londres est jolie' with our use (or Pierre's, for that matter) of 'London is pretty'? The suggestion just made is that the question can be taken in two ways, as a question about linguistic interpretation, or as one about individual interpretation. We can give a linguistic translation of Pierre's utterances. We can also give a piecemeal individual interpretation of Pierre's utterances as expressive of what he believes. We can, after all, focus simply on his "French beliefs," ignoring his English ones. And then we can pretty much preserve what needs preserving, in the way the world looks to Pierre, by using a linguistic translation of those utterances. We can do the same thing should we focus solely on his "English beliefs." What we can't do – at least not without making use of an idiom whose syntactic resources reflect the structure of Pierre's conceptual system – is give an interpretation of all of his beliefs at once.

10

The linguistic interpretation – the translation, if you will – of Pierre's sentence 'Londres est jolie' is 'London is pretty'. We do not have to know very much about Pierre, beyond the fact that he speaks French, to know that. The linguistic interpretation of 'Pierre croit que Londres est jolie' is 'Pierre believes that London is pretty'. This we know, as it were, once and for all, and not on a one-off basis.

When Pierre sincerely says 'Londres est jolie', *he* knows that he is expressing a belief; *he* knows how to interpret himself: je crois que Londres est jolie. Can *I* interpret him by saying that he believes that London is pretty? That all depends. It depends, in particular, on what I have already done in the way of interpreting him. If I have been discussing the beliefs he is wont to express in English about London, I will most probably have been using sentences in which the word 'London' occurs, saying that Pierre is convinced that London is not pretty. I cannot then just turn around and say that he believes that London is pretty; at the very least, some contextualization of such a claim is needed.

This may seem weird. Given the facts about linguistic interpretation – about translation – how can there be any doubt about whether I can interpret Pierre's 'je crois que Londres est jolie' with 'Pierre believes that London is pretty'? The two sentences mean the same thing, for goodness' sake.

Indeed. But whether I can describe another's beliefs in a particular way very much depends upon the context of description. My descriptions of others' beliefs – my ascriptions thereof – are sensitive to the context in which they are made. And as we all know, when a sentence is context-sensitive, its truth in one context does not assure its truth in others. Likewise, there is no guarantee that the translation of a context sensitive sentence will, in the context of translation, have the truth value of the translated sentence in the context from which it is translated. The two sentences 'Pierre croit que Londres est jolie' and 'Pierre believes that London is pretty' mean the same thing. So do the sentences 'je suis fatigué' and 'I'm tired'. But one wouldn't infer from this synonymy that when Pierre says '[je crois que] je suis fatigué', I can interpret him as saying '[Pierre thinks that] I'm tired'.

The banal principle (T) is *of course* subject to qualification: If S translates as T from your language to mine, and S is true as you use it, T will be true as I use it *if* S (and T) are free of context-sensitive vocabulary. I suspect that Kripke, in framing (T), thought that such qualification was unnecessary. He was, after all, concerned with sentences like 'Pierre believes that London is pretty' and its French translatation; tense aside, he probably thought, there is nothing context-sensitive in such sentences. As I see it, Kripke's puzzle arises, in part, because such sentences *are* contextually sensitive in the way I have been suggesting. Given the sort of contextual sensitivity I am suggesting they have, given someone suffering from the sort of confusion from which poor, poor Pierre suffers, *and* given the lack of multiple words for London in English, we are in a bit of a pickle, when we try to answer the question, Does he, or does he not, believe that London is pretty?[25]

Let us take stock. Schematic principles such as

> (D2) Pierre's uses (in the language he speaks in London) of instances of 'If I, Pierre, on reflection, sincerely assent to 'p', where 'p' is a sentence of my language, then I, Pierre, believe that p' are true in the language Pierre speaks in London

are surely true. Uses of instances of (D), the schematic, third-person ancestor of (D2), are perhaps invariably true when taken relative to contexts in which no substantive interpretation has already occurred. We can reliably *begin* interpreting another by using the linguistic interpretation of his speech. If, however, he suffers from some sort of confusion (which may become manifest when we look at linguistic translations of his speech), we may not be able to completely interpret him via linguistic translation.

Construed as principles about linguistic interpretation and suitably qualified, principles such as (T) are banal truths. But they do not yield puzzling or paradoxical consequences about Pierre's beliefs. Indeed, given the ubiquity of context dependence in natural language – is there, for example, a comparative adjective which is *not* context-dependent? – there is very little which a suitably qualified version of (T) tells us. The principle

> (R) Multiple occurrences of an expression within ascriptions of attitude to a single person indicate that the attitudes involve multiple occurrences of a single way of thinking in the attitudes ascribed

seems (to me) to tell us something important about how we ascribe attitudes to others. It is, in my opinion, in part because something along the lines of (R) is true that we find Kripke's puzzle genuinely puzzling. (R) is craftily phrased ("indicate") so that it can be taken as a principle about the semantics of attitude ascription, or as one about its

---

[25] At this point, one wants to hear a story about the precise nature of the context sensitivity I allege for sentences like 'Pierre believes that Paris is pretty'. Different authors will tell different stories here, and an essay on Kripke's essay is not the place for that literature review. A reader interested in my own views of the matter might look at the close of my "Propositional Attitude Ascriptions."

"pragmatics"; only those who take it to be a semantic principle are likely to be moved by the argument of the last two sections, that what Kripke's puzzle shows us is that interpreting others by assigning them beliefs is a contextually sensitive affair. I hope that even those who reject this will at least assent to the pragmatic version of (R), and the diagnosis of Kripke's puzzle that I've offered.

Do we say, when we say 'Pierre believes that London is pretty, and Pierre believes that London is not pretty' that Pierre's beliefs are contradictory? Since the language we use to ascribe belief is context-sensitive, there need be no unequivocal answer to this question. It would not be surprising, I think, to discover that the answer was that it depends: a *normal* use of this would entail that he had contradictory beliefs, but unusual uses of this – ones in a special context in which our interests are simply to convey the truth conditions of various pieces of Pierre's unfortunate mental landscape – may not have such an entailment.[26]

"Does Pierre, or does he not, believe that London is pretty?" If there were a Pierre, and someone asked such a question about him – in the course of an everyday, "nonphilosophical" conversation, with interests of a more or less normal sort – the question might well have a straightforward answer. What that answer would be would depend on the situation in which the question was asked, the interests and focus of conversants, what had been said already, and what was presupposed. If the question were asked when our philosophical noses were being rubbed in the sordid details of Pierre's intellectual history, the question probably wouldn't have a straightforward answer. That doesn't seem terribly problematic to me – lots of questions don't have a straightforward answer.[27]

---

[26] This is my own view of the matter. I take (R) to be a rule of thumb about the truth conditions of ascriptions of attitude. Normally, ascriptions of attitude to an individual will be *true* only if the identity and difference of vocabulary in the ascriptions faithfully reflects identity and difference among ways of thinking involved in the attitudes ascribed. But (R) is a rule of thumb, and when pressure is put upon it, by a case like that of Pierre's, it may be broken. Again, the interested (or puzzled) reader can look at "Propositional Attitude Ascriptions."

[27] Thanks to David Braun for comments. And thanks to Saul Kripke for providing a model of how philosophy can be rigorous and accessible, genuinely significant and still fun.

This essay was finished almost six years ago. I have resisted the urge to revise to discuss recent work – especially that of Kit Fine and Scott Soames – that bears on the essay's topic.

A Note on Kripke's Puzzle about Belief

Nathan Salmon

ABSTRACT

Millianism is the doctrine that the semantic content of a proper name is just the name's designatum. Without endorsing Millianism Kripke uses his well-known puzzle about belief as a defense of Millianism against the standard objection from apparent failure of substitution. On the other hand, he is not resolutely neutral. Millianism has it that Pierre has the contradictory beliefs that London is pretty and that London is not pretty – that Pierre both believes and disbelieves that London is pretty. I argue here for hard results in connection with Saul Kripke's puzzle and for resulting constraints on a correct solution. Kripke flatly rejects as incorrect the most straightforwardly Millian answer to the puzzle. Instead he favors a view according to which not all instances of his disquotational principle schema and its converse (which taken together are equivalent to his strengthened disquotational schema) are true although none are false. I argue in sharp contrast that the disquotational schema is virtually analytic. More accurately, every instance of the disquotational schema (appropriately restricted) is true by virtue of pure semantics. Moreover, there is an object-theoretic general principle that underlies the disquotational schema, is itself analytic, and entails each of the instances of the disquotational schema. By contrast, the converse of the disquotational principle leads to a genuine contradiction and is thereby straightforwardly falsified by Kripke's own example.

Much of the present material was presented in a nutshell to the Gala Opening of the Saul Kripke Center at the Graduate Center of the City University of New York on May 21, 2008. I am grateful to my audience, especially Saul Kripke, for their reactions and comments. I also thank David Kaplan for prior discussion. I am equally grateful to the participants in my seminar at the University of Southern California during fall 2008, especially Daniel Kwon and Lewis Powell, for their many helpful comments.

I

I argue here for relatively hard results in connection with Saul Kripke's well-known puzzle about belief, and for resulting constraints on a correct solution.[1] Kripke uses the puzzle as part of a defence of Millianism against the standard objection from apparent failure of substitution. He does not endorse Millianism, however. Indeed, he is not even resolutely neutral, for he also flatly rejects as incorrect the most straightforwardly Millian answer to the puzzle. The defense consists in exposing that the traditional objection from substitution failure implicitly invokes a set of supplementary assumptions that, by themselves, generate the same counterintuitive consequence completely independently of Millianism (pp. 1018–19).

In presenting the puzzle, Kripke follows a sound methodology championed in Alfred Tarski's classic discussion of the liar paradox ("antinomy"). Tarski wrote:

> In my judgment, it would be quite wrong and dangerous from the standpoint of scientific progress to depreciate the importance of this [the liar paradox] and other antinomies, and to treat them as jokes or sophistries. It is a fact that we are here in the presence of an absurdity, that we have been compelled to assert a false sentence.... If we take our work seriously, we cannot be reconciled with this fact. We must discover its cause, that is to say, we must analyze premises upon which the antinomy is based; we must then reject at least one of these premises, and we must investigate the consequences which this has for the whole domain of our research.[2]

In this same scientific spirit, Kripke enumerates each of the assumptions involved in obtaining the unacceptable conclusion, in order to identify and isolate the faulty assumption. There is to begin with the *principle of translation*:

T: If a sentence of one language expresses a truth in that language, then any literal (that is, semantic-content-preserving) translation of it into any other language also expresses a truth in that other language.[3]

---

[1] "A Puzzle about Belief," in A. Margalit, ed., *Meaning and Use* (Dordrecht: D. Reidel, 1979), pp. 239–83; reprinted in M. Davidson, ed., *On Sense and Direct Reference* (Boston: McGraw Hill, 2007), pp. 1002–36. Page references throughout are to this reprinting.

[2] Tarski, "The Semantic Conception of Truth," *Philosophy and Phenomenological Research*, 4 (1944), pp. 341–75, at p. 348; reprinted in L. Linsky, ed., *Semantics and the Philosophy of Language* (Urbana: University of Illinois Press, 1952), pp. 13–47, at p. 20.

[3] I have inserted the phrase 'literal (that is, semantic-content-preserving)' on Kripke's behalf. This notion of literal translation is clearly intended, both by Alonzo Church and by Kripke; nonliteral translation is irrelevant. See my "The Very Possibility of Language," in C. A. Anderson and M. Zeleny, eds., *Logic, Meaning and Computation: Essays in Memory*

At the center of the puzzle is the *disquotational schema* for English:

$D_{English}$:　　If a normal English speaker, on reflection and under normal circumstances, sincerely assents to 'φ' then he/she believes that φ.[4]

Infinitely many disquotational principles are thus obtained by replacing both occurrences of the schematic letter 'φ' "by any appropriate standard English sentence lacking indexical or pronominal devices or ambiguities" (p. 1014).

There is an analogous French schema D_{French} for French, an analogous Italian schema $D_{Italian}$ for Italian, and so on. The translation of D_{French} into English is the following schema, where '$φ_F$' is to be replaced (within the quotation marks) by any appropriate standard French sentence lacking indexical or pronominal devices and '$φ_E$' by that sentence's translation into English:

D_{French}*:　　If a normal French speaker, on reflection and under normal circumstances, sincerely assents to '$φ_F$' then he/she believes that $φ_E$.

There is also a strengthened disquotational schema for English:

$SD_{English}$:　　A normal English speaker who is not reticent will be disposed under normal circumstances to sincere reflective assent to 'φ' if and only if he/she believes that φ. (p. 1015)

---

of *Alonzo Church* (Boston: Kluwer, 2001), pp. 573–95; reprinted in my *Metaphysics, Mathematics, and Meaning* (Oxford: Oxford University Press, 2005), chapter 17, pp. 344–64, at 352–4.

It must be noted that *T* extends to attributions of belief. Thus, if 'Pierre croit que Londres est jolie' is true in French then its literal translation into English is equally true in English. Assuming that the normal translation preserves semantic content, if 'Pierre croit que Londres est jolie' is true in French then 'Pierre believes that London is pretty' is true in English. Kripke demonstrates with his Paderewski example that this assumption is not essential to the puzzle.

[4] Kripke's formulation omits the phrase "under normal circumstances." I regard this as a minor oversight. Kripke says the following of his formulation: "I fear that even with all this some astute reader – such, after all, is the way of philosophy – may discover a qualification I have overlooked, without which the asserted principle is subject to counterexample. I doubt, however, that any such modification will affect any of the uses of the principle to be considered below. Taken in its obvious intent, after all, the principle appears to be a self-evident truth" (pp. 1014–15). The phrase "normal circumstances" is to be understood so that Pierre's inability to translate 'London' as 'Londres' or vice versa does not in itself disqualify his circumstances from being normal. Rather, the spirit of the principle schema excludes genuinely bizarre circumstances – as, for example, in which a normal speaker is under a hypnotic spell, or under the control of a Cartesian demon, and as a result signals assent when he/she intends to dissent.

(See note 4.) This strengthening of $D_{English}$ leads to a stronger form of the puzzle.

Of the various principles just enumerated, the translation principle T is the most immune from reasonable doubt. It is surely not the culprit. Indeed, Kripke demonstrates with his Paderewski example that T plays no crucial role in the puzzle. (See note 3.) I shall simply assume T throughout the present discussion.

To construct the puzzle, Kripke describes a hypothetical scenario in which a bilingual English-French speaker, Pierre, is unaware that the cities he calls 'London' and 'Londres' are in fact one and the same. The puzzle is generated through application of these various principles to the following stipulations taken to be true *by hypothesis*:

$H1$:   Pierre is a normal French speaker.

$H2$:   Pierre is a normal English speaker.

$H3$:   Pierre is rational/logical.

$H4$:   When confronted with 'Londres est jolie', 'London is pretty', or their negations, Pierre reflectively interprets the sentence.

$H5$:   Pierre is not reticent to reveal his position with respect to the issue of whether London is pretty.

$H6$:   Under normal circumstances Pierre sincerely assents to 'Londres est jolie' and is not at all disposed to assent to 'Londres n'est pas jolie'.

$H7$:   Under normal circumstances Pierre sincerely assents to 'London is not pretty' and is not at all disposed to assent to 'London is pretty'.

We may supplement these stipulative hypotheses with the following trivially true hypotheses:

$H8$:   English is a language; French is a language; 'London is pretty' and 'London is not pretty' are commonplace English sentences, which express as their English semantic contents, respectively, that London is pretty and that London is not pretty; and 'Londres est jolie' is a commonplace French sentence, which expresses as its French semantic content that London is pretty.[5]

$H9$:   'Pierre believes that London is pretty', 'Pierre does not believe that London is pretty', and 'Pierre believes that London is not pretty' are commonplace English sentences, which express as

---

[5] Normal French speakers (in Kripke's sense) inform me that '*jolie*' correctly applies in idiomatic French to a creature, not to a city. I shall follow the literature in ignoring this departure.

their English semantic contents, respectively, that Pierre believes that London is pretty, that Pierre does not believe that London is pretty, and that Pierre believes that London is not pretty; and 'Pierre croit que Londres est jolie' is a commonplace French sentence, which expresses as its French semantic content that Pierre believes that London is pretty.

Hypothesis *H8* has the straightforward consequence that the French sentence 'Londres est jolie' translates into English literally (preserving semantic content) as 'London is pretty', and vice versa. Hypothesis *H9* has the consequence that the French 'Pierre croit que Londres est jolie' translates into English literally as 'Pierre believes that London is pretty'. Again, Kripke demonstrates through his Paderewski example that these consequences concerning literal translation are in any event at least largely inessential to the puzzle.[6]

Kripke's puzzle presses a pair of questions:

Q1:   Does Pierre believe that London is pretty?
Q2:   Does Pierre disbelieve that London is pretty?

To *disbelieve* a proposition *p* is (at least for present purposes) to believe its negation, ~*p*. It is thus a kind of believing.[7] The second question is thus whether Pierre believes that London is *not* pretty.

The preceding presentation is more explicit than Kripke's. Kripke focuses almost exclusively on *Q1*, though *Q2* is equally relevant and, strictly speaking, a distinct question from *Q1* (which might even be answered independently of *Q1*). More significantly, in presenting the puzzle Kripke avoids talk of propositions nearly altogether. This is not because he disbelieves in propositions or is skeptical of their existence. Rather he wishes to rest the puzzle on as meager resources as possible. Yet acknowledgment of propositions is at least implicit in the puzzle, and is crucial to solving it. Indeed, talk of propositions is already explicit at least in hypothesis *H4*, if not also in *H5*, neither of which does Kripke

---

[6] One purported solution that is Fregean in spirit (although it deviates significantly from Frege's own theory) has the implausible consequence that whereas 'Londres est jolie' translates literally into English as 'London is pretty', contrary to *H9* 'Pierre croit que Londres est jolie' does not translate literally as 'Pierre believes that London is pretty', and is translatable literally only insofar as the sense of 'Londres' in Pierre's French idiolect is expressible in English, as perhaps by a definite description. (See note 3.) Any purported solution is discredited to the extent that it is committed to rejecting trivial hypotheses.

[7] The interrelationships among belief, disbelief, suspension of judgment, and failure to believe are significantly more complicated than might first appear. See my "Being of Two Minds: Belief with Doubt," *Noûs*, 29, 1 (January 1995), pp. 1–20; reprinted in my *Content, Cognition, and Communication* (Oxford: Oxford University Press, 2007), pp. 230–48.

explicitly and fully state as such. If I am correct, as we shall soon see, talk of propositions is implicit also in $H1$, $H2$, $H6$, and $H7$. More important, reference to propositions, as we shall also see, underlies the disquotational schemata.

The relevant instances of $D_{French}*$ and $D_{English}$ are the following:

D_{French}':   If Pierre is a normal French speaker and, on reflection and under normal circumstances, he sincerely assents to 'Londres est jolie', then he believes that London is pretty.

$D_{English}'$:   If Pierre is a normal English speaker and, on reflection and under normal circumstances, he sincerely assents to 'London is not pretty', then he believes that London is not pretty.[8]

Invoking $H1$, $H2$, $H4$, $H6$, $H7$, $H8$, and $H9$, one obtains the bizarre result that Pierre both believes and disbelieves that London is pretty:

R1

a:	D_{French}, T	$\vdash$	$D_{French}*$.
b:	$D_{French}*$, $H1$, $H4$, $H6$, $H8$, $H9$	$\vdash$	Pierre believes that London is pretty.
c:	$D_{English}$, $H2$, $H4$, $H7$, $H8$	$\vdash$	Pierre disbelieves that London is pretty.
d:	$D_{English}$, D_{French}, T, $H1$, $H2$, $H4$, $H6$–$H9$	$\vdash$	Pierre has contradictory beliefs.

The weaker disquotational schemata together with T, the stipulative hypotheses, and the trivial hypotheses thus yield affirmative answers to both $Q1$ and $Q2$. The primary version of the puzzle presses the obvious objection: Answering both questions affirmatively is evidently incompatible with $H3$. This conflict casts serious doubt on the disquotational schemata.

There is worse yet to come. The relevant instance of $SD_{English}$ is the following:

---

[8] Strictly speaking, these do not qualify as admissible instances, in light of the ambiguity in English of 'London is pretty', which can be used to describe London, Ontario, instead of London, England. The example illustrates that the disquotational schemata can be extended to ambiguous sentences, provided the sentence in question is given the same reading in the metalanguage that the speaker gives it in assenting or not assenting to it.

On the other hand, the disquotational schemata need to be restricted to sentences that are commonplace – that is, not technical, not especially long, with no arcane vocabulary, and so on. (See the preceding note.) For Kripke's purposes, what are needed are plausibly restricted schemata for which $SD_{English}'$ and SD_{French}' qualify as legitimate instances.

$SD_{English}{}'$:   If Pierre is a normal English speaker and not reticent, then he will be disposed under normal circumstances to sincere reflective assent to 'London is pretty' iff he believes that London is pretty.

Invoking $H5$ in combination with the same hypotheses as before, one now obtains results that are not merely implausible or mysterious, but utterly unacceptable – for example, that Pierre both believes, and also does not believe, that London is pretty.[9] In the spirit of Tarski's analysis of the liar paradox, Kripke's puzzle generates a fundamental result, which any solution must accommodate:

R2

a:	$H1, H2, H4–H9$	$\vdash$	$\neg(SD_{English} \wedge D_{French} \wedge T).$[10]
b:	$H1, H2, H4–H9, T$	$\vdash$	$\neg(SD_{English} \wedge D_{French}).$

Assuming T together with the hypotheses listed, this result excludes the prospect that all instances of the strengthened disquotational schemata are true. On the other hand, it leaves open the issue of whether the weaker disquotational schemata might yet obtain.

II

Unlike Tarski, Kripke does not make any official pronouncement concerning which principles are guilty. Instead he considers a variety of possible answers to the puzzle without officially endorsing any of them. He does clearly favor one answer to the puzzle and flatly rejects some specific answers as incorrect – including the most straightforwardly Millian conclusion, to wit, that Pierre indeed has contradictory beliefs. Kripke objects that, given $H3$, "it is clear that Pierre, as long as he is unaware that the cities he calls 'London' and 'Londres' are one and the same, is in no position to see, by logic alone, that at least one of his beliefs must

---

[9] Kripke presents a third version of the puzzle on which $H7$ is replaced with the following:

> $H7'$: Pierre is not at all disposed to assent to either 'London is pretty' or 'London is not pretty'; instead his attitude is one of suspension of judgment. (p. 1022)

> This replacement leads equally to the unacceptable conclusion that Pierre both believes and does not believe that London is pretty.

[10] The negation sign '$\neg$', as contrasted with '$\sim$', will be used throughout to indicate that not all instances of the schema to which the sign is prefixed are true. (It does not in general follow that all instances of the schema are false, or even that any are.)

be false. He lacks information, not logical acumen. He cannot be convicted of inconsistency; to do so is incorrect" (p. 1022).

The solution Kripke favors accepts the translation principle *T*, but does not accept all admissible instances of any of the disquotational schemata. At the same time the favored solution does not reject any instance as false. Instead all problematic instances – Pierre vis-à-vis 'London is not pretty' and 'Londres est jolie', the ancients vis-à-vis 'Hesperus appears in the evening sky' and 'Phosphorus does not appear in the evening sky', Lois Lane vis-à-vis 'Superman can fly' and 'Clark Kent cannot fly', and so on – are deemed not true but also not false. On this solution it is neither true nor false that the ancients believed that Hesperus was Phosphorus, and neither true nor false that they believed that Hesperus was not Phosphorus. Analogously, on this solution it is neither true nor false that Lois Lane believes that Superman can fly, and neither true nor false that she believes that he cannot fly. And likewise, it is allegedly neither true nor false that Pierre believes that London is pretty, and neither true nor false that he believes that London is not pretty. Instead the phrase 'believes that', and perhaps even the simple proposition-designation forming operator 'that' by itself, are evidently undefined for these notorious problem cases. In the preface to *Naming and Necessity* Kripke writes:

> Some critics of my doctrines, and some sympathizers, seem to have read them as asserting, or at least implying, a doctrine of the universal substitutivity of [codesignative] proper names. This can be taken as saying that a sentence with 'Cicero' in it expresses the same 'proposition' as the corresponding [result of substituting 'Cicero'] with 'Tully', that to believe the proposition expressed by the one is to believe the proposition expressed by the other, or that they are equivalent for all semantic purposes. Russell does seem to have held such a view for 'logically proper names', and it seems congenial to a purely 'Millian' picture of naming, where only the referent [designatum] of the name contributes to what is expressed. But I. . . . never intended to go so far. My view that the English sentence 'Hesperus is Phosphorus' could sometimes be used to raise an empirical issue while 'Hesperus is Hesperus' could not shows that I do not treat the *sentences* as completely interchangeable. Further, it indicates that the mode of fixing the reference is relevant to our epistemic attitude toward the sentences expressed.[11] How this relates to the question what 'propositions' are expressed by these sentences, whether

---

[11] Our epistemic attitude toward the *sentences expressed?* Is this a slip of the pen? Sentences are not expressed *by* anything; sentences express propositions. Does Kripke mean our cognitive attitude toward *what* the sentences express, that is, toward the *propositions* that the sentences express? Does he mean our cognitive toward the *sentences* themselves – as opposed to the propositions they express? Neither? Both?

these 'propositions' are objects of knowledge and belief, and in general, how to treat names in epistemic [i.e., propositional-attitude] contexts, are vexing questions. I have no 'official doctrine' concerning them, and in fact I am unsure that the apparatus of 'propositions' does not break down in this area. [*Footnote:* Reasons why I find these questions so vexing are to be found in my 'A Puzzle about Belief'.] (pp. 20–1)

In "A Puzzle," Kripke voices his worries in a similar manner:

> The point is *not*, of course, that codesignative proper names *are* interchange-able in belief [propositional-attitude] contexts *salva veritate*, or that they *are* interchangeable in simple contexts even *salva significatione*. The point is that the absurdities that disquotation plus substitutivity would generate are exactly paralleled by absurdities generated by disquotation plus translation, or even 'disquotation alone' (or: disquotation plus homophonic transla-tion).... When we enter into the area exemplified by ... Pierre, we enter into an area where our normal practices of interpretation and attribution of belief are subjected to the greatest possible strain, perhaps to the point of breakdown. So is the notion of the *content* of someone's assertion, the *proposition* it expresses. (pp. 1033–4)

It can be forcefully argued – and I am persuaded – both that the solution Kripke favors is incorrect and furthermore that the answer he rejects is in fact correct. Pierre does indeed have contradictory beliefs. Whereas believing contradictions is typically a violation of even the most lenient of reasonable cognitive norms, in Pierre's circumstances the transgres-sion is completely excused. What are at issue are precisely the weaker disquotational instances D_{French}' and $D_{English}'$. Whereas Kripke is inclined to deem them neither true nor false, because not all instances are true even if none are false, it can be demonstrated that they may be plausibly inter-preted in such a way that they are basically *analytic* – or at least nearly enough so that they are straightforwardly true – even while hypotheses H_1–H_7, understood correspondingly, remain true by stipulation.

To substantiate the case, I shall propose definitions for 'normal speaker', 'reflect', 'sincere assent', and 'reticent', as these terms arise in Kripke's puzzle. In proposing these definitions I am guided by Kripke's own clarifications (at p. 1014). The point of these proposed definitions is not to capture the terms' standard English meanings. The point, rather, is to provide a set of concepts – core *potential* meanings – that are not implausible as contents for the terms, and that play the roles of such concepts as that of *normal speaker, sincere assent,* and so on in a fruitful reformulation of Kripke's puzzle, with the result that relevant speculative principles and stipulated hypotheses, so interpreted, are more readily assessed as legitimate or not.

The definition for 'normal speaker' is straightforward:

D1:   Agent *A* *speaks* language *L* *normally* =$_{def}$ *A* speaks *L* sufficiently
well that for every commonplace expression of *L*, *A* would nor-
mally use and take it to mean exactly what the expression in
fact means in *L*; in particular, for every commonplace sentence
S of *L*, if confronted with *S*, *A* would normally take it to express
exactly the very proposition p_S that *S* in fact expresses in *L*.[12]

The issues surrounding the notions of reflection and sincerity are more
complex and require more careful consideration. We begin by considering the following natural definitions as at least first approximations:

D2:   Agent *A* *reflects with respect to* sentence *S* =$_{def}$ *A* considers *S* sufficiently that he/she thereby interprets it as expressing exactly
the proposition p_{AS} he/she would normally take it to express.

D3:   Agent *A* *sincerely assents to* sentence *S* =$_{def}$ *A* assents verbally to *S*;
furthermore *A*'s verbal assent to *S* is appropriately occasioned by
A's believing p_{AS}, where p_{AS} is the very proposition he/she therewith takes *S* to express.

These definitions are in fact better than mere approximations. They
closely reflect Kripke's own explanations of the relevant notions.[13] They
also suffice, when taken in conjunction with *D1* and the stipulative and
trivial hypotheses, for the purpose of establishing, contrary to Kripke
himself, that Pierre indeed harbors contradictory beliefs. We shall consider a variety of possible refinements of *D2* and *D3*, but for simplicity's
sake we shall take these to be our official definitions.

A more subtle pair of concepts is available, and equally sufficient for
the purpose at hand. It might be supposed that the relevant notion of
sincere assent essentially involves taking a metaperspective, specifically,
taking oneself to believe the proposition expressed by the sentence to
which one assents. Correspondingly, the relevant notion of reflection
would involve getting oneself right. As such the following alternative
definitions might be taken in lieu of *D2* and *D3*:

[12] See note 8. Kripke says, "When we suppose that we are dealing with a normal speaker
of English, we mean that he uses all words in the sentence in a standard way, combines
them according to the appropriate syntax, etc.: in short, he uses the sentence to mean
what a normal speaker should mean by it" (p. 1014).

[13] Kripke: "The qualification 'on reflection' guards against the possibility that a speaker
may, through careless inattention to the meaning of his words or other momentary conceptual or linguistic confusion, assert something he does not really mean, or assent to a
sentence in linguistic error. 'Sincerely' is meant to exclude mendacity, acting, irony, and
the like" (p. 1014).

D2':   Agent *A reflects with respect to* sentence $S =_{def} A$ considers S sufficiently that he/she thereby interprets it as expressing exactly
the proposition p_{AS} he/she would normally take it to express;
furthermore, in so doing A considers p_{AS} sufficiently thoroughly
that, under normal circumstances, if he/she takes him/herself
to believe p_{AS}, to disbelieve p_{AS}, or to suspend judgment, he/
she so takes him/herself appropriately precisely because he/she
does so believe, disbelieve, or suspend judgment.

D3':   Agent *A sincerely assents to* sentence $S =_{def} A$'s assent to S is appropriately occasioned by A's *taking him/herself to believe p_{AS}*, where
p_{AS} is the very proposition he/she therewith takes S to express.

Compared to these alternative definitions, the notions of reflection and
sincere assent captured in *D2* and *D3* are somewhat crude. Although
they yield cruder notions, the original definitions seem entirely faithful
to Kripke's expressed intent. More important, the notions captured in
D2' and *D3'* complement each other in such a way that the net effect
of the replacements leaves the puzzle and the constraints on its correct
solution exactly the same as with the cruder notions they replace.

Reflection on each of these various definitions confirms that each of
the stipulated hypotheses *H1–H7*, as thus interpreted, may be taken to be
true by hypothesis. For example, it may be taken as stipulated that if confronted with any commonplace French sentence, Pierre would normally
take the sentence to express the very proposition it in fact expresses in
French. Similarly for *H2* and each of *H4–H7*.

One might hesitate over *H4*. The proposed definition *D2'* defines
'reflection' in such a way that if an agent "reflects" with respect to a
sentence, and judges under normal circumstances that he/she believes
the proposition he/she therewith interprets the sentence as expressing,
this is precisely because he/she does believe the proposition. Is it really
legitimate simply to stipulate that in the scenario under consideration,
if Pierre takes himself to believe the very proposition he interprets a
sentence as expressing then he takes himself correctly? Or does such a
verdict simply beg the question?

Controversy about Pierre's case notwithstanding, the stipulation must
be deemed entirely legitimate. First, *H4* does not by itself settle the issue
raised by *Q1* or *Q2* any more than any other enumerated hypothesis
does; *H4* is no more question-begging, in any significant sense, than any
of the other hypotheses are. It is also important to recognize exactly what
H4 stipulates. Interpreted through *D2'*, *H4* does not amount to a claim

that Pierre is infallible concerning whether he believes. It does not even stipulate that Pierre is immune from error, that he *could not* be mistaken, in judging that he has a certain opinion. It stipulates a truth-functional relation: either Pierre does not judge that he believes, disbelieves, or suspends judgment about something, or else he does so judge but not under normal circumstances, or else he does so judge under normal circumstances and in so doing he considers matters sufficiently thoroughly so that in those circumstances his judgment is not mistaken. Taking oneself to be of a certain opinion is not like taking oneself to be healthy, wealthy, and wise. Careful, thoughtful, and thorough consideration normally provides considerably greater warrant, and greater likelihood of being correct, in the former case than in the latter. In judging that one is indeed of a certain opinion, for one to base that judgment on a cold, hard look at oneself in a careful and probing way is for one to examine thoroughly all the relevant evidence available. Normally, if one thoroughly considers the question of whether one believes something, and concludes that one does indeed believe, that conclusion is not merely a coincidently correct conviction. It is normally a firm case of knowledge. *D2′* might even be revised as follows:

> D2″: Agent *A reflects with respect to* sentence $S =_{def} A$ considers S sufficiently that he/she thereby interprets it as expressing exactly the proposition p_{AS} he/she would normally take it to express; furthermore, in so doing A considers p_{AS} sufficiently thoroughly that, under normal circumstances, if he/she takes him/herself to believe p_{AS}, to disbelieve p_{AS}, or to suspend judgment, then he/she *knows* that he/she does so believe, disbelieve, or suspend judgment.

Replacing *D2′* with *D2″* has no significant effect on the puzzle or the constraints on its correct solution.

Furthermore, the notion of reflection defined in *D2′* does not guarantee that if the reflective speaker takes him/herself under normal circumstances *not* to believe a proposition, he/she so takes him/herself correctly. Such an additional requirement would be excessive. In particular, I shall argue, although he is reflective, Pierre is very much mistaken *about himself* when under normal circumstances he continues to refrain in all sincerity from assenting to 'Londres n'est pas jolie'. Though he does not realize it, he arguably believes exactly what he takes that sentence to express. Taking oneself not to believe is significantly different in this respect from taking oneself to believe. One can normally determine whether one believes a proposition *p* through careful consideration of the issue of whether p or $\sim p$, and deciding between them. Deciding in favor of p in such circumstances is a way of believing p. Opting instead for $\sim p$ is a way of disbelieving p. As noted earlier, disbelieving is a kind of believing. It is not ipso facto a way of *not believing p*, of failing to believe p. Even failing to decide between p and $\sim p$ is not itself a way of failing to believe p. Deciding is not a way of not believing, and neither is failing to choose. Careful consideration of whether one believes provides some likelihood of being correct if one concludes that one does not believe. But it provides a *guarantee* of being correct if one concludes that one does believe. (See note 7.) In the case of $H4$ the stipulation concerns the quality and character of Pierre's consideration: it is sufficiently thorough – sufficiently self-aware, truth-guided, thoughtful, careful, probing, dispassionate, unbiased, and so on – that if his circumstances are normal – if he is not under a hypnotic spell, not under the influence of hallucinogenic drugs, not manipulated by a Cartesian demon, and so on – and if he concludes that he really is of a certain opinion, this is appropriately precisely because he is in fact of that opinion. This may be taken to be every bit as *true by hypothesis* as any of $H1$–$H7$.

The notion of one act, event, or state of affairs appropriately occasioning another stands in need of clarification. Precisely what this amounts to does not affect the central issue. Pierre does sincerely assent, and he therefore has contradictory beliefs. Still, it is well to inquire into the relationship between verbal assent and belief. As I have argued at some length elsewhere, underlying the weaker disquotational schemata $D_{English}$, D_{French}, and so on, is the very nature of belief itself. Belief of a proposition is a favorable cognitive attitude. Embracing a proposition by believing it – as opposed to mere wishing or hoping – is, fundamentally, a kind of assenting. Belief is not mere outward, verbal assent to a sentence, however; more directly, it is a kind of inward, cognitive assent to the proposition itself.[14] This suggests a deeper definition for 'sincere assent':

> $D3''$: Agent A *sincerely assents to* sentence $S =_{def} A$ assents verbally to S; furthermore A's verbal assent to S is appropriately an outward manifestation of A's *cognitive* assent to p_{AS}, and therewith of his/her belief thereof, where p_{AS} is the very proposition he/she therewith takes S to express.

This alternative definition is significantly more illuminating than $D3$, especially in regard to understanding the legitimacy of $D_{English}$ and D_{French}.

---

[14] *Frege's Puzzle* (Atascadero, Calif.: Ridgeview, 1986, 1991), at pp. 80, 103–5, and passim.

Finally, the proposed definition for 'reticent' is straightforward:

> D_4:   Agent A is *reticent* (to reveal his/her attitudes) *with respect to*
> proposition $p =_{def} A$ is not strongly disposed, or else is counter-
> disposed, to reveal (through assent, dissent, or abstention in
> response to queries) that he/she believes p, that he/she disbe-
> lieves p, or that he/she suspends judgment.[15]

It emerges from the proposed definitions, as well as from their potential replacements, that the stipulative hypotheses do invoke propositions – at least implicitly if not explicitly. For example, qua normal French speaker, Pierre stands in a specific relation to certain propositions. He interprets 'Londres est jolie' to express that London is pretty. What Pierre therewith takes the sentence to express – that London is pretty – is, even if Pierre does not recognize it, nothing more nor less than a proposition.[16]

III

The following important principle follows logically from definitions $D_1–D_3$. (As the reader can readily verify, it equally follows from D_1, D_2', and D_3', and from D_1, D_2, and D_3''.) The principle may be regarded as therefore analytic, on relevant interpretations of 'normal speaker', 'reflect', and 'sincere assent'.

> B: For every commonplace sentence S of any language L, if a nor-
> mal speaker of L, on reflection and under normal circumstances,
> sincerely assents to S, then he/she believes the proposition S
> expresses in L.

Put another way, substitution within B of the definitions of 'normal speaker', 'reflect', and 'sincere assent', results in a classical logical truth. This analytic truth can be employed in lieu of the disquotational sche-mata to generate the first version of Kripke's puzzle. Principle B together with H_1, H_4, and H_6, and the further observation that French is a lan-guage and 'Londres est jolie' a commonplace French sentence, are

---

[15] Kripke: "The qualification about reticence is meant to take account of the fact a speaker may fail to avow his beliefs because of shyness, a desire for secrecy, to avoid offense, etc.... Maybe again the formulation needs further tightening, but the intent is clear" (p. 1015).

[16] Arguably the solution Kripke favors entails a rejection of H_1, not as false but as untrue, on the ground that the phrase 'the proposition expressed in French by 'Londres est jolie" is not well defined (is *improper*). I regard the rejection of H_1 on this ground as ill-motivated and excessively implausible. A similar situation obtains in connection with other hypotheses.

already sufficient to yield the result that Pierre believes the proposition expressed in French by 'Londres est jolie'. (See note 16.)

Affirmative answers to *Q1* and *Q2*, and therewith a hard constraint on any solution to Kripke's puzzle, are obtained as follows, using the proposed definitions *D1–D3* in place of the weaker disquotational schemata:

R3

a:	*D1–D3*	⊢	*B.*
b:	*B, H1, H4, H6, H8*	⊢	Pierre believes that London is pretty.
c:	*B, H2, H4, H7, H8*	⊢	Pierre disbelieves that London is pretty.
d:	*D1–D3, H1, H2, H4, H6–H8*	⊢	Pierre has contradictory beliefs.[17]

The analytic principle *B* does the primary work performed by the weaker disquotational schemata in Kripke's original formulation. Indeed, there is a clear sense in which *B*, which explicitly concerns propositions, underlies the weaker schemata. Though it is analytic, *B* might even be regarded as simply a more explicit rendering of those schemata. For example, $D_{English}$ and D_{French}, with substituends for 'φ' restricted to commonplace sentences, are derivable from *B* together with the following trivial schemata, respectively:

E: In English, 'φ' expresses (the proposition) that φ, and nothing else.

F: In French, 'φ_F' expresses (the proposition) that φ_E, and nothing else.

The schematic letter 'φ' is to be replaced by any suitable English sentence (containing no indexicals, etc.), 'φ_F' by any suitable French sentence, and 'φ_E' by its literal translation into English. This hard result may be formulated as follows:

R4

a:	*B, E*	⊢	$D_{English}$
b:	*B, F*	⊢	D_{French}^{*}
c:	*D1–D3, E*	⊢	$D_{English}$
d:	*D1–D3, F*	⊢	D_{French}^{*}

[17] As mentioned, these results, as well as the results to follow, are preserved if definition *D3* is replaced with *D3″*, or if *D2* is replaced with either *D2′* or *D2″* and *D3* is simultaneously replaced with *D3′*.

Instances of the schemata E and F are, strictly speaking, not themselves analytic. One does not know simply by virtue of one's knowledge of English that 'Londres est jolie' expresses in French that London is pretty. The instances of E and F are not themselves trivial. What is trivial is something meta-meta-theoretic: that every suitable instance of those schemata is true. By the same token, then, insofar as B is analytic it is trivial that every suitable instance of $D_{English}$ is true without exception, and similarly for D_{French}, $D_{Italian}$, and so on. This result supports $D_{French}{}'$ and $D_{English}{}'$, and therewith (given the appropriate stipulative hypotheses) the conclusion that Pierre indeed has contradictory beliefs. This result thus yields the same constraint on any solution to Kripke's puzzle.

As we have seen, Kripke objects to any such solution. His objection evidently makes use of a further hypothesis, one that is clearly more speculative than the purely stipulative hypotheses H_1–H_7 and the trivially true $H8$ and $H9$, to wit,

H_{10}:   If H_3, then Pierre does not have contradictory beliefs.

As Kripke undoubtedly recognizes,

R5a: H_1–H_4, $H6$–$H_{10} \vdash \neg(D_{French}{}^* \wedge D_{English})$.

By insisting on H_{10} in addition to the stipulative hypotheses, Kripke is committed to denying – erroneously if the foregoing is correct – that every instance of the weaker disquotational schemata is true. In particular he must reject as untrue (even if they are not false) the conjunction of $D_{French}{}'$ together with $D_{English}{}'$.

On the other hand, as we have seen in R_3, the proposed definitions D_1–D_3 together with the stipulative hypotheses H_1, H_2, H_4, and $H6$–$H9$ yield the result that, for better or for worse, Pierre has contradictory beliefs. This yields an additional hard result, and with it an additional constraint on any solution to the puzzle:

R5b: D_1–D_3, H_1–H_4, $H6$–$H9 \vdash \sim H_{10}$.

This result discredits Kripke's objection. As already noted, hypothesis H_{10} is speculative. Certainly it is more speculative than any of the hypotheses enumerated in R_5b, each of which is either stipulated to be true by hypothesis or trivially true. Furthermore each of D_1–D_3, qua definition, is analytically true. Thus, true premises entail H_{10}'s falsity. For better or for worse, H_{10} is untenable. This result does not in itself solve Kripke's puzzle. A complete solution must acknowledge that Pierre has contradictory beliefs, and will also provide some account of how it happens that a rational agent in Pierre's situation excusably harbors contradictions.[18]

IV

Though the proposed definitions together with schemata E and F entail the weaker disquotational schemata, they do not also entail any of the strengthened disquotational schemata. In particular,

R6:	*D1–D4, E*	$\not\models$	$SD_{English}$

There are interpretations (models) on which D_1–D_4 together with E are verified but $SD_{English}$ fails. As we shall see, one such interpretation is precisely the understanding of standard meta-English on which each of the definitions D_1–D_4 provides the interpretations for 'normal speaker', and so on.

Although the strengthened disquotational schema cannot be deemed analytic or trivial, there are plausible, speculative hypotheses that support that schema. The most natural such speculative hypothesis is the following:

H_{II}: If a speaker takes a sentence S to express a proposition p, believes the very proposition p, is disposed to reveal verbally that he/she believes p, and is not also counterdisposed, then under normal

---

[18] Kripke presents a fourth version of the puzzle (see note 9) on which *H6* is replaced with the following:

> *H6′*: Pierre sincerely assents to 'Si New York est jolie, Londres est jolie aussi' and is not at all disposed to assent to 'Ce n'est pas que si New York est jolie, Londres est jolie aussi'. (p. 1022)

Correspondingly, H_4 is generalized and Q_1 is replaced with $Q_1′$: 'Does Pierre believe that if New York is pretty then so is London?'. Pierre's inability to infer legitimately that New York is not pretty is evidently incompatible, given H_3, with affirmative answers to both $Q_1′$ and Q_2. A complete solution to this puzzle will answer both questions affirmatively and also provide an explanation of why Pierre's rationality does not enable him in this case to draw a simple modus tollens inference. Cf. my *Frege's Puzzle*, at pp. 103–18, 129–32; and "Illogical Belief," in J. Tomberlin, ed., *Philosophical Perspectives, 3: Philosophy of Mind and Action Theory* (Atascadero, Calif.: Ridgeview, 1989), pp. 243–85, reprinted in M. Davidson, ed., *On Sense and Direct Reference* (Boston: McGraw Hill, 2007), pp. 1037–67, and in *Content, Cognition, and Communication*, pp. 193–223.

circumstances he/she will be (more or less equally strongly) disposed to assent to *S*.

We have the following result:

R7:	*D1–D4, E, H11*	$\vdash$	$SD_{English}$

I submit that the strengthened version of Kripke's puzzle, which employs the strengthened disquotational schemata, derives the bulk of its force from the plausibility of this hypothesis $H11$ (or from that of similar speculative hypotheses).[19]

By the same token, $H11$ is as untenable as $H10$. This follows from the preceding result:

R8

a:	$D_{French}*, H1, H2, H4–H9$	$\vdash$	$SD_{English}$
b:	$D1\text{-}D4, H1, H2, H4–H9$	$\vdash$	$\sim H11$

That is, the weaker disquotational schemata together with the listed stipulative hypotheses entail that not all instances of the strengthened disquotational schema is true. Insofar as $H11$ is more speculative than the premises enumerated in *R8b*, this refutes $H11$. The stronger version of the puzzle is virtually an ironclad proof that $\neg SD_{English}'$ is not true.

The latest result also yields a further constraint on any solution to Kripke's puzzle. The correct solution to Kripke's puzzle upholds the weaker disquotational schemata, providing affirmative answers to *Q1* and *Q2*, while rejecting the strengthened disquotational schema. A complete solution must also provide an explanation of how $H11$ fails in cases like Pierre's. (See note 18.)

---

[19] The derivation of $SD_{English}$ from $H11$, $D1–D4$, and *E* involves construing *D1* in such a way that for any commonplace English sentence *S* that univocally expresses only one proposition (with respect to a context), that same proposition is the only thing that a normal English speaker takes *S* to express (with respect to the context in question).

11

On the Skepticism about Rule-Following in Kripke's Version of Wittgenstein

George Wilson

I. INTRODUCTION

Many commentators on Kripke's *Wittgenstein on Rules and Private Language* (hereafter *WRPL*)[1] have found it flatly incredible that Kripke would suppose that Wittgenstein was some kind of skeptic about meaning. But often, it seems to me, these commentators have not paid adequate attention to the character of the putative meaning of skepticism that is chiefly at issue in Kripke's reconstruction. The questions here are confusing, but it will be useful to begin with Kripke's well-known comparison to Hume.

Kripke asserts, "It is important and illuminating to compare Wittgenstein's new form of skepticism with the classical skepticism of Hume: there are important analogies between the two. Both develop a skeptical paradox, based on questioning a certain *nexus* from past to future. Wittgenstein questions the nexus between past 'intention' or 'meanings' and present practice: for example, between my past 'intentions' with regard to plus and my present computation '68 + 57 = 125'" (*WRPL*, p. 62). Hume, of course, is a skeptic about the idea that past causes necessitate their future effects. The nexus questioned by Kripke's Wittgenstein, on the other hand, is this: what the speaker means *now*

---

[1] Saul Kripke, *Wittgenstein on Rules and Private Language* (Cambridge: Harvard University Press, 1982).

This paper is a rather distant descendant of talks I gave some time ago at UCLA, The Australian National University, and the Third Meeting of Italian-American Philosophy in Rome in 2001. A shortened version of the talk in Rome was printed in the proceedings of the conference: *The Legitimacy of Truth*, ed. Riccardo Dottori (Munster: Lit Verlag, 2003), pp. 171–87. Sections II and IV of the present paper are adapted from the sections of the proceedings version. I would like to thank Brian Bowman, Goeff Georgi, and Jonathan Weil for a host of suggestions, both substantive and editorial.

by a term determines how the term, in its present meaning, is to be applied correctly in an indefinite range of yet to be examined cases. Let us say, for brevity, that what is claimed to be questioned in Wittgenstein is the idea that the meaning of a term *semantically determines in advance* whether or not the term, so meant, applies to various actual and possible candidate items. In Section I, I will spell out more carefully what I think the targeted notion of "prior semantic determination" amounts to, and I will sketch the outlines of the critique of that notion that Kripke's Wittgenstein elaborates.

It seems to me that it is a great achievement of Kripke's book to stress the centrality of the skeptical doubts about semantic determination in Wittgenstein's rule-following reflections and to develop an original and powerful challenge to this fundamental idea. Actually, a certain number of commentators, John McDowell, David Pears, and most notably Crispin Wright,[2] have been in broad agreement with Kripke about *this* objective of the rule-following considerations, although, of course, they differ about the precise character of the challenge and on a host of related matters. But Kripke's discussion takes two crucial further steps. First, he brings out the way in which that intuitive conception rests in turn upon an apparently natural view of what it is for a speaker to mean something by a term. This view, which I will elaborate shortly, is the view that Kripke refers to as "classical realism" about meaning. Second, in the course of developing the Skeptical Argument that he finds implicit in Wittgenstein, Kripke puts together a critique of classical realism and its associated conception of semantic determination – a critique that is distinctive in its strategy and richly suggestive.

Unfortunately, the power and interest of this challenge are somewhat obscured in Kripke's presentation by what appears to be a repeated invocation of a striking "nonfactualism" concerning the meanings of terms or expressions, either as used by an individual speaker or within a linguistic community as a whole. For instance, he says that Wittgenstein "does not give a 'straight' solution, pointing out to the silly skeptic a hidden fact he overlooked, a condition in the world which constitutes my meaning

---

[2] John McDowell, *Mind, Value, and Reality* (Cambridge: Harvard University Press, 1998); see especially "Wittgenstein on Following a Rule," pp. 221–62 and "Meaning and Intentionality in Wittgenstein's Later Philosophy," pp. 263–78. David Pears, *The False Prison*, vol. 2 (Oxford: Oxford University Press, 1988). Crispin Wright, of course, has written a great deal on the subject. See, for instance, *Wittgenstein on the Foundations of Mathematics* (London: Duckworth, 1980), especially chapters 2 and 12, and *Rails to Infinity* (Cambridge: Harvard University Press, 2001).

addition by 'plus'. In fact, he agrees with his own hypothetical skeptic that there is no such fact, no such condition in either the 'internal' or 'external' world" (*WRPL*, p. 62). It is easy to provide a fairly long list of similar passages.[3] If these passages are taken at face value, then, according to Kripke, Wittgenstein agrees with the skeptic in holding that

> (NF) There are no facts, individualistic or social, about the speaker that constitute his meaning one thing rather than another (and, rather than nothing at all) by his use of any given term or sentence.

Actually, for most readers of Kripke's book, it is precisely this non-factualism about meaning that expresses "*the* skeptical conclusion" – the general thesis that the notorious Skeptical Argument purports to establish. What is more, since Kripke holds that Wittgenstein accepts the conclusion, it is the overarching skeptical principle that constrains the framework of the Skeptical Solution. In Kripke's book, we find many prima facie affirmations of semantic nonfactualism, but its status in *WRPL* is problematic. First, many critics have complained that it is not easy to be sure just what it is that (NF) does or does not say, and we will explore some of these narrower exegetical issues as we proceed. Second, it seems to me that it is also difficult to understand how something like (NF) fits into the broader argumentative structure of Kripke's discussion. In fact, I will argue that it is doubtful that Kripke should claim that his reconstructed Wittgenstein endorses (NF) at all. As I interpret the Skeptical Argument, it is not at all obvious that (NF) should be its upshot. Finally, I'll argue that, on its most natural interpretation, (NF) is actually incompatible with the perspective of the so-called Skeptical Solution. This may sound a bit liking trying to cut Raskolnikov out of *Crime and Punishment*, but it's more like taking him out of an adaptation of *Vanity Fair*. (NF) is simply not the right character for the story that is told within the positive framework of the Skeptical Solution. In fact, it is the nonfactualism about meaning, especially when it is taken to

---

3 Here are two additional passages in which Kripke seems to endorse, as Wittgenstein's skeptical conclusion, the nonfactualism formulated here as (NF). On p. 21, he says, "It [the skeptical challenge] purports to show that nothing in my mental history of past behavior – not even what an omniscient God would know – could establish whether I meant plus or quus. But then it appears to follow that there was no *fact* about me that constituted my having meant plus or quus." Or on p. 70, he notoriously asserts, "Nevertheless I choose to be so bold as to say: Wittgenstein holds, with the sceptic, that there is no fact as to whether I meant plus or quus." Other quotations tending toward nonfactualism could be added to the list. However, as we will see later, there are still other formulations of "the skeptical conclusion" that give a rather different impression of its import.

be Wittgenstein's supposed skeptical conclusion, that has been deemed most objectionable, philosophically and exegetically, in Kripke's exposition of Wittgenstein's "rule-following considerations." So, if we can see how it might be reasonably excised from the core of Kripke's account of Wittgenstein, it would seem that the account is bound to benefit. Nevertheless, I will need to spend some time developing the preceding claims. Specifically, I will explain my interpretation of the Skeptical Argument as an argument chiefly directed against an intuitive conception of "semantic determination." I will also explain at some length why the apparent nonfactualism about meaning strikes me as so puzzling in the overall context of Kripke's book. These explanations are found in Section II.

In Section III, I argue for three related claims. (A) Implicit in the Skeptical Solution is the idea that ascriptions of meaning to a speaker at a time are directly committed to the claim that the speaker's relevant linguistic dispositions at that time are properly in agreement with relevant standards of correctness settled upon within the wider linguistic community. (B) Given that meaning ascriptions carry this commitment, according to the Skeptical Solution, they cannot be coherently construed, within that framework, as being nonfactual in content. Meaning ascriptions express purported facts about the relations between a designated speaker's linguistic dispositions and the community's stable linguistic practices and norms. (C) We need to draw a distinction between different senses in which a set of facts might *constitute* a speaker's meaning *so and so* by his use of a term during a specific period of time. This distinction allows us to discriminate between a modest version of the view that a speaker's dispositions constitute his meaning and a stronger version of the view. I claim that the Skeptical Solution is actually committed to the modest version but not the stronger one, and I explain why it is only the stronger version of what Kripke calls "the dispositionalist account" of meaning that the Skeptical Argument addresses and arguably defeats. In my opinion, the failure to draw this distinction has been the source of considerable confusion both in Kripke's discussion and in critical commentary on it. Finally, in Section IV, I take a brief look at some key passages in the *Philosophical Investigations* (hereafter *PI*)[4] to bring out the particular way in which Wittgenstein is not a nonfactualist about meaning ascriptions. Wittgenstein has a special understanding of the kinds of

---

[4] Ludwig Wittgenstein, *Philosophical Investigations*, 3rd edition, trans. G. E. M. Anscombe, (Oxford: Blackwell, 2001), hereafter referred to as *PI*.

facts that correct meaning ascriptions describe, an understanding that the Skeptical Solution at least partially succeeds in capturing.

II. Nonfactualism and the Skeptical Conclusion

In the enormous literature on *WRPL*, there is really no consensus about what it is that Kripke's skeptic is questioning. Hence, I want to begin by making an important but controversial point about the way in which I understand the skeptical challenge. To do so, let us consider, for instance, Kripke's chief example of the speaker whose use of the term '+' comes under skeptical investigation. We can suppose that this speaker has at least heard of addition, say, from the teachers who have instructed him about the procedure of adding and about the meaning of the term '+'. And we can suppose as well that the speaker takes himself to know, on the basis of this instruction, how the operation of addition is to be performed. Then, on at least one obvious reading of the statement, it will be true that,

(1) In using '+', the speaker intended to be adding.

However, it doesn't follow from this that

(2) The term '+', as the speaker used it, actually meant *addition*.

For it could be that the operation that the speaker actually learned to perform and did, in fact, perform was quaddition. That is, the speaker might wrongly suppose that what he has learned to do is the same as the procedure or operation that others call "addition," and, in carrying out a particular calculation, he may aim at and take himself to be adding. In these circumstances, the speaker would be mistaken in believing that (2) expressed a truth about him, and '+', as he was disposed to use it then, actually meant *quaddition*. This is so, despite the speaker's own description of what he was doing as "addition." In my opinion, the skeptical challenge asks for a fact or constellation of facts that could somehow *constitute* its being the case that (2). I believe that the skeptic can allow, throughout his challenge, that, at the relevant time, the speaker meant (intended) to be adding and even that

(1′) The speaker intended that '+', as he used it then, was to mean *addition*.

What the skeptic questions is whether there could be a fact that constituted the speaker's succeeding in what he then intended. The skeptic is not asking, quite generally, what a person's intending anything at all might consist in. And he is not asking, quite generally, what makes it the case that a person's intentions have the content that they do. His question is a question in what Stalnaker dubs "foundational semantics" – a metasemantic question about the facts, if any, that constitute a term's having the meaning that it does for a speaker (in his idiolect) or within a broader linguistic community.[5] What makes it the case that a term stands in the relation of meaning (or denoting) to one appropriate semantic value or another? Moreover, this question, as we will see later, does not request some sort of analysis or reduction of the semantic relation mentioned in (2) to facts describable in purely nonsemantic and/or nonintentional concepts.[6] For obvious reasons, it is easy to mix up issues about the nature of the putative fact described by (2) and about the nature of the facts described by (1) or (1'), but, if we do, we are bound to suffer for the confusion. This point also has the consequence that there is no categorical proscription, in the dialectic of the Skeptical Argument, against making certain limited appeals to the speaker's intentions or, more generally, to the speaker's intensional states (for example, his beliefs and desires) when offering either a straight or skeptical solution to the puzzle.[7]

In any case, Kripke affirms that there is a "skeptical conclusion about meaning" that Wittgenstein himself elaborates and endorses, but Kripke's

---

[5] "Reference and Necessity," in *Ways a World Might Be: Metaphysical and Anti-Metaphysical Essays* (Oxford: Oxford University Press, 2003), pp. 166–68.

[6] When the skeptic asks what kind of fact constitutes addition as the operation that the speaker means by '+', his question should be understood with a certain philosophical naivete. The only requirement with which the challenge is initially raised is that a potential answer should be informative (not blatantly circular) and draw the right discriminations between cases. Thus, there are no strong restrictions at the outset on the kinds of terms in which the answer is to be framed. In *Naming and Necessity* (Cambridge: Harvard University Press, 1980), after Kripke has finished his critique of descriptivism, he asks, in effect, about the kind of fact that might link the uses of names with their bearers. He investigates this question without supposing that an answer must satisfy any notably reductive conditions. See pp. 90–7. I am suggesting that Kripke's skeptic should be understood to be raising *his* question in much the same spirit.

[7] Of course, there are many beliefs and intentions that a person could not have unless he or she had the capacity to express their contents in a language that the subject knows. Call members of this vaguely defined category "language-bound" beliefs, intentions, and so on. I am not denying that the danger of circularity is introduced into a solution of the skeptical problem that appeals to language-bound propositional attitudes. My point is simply that Wittgenstein surely does not hold that all propositional attitudes are language-bound in this sense. From Wittgenstein's perspective, an appeal to propositional attitudes that are not language-bound does not automatically threaten circularity. Naturally, it is often hard to say whether a given propositional attitude, such as a particular intention, is or is not language-bound.

formulation of the thesis has a confusing tendency to vary from passage to passage. However, if we attend to the basic target and tactics of the Skeptical Argument and to certain key aspects of the skeptical response to that argument, we see that there is a fundamental skeptical conclusion that figures as the focus of both the argument and the response. Moreover, this conclusion does involve a kind of nonfactualism or, better, a kind of factual indeterminacy, about what standards of correctness, if any, govern the correct application of expressions in the idiolect of an arbitrary speaker.[8] It is precisely this thesis of factual indeterminacy about preestablished standards of correctness that seems to undermine the intuitive conception of prior semantic determination. Here is a bare sketch of the content of and argument for the *basic* skeptical conclusion I have in mind.

Let 'Φ' be any basic term a speaker S proposes to use as a general term or predicate. That is, 'Φ', as S plans to employ it, is to apply correctly or incorrectly, as the case may be, to the members of some open-ended domain of objects D. We can assume that 'Φ' is a descriptive term for S, a term that applies correctly or incorrectly, in a given instance, depending upon the facts about the specific character of the candidate item in question. Now, if this is to be so, there needs to be a standard of correctness for S's envisaged ascriptions of the term, that is, there needs to be a determination of the *type of fact* required for the correctness of these prospective ascriptions. Somehow S needs to adopt an intention or, at least, a linguistic policy or commitment that 'Φ', as he is to use it, is true of something just in case that thing is an instance of the type of fact that he has "suitably" in mind. Or, in other words, the standard of correctness for S's use of 'Φ' needs to be established by S in terms of the *properties* that the D-members might exemplify – in terms of those objective, predicable conditions in the world, realized or not as they may be – by the various objects in D. If S is to mean something by 'Φ', then there must be certain properties, P_1 through P_n, to which S is committed as the standards of correctness for his use of 'Φ'. S is to follow the semantic rule or guiding principle, constitutive of the term's meaning, that, for any object in the domain of 'Φ', the term is to be applied to a D-item *o* just in case *o* exemplifies the specified mix of P_1 through P_n. These properties or

---

[8] I have discussed various key aspects of Kripke's reading of Wittgenstein in "Kripke on Wittgenstein and Normativity," *Midwest Studies in Philosophy* XIX (1994), pp. 366–90, and in "Semantic Realism in Kripke's Wittgenstein," *Philosophy and Phenomenological Reasearch* 58 (1998), pp. 99–122.

conditions, then, give the robust truth or satisfaction conditions for the term 'Φ' in S's idiolect.

This is an appealing conception of what is involved in meaning something by a primitive general term. It is appealing because it ensures that meaning involves a straightforward form of prior semantic determination. If S has adopted such a suitable semantic commitment and the relevant facts about candidate objects are taken to be fixed, then it is thereby already determined conclusively, for an unbounded range of candidates in D, whether 'Φ' applies correctly to those objects or does not. As this formulation indicates, the semantic determination here depends on two distinct but related factors. In coming to mean something by the term, S establishes which language-independent conditions a candidate for 'Φ' ascription is to exemplify, that is, S establishes the robust satisfaction conditions for his use of 'Φ'. But now, whether 'Φ' does apply to an object *o* (as it is at a certain time) depends also upon whether *o* actually realizes the stipulated conditions or not. With this qualification understood, we can say that, on the present conception, meaning determines *correct* application instance by instance, and so, in this sense, it is *normative* in relation to the correctness of the speaker's future ascriptions of 'Φ'. The conception of the meaning of a general term outlined above is, I believe, the conception that Kripke refers to as "the classical realist picture of meaning" (*WRPL*, p. 73).[9] I have just stated that "picture" as an account of the meaning of general terms, while, as we will discuss shortly, Kripke explains classical realism, named as such within his text, as a view about the meaning of (indicative) sentences.

Here is how Wittgenstein sets up the problem of "prior semantic determination" in remark §186 in *PI*. After introducing the incorrigibly deviant "+2 adder" in §185, the question arises how it is to be decided how one is to go on in following the relevant instructions. Wittgenstein asks if his interlocutor, the +2 instructor, already meant each of the infinite number of propositions that identify what the next continuation of the series ought to be. The interlocutor says, "No, what I meant was, that he should write the next but one number after *every* number that

---

[9] Kripke introduces the phrase "the classical realist picture of meaning" almost in passing. However, it is possible to reconstruct from the surrounding discussion the chief features of the position that the phrase is meant to designate. For a somewhat different understanding of Kripke's use of the phrase, see Martin Kusch, *A Sceptical Guide to Meaning and Rules* (Montreal & Kingston: McGill-Queen's University Press, 2006), pp. 10–12.

he wrote; and from this all those propositions *follow* [my emphasis] in turn." Wittgenstein replies, "But that is just what is in question: what at any stage does *follow* from that sentence. Or, again, what, at any stage, are we to call 'being in accord' with that sentence (and with the *mean*-ing you then put into the sentence – whatever that may have consisted in)." And, in what seems to be a partial, rather guarded answer, he continues, "It would almost be more correct to say, not that an intuition was needed at every stage, but that a new decision was needed at every stage." By §190, these issues are announced by, "It may now be said: 'The way the formula is meant *determines* which steps are to be taken,'" and the investigation proceeds in these terms. What is it for the meaning of a term or formula to determine the steps that should be taken next? And Wittgenstein repudiates the "queer" mode of determination upon which the interlocutor recurrently insists.

To underscore the puzzle about "'prior semantic determination," I have stated what Kripke refers to as the "classical realist" conception of "meaning" for the case of predicates, emphasizing its correlative view of how meaning determines application. But the classical realist conception can be formulated just as well for the case of whole declarative sentences, and when Kripke officially introduces "classical realism" into his discussion, he presents the second formulation. We can indicate the connection in the following way. Just as a predicate 'Φ' represents, as we might say, a *type of fact* which properly constitutes its satisfaction conditions, similarly a "descriptive" sentence 'Σ', as it is used by speaker S, represents a particular possible fact PF – a possible fact that represents the (classical realist) truth conditions for that sentence as it functions in the setting of S's idiolect.[10] 'Σ' expresses a truth just in case the possible fact PF is realized. To allow for the occurrence of context-sensitive devices in the relevant sentence Σ, we should probably say that 'Σ', as S uses it, represents a schematic possible fact PF* and that it is only contextualized utterances of 'Σ' that express specific possible facts, that is, specific instances of the schematic fact PF*. However, I will continue to employ the simpler formulation. Thus, according to classical realism, the meaning of a sentence determines the possible fact (if any) whose realization will make the sentence true. The meaning of a sentence, so conceived, together with the character of the relevant segment of the

---

[10] One might think of what Kripke calls "possible facts" in this connection as being structured propositions of some sort. For a critical overview of theories of the nature and semantic function of structured propositions, see Jeffery C. King, *The Nature and Structure of Content* (Oxford: Oxford University Press, 2007).

world determines whether the represented possible fact is realized or not, that is, it determines whether what the sentence says is or is not true.[11]

Naturally, it is possible to develop a form of skepticism about this sort of classical realism from different directions. One may be skeptical about the coherence of the robust notion of facts or properties (the "platonistic" truth or satisfaction conditions) that, according to classical realism, are supposed to constitute the semantic standards of correctness for the relevant expressions. One may object, on nominalistic grounds, to the relatively abstract and the mind- and language-independent conception of these "standards" upon which classical realism relies. Nevertheless, this is not the strategy that Kripke's semantic skeptic pursues. The skeptic argues, in effect, that although such extralinguistic standards of correctness may be metaphysically wholly reputable and may be abundant in profusion, they necessarily remain "idle wheels" in relation to the enterprise of setting any real standards in place, standards that can determinately govern the correctness and incorrectness of a speaker's employment of his terms and sentences.

More specifically, the skeptic argues that there can be no fact of the matter about which would-be standard of correctness, out of a host of equally admissible options, is supposed to govern a speaker's use of a term 'Φ'. And in the same vein, the skeptic argues that it is always factually indeterminate as to which possible fact, out of a comparable range of options, is represented, in virtue of S's prior semantic commitments, by a sentence 'Σ' in S's idiolect. Given any one intuitively plausible standard of correctness, it is possible to think of "yet others standing behind it" whose patterns of "accord and conflict" differ from the first, but where each of the deviant alternatives is completely compatible with every fact, inner and outer, associated with S's use of 'Φ' or 'Σ'. This, then, is what I take to be the *basic* Skeptical Conclusion – the conclusion for which Kripke's skeptic argues and Kripke's Wittgenstein affirms. Stated somewhat more carefully it says,

---

[11] It is useful to distinguish between classical realism (in semantics) as a theory (or picture) of truth or satisfaction conditions and as a theory of meaning for the terms or sentences in question. Classical realism about the satisfaction conditions for a general term holds that they are mind- and language-independent conditions in the world that have been associated with the term as the standards of correctness for its application. Classical realism about the meaning of general terms claims that a given general term has the meaning that it does *in virtue of* its antecedent association with satisfaction conditions so conceived. I am indebted to Scott Soames for emphasizing the importance of this distinction to me.

(BSC) a) There are no facts about a speaker, taken individually or socially, that establish any single set of properties – out of an indefinite range of alternatives – as the standards of correctness for his/her use of 'Φ'. And b) there are no individual or social facts that establish any single "possible fact" as that which is represented by the speaker's use of 'Σ'.[12]

The skeptic argues for this conclusion by considering and rejecting a range of facts about the speaker, supposedly exhaustive of the viable possibilities, that might be thought to determine which property or which possible fact the term or sentence in question actually represents.[13]

What a "standard of correctness" might be will vary, to some extent, from one kind of term to another. For descriptive predicates, as I have said, it is natural to take the standards to be empirical properties, realized or not, as they may be, by various relevant items in the world. In Kripke's example of S's use of '+', the standard of correctness for the sign is supposed to be a particular method or procedure of calculation that yields a unique numerical value for any pair of natural numbers (or numerals). The speaker takes himself to have mastered such a calculation procedure and believes that the procedure he has mastered is exemplified in those calculations that are prompted for him by the term '+'. Since, in one sense of the treacherous word "rule," the steps and the recursive ordering of those steps that make up the computational procedure are themselves rules of the procedure, the speaker takes himself to have mastered those computational rules. (Rules in this sense should be distinguished from various *linguistic formulations* of them – from various "expressions" of those rules.) And, of course, the procedure in question is supposed to be a procedure for computing the result of *adding* any pair of numbers. The computational procedure (the algorithm) that S has mastered purportedly determines, for *any* pair of numerals 'j' and 'k', how S's calculations, elicited by '+', should properly proceed, and S's

---

[12] It is important that I formulate the thesis here by saying that there are no facts about the speaker or the linguistic community that constitutes one property rather than another *as* standards of correctness for the term in question. Later I will argue that the question "What are the facts that constitute someone's meaning *so and so* by a term?" is importantly ambiguous in a crucial way. The present formulation withstands the complications engendered by that ambiguity.

[13] Especially in "Semantic Realism in Kripke's Wittgenstein," I stress that the overall argument for the basic Skeptical Conclusion is not a regress argument, although a regress argument figures in the consideration of certain potential straight solutions. This point about the structure of the argument makes a difference to the way in which I think *PI* § 201 is to be reconstructed. On this, see pp. 110–14 of "Semantic Realism."

mastery of the procedure involves S's having generally reliable, although not infallible, intuitive access to what it is that the procedure step by step requires for specific arguments. Correlatively, the truth conditions of an arbitrary atomic equation framed by S with '+', that is, an equation of the form '$j + k = l$', are centrally defined for S in terms of the procedure that S's '+' calculations are meant to execute. For S, such statements are to count as true just in case the result of performing *this* procedure (the one he has in mind) on j and k is l.

It is important to notice that two different but related kinds of rules are involved in S's establishing a meaning for '+'. There are the *computational rules* that S is supposed to have learned through his training in performing suitable calculations and in seeing them performed by others. And, of course, these are supposed to be computational rules for carrying out *addition* on the natural numbers. But there is also the *semantic rule* that is also involved in S's establishing a meaning for his use of '+'. He commits himself to the semantic rule stated above, the rule that is to assign truth or satisfaction conditions to his present and prospective applications of the term in '+' equations. The conditions thus assigned by the semantic rule for '+' are grounded in the rules of calculation that S takes himself to have learned. So whether S, in any given instance, has carried out a specific calculation "correctly" depends upon whether his actual computational performance is in accordance with what his internalized procedure prescribes for the computation in question. And the truth or falsity of a corresponding '+' equation depends upon the specific arithmetic facts concerning the application of the procedure in that case. It depends, more specifically, upon which number is generated as the upshot of the intended method of calculation when it has been carried out correctly for the arguments in question.

But of course, what the skeptic argues is that there simply are no facts about which procedure the speaker has learned and made the subject of his semantic rule. There are no facts about the speaker that make it the case that the procedure he purportedly has mastered and thereby has in mind as governing '+' really is a procedure of addition, rather than quaddition, and rather than some other oddball operation defined upon the natural numbers. Similarly, he insists, there are no facts about the speaker which establish whether the truth or falsity of any '+' equation affirmed by S turns on the mathematical facts about addition, or turns instead on counterpart facts about quaddition, or, again, turns on counterpart facts about still another deviant method of calculation. Thus, there are no facts about whether '+', as the speaker uses it, is governed by any one arithmetical operation (algorithm) or another. Kripke's argument proceeds by rejecting various proposals about the facts that might provide a "straight solution" to the skeptic's challenge, and, taken together, these proposals are supposed to exhaust all of the possibilities. I will not attempt to evaluate the success or failure of the cumulative argument for (BSC), although I will suppose, for purposes of the present discussion, that it is successful.

The Skeptical Solution is defined as *skeptical* because of its acceptance and incorporation of (BSC). And the first step in the Skeptical Solution is to grant that terms and sentences do not have classical realist truth (or satisfaction) conditions, and, a fortiori, that their meaningfulness does not depend on truth conditions in this sense. Note that this is the crucial step in establishing the framework of the Skeptical Solution. Kripke says, "If Wittgenstein is right, we cannot begin to solve it [the skeptical problem] if we remain in the grip of the natural presupposition that meaningful declarative sentences must purport to correspond to facts: if this is our framework, we can only conclude that sentences attributing meaning and intention are themselves meaningless.... The picture of correspondence-to-facts must be cleared away before we can begin with the sceptical problem" (*WRPL*, pp. 78–9). On the basis of the Skeptical Argument, Kripke's Wittgenstein denies that terms even purport to have classical realist standards of correctness and, as in the passage just quoted, he denies, more or less equivalently, that sentences purport to represent classical realist "possible facts." In other words, Kripke's Wittgenstein denies that sentences and predicates have the meanings they do in virtue of their having classical realist truth or satisfaction conditions at all.

For the classical realist, the statement

(3) Sentence 'Σ', as S uses it, means that *such and such*

says roughly the same as

(4) 'Σ', as S uses it, represents the possible fact that such and such,

where (4) records a genuine relation, univocally understood, between 'Σ' and the "possible fact" in question. Similarly,

(5) The term 'Φ', as S uses it (during t), means *so and so*

says that

> (6) 'Φ', as S uses it (during t), is governed by its antecedent name-like
> correlation with the language independent property of being so and
> so.[14]

Consequently, as Kripke affirms, the Skeptical Solution also rejects the
classical realist parsing of the content of

> (7) The meaning of a term or sentence determines what has to be the
> case in order for the term to be satisfied in a given instance or for
> the sentence to be true.

It rejects, that is, the classical realist conception of "semantic determination," and it offers alternative accounts, constrained by (BSC), of both the
content of meaning ascriptions and the nature of prior semantic determination. To arrive at the basis of such an alternative account, Kripke says,
"we must consider how we actually use: (i) the categorical assertion that
an individual is following a given rule (that he means addition by '+'); (ii)
the conditional assertion that 'if an individual follows such-and-such a rule,
he must do so-and-so on a given occasion'" (*WRPL*, p. 108). We will take a
brief look at these 'skeptical' accounts of meaning a little later in the discussion. They represent the central positive strands of the Skeptical Solution.

However, none of the considerations so far provides us with grounds
for understanding Kripke's apparent claims that Wittgenstein himself sub-
scribes to the sort of nonfactualism about *meaning* mentioned earlier. I have
insisted that it is crucial to the attack on the classical realist idea of "semantic determination" that Kripke's Wittgenstein accepts (BSC), and that result
tells us that there are and there can be no facts about the speaker that constitute suitable classical realist standards of correctness for his use of terms
and sentences. It is this result that questions whether any robust truth conditions can be put in place to settle in advance semantic questions of accord
and conflict over an unbounded range of actual and potential cases. What
is more, the skeptic, who is himself a classical realist about semantics, has a
characteristic conception of what it is for a speaker to mean something by
an expression – a conception that is partly framed in the purported equivalence of (3) and (4) and (5) and (6). It follows, therefore, that Kripke's
skeptic does adopt a radical semantic nonfactualism about meaning. That

---

[14] I stress that these equivalences are part of the implicit framework of classical realism about
meaning for the following reason. Although the equivalences can seem almost trivial and
inevitable, especially the purported equivalence between (5) and (6), it is rather clear that
Wittgenstein rejects them. I take up this point in the last section of the paper.

is, the skeptic accepts the thesis that there are no facts that constitute the speaker's meaning something by his uses of the terms and sentences in a speaker's idiolect. But it is hard to see why Kripke's Wittgenstein should agree. On Kripke's own account, Wittgenstein rejects the classical realist conception of meaning and meaning ascriptions, and he offers another in its place. So it should mark a distinction between Kripke's skeptic and Kripke's Wittgenstein that the latter but not the former is tempted by (BSC) into nonfactualism about meaning.

On the other hand, it is true that Kripke's Wittgenstein maintains that meaning ascriptions like (3) and (5) and their variants do not purport to represent classical realist possible facts. Thus, Kripke asserts, "Wittgenstein's sceptical solution concedes to the sceptic that no 'truth conditions' or 'corresponding facts' in the world exist that make a statement like "Jones, like many of us, means addition by '+'" true" (*WRPL*, p. 86). At this juncture, we *do* arrive at the result that meaning ascriptions are not "fact-stating" in this quasi-technical sense. However, the emphasis on this specific *claim* is also puzzling. Under the regime of the Skeptical Solution, *no* meaningful declarative sentence purports to represent a classical realist possible fact, and it therefore marks out nothing special about meaning ascriptions to note that they fail to "state facts" under such a theoretically loaded interpretation of the phrase. Kripke's Wittgenstein would turn out to be a nonfactualist about everything under *the present* interpretation. In this sense, no sentence whatsoever states or depicts facts, when (BSC) has been embraced. For the same reason, it is doubly puzzling when Kripke says, "Recall Wittgenstein's sceptical conclusion: no facts, no truth conditions, correspond to statements such as, 'Jones means addition by '+'" (*WRPL*, p. 77). If we assume that the talk here of "facts" and "truth conditions" is to be construed within the classical realist framework, one would have thought that the "sceptical conclusion" was something much stronger and specific to the special case of meaning ascriptions – a thesis like our (BSC), for example.

It looks to me, therefore, as though Kripke may have confused (BSC) with the thesis that meaning ascriptions don't have classical realist truth conditions and, moreover, confused (BSC) with the nonfactualism about meaning you get if you arrive at (BSC) from within the context of a classical realist account of meaning.[15] What is more, if these issues are kept

---

[15] Scott Soames makes a similar suggestion that Kripke may have confused two distinct conclusions about meaning facts and about two corresponding lines of argument concerning them. See his article, "Facts, Truth-Conditions, and the Skeptical Solution to the Rule-Following Paradox," *Philosophical Perspectives* 12 (1998), pp. 313–48.

straight, it appears that the Skeptical Solution is *not* directly committed to any notable nonfactualism about meaning. Its mere acceptance of (BSC) does not so commit it. However, it is more difficult to decide whether the Skeptical Solution, in its further ramifications, supports an interesting, substantial form of nonfactualism about meaning. After all, the Skeptical Solution does not deny the somewhat schematic claim that meaning is, in some sense, *normative*, despite the fact that it jettisons the classical real-ist account of the normativity of meaning. It remains an open question whether whatever alternative conception of normativity the Skeptical Solution constructs, might lead, together with additional considerations, to some sort of nonfactualism about meaning ascriptions. This question is delicate and difficult because it is less than clear just how certain key aspects of the Skeptical Solution are supposed to work. We will address this topic in the next section.

III. THE SKEPTICAL SOLUTION AND NONFACTUALISM

Let me attempt a brief overview of the key aspects of the Skeptical Solution. In particular, I will follow Kripke in stating these aspects as they apply to the paradigmatic case of the term '+' and the arithmetic operation of addition. There are some special features of the case of arithmetic truth that call for some comment here, although, of course, the Skeptical Solution is supposed to offer us a framework that explains what it is for an arbitrary term 'Φ' to have meaning and what it is to say that the term, as used by a particular speaker, means *so and so*. However, without commenting on the special features of the arithmetic case, it is hard to state how the account of meaning ascriptions in the Skeptical Solution is supposed to work for the term '+', and if there is confusion about this central example, that confusion is liable to infect our under-standing of the more general framework.[16]

So, to reprise, the Skeptical Solution, accepting (BSC), assumes that there is no general computational procedure, potentially present in S's mind at t, that determines in advance, for each pair of possible argu-ments, the patterns of derivations that correct calculations for '+' by S

---

[16] The example of '+' and the operation of addition works very effectively for setting up the skeptic's challenge. However, there are special features of arithmetic truths (their necessity, their grounding in computation, and so on) that make it hard to state the pos-itive framework of the Skeptical Solution, as it applies to the case of '+', in a minimally plausible way. To even attempt to cover that case, one is forced to speculate about the character of Wittgenstein's difficult and sometimes puzzling remarks about calculation and arithmetic truth.

must realize. As a consequence, there is nothing that assigns classical realist truth conditions, grounded upon the intended preestablished computational procedure, to sentences of the form '$j + k = l$' (as they are used by S). Nevertheless, in opening his account of the Skeptical Solution, Kripke explains, "[The skeptical paradox] holds no terrors in our daily lives; no one actually hesitates when asked to produce an answer to an addition problem! Almost all of us unhesitatingly produce the answer '125' when asked for the sum of 68 and 57, without any thought to the theoretical possibility that a quus-like rule might have been appropriate!" (*WRPL*, p. 87). And it is a crucial part of the Skeptical Solution that we are wholly right to proceed "blindly" in this fashion. An individual calculator who is seemingly competent in the use of '+' is justified in performing a particular calculation "on his own" and even in taking his result, defeasibly, to be right.

Naturally, some computations performed by S may contain "mistakes" and may be "corrected" by others in the community. But S, although wrong in these instances, remains defeasibly justified in his practice of calculating *on his own* as long as his computations for '+' remain in overall agreement with the way in which others carry out the calculations for the same range of numerical arguments. If this overall agreement were to lapse and the general expectation of agreement were to fade, then the justification that each "competent" individual has for proceeding on his own would lapse as well. On the other hand, when a framework of overall agreement has been successfully sustained, by initial training and by subsequent instruction and correction, then the individual calculator can take his concrete calculations as the derivation of a genuinely correct arithmetic result. Given a particular addition problem, if there is suitable concordance among adders on the pattern that their token calculations for that problem are to realize, the framework of global agreement justifies them defeasibly in accepting calculations of that pattern as correct. The community adopts that pattern and, in Wittgenstein's phrase, they "put it in the archives." If 'j' and 'k' are the arguments in question and 'l' is the numerical result that the accepted pattern of calculation yields, then the equation '$j + k = l$' is effectively accepted in the community as an arithmetic truth.[17]

---

[17] Here and in the following two paragraphs, I go beyond anything that Kripke says about Wittgenstein's views on the subject of arithmetic truth. Also, what I say is too brief and oversimplified, but I have hoped to say enough to make it possible to develop the ensuing presentation of the Skeptical Solution, especially as it applies to '+'. In particular,

Wittgenstein himself seems to regard these accepted equations as having the character of particularized "rules" that, given a stable background of community agreement, "fix" the unique result that correct '+' calculations with *j* and *k* must produce. An individual adopts such a rule for '*j*', '*k*', and '*l*' when he accepts his own '+' computation (resulting in '*l*') as a "model" for – as paradigmatic of – how any '+' computation on '*j*' and '*k*' ought to go. He sees his own concrete calculation as instantiating the pattern to which any other counterpart concrete calculation must conform. Of course, the community's acceptance of such rules or problem-specific arithmetic standards is not just an accident. How individual calculators will, in favorable circumstances, perform *is* determined, that is, it is causally determined, both by the regimen of training in '+' computations they have received, together with their natural propensities in learning to go on from that training in the familiar and mutually expected way. So the acceptance by various calculators of the correctness of a given pattern of calculation will normally take place as a matter of course, and the pattern that each of them derive is likely to strike them as the "natural and inevitable" right result.

Of course, it is no part of the conception here that an equation '*j* + *k* = *l*' means the same as "We mostly agree in getting *l* when we compute the sum of *j* and *k*." If a community of game players agree in accepting the rule of chess (in these words), "The King in chess moves one square in any direction," then the words themselves simply express that familiar rule of chess. These words do not express the anthropological truth that the community of chess players has concurred in setting up and sustaining such a rule. Similarly, it is true, within the framework of the Skeptical Solution, that the patterns of correct calculation with '+' and the counterpart simple truths about addition are, in effect, settled upon over the course of time. It is critical here that, according to Kripke's Wittgenstein, nothing establishes in advance even the truth conditions (let alone the truth value) of every atomic equation framed in terms of '+'. So it is left to the community to settle upon those truth conditions and the patterns of calculation that support them, and this is a process with an indefinitely

the Wittgenstein I describe comes across as a strict finitist, and there is evidence in favor of such a reading of him. However, the whole topic is complicated and controversial. See *Remarks on the Foundations of Mathematics*, ed. G. H. Wright, R. Rhees, and G. E. M. Anscombe (Cambridge: MIT Press, 1978). For the idea that proofs, including calculations, are accepted as "models" of how the pertinent procedure is to go and the proposal that "the proved proposition is a rule," see especially the remarks § 25 through § 28 in part III.

extendable history over time. Nevertheless, the results that get accepted – the '+' equations that come to be adopted – are themselves timeless or tenseless statements. The truths that they express make no reference to time nor to particular instances of calculating in terms of '+'.

The Skeptical Solution incorporates an account of meaning. It tells us that the meaning of a term 'Φ', in a given linguistic community, depends upon (a) the assertability or justification conditions that the community accepts in practice for (basic) sentential completions of 'Φ' and (b) the characteristic role or utility of the predicate, so employed, within the language games in which it figures. In the highly simplified story about the use of '+' that I have adumbrated above, the assertability conditions for basic '+' equations are given by the computations from which the equations are to be read off. However, the status of particular computations as *justifying* the assertion of a specific '+' equation presupposes that the community is implicitly in agreement or, at least, is in a position to reach agreement about how the pertinent computation types should be performed. Presumably, a central language game role or function of the assertible '+' equations is provided by the way that these equations mediate inferences between judgments about the cardinality of sets and ordinal positioning in a series. In point of fact, any minimally acceptable account of the language game role of the term '+' and of the '+' equations would have to go well beyond these basic applications, and a more extended account would quickly become quite complicated. But perhaps this is enough to suggest a rough idea of the approach of the Skeptical Solution to questions of meaning. The Skeptical Argument purports to show that the meaning of a term cannot be explained in terms of facts about its classical realist truth conditions. It purports to have demonstrated that there simply are no such facts. The alternative account of meaning that the Skeptical Solution offers in place of the discredited classical realism maintains that the meaning of a term depends instead upon facts about (a) and (b) above – the justification conditions of the term and the functions that it serves in relevant language games.

However, just these considerations are enough to raise a puzzle about how questions of linguistic meaning can fail to be factual according to the Skeptical Solution. First, the Skeptical Solution does not deny that there are genuine *facts* concerning categories (a) and (b).[18] Second, the

[18] Actually a good deal turns here on questions about how the concept of "assertability conditions" is explicated. One might imagine that a set of circumstances K warrants the assertion of a sentence Σ for a speaker (or linguistic community) only if the speaker (or community) has adopted an internalized rule that says that the assertion is warranted

Skeptical Solution affirms that what it is for a term to mean something at or during a certain time *depends* upon constellations of facts from these two categories. It is true that we are never given any clear articulation of what the nature of this "dependence" is supposed to be. Kripke tells us that the Skeptical Solution does not propose that necessary and sufficient conditions for meaning ascriptions can be given in terms of considerations drawn from (a) and (b). In fact, he also tells us that the Skeptical Solution proposes no "analysis" of what meaning something by a term or sentence consists in. In particular, no analysis or reduction of meaning in terms of factors from categories (a) and (b) is envisaged. Nevertheless, this rather underspecified thesis of factual dependence is central to the Skeptical Solution. Even if we were to suppose that matters of linguistic meaning stand only in some kind of weak supervenience relation to the facts in (a) and (b), it is puzzling to grasp, from the "skeptical" perspective, how questions about what a term or sentence means could *fail* to be in factual in nature. Indeed, questions of meaning should be just as factual as the undisputed facts about linguistic practice that figure in (a) and (b). After all, the Skeptical Solution seems to maintain that what a term or expression means is somehow explained by the prior facts that these two categories subsume.

These reflections are reinforced if we focus specifically on what the Skeptical Solution proposes concerning the assertability or justification conditions for ascriptions of meaning to an individual speaker's use of a term. For instance, what are the justification conditions for meaning ascriptions that say that '+', as used by a speaker S, does or does not mean *addition*? More narrowly, what are the (third-person) assertability conditions for judgments of this type?[19] Having stressed once more the importance of the background presupposition that the community is

when circumstances K have been realized. Given a conception of this ilk, it is difficult to see why an analogue of the Skeptical Argument couldn't be constructed to show that there can be no fact of the matter about what assertability conditions (in this sense) govern any term or sentence. I think that Kripke is at some pains to make it clear that assertability or justification conditions are *not* to be understood in this fashion. It is an essential part of the Skeptical Solution that assertability conditions are supposed to be concretely *manifest* in the speech activities of the community. It would be an enormous project to try to spell out in any detail what this notion of "assertability conditions" amounts to. And it would be a comparable project to decide whether the Skeptical Solution, invoking assertability conditions so construed, succeeds in evading an adjusted version of the skeptical challenge. I say more (but only a little more) about this crucial issue in "Is Kripke's Wittgenstein a Temporal Externalist?" forthcoming in *Meaning Across Time*, ed. Tom Stoneham.

[19] As Kripke very briefly indicates, some special attention has to be given to the assertabilty conditions for statements of the form, 'Φ', as *I* use it now, means *so and so*.

roughly in agreement about how a range of tractable '+' calculations are to proceed, Kripke says:

> Any individual who claims to have mastered the concept of addition will be judged by the community to have done so if his particular responses agree with those of the community in enough cases, especially the simple ones (and if his 'wrong' answers are not often *bizarrely* wrong, as in '5' for '68 = 57', but seem to agree with ours in *procedure*, even when he makes a 'computational mistake.') An individual who passes such tests in enough other cases is admitted as a normal speaker of the language and member of the community. Those who deviate are corrected and told (usually as children) that they have not grasped the concept of addition. (*WRPL*, pp. 91–2)

Thus, the favorable justification conditions that the Skeptical Solution assigns to judgments of the form

(7)   '+', as S uses it at or during a time t, means *addition*

seem to correspond roughly to the type of *inductive evidence* appropriate for confirming counterpart factual judgments of the form

(7′)   At or during t, S is disposed to use '+' in adequate alignment with the patterns of calculation for '+' that are actually or prospectively accepted by his linguistic community and in suitable agreement with the reports of the results of these calculations that members of the community would consequently endorse.

Actually, to reflect properly some of the nuances and qualifications in Kripke's discussion of the assertability conditions for '+' equations, my formulation of (7′) should be expanded and refined.[20] But the simplified version should be adequate for stating the points I want to make. If the speaker S passes the tests that Kripke mentions in the quoted paragraph, then members of the community are supposed to be warranted or justified in judging that (7). But what is the character of the epistemic entitlement that the community is thereby supposed to have? The simplest answer to the question is the following. S's passing the indicated

---

These will be the "first-person" assertability conditions for judgments of type (5). The questions raised by the first-person case are extremely interesting, but the interest of these questions is tangential to the present line of argument. For the purposes at hand, it seems legitimate to focus on the third-person assertabilty conditions.

[20] In fact, Kripke makes it clear that even his own, somewhat fuller characterization of the assertability conditions in question here is too simple. However, it is the basic theoretical approach that needs to be sketched without filling in all of the laborious detail that greater accuracy would demand.

criterial tests is understood to provide *factual evidence* or *empirical confirmation* for proposition (7). *That* identifies the nature of the warrant or justification that these assertability conditions supply for instances of (7). However, this natural supposition makes sense only if it is assumed that (7) expresses, in part or whole, the content of the patently factual proposition (7'). Since the assertability conditions proposed for (7) describe confirming evidence for (7'), it is utterly opaque how those same conditions could warrant (7) in some quite different way. So the Skeptical Solution had better grant that (7) says something distinctively factual itself – something akin to (7').

Here is a more general formulation of the way that the Skeptical Solution contends that ascriptions of meaning of the form

(5)   The term 'Φ', as S uses it during t, means *so and so*

are related to the conditions that warrant their assertion. An instance of (5) will be defeasibly warranted if

(i)   facts about how S actually ascribes 'Φ' to candidate instances are in adequate alignment with the justification conditions in his community for judgments about suitable test cases that they are so and so;

(ii) facts about S's use of 'Φ' reflect adequate sensitivity to the role and utility of 'Φ' within the wider activities of the linguistic community;

and

(iii) facts that indicate that the way that S is disposed to use 'Φ' would continue to be adequately in alignment over time with community justification conditions for 'Φ' and sensitive to the future role and utility of the term in pertinent language games.

But now, we ask as we asked before, *how* is it that these facts – the positive justification conditions for meaning ascriptions of form (5) – constitute an intelligible kind of warrant for asserted instances of (5)? What kind of epistemic entitlement can the facts falling under (i) through (iii) provide for the content expressed by the meaning ascriptions subsumed by (5)? It is worth reminding ourselves that there are various kinds of warrant that relevant facts can supply for different kinds of linguistic acts. Thus, facts about a speaker and his situation may warrant him in *ordering* someone to do something. Other sorts of fact may warrant him in *making a promise* to do something himself, and still others may warrant him in *conferring a special kind of authority* on another person. And so on. From case to case the general character of the warranting facts will vary and so will the character of the warrant they confer. The present question is: what kind of warrant do the facts in (i) through (iii) provide for asserted instances of (5)? The Skeptical Solution is not entitled to assume blankly that the warranting force of the justification conditions it assigns to meaning ascriptions is a matter about which nothing needs to be spelled out.

It is tempting to believe that there is nothing much to say here because what there is to say is so obvious. Surely, one might allow, the proponent of the Skeptical Solution thinks that the facts in (i) through (iii) warrant meaning ascriptions by supplying adequate but defeasible evidence for them. Perhaps this is the obvious idea. Perhaps this is all there is to the matter. But then, the Skeptical Solution had better incorporate a still more obvious consequence of this concession. Meaning ascriptions, understood to be potentially licensed by such evidence, must consequently express a content about *matters of fact*. It must express a factual content that the confirming evidence in question can legitimately support. Therefore, strict nonfactualism about ascriptions of meaning can form no coherent part of the Skeptical Solution.

It could be allowed that meaning ascriptions express something *more* than a narrowly factual content. Maybe, as Kripke sometimes seems to claim, assertions of (5) carry some additional speech act force like "acknowledging" the competence of S as a 'Φ' user and/or "endorsing" his license to continued employment of the term. Still, even if some such qualification were to be countenanced, the point remains that meaning ascriptions about a speaker S at a time t will, among other things, express a factual commitment about the relation of S's actual and prospective use of 'Φ' to the established norm-determining practices of the community. I don't see how this conclusion can be avoided. That is, it is absolutely central to the positive framework of the Skeptical Solution that the relevant meaning ascriptions are warranted by the facts in (i) through (iii), and it is utterly mysterious what other explanation can be constructed concerning the nature of the warrant or entitlement that this framework seeks to posit.

Finally, I want to return to a point with which we began. If the Skeptical Argument constituted a persuasive general argument for the nonfactualism of meaning, then overall exegetical consistency would motivate an attempt to avoid this last conclusion. But I have insisted from the outset that the Skeptical Argument does not support nonfactualism about meaning, and I have even questioned the common impression that it purports to do so. For all these reasons then, I strongly favor a reading of the Skeptical Solution that grants that the meaning ascriptions in (5) have a factual subject matter – roughly, the subject matter I have just described.[21]

However, there are several questions that need to be addressed. First, haven't I just proposed, in effect, that the Skeptical Solution endorses a certain version of what Kripke calls "the dispositionalist account of meaning"? After all, I have pointed out that the Skeptical Solution seems implicitly committed to the claim that instances of the meaning ascriptions in (5) make a factual claim about how the speaker S is disposed at t to apply the term 'Φ' and about how his dispositions are related to his community's standards of correctness for 'Φ'. And yet, in the course of developing the Skeptical Argument, Kripke's Wittgenstein argues at length against a dispositionalist account of meaning (*WRPL*, pp. 22–38). Haven't I just argued that the so-called Skeptical Solution really turns upon embracing a "straight solution" to the skeptical challenge – a straight solution that says that meaning something by a term is constituted by the speaker's dispositions to apply and otherwise deploy the term in question? If this is so, then there *is* a fundamental incoherence here, but the incoherence lies in my explication of Kripke's overall dialectic.

It will come as no surprise that I believe that this impression rests on a serious misunderstanding of "the dispositionalist account of meaning" that is criticized and rejected in the course of the Skeptical Argument. There *is* a perfectly natural sense in which, given the outlook of the Skeptical Solution, S's meaning "addition" by "+" at a time t *is* constituted by S's dispositions to use '+'. But there is also another equally natural sense – a stronger sense – in which what S means by '+' at t cannot be determined or constituted by those dispositions. It is only the stronger version of the dispositionalist account that is rejected in the course of the Skeptical Argument. There is plenty of room for confusion about this matter, and it will be worth taking some pains to sort the confusion out.

We can't advance far with these issues unless we start by registering the fact that there is a significant ambiguity that potentially arises when we ask whether there are certain facts or states or processes that *constitute* a speaker's meaning something by a term at or during a certain time. To

---

[21] Toward the end of the section, I will discuss a specific concern that suggests that even (7′) may not express a straightforwardly factual judgment. The concern turns out to call for an interesting qualification, but it will not effect the basic conclusion developed in the last few paragraphs.

bring out the potential ambiguity, consider, first, the following simple case. Someone may assert truly that

(8) Jones murdered Smith in the library at midnight,

and this may be true despite the fact that the death of Smith that Jones's action caused occurred in the hospital at noon of the following day. Suppose that Jones murdered Smith by stabbing him, and the stabbing took place in the library at midnight. In one sense, the stabbing constituted the murder and explains why it was in the library and at midnight that the murder was performed. But in another sense, the fact that Jones stabbed Smith in the library at midnight is not sufficient to constitute the fact that (8) reports. Something more was needed to constitute the stabbing *as a case of murder*. For instance, it is required that the stabbing brought about Smith's demise in the right way. So, we can say that the murder was *constituted in time* (and location) by the stabbing, but the stabbing was *constituted as* a case of murder by further facts about the causal upshot of the stabbing.

Or here is another slightly more delicate example. Consider the fact (as we will suppose) that

(9) Lucy already knew, at a certain time t, that Fred and Ethel would erect a duplex on this site in six months' time.

On the one hand, we can ask, "What was it about Lucy that constituted her knowing about the prospective duplex *at the earlier time t?*" (What made it the case, concerning Lucy at that time, that she already knew then that her friends were going to build a duplex on the site?) And the answer to this question – a question, so to speak, about the *constitution in time* of her prior knowledge – is answered, at least to a first approximation, by pointing out that, *already at t*, Lucy *believed* that Fred and Ethel would erect a duplex on that site in six months. Nevertheless, there is a different constitutive question that can be raised in the same context. One can also inquire about the conditions that Lucy's relevant belief at t has to satisfy in order for it to *constitute* a case of her *knowing* (at t) that Fred and Ethel would build the duplex. That is, we can ask, "But what made it the case that Lucy's belief was an instance of her *knowing* that her friends would construct a duplex at the site?" A chief part of the answer to this question includes the following: the fact that Fred and Ethel *did* build a duplex at the site within the envisaged period, and the additional fact that Lucy's reasons for holding her belief were related, in the right epistemic way, to the etiology of the ensuing duplex construction.

Therefore, if we ask, "What constituted Lucy's knowing, already at t, that Fred and Ethel would erect a duplex there and then?" we can either be asking a more ambitious question: roughly, "What are the necessary and sufficient conditions for the truth of proposition (9)?" Or we can be asking the more modest question, "What was the state of Lucy at t that constituted (given the realization of appropriate further conditions) her having prior knowledge of an ensuing duplex?" Thus these examples illustrate that an action or state or process *x* can constitute an instance of Θ as something that takes place at or during a certain time (*x* constitutes in time that instance of Θ) although the facts about *x* that constitute it as (are sufficient for its being) an instance of Θ are not all realized prior to or at the time that *x* occurs.

Wittgenstein says in part II of the *Philosophical Investigations*, "In saying, 'When I heard this word, it meant ... to me' one refers to a *point of time* and to *a way of using the word*. (Of course, it is this combination we fail to grasp.)" (*PI*, part II, p. 175e). It is not clear what conceptual failure he has in mind in this passage. Obviously, he thinks that we tend to misinterpret the role of temporal reference in some of our basic talk about meaning and understanding. Certainly, a related thought is expressed at *PI* §187, a remark that occurs in the heart of the rule-following considerations.

> "But I already knew, at the time when I gave the order, that he ought to write 1002 after 1000." – Certainly; and you can also say you *meant* it then; only you should not let yourself be misled by the grammar of the words "know" and "mean". For you don't want to say that you thought of the step from 1000 to 1002 at that time – and even if you did think of this step, still you did not think of other ones. When you said "I already knew at the time..." that meant something like: "If I had been asked what number should be written after 1000, I should have replied '1002'." And that I don't doubt. This assumption is rather of the same kind as: "If he had fallen into the water then I would have jumped in after him". – Now, what was wrong with your idea?

It is striking that, in this passage, he links together the "grammar" of "He already knew it then" with the "grammar" of "He meant it then" as having a similar potential to mislead. How do they mislead? In §188, he goes on:

> Here I should first of all like to say: your idea was that the act of meaning the order had in its own way already traversed all those steps: that when you mean it your mind as it were flew ahead and took all the steps before you physically arrived at them.

Thus you were inclined to use such expressions as: "The steps are *really* already taken, even before I take them in writing or orally or in thought." And it seemed as if they were in some *unique* way pre-determined, anticipated – as only the act of meaning can anticipate reality.

Without attempting a detailed exegesis of these remarks, it seems that we can say this much. The "grammar" of temporal reference in our talk about meaning and prior knowledge misleads us about what meaning and prior knowledge amount to – what constitutes meaning something at a certain time or what constitutes knowing something in advance.[22] Moreover, it is worth noting that the misunderstanding in question is said by Wittgenstein to involve a corresponding misunderstanding about what it is for meaning to determine the speaker's prospective steps in advance. In any case, whatever Wittgenstein may have had in mind here, we have observed that the question "What facts constitute S's having already known that P?" exhibits a recognizable ambiguity. Thus, when we ask, "What facts constitute S's meaning *so and so* by Φ at t?" we do well to be alive to the possibility that this question also involves a troublemaking ambiguity of a similar type.

In fact, Kripke seems implicitly to allow conceptual space for some such distinction when, at the very outset of his discussion, he formulates the basic ground rules of the skeptical challenge. He says,

> An answer to the skeptic must satisfy two conditions. First, it must give an account of what fact it is (about my mental state) that constitutes my meaning plus, not quus. But, further there is a further condition that any putative fact must satisfy. It must, in some sense, show how I am justified in giving the answer '125' to '68 + 57'. The 'directions' mentioned in the previous paragraph that determine what I should do in each instance, must somehow be 'contained' in any candidate for the fact as to what I meant. (*WRPL*, p. 11)

As the sprinkling of scare quotes in the passage suggests, its import is somewhat murky. Nevertheless, it is not implausible to read the passage in the following way. First, an answer to the skeptical challenge must specify the kind of psychological or other state that S, the '+' user, was in at t – the state that provided the constitution in time of S's meaning something by '+'

---

[22] Suppose that meaning something by a term necessarily involves *knowing how* the term is to be used in cases not yet encountered. This skeletal supposition is hardly in conflict with Wittgenstein's thinking about meaning. What is more, just as a person can know in advance that P, so a person can know in advance how to Q. This link suggests a way in which the "grammar" of "meaning" and of "prior factual propositional knowledge" might be intimately related.

when he did. Second, if Ψ is the putative state in question, then there must be facts about Ψ that *constitute it as* a case of S's meaning *addition* rather than *quaddition* during the designated period. However, the passage also indicates that the skeptic understands this constraint in a very strong way.

The constraint is this. If state Ψ is genuinely to constitute S's meaning *addition* by '+' at t, then the facts about Ψ (at t) must, as Kripke puts it, "determine what [the speaker] must do in each instance." That is, the facts about state Ψ, as it occurs at t, should already determine *then*, for any pair of arguments for '+', the specific conditions (the specific computational pattern) that a particular calculation for those arguments has to satisfy in order for the calculation to have been performed correctly. Correlatively, given S's intentions in ascribing '+' to various number triples, these same conditions should also settle the conditions under which the '+' equations that S employs would count as true. The preestablished conditions on the correctness of S's calculations are "the directions" that Kripke refers to in the previous quotation – the facts about how a given calculation ought to be carried out. And I take it that the stipulation that these "normative conditions" are to be "contained in" facts about state Ψ requires that those conditions must somehow be determined by the pertinent facts about Ψ – by facts about Ψ that are already realized at t. Indeed, it is a part of the skeptic's further idea that facts about Ψ should determine the computational patterns in such a way that S has privileged but fallible intuitive access to the step-by-step unfolding of those patterns. S's intuitive access should "guide" him in performing his calculations. It should "tell" him what to do. Finally, the series of correct calculations that satisfy the case-by-case correctness conditions must correspond, in the expected way, to the infinite table for *addition*. In other words, the constraint that is being imposed on candidate states of meaning for an individual speaker is one that is derived directly from a classical realist conception of meaning. The desired facts about the putative state of meaning must explain how '+', as S uses it, is antecedently governed at t by a standard of correctness that suitably tracks the predetermined facts about addition on the natural numbers.

The nature and strength of this constraint emerge sharply in Kripke's discussion of the way in which "the dispositionalist account" proposes to respond to the skeptical challenge. The constraint, applied to the dispositional account, requires that it be possible, as Kripke puts it, to "read off," from some specified range of facts concerning S's dispositions, the "normative" conditions that specify how S's calculations are to be performed. And this means, I assume, that the relevant facts about

S's dispositions at t (partially idealized perhaps) are themselves to determine how correct calculations for '+' are, at any given stage, to be carried out. What Kripke argues at some length is that this constraint on the dispositional account cannot be met without introducing some form of unacceptable circularity. In other words, what Kripke's arguments aim to show is that facts about S's dispositions concerning '+' cannot provide a "straight solution" to the skeptical challenge.

Nevertheless, it seems to me that the skeptic's implicit constraint on dispositionalist accounts of what constitutes a speaker's meaning something by a term is too strong. (Paul Horwich has raised a similar objection.[23]) It does not reasonably apply to a significantly more modest version of the dispositionalist account. Suppose that this account purports to answer only what I have called "the modest question" about what constitutes (in time) S's meaning something by a term at a given time. The modest account will grant that facts about S's dispositions in arithmetic calculation do not themselves determine standards of correctness for the '+' calculations that S performs. It grants, in other words, that the truth conditions for S's use of '+' equations cannot be "read off," by S or others, from S's computational (and related linguistic) dispositions. Those standards, it may be allowed, are established in some other fashion quite independently of S and his proclivities in computing '+' and in asserting '+' equations. Nevertheless, the modest account maintains, first, that what makes it the case that, *at time t*, S meant *addition* by his use of '+' is the fact that, at that time, S was disposed to perform '+' calculations in such-and-such a way. Thus, these dispositions represent the constitution in time of S's meaning *addition* by '+'. And second, the modest version requires that the calculations he was thereby disposed to perform must have been roughly in accord – give and take some errors – with the independently established standards or conditions of correctness for the various specific calculations keyed to '+'. According to this modest dispositionalism, it is just the fact of approximate accord with appropriate standards accepted in the community that stands as the constitutive requirement for S's dispositions, concerning calculation with '+', to count as a genuine instance of his using that term to mean *addition*.[24] Thus, the Skeptical Solution embraces a modest version of dispositionalism about meaning.

[23] Paul Horwich, chapter 10 of *Meaning* (Oxford: Oxford University Press, 1998), pp. 212–25.
[24] On p. 25 of *WRPL*, Kripke says, "Wittgenstein's views have dispositional elements." Modest dispositionalism about meaning captures, I believe, the dispositional elements that Kripke discerns in Wittgenstein's outlook.

The following example illustrates what the modest dispositionalist has in mind. Suppose it is true that Oscar knew how to play the Brighthurst piano sonata during a certain time t, and we ask what constituted Oscar's knowing how to play the sonata at that time. One obvious possibility – there is an assortment of cases here – is that Oscar's knowing how to play the sonata was constituted in time by his ability or disposition to produce performances at the piano, when prompted to play the Brighthurst sonata, that have such-and-such a detailed character.[25] Of course, what constitutes this "narrow" ability *as* an instance of knowing how to play the sonata is the fact that all or most of these actual and counterfactual performances match nearly enough the way in which the Brighthurst composition should be played. We don't imagine that it is facts about Oscar's "Brighthurst"-piano-playing dispositions that establish the "normative" facts about how the sonata is to be played. The Brighthurst sonata cannot be "read off" from Oscar's significantly flawed and sometimes incomplete performances. Those "normative" facts are presumably settled by what Brighthurst specified when he composed his work and, perhaps, by facts about the evolving traditions of performance that have come to be recognized in connection with this piece. In any event, these "normative facts" are plainly settled quite independently of any facts about Oscar and his ability to play the Brighthurst composition. Still, it seems right that Oscar's Brighthurst sonata dispositions are sufficient to constitute his knowing how to play it, or, more specifically, that they are sufficient, in the imagined case, to constitute the temporal basis of his knowing how to play it during t. What is more, the sentence, "Oscar knew, at time t, how to play the Brighthurst sonata" surely *states* or *reports* a determinate (if somewhat vague) *fact* about Oscar and about his piano repertoire at the time.

The modest dispositionalism about meaning that I described two paragraphs earlier rejects the thought that the case-by-case conditions for the correctness of S's calculations for '+' are themselves determined

---

[25] Oscar's relevant disposition is to produce performances that are *intended* to be instances of the Brighthurst sonata. In virtue of that disposition, Oscar knows how to play the sonata if those performances would be regularly in adequate conformity with the way the sonata is to be played. Notice that Oscar can produce a performance with the intention of playing the Brighthurst sonata without knowing that the piece bears that title or any other name. More broadly, the intention with which he plays is not language-bound in the sense explained in note 4. Similar remarks apply to the person who knows how to add. His relevant disposition is to perform calculations with the intention of adding, but I contend that the intention with which he thereby acts or would be acting is also not language-bound. He certainly need not know that the computational procedure he has mastered is a procedure called "addition." As I explained at the beginning of Section II, this is why the account that is offered by the Skeptical Solution is not circular.

by facts about S's dispositions to use '+'. Therefore, it agrees with the Skeptical Argument's objections to the strong version of the dispositionalist account of meaning, while rejecting the skeptic's constraint on what it takes for a state of the speaker to constitute his thereby meaning what he does. (And the rejection of that constraint is tantamount to the rejection of the classical realist's view of meaning.) Nevertheless, modest dispositionalism does assume, in effect, that case-by-case correctness conditions for '+' calculations have somehow been independently established. And yet, isn't even this assumption in conflict with (BSC)? Doesn't the assumption contradict (BSC) – at least on its broadest interpretation? That is, if it is assumed that facts about the collective computational dispositions of the community of '+' calculators, or facts about the dispositions of some designated part of that community, are supposed to determine case-by-case correctness conditions for the calculations they perform with '+', then Kripke explicitly (although rather tersely) contends that this assumption is also defeated by an extended version of that part of the skeptical argument directed at the original dispositionalist account. He suggests that many of the arguments against the thesis that a single speaker's dispositions can determine how his or her calculations for '+' should go will equally defeat the similar idea that dispositions to calculate, pooled from the wider community, determine correctness conditions for the community's use of "+". (See *WRPL*, p. 111.) Once again, I will not question whether the skeptical argument against such a "community" version of the dispositionalist account is sound.

The Skeptical Solution, accepting (BSC), denies that there is a fact about individual speakers or about the community as a whole that establishes something as the meaning that guides them in their computations for '+' and determines in advance, for each pair of arguments, the conditions that a correct individual calculation for '+' must satisfy. Nevertheless, as I discussed at the beginning of this section, the Skeptical Solution does affirm, for a large but rather indeterminate range of cases, that it *is* established (perhaps defeasibly) within the community that certain of the '+' calculations they perform are to be accepted as correct and that the corresponding '+' equations are to be accepted as true. These are the basic standards for correct addition against which the competence of individual '+' users are to be tested. The Skeptical Solution provides, along these lines, for the establishment of patterns of correct calculation performed for '+'. It thereby provides for computational patterns that have the status of established requirements imposed on the practice of adding natural numbers, requirements that are independent of the computational vagaries of any single individual. This, then, is the schematic perspective of the Skeptical Solution, incorporating the modest dispositionalism about what constitutes meaning sketched above. The term '+', as a given speaker uses it, means *addition* if the speaker, in performing calculations for '+', is disposed, under favorable circumstances, to produce computations that, taken as a package, are roughly in accordance with the standards for these calculations that the community has or is prepared to put in place. On this approach, what constitutes the basis in time of S's meaning *addition* by '+' during t are S's dispositions concerning the use of '+' at that time. And what constitutes those dispositions *as* instances of meaning *addition* by '+' is the substantial but imperfect conformity of what S is disposed to calculate with the indeterminately large and open-ended set of standards for correct calculation that have come to be instituted within the community. In fact, I've argued at length that the Skeptical Solution is committed to just such an outlook. Therefore, it *is* committed to a kind of modest dispositionalism, and it seems simply wrong for Kripke's Wittgenstein to deny, if he does, that correct ascriptions of meaning state facts about the speaker and his dispositions concerning the proper use of the term. This explains why I have insisted that it is so important to keep the thesis of factual indeterminacy about standards of correctness in (BSC) distinct from any kind of significant nonfactualism about ascriptions of meaning.

There is one final complication that deserves comment. Although the truths of addition that the community has adopted up to a given time may be very large, they still are finite, and the truth or falsity of a potential infinity of '+' equations still remains to be fixed. This means that, even if a speaker's dispositions concerning '+' have so far matched all the established standards closely enough, there is still a possibility that, as the community extends its range of standards for addition, the course of these new determinations and the individual speaker's evolving dispositions may diverge. If this were to happen, then any earlier warranted judgment that the speaker meant *addition* by '+' would come to be defeated. This consideration shows that, at any time, there is no fact about the speaker and his dispositions that simply "make it true" that, at the time in question, he has meant *addition* by '+'. And yet, this concession could sound as if it represents the sort of significant nonfactualism about meaning ascriptions that I have said the Skeptical Solution can and should avoid. In my opinion, however, it is an illusion that whatever "nonfactualism" these observations might support is a substantial one.

Let's go back to the case of Lucy's prior knowledge, but slightly change the content of what she is supposed to know in advance. Let us imagine that it is claimed that, at a certain point in time, Lucy already knew that

(10) No duplex would ever be erected on this site.

Of course, there is no point in time such that the state of the world up until that time has *fully validated* (10), but this trivial truth hardly impugns the factual character of that proposition. However, since the meaning ascriptions in (5), unlike (10), contain a reference to a specific period of time, the question of truth validation might seem to be less trivial. Nevertheless, it *is* trivial in the same way that there is no time by which the state of the world has already made it true that

(11) Lucy already knew at t that no duplex would ever be erected on this site.

Just as the relevant facts about the site continue to *sustain* the truth of (10), as time goes by, these same facts, together with further facts about the evolving epistemic relations of Lucy's belief to what does or doesn't happen at the site, may also continue to *sustain* the truth of (11). So, yes! There is no point in time at which a set of facts have been realized that constitute Lucy's belief as a case of knowing that (10) – no facts that fully validate the credentials of her belief in (10) as knowledge. And maybe, in the light of these considerations, there is some temptation to deny that (11) can have the function of "describing," "reporting," or even "stating" some configuration of already realized facts. But be this as it may, such a denial could hardly represent an interesting or substantial nonfactualism about prior knowledge. After all, either (11) is indefinitely sustained through time or it is not, and, the issue, at each juncture, is a question of the existing facts. Despite the complication of its internal reference to a specific time, (11) is no more nonfactual than (10).

Similarly, if things go well, the claim that S meant *addition* by '+' will continue to have been factually sustained despite the fact that it will never be fully validated. The issues would be the same if the Brighthurst sonata were both unfinished and endlessly a work in progress, while Oscar had boundless endurance at the piano. In the case of meaning, as in the case of prior knowledge (both knowing that and knowing how), the continuing absence of full validation by the facts is not enough to institute anything more than a philosophically tame nonfactualism. All that is established by these deliberations is the unsurprising point that the constitutive credentials of a speaker's meaning a certain something by a term may remain, at any given stage, incomplete and open-ended.

IV. THE FACTUALISM OF MEANING ASCRIPTIONS
IN WITTGENSTEIN

Kripke calls attention to the famous remark at §10 in *PI*, and he uses it to summarize and underscore key aspects of his interpretation of Wittgenstein on meaning (*WRPL*, pp. 76–7). In conclusion, I want to comment briefly on some of the themes that this well-known passage inaugurates and on the interesting gloss that Kripke gives them. I will suggest that it is already clear in §10 and neighboring passages that Wittgenstein certainly is a factualist about meaning ascriptions, although his conception of the facts that correct ascriptions describe stands in stark opposition to the classical realist account. Kripke's exegesis here is highly suggestive, and it fits rather well with the version of the Skeptical Solution that I have tried to elaborate.

Having described the second simple builder's language game, Wittgenstein says,

> Now what do the words of this language *signify*? – What is supposed to show what they signify, if not the kind of use they have? And we have already described that. So we are asking for the expression, "This word signifies *this*" to be made a part of the description. In other words the description ought to take the form: "The word ... signifies...."

> Of course, one can *reduce* [italic my own] the description of the use of the word 'slab' to statement that this word signifies this object.... but the kind of '*referring*' this is, that is to say the use of these words for the rest, is already known....

> But assimilating the descriptions of the uses of words in this way cannot make them more like one another. For, as we see, they are absolutely unlike.

There is a great deal in this passage that deserves careful scrutiny, but it seems to me that each of the following claims are either directly asserted or pretty plainly suggested.

First, Wittgenstein asserts that a statement of the form

Word W signifies (means, refers to, stands for) so-and-so

is itself a *description of the use* of word W in a contextually identified language. Second, it is held to be a kind of "reduced" form of description that will convey something significant about the facts of W's use only to someone who already knows a great deal about the kind of "signifying" that is in question in the particular case. Notice Wittgenstein's talk here about *kinds* of "referring" or "signifying" in this remark. He seems to claim that semantic verbs like "signify," "refer," and "mean," at least in this kind of employment, do not stand for univocal semantic relations that ground and explain, through the speakers' knowledge of the relata, the actual practice of using the signifying terms or phrases in question. In important ways, such ascriptions of meaning might be compared to, for example,

This piece of ivory stands for the king in chess.

Here we have an apparently relational statement that conveys information to knowledgeable chess players about how that piece of ivory is to be deployed in games of chess. Third, even particular meaning ascriptions, like "The numeral 'c' means the number three," are likely to function in a family resemblance manner. In the builders' language game, the numeral 'c' is used in the very simple way that Wittgenstein lays down. It is used only in basic counting and in reports of the results of counting. But numerals that "refer to" or "mean" the number three in more elaborate, more sophisticated settings exhibit additional uses – uses that are interconnected in complicated ways. And one can imagine a host of further variations on the relevant "language games" of counting, ordering, calculating, and reporting cardinality, every one of which will include a use of numerals that stand for (or mean) the various natural numbers.

In §10, Wittgenstein is discussing simple ascriptions of meaning made in relation to the expressions of his uncomplicated hypothetical language, and what he says clearly bears on some of our present issues. As I have just emphasized, Wittgenstein characterizes these meaning reports as *descriptions* – as descriptions of facts about the roles of these terms in the builders' language game. And although Wittgenstein does not here present matters in these terms, he surely would allow that such ascriptions are sometimes true and that, when they are, they are true in virtue of the facts about the overall linguistic use of the terms that the pertinent ascriptions concern. What is more, in later remarks in *PI*, Wittgenstein makes similar claims about, for example, names of colors, of shapes, and of sensations. In short, Wittgenstein gives every indication of being some kind of a factualist about meaning ascriptions of these sorts. And other than the relative simplicity of the language games he invokes, it is hard to see what is supposed to be special about the examples he supplies.

Imagine a more complicated version of the builders' language that contains, for instance, a richer vocabulary for kinds of things and a limitless, computationally transparent series of numerals. Let it be further stipulated that these better builders have mastered, in their own notation, the four basic operations of arithmetic. Now, someone characterizing this slightly more complicated language could say,

(12) '+', as the builders use it, means *addition*,

and, from the standpoint Wittgenstein presents in §10, this meaning ascription can represent a correct description of the builders' use of '+'. (12), for him, would state facts about "the post or place in grammar" of '+' within the language of the builders.[26] It does not state that

> (12′) '+', as the builders use it, is governed by its name-like correlation with an antecedently established, result-determining operation of addition.

In his own discussion of §10, Kripke points out that one suspects that Wittgenstein implicitly rejects as confused the classical realist construal of a meaning ascription such as (5) – the construal that takes instances of (5), such as (12), to be roughly equivalent to counterpart instances of (6), such as (12′). This emerges at several points in Kripke's discussion, but one such place is in his comments on Wittgenstein's treatment of the builders' numerals (*WRPL*, p. 77). The following is a minimal adaptation by me of these remarks. It is an adaptation that only changes Kripke's references to numbers to references to arithmetic operations and substitutes the phrase "the classical realist" where Kripke speaks of "the Platonist." I have italicized the words and phrases that I have substituted for Kripke's original wording.

> Wittgenstein suggests that such an expression as 'stands for *the arithmetical operation of addition*' is in order, but is dangerous if it is taken to make a certain metaphysical suggestion. In the sense this is intended by '*classical realists*,' one suspects him of *denying* that the plus sign stands for *an abstract arithmetic operation called* '*addition*'. Most important for the present purpose, the case exemplifies the central questions he wishes to ask about the use of language. Do not look for 'entities' and '*possible* facts' corresponding to numerical assertions, but look at the circumstances under which utterance involving numerals *and other arithmetic terms* are made, and the utility of making them under those circumstances.[27]

This is a succinct statement of some of the fundamental theses of the Skeptical Solution. It illustrates very clearly two of the points that

---

[26] For two instances in which Wittgenstein invokes the concept of a word's having a "post" or "place" in grammar, see *PI* § 29 and *PI* § 257.

[27] Here is the original passage from Kripke. "Wittgenstein suggests that such an expression as 'stands for a number' is in order, but is dangerous if it is taken to make a certain metaphysical suggestion. In the sense this is intended by 'platonists', one suspects him of *denying* that numerals stand for entities called 'numbers'. Most important for the present purpose, the case exemplifies the central questions he wishes to ask about the use of language. Do not look for 'entities' and 'facts' corresponding to numerical assertions, but look at the circumstances under which utterances involving numerals are made, and the utility of making them under these circumstances."

I have wanted to highlight, while keeping them disentangled from one another. Kripke contends that Wittgenstein rejects classical realism about meaning, and his rejection is based on an extended argument that purports to establish its ultimate incoherence. In repudiating that philosophical outlook, Wittgenstein rejects, across the board, the idea that sentences represent classical realist possible facts and have their particular meanings in virtue of the possible facts they semantically represent. This, of course, constitutes a repudiation of the view that Wittgenstein had endorsed in the *Tractatus.* So ascriptions of meaning, like all other sentences, do not even purport to depict classical realist possible facts. But this important point should not be mixed up with another. It does not follow that correct meaning ascriptions do not, in some substantial sense, state, describe, or report facts concerning the use of the terms or sentences to which meaning is therein ascribed. And, in fact, it is clear that Wittgenstein thinks these ascriptions do state facts about "use" in appropriate language games. (Of course, linguistic use, within Kripke's reconstruction, is primarily a matter of epistemic warrant and language game utility.) What is more, if we eliminate from Kripke's formulations of the Skeptical Solution the repeated apparent affirmations of nonfactualism about meaning that mar it, we can present, within the framework of his reconstruction, many of Wittgenstein's major positive themes concerning meaning and use, normativity and truth.

12

Kripke on Color Words and the Primary/ Secondary Quality Distinction

Mario Gómez-Torrente

1. THE LOCKEAN PRIMARY/SECONDARY QUALITY DISTINCTION AND KRIPKE'S REACTION TO IT

Many philosophers, especially since the seventeenth century, have thought that the sensible properties of objects divide into two very different kinds. For these philosophers, determinate properties of color, sound, heat or cold, taste, and smell are in a way subjective or less real than properties such as solidity and determinate shape, motion and mass. In the seventeenth century, in particular, arguments for this divide played a role in defenses of the superior objectivity of the new physics, which was formulated in terms of properties of the latter group. In his influential treatment, Locke proposed that properties of color, sound, and so on are merely "powers to produce various sensations in us" (*Essay Concerning Human Understanding*, II.viii.10), dispositions that an object has to produce certain sensations in humans; he called these dispositions *secondary qualities*.[1] He also postulated that solidity, the shapes, and so on are nondispositional, or *primary qualities*. Thus, for example, on Locke's view, an object's being yellow consists in its power or disposition to produce sensations of yellow, not in any intrinsic causal ground of that power. On the other hand, an object's being spherical is an intrinsic property of it, different from its disposition to produce sensations of spherical shape in us under some circumstances, or from any other disposition it may have.

---

[1] Locke's secondary qualities also included other dispositions (see *Essay* II.viii.23 and 25). In the current usage, which I will follow, "secondary qualities" is reserved for powers to produce sensory effects. It is a matter of exegetical dispute whether this characterization is compatible with other claims Locke makes about secondary qualities, and even whether the phrase just quoted is to be interpreted as it usually is. Stuart (2003) is a recent discussion of these issues.

The Lockean view appears to have been a dominant view on color, sound, and so on among analytical philosophers until about the mid-1980s.[2] One of the exceptions had been Kripke in *Naming and Necessity*:

> To understand [the dispute over primary and secondary qualities], it is especially important to realize that yellowness is not a dispositional property, although it is related to a disposition. Many philosophers for want of any other theory of the meaning of the term 'yellow', have been inclined to regard it as expressing a dispositional property. At the same time, I suspect many have been bothered by the 'gut feeling' that yellowness is a manifest [nondispositional] property, just as much 'right out there' as hardness or spherical shape. The proper account, on the present conception is, of course, that the reference of 'yellowness' is fixed by the description 'that (manifest) property of objects which causes them, under normal circumstances, to be seen as yellow (i.e., to be sensed by certain visual impressions)'; 'yellow', of course, does not *mean* 'tends to produce such and such a sensation'; if we had had different neural structures, if atmospheric conditions had been different, if we had been blind, and so on, then yellow objects would have done no such thing. If one tries to revise the definition of 'yellow' to be, 'tends to produce such and such visual impressions under circumstances *C*', then one will find that the specification of the circumstances *C* either circularly involves yellowness or plainly makes the alleged definition into a scientific discovery rather than a synonymy. If we take the 'fixes a reference' view, then it is up to the physical scientist to identify the property so marked out in any more fundamental physical terms that he wishes. (Kripke 1972, 140, n.71)

On the "fixes a reference" view, the property of being yellow is (if anything) the nondispositional property, whatever it is, that causes sensations of yellow in certain paradigmatic circumstances.[3] In this, 'yellowness' is similar to terms for natural substances, phenomena, and kinds, whose referent, but not their meaning, is given by descriptions that mention a paradigmatic sample, described in terms of overt properties of its members. Thus, for example, the reference of 'gold' is rigidly fixed by some

---

[2] Such is McGinn's historical appraisal in (1983, 5), and (1999, 313), though Mackie's in (1976, 7) differs. Since the late 1980s there has been a boom of publications about color, in which positions such as physicalistic realism and eliminativism have also taken an important following.

[3] Kripke's use of the phrase "normal circumstances" is to be distinguished from the use of similar phrases in the dispositionalist literature discussed later. As we will see, the typical dispositionalist will need to specify a priori an exhaustive list of "normal conditions" in which an object is yellow iff it produces a sensation of yellow. Kripke merely uses "normal circumstances" as short for some minimally comprehensive list of paradigmatic circumstances in which we call certain objects yellow, and claims that the specification of an exhaustive list of "normal conditions" in the dispositionalist's sense would either be circular or involve a posteriori discoveries. This will be a theme developed in his work expounded below.

such description as 'the substance instantiated by the items over there, or at any rate, by almost all of them' (Kripke 1972, 135). The fact that, in the case of 'yellowness', the description in question mentions the production of certain sensations as a relevant overt property does not imply that yellowness is the mere disposition to produce them. From this perspective yellowness is, if anything, a primary quality,[4] closely related to natural substances, phenomena, and kinds.

The 1980s saw a strong interest in renewed defenses of broadly Lockean dispositionalist views of color, sound, and so on.[5] These defenses often share a number of new features. First, contemporary Lockeans sometimes formulate their doctrine in terms of biconditionals of the form 'an object is yellow iff ...', not in terms of the stronger Lockean statement of property identity.[6] Second, it is not simply claimed that an object is yellow iff it would produce sensations of yellow in us. What is postulated is that an object is yellow iff it would produce sensations of yellow *in normal humans under normal conditions*.[7] The reason for the qualification in italics is that contemporary dispositionalists want to accommodate the fact that in many cases we talk of the real as opposed to the perceived color of an object, for example in cases where the perceiver we have in mind is color-blind, or in cases where illumination is provided by some unusual light. The phrase "in normal humans under normal conditions" is taken to be short for a complete, non-trivial specification of the cases where the color of an object is the color it appears to have.[8] Kripke noted,

---

[4] Other nondispositional philosophical views of color had been defended, for example, by Smart (1963) and Armstrong (1968) (see also Smart 1975), though with a motivation and apparatus very different from Kripke's. Averill (1985) usefully brings out some of these differences.

[5] Among the authors who defend dispositional views in this period one may mention Evans (1980), McGinn (1983), Peacocke (1984), McDowell (1985), Nagel (1986), Wright (1988, 1989), and Smith (1990). Part of this literature grew out of attempts to argue that certain philosophically problematic nonsensible properties (such as moral properties) are also dispositions to produce certain subjective responses.

[6] Though some dispositionalists (for example, Wedgwood 1998) argue that some stronger formulation in terms of properties is needed.

[7] In some slightly different alternative formulations, sensations are replaced with either experiences or immediate perceptual judgments (that the relevant object is yellow). Sensations are taken to be items with a phenomenal quality but no intentional content, while experiences are taken to possess both a phenomenal quality and a content, and judgments a content but (perhaps) no peculiar phenomenal quality. The considerations in this essay (and in particular Kripke's arguments expounded below) seem to apply indifferently to all these formulations (with little modifications).

[8] A trivial specification would be, for example, "under conditions in which the object is yellow iff it looks yellow."

however, that the intended biconditional should presumably be something like "an object is yellow iff (it can be observed by normal humans under normal conditions and it would produce sensations of yellow in normal humans under normal conditions)." (Given the standard understanding of counterfactuals, the unmodified biconditionals imply that if there is an object that could not be observed under normal conditions, it is of all colors.) Finally, a third typical feature of the defenses alluded to is that they postulate that the relevant biconditionals are a priori or true as a matter of conceptual necessity.[9] This thesis is meant to sustain the required Lockean division of the sensible qualities. Perhaps there is a complete, nontrivial spelling out of "in normal humans under normal conditions" for which it is true as a pure matter of fact that, for example, an object is spherical if and only if it would produce sensations of sphericality in normal humans under normal conditions. But on the views in question, for no such spelling out is this biconditional a priori.

Partly in reaction to this literature, Kripke expanded and refined his opposition to dispositionalist views of color, sound, and so on in seminars at Princeton in 1987 and 1991, and also in some talks in the late 1980s, notably in a long talk at the University of Michigan in 1989.[10] In these lectures, Kripke began by criticizing several arguments for Lockean dispositionalism and for Locke's division of the sensible qualities. He was almost exclusively concerned with discrediting arguments designed to establish these doctrines a priori, but he criticized some attempts to use empirical evidence as well. Kripke also presented a battery of direct counterexamples to the thesis that the dispositionalist biconditionals could be formulated a priori, and also, less crucially, to the thesis that some of the biconditionals actually proposed are metaphysically necessary; these examples parallel, respectively, his epistemic and modal arguments against descriptivist theories of proper names in *Naming and Necessity*. Finally, he qualified the "fixes a reference" view of color by developing new positive views about the semantics and overall functioning of words for colors and other sensible qualities, views that help explain our intuitions about his counterexamples to dispositionalism.

---

[9] See, for example, McGinn (1983, 11), Nagel (1986, 75), and Wright (1988, 14ff). Mackie (1976) seems inclined to think that the biconditionals would be a posteriori if they were true.

[10] Like other of his unpublished ideas, Kripke's basic views in this area have managed to get some exposure, and in several cases they clearly shape the later discussion. See Johnston (1992, 262, n.29), Broackes (1992, 442, n.32), and Wright (2002, 402, n.1) for references to Kripke's unpublished views.

Most of what follows (Sections 2 to 4) is an attempt to summarize these Kripkean ideas, based especially on a transcript of a recording of the Michigan talk, on recordings of lectures of the 1987 seminar, and to a lesser extent on seminar notes and personal recollections. In Section 5 I briefly review some recent defenses of dispositionalism about color, and I sketch some objections that could be made to them from a broadly Kripkean perspective.[11]

2. KRIPKE ON ARGUMENTS FOR DISPOSITIONALISM AND FOR LOCKE'S DIVISION OF THE SENSIBLE QUALITIES

In the first part of his critique, Kripke sought to undermine the main kinds of considerations usually adduced in favor of Lockean dispositionalism or of Locke's divide of the sensible qualities. These include: first, arguments using the possibility of intramodal sensory inversion; second, considerations based on the thesis that secondary qualities are accessible only to one sense, whereas primary qualities are accessible to more than one sense; third, considerations based on the claim that fundamental science uses primary but not secondary qualities as primitives; and fourth, arguments based on the alleged fact that the causes of perceived color are physically diverse.

The first kind of arguments appeal to the idea that the objects that cause sensations of red in us might cause sensations of green in a race of Martians.[12] This is taken to imply that there is no genuine disagreement between us and the Martians when we say that ripe tomatoes are red and they say that they are green (see, for example, McGinn 1983, 9–10). Dispositionalism about color is supposed to explain this alleged relativity, for it generalizes easily to the doctrine that, given a certain object, each population of "normal" perceivers determines a peculiar color property for it: the object is red relative to a population of perceivers in

---

[11] Needless to say, Kripke may not agree with my claims in Section 5. It is also important to emphasize that the exposition in Sections 2 to 4 is very brief and sketchy due to space limitations, and does little justice to the wealth and precision of the discussion in Kripke's seminars. Besides, since the exposition is based on oral presentations by Kripke, there is a considerable risk that I have misrepresented his views at some points. However, I hope the exposition may be of some use as a rough picture of these views before they can be published in a more satisfactory way.

[12] In the 1987 seminar, Kripke developed an original argument against the possibility of behaviorally undetectable full color spectrum inversion, which I cannot go into for lack of space. At any rate, the arguments we are examining do not require the strong assumption of such a possibility.

whom it is disposed to cause sensations of red, and it is green relative to a population of perceivers in whom it is disposed to cause sensations of green. Since there are similar arguments for this relativity in the case of secondary qualities quite generally, we have a similarly general argument for Lockean dispositionalism.

In reply, Kripke recalls an example from the first of Berkeley's *Dialogues* (which he borrowed from Malebranche). Berkeley asks us to imagine a race of small creatures with suitably microscopic vision, in whose visual field objects that look, say, one foot long to us appear the way a one-hundred-foot-long object appears to us. Kripke notes that no one would draw from this possibility the idea that size is relative, or that the property of being one foot long is dispositional. The only proper conclusion is that different organisms can have different sensations caused by the same property. But if a dispositionalist thesis about size and a distinction between the sensible qualities are not supported by Berkeley's example, no such distinction and no dispositionalist thesis about color are supported by a color inversion example.

Considerations of the second kind have a long history, and reappear frequently in the recent literature.[13] Dispositionalism is a natural explanation of the alleged fact that Locke's secondary qualities are accessible only to one sense. For it is natural to think that, say, the disposition to produce a sensation of red is only accessible to the sense that registers that sensation; on the other hand, a primary property is not defined by its effects on any particular sense, and so is presumably accessible to more than one sense, if accessible at all. But is it true that Locke's secondary qualities are accessible only to one sense, whereas primary qualities are accessible to more than one sense? Even if it is true as a matter of fact, is it a priori true, as needed if it is to be used in an a priori argument for dispositionalism?

Kripke notes that it appears to be false even as a matter of fact. Presumably, the phenomenally similar sensations that we get when we smell and taste bourbon are best seen as caused by the same property. On the other hand, mass appears to be immediately accessible only to the sense of feel.[14] But in any case, the thesis does not seem a priori true. We can easily imagine red objects giving off a characteristic squeak,

[13] See, for example, Evans (1980, 270), McGinn (1983, 8–9), and Smith (1990, 241ff.). Aristotle's distinction between "common" and "special" sensibles in *De Anima* is sometimes cited as a precursor.

[14] We might speculate that a sixth sense is *possible* that detects mass. But we might make the same speculation about color.

which we might have learnt to recognize by hearing. It is equally easily imaginable that after long correlation, our linguistic usage could have developed in such a way that we had used the word "redness" to refer to the property that causes both the visual sensation of red and the squeaky sensation.[15] As far as we know, it is not true that red objects give off such a squeak. But we cannot conclude a priori that they do not or could not. The dispositionalist must dismiss this example, claiming that, even if red objects do or could give off such a squeak, the qualities perceived by sight and by hearing when in the vicinity of a red object are or would still be different.[16] The problem is then how to argue for this last claim so that, say, the qualities perceived by sight when one looks at a sphere are not all different from the qualities perceived by feel when one touches the same sphere.

Obviously one cannot argue for the claim at stake by appealing to the thesis that redness and squeakiness are dispositional properties defined by reference to different sensory effects on us, on pain of begging the question. The dispositionalist may propose that the visual sensation of shape resembles the tactile sensation of shape in a way in which the visual sensation of red and the auditory squeaky sensation do not resemble each other. But it is just as hard to see any purely phenomenal resemblance in the first case as it is in the second case. The dispositionalist must claim that there is some other way to see unity in the first case and contrast in the second, a way that does not rely either on phenomenal resemblance or on the actual experience of correlation or lack of it. But it is thoroughly unclear that such a way exists.[17]

A related claim of some Lockeans and of Locke himself is that the sensations corresponding to primary qualities bear a perceptually detectable

---

[15] Kripke would not deny that in a sense a person who detected colors by squeaks would have a different concept of the colors. But this still does not establish the intended divide. A batlike creature who detected shapes by hearing would in the same sense have a different concept of the shapes.

[16] A similar response seems mandatory in the bourbon example; cf. Mackie (1976, 29).

[17] One dispositionalist line is to insist that the development of abilities of shape recognition by sight alone can lead to a kind of intuitive geometry which is the same, or a priori isomorphic to, a corresponding kind of intuitive geometry that one can figure out through the development of abilities of shape recognition by touch alone (see Evans [1980, 269ff.] and Smith [1990, 242f.] for views of this sort). Even if this were true, Kripke would reply that the development of abilities of color recognition by means of different types of squeaky sounds alone can lead to an intuitive mathematical representation which is the same, or a priori isomorphic to, a corresponding intuitive mathematical representation of "color space" given rise to by the development of abilities of color recognition by visual sensations alone.

resemblance to these qualities, while the sensations corresponding to secondary qualities do not resemble anything in the object.[18] But it's hard to make sense of the claim that *any* quality perceptually resembles a sensation, even granting that a quality may resemble another quality in some respect and that a sensation may phenomenally resemble another sensation. Furthermore, there is an easy argument against the Lockean claim that the quality of sphericality resembles both visual and tactile sensations of sphericality. Provided that the relation of resemblance at stake is transitive, as seems reasonable in the Lockean context, this claim implies that these sensations resemble each other, which is, as we said, hard to see.[19] Also the examples of phenomenal inversion or distortion, which, as we just noted, can be reproduced for the primary qualities, show the dubiousness of the talk of resemblance between qualities and the sensations corresponding to them.

A third important kind of traditional and recent considerations for dispositionalism and the Lockean divide of the sensible qualities relies on the claim, taken either as a priori or as a posteriori, that fundamental scientific explanations do not use Locke's secondary properties, and do use the traditionally primary properties.[20] For Kripke, it is very doubtful that such a claim is a priori. It does not seem a priori impossible that color words (and words for felt properties like warmth and coldness, or for auditory properties) could have been used in the most fundamental physics, an unimprovable physics in which they appeared as irreducible qualities. Besides, it is in any case doubtful that even as a matter of fact the qualities that appear in fundamental science are not secondary. Kripke notes that highly fundamental levels of current physics, such as relativity theory and quantum mechanics, might be interpreted as challenges to the idea that the notion of shape that appears in them is nondispositional. Thus, for example, special relativity implies that the shape of an object is relative to

---

[18] Similar claims are characteristic also of some color eliminativists like Mackie (1976) and Boghossian and Velleman (1989).

[19] Molyneux's question is related. He asked whether a man born blind could, on recovering vision as an adult and before learning to establish any correlation by experience between sight and touch, tell by sight alone which of two objects of similar size presented to him was a sphere and which a cube (see Locke, *Essay*, II.ix.8). Significantly, Locke favored a negative answer, which goes against his view on primary qualities and resemblance.

[20] See, for example, McGinn (1983, 14–15) and Nagel (1986, 75–6), for versions of the a priori claim. Smith (1990, 248ff.) claims that it is a priori that the qualities traditionally taken as secondary are not suitable for science, but also says that it is not a priori that the qualities traditionally taken as primary are so suitable. Mackie (1976, 17ff.) maintains the a posteriori claim.

the coordinate system the observer is at rest in. And we can easily modify the famous Schrödinger's cat thought experiment so that what is quantum mechanically indeterminate in the modified scenario is whether a block of ice receives the shape of a sphere or that of a cube (depending on whether a certain particle is emitted by a source or not); at least on standard interpretations of quantum mechanics, the block of ice is neither spherical nor cubical before an observation of it has been made. And there seems to be less room for Locke's primary properties as traditionally conceived as we move to even more fundamental levels of current physics. The a posteriori version of the argument from fundamental science may have looked plausible to a seventeenth- or eighteenth-century philosopher, but it now appears far from compelling.

It is also worth noting that (currently) less fundamental but well-developed levels of science do use terms for traditionally secondary qualities without incurring any obvious error. Thus we are taught in chemistry classes that we can test for acidity and alkalinity by seeing whether litmus paper turns red or blue. And thermodynamics states a good number of laws about heat and temperature. The right picture is probably that all sensible qualities, for all we know a priori, can appear in different parts or levels of science, and that whether they can or not is independent of the question whether they are dispositional or not. No argument for dispositionalism or for the intended dividing line of the sensible qualities should be expected from this kind of consideration.

A fourth kind of argument for Lockean dispositionalism, which has perhaps been presented only for color, is that since physics tells us that the causes of any given perceived color are diverse, objects of the same color cannot have anything in common other than that they all share a disposition to produce perceptions of that sort.[21] This is a purely a posteriori argument. Kripke was ready to concede that there could be some diversity in the causes of perceived color at some fairly fundamental level of physical description, but he doubted that this is relevant even if true.[22] Even if the causes of color sensations turn out to be diverse to some extent according to fairly fundamental levels of physics, this would provide no

---

[21] See Hardin (1988, 1ff.) for an exposition of the variety of physical causes of perceived color, which suggests to its author that "it would be in vain to suppose that objects sharing a common color resemble one another in physical structure" (1988, 4). Hardin rejects dispositionalism, but he defends color eliminativism on the basis of broadly similar subjectivist grounds.

[22] Still, he thought that one should examine in detail the extent to which diversity claims hold when restricted to the perceived color of objects (the primary case of application of color predicates). Like Averill (1992), Kripke conjectured that at least some of the

argument for dispositionalism. Call a system of classification *Goodmanian* with respect to another if it classifies together things that according to the other system are quite disparate. (Compare the definition of the property of "grueness" in Goodman 1955, 74.) Even if our system of color classification is Goodmanian with respect to the systems of classification of fairly fundamental levels of physics,[23] this does not imply that the predicates in our system of color classification stand for Lockean dispositional properties, or even for disjunctive properties. The properties in question may well be best seen as nondispositional within their own system of classification or even within systems of classification of not so fundamental levels of science; think again of the use of the notion of heat in thermodynamics, which is compatible with the causes of heat being diverse from the point of view of more fundamental levels of physical description.[24] (Recall that Kripke's "fixes a reference" view of note 71 in *Naming and Necessity* was explicitly consistent with the properties in question being taken from nonfundamental levels of physics.[25]) As noted earlier, presumably many or all predicates for sensible qualities fail to appear as usually understood in the system of classification of fundamental levels of current physics, which makes our system of classification of primary qualities Goodmanian also on these grounds. But this is no reason to adopt a dispositionalist view of the traditionally primary qualities, as understood within comparatively more rudimentary systems of classification.

usual examples are directly irrelevant, for they do not concern objects, and may be explained as illusions. The blue appearance of the sky has a different physical cause from that of a blueberry, but it may be just as illusory as the appearance that "the sky" has the shape of a vault.

[23] Kripke noted several respects in which our color perception system is Goodmanian with respect to the presumable underlying physics, respects that can be discerned without much specialized knowledge. For example, our perception system imposes radical phenomenal breaks on the continuum of light wavelengths.

[24] Though thermodynamics does not seem to be too Goodmanian with respect to the "next" level of physics, statistical mechanics.

[25] Kripke often noted, however, that color science is far from having reached the reasonably definitive results that might turn it into an established though nonfundamental part of physics, in the style of thermodynamics. The relevant scientific work about color is not all in yet. Among some of the polemics and surprising disagreements, he mentioned the fact that some books assert that three appropriately chosen color lights ("primaries") can be mixed (in different intensities) to obtain a color match for any arbitrary light, but others, presumably correctly, deny this. See, for example, Feynman, Leighton, and Sands (1963, section 35–3), where the truth is said to be that for every such trio there will be some color light that can only be obtained from the trio in the sense that, when mixed with one of the chosen primaries, it matches the mixing of the other two. In any case, Kripke thought it extremely implausible that science would in the long run embrace dispositionalism or eliminativism about color.

3. KRIPKE ON COLOR WORDS IN NATURAL LANGUAGE

According to Lockean dispositionalists, redness is a priori radically different from a natural kind or substance like gold. As McGinn puts it, "we cannot envisage cases in which the identity of a given colour comes apart from its appearance – there cannot be 'fool's red' as there can be fool's gold" (1983, 13). (Strictly speaking, as noted earlier, modern dispositionalists postulate that it is a priori that there cannot be fool's red "for normal humans under normal conditions.")

Kripke notes a tension in this dispositionalist view. If one is allowed to use qualifications of this sort, then one can presumably equally hold that there cannot be fool's gold for normal humans under certain conditions. There seems to be no obstacle to the idea that if one can specify these conditions in the color case, then one can specify them in the gold or sphericality case. Thus the dispositionalist is led to hold that, even if we can specify both the cases where we will not be fooled about redness and the cases where we will not be fooled about gold or sphericality, only in the redness case can we reach that specification a priori. The problem then, Kripke objects, is that "normal humans" and "normal conditions" in the redness case must be specifiable in advance of any relevant empirical discovery; the dispositionalist cannot appeal to empirical findings when drawing up his list. But even the list of known cases where we actually distinguish between apparent and real color could hardly have been drawn in advance. Some of these cases will be mentioned in Section 4.

The dispositionalist rejects the idea, embraced in *Naming and Necessity*, that color terms are much like terms for natural kinds, substances, or phenomena. He thinks that it is even a priori that 'redness' is not a natural kind term. Now, by this he does not mean that in the case of a natural kind you can be fooled without making any gross mistake in perceptual judgment, but you cannot be fooled in the case of red. Certainly you cannot be fooled about perceptual judgment in either case, unless you include as perceptual judgments things of the form "this is gold." But if so, you should include as perceptual judgments things of the form "this is red," and you can be fooled about these. What the dispositionalist must mean is that if something looks red to us, then no amount of saying that it is just totally unlike the other things that are red will have any force against the judgment that it is red. In the case of gold, the dispositionalist accepts Kripke's view that the reference of 'gold' is fixed by "the substance instantiated by the items over there, or at any rate, by almost all of them." Given that we have found out that there is indeed a substance instantiated by most of the things paradigmatically called 'gold', we are content to classify the exceptional things that look like gold but differ from it in more subtle properties as not being really gold. But no such thing can happen with 'red', according to the dispositionalist.

It is important not to confuse what is (allegedly) the scientific truth about color with the way color terms function in natural language. As we have seen, a view sometimes derived from science is that red things do not have much in common.[26] Even if this were so, it would not mean that color terms are not like natural kind terms in the relevant respect. The important question is: if almost all the red things *had* enough in common, would there be a pressure to classify some exceptional things that looked red but differed from the other things in more subtle properties as not being really red? Intuitively, the answer is yes. The (alleged) empirical fact that paradigmatically red things do not have much in common does not show that 'red' is not a natural kind term,[27] just as the discovery that paradigmatic cases of gold did not have much in common would not have shown that 'gold' is not a natural kind term.

Beliefs such as the belief that most paradigmatic cases of gold belong to a single substance, or that most paradigmatically red things share a certain nondispositional property, are examples of what Kripke calls *prejudices*. Although not perforce a priori, a prejudice is a belief that we hold onto pretty firmly, and that we try to retain with as little modification as possible in the face of pressures from empirical data. For Kripke, our language is replete with working prejudices. Many of them have a semantic role, though not the role of an analytic definition. One semantic role of the belief that most paradigmatic cases of gold belong to a single substance is that of setting a condition for the assignment of an extension to 'gold', in case the prejudice is true. If we find out that it is not true, the semantics we give to 'gold' will depend to a great extent on our new decisions in view of the empirical data, and one semantic role of the relevant remaining prejudices will be to guide these decisions. A similar thing happens with 'red'. If the prejudice that most paradigmatically red things share a certain nondispositional property turns out to

---

[26] It should be mentioned that the view is by no means universal or even majoritarian. A good many authors propose realist physicalist theories of various kinds which see a unity in the red things. See, for example, Byrne and Hilbert (1997), Hilbert (1987), and Jackson (1996).

[27] As we will see, Kripke's ultimate view is that 'red' is not exactly a natural kind term. He just wants to note that a certain argument against the view that it is a natural kind term is flawed.

be empirically false, this may eventually incline us to make some new semantic decisions, perhaps to choose an extension for the term, guiding ourselves by other prejudices such as those mentioned below. (Of course, on Kripke's view any such inclination in the case of color is totally premature at this moment.)

Two other examples of prejudices spotted by Kripke, and highly relevant in the discussion about the primary/secondary quality distinction, involve the notion of solidity. A. S. Eddington said that science has shown that a table is not really solid because there are big gaps in it, and Susan Stebbing replied that tables are paradigmatic cases of solidity. (See Eddington 1928, 1ff., and Stebbing 1937, 51ff.) Both can be seen as relying on prejudices. Stebbing relies on the prejudice that (most) paradigmatic instances of application of a predicate are indeed instances of the predicate. Eddington relies on the prejudice that if something is really solid then it does not have gaps. This latter belief strikes some as analytic or quasi-analytic, but one indication that it isn't is presumably that people like Stebbing want to claim that ordinary objects are solid and yet are full of gaps.

There are many other prejudices that we have about colors, besides the mentioned prejudice that most paradigmatically red things share a certain nondispositional property. One is analogous to Stebbing's paradigms prejudice: (most) paradigmatic instances of a color predicate are indeed instances – grass is green, lemons are yellow, English pillar boxes are red. Another prejudice is the famous color incompatibility principle, as applied to red and green, say: something cannot be both red and green all over.[28] Yet another prejudice, related to the incompatibility principle, is analogous to Eddington's "no gaps" prejudice; it's the so-called principle of the dissectiveness of color, as applied to yellow, say: if something is yellow all over, then all its ordinary parts are yellow. (Or at least: if something is yellow all over, then all its ordinary parts are not colored with some color incompatible with its being yellow.) The dissectiveness principle may or may not be true, but it is certainly a strong prejudice, and in fact it seems to be by and large valid.[29]

---

[28] For Kripke there is no reason in principle why an object could not be both red and green all over, since the properties that cause red and green impressions in paradigmatic circumstances may turn out to be co-instantiable. What does seem impossible in principle is that an object can look both red and green all over.

[29] Armstrong (1961, 162–3), accepts the principle (see also Armstrong 1969). Hilbert (1987, chapter 2), rejects it. The name "dissective" comes from Goodman (1951).

Another prejudice about color is the belief that every normal opaque object must have a color. Kripke acknowledged that this prejudice confers to color words a functioning different from that of pure natural kind terms. If something had little in common with most red things *but* we had no reason to call it other than red, we would have a strong pressure to give it some color, and with further pressure from the paradigms prejudice, probably the red color that it appears to have.[30] Note, however, that while we feel embarrassed to count a normal opaque object as having no color at all, the dispositionalist theory is compatible with the claim that some objects are colorless: in order to be colorless, an object must simply fail to be observable under normal conditions, or fail to produce a sensation of color under normal conditions (perfectly imaginable possibilities, as we will see in Section 4). So the dispositionalist theory is in tension with this prejudice.[31]

Kripke's methodology postulates that there is a rough procedure that we follow as members of a linguistic community, which consists in that we try to preserve as many prejudices as possible, and with as little modification as possible, in the face of conflicts with empirical data. What prejudices about a certain term are modified and to what extent is dictated by the relative frequencies and strengths of the empirical conflicts that arise between the different prejudices. Most of the examples in the next section are designed both as counterexamples to the thesis that the specification of "normal conditions" needed by the dispositionalist can be done a priori, and as thought tests for the hypothesis that we apply the procedure just roughly described.

---

[30] Kripke also noted that an obvious difference between the sensible qualities and natural kinds is that, while something cannot look red or spherical and not be red or spherical *if the senses are not deceiving us*, something may look like gold and not be gold without any sense deception. Yet another difference is that, if most tables were gappy but a few had turned out to be gap-free, we would have been inclined to call the latter solid; most paradigmatic instances of a natural kind term turn out to have nothing in common, it seems we are more likely to withdraw the term.

[31] Kripke also emphasized a difference between color terms and terms generally agreed to express dispositional properties, such as 'nauseating', 'sexy', or 'painful' (as a predicate of objects such as a torture instrument). In the case of color, we say that the observers that the dispositionalists exclude as abnormal, such as the color-blind, are in error when they make certain color judgments. In the case of 'sexy', for example, we don't say that the people who deviate from the norm, such as the shoe fetishist who finds shoes sexy, are in error; we just call them exceptional cases. If color words are purely dispositional terms, why don't we call the color-blind merely exceptional cases? The fact that we don't speaks against the dispositional view.

4. SOME OF KRIPKE'S COUNTEREXAMPLES
TO LOCKEAN DISPOSITIONALISM

Modal Considerations

On McGinn's and other dispositionalist views, the equivalence between being red and looking red (to normal observers under normal conditions) is not just a priori but metaphysically necessary, so these views imply that if humans had been so physically constituted that lemons had looked red to them, lemons would have been red (see, for example, McGinn 1983, 13, n.12). Kripke's view of 'yellowness' as a rigid term implies that in the world described by McGinn lemons would still be yellow (provided 'yellowness' refers), and Kripke noted that we do have the intuition that lemons would still be yellow (though they would look red).[32] This is thus a modal counterexample to a number of dispositionalist views, analogous to the modal counterexamples of *Naming and Necessity* against some descriptivist theories.

Nagel (1983) and Shoemaker (1986, 410–11), though agreeing with McGinn that being red and looking red are actually (and a priori) coextensional, concur with Kripke's modal intuition and propose "rigidifying" repairs of the dispositionalist view. Nagel's repair consists in proposing that being red is, in all possible worlds, the property of looking red to us in the actual world. This is clearly defective, as it implies that a piece of litmus paper that is dipped in an acid in the actual world and dipped in an alkali in a counterfactual world is red in the counterfactual world. On Shoemaker's fix, redness is "the disjunction of all those properties, actual and possible, whose instantiation would produce (under certain circumstances) [experiences of red] in creatures constituted as we in fact are" (1986, 410). This seems to fix the modal problem, but it does not go well with Shoemaker's intuition that being red and looking red are a priori coextensional. Note, for example, that Shoemaker's theory is a priori consistent with the negation of the color incompatibility principle, but the principle is a priori if being red and looking red are a priori coextensional; also, an object's possessing one of the properties in the disjunction is not a priori incompatible with its also having an interfering property that

---

[32] McGinn (1983) claims to have the opposite intuition, but it's hard to avoid thinking that he is in the grip of his own theory. He sticks to this view in (1996), where he proposes a different analysis of the color properties, which is nevertheless necessarily coextensional with his old analysis.

makes the object look yellow (such as the property discussed in the jaundice example of the next subsection).

The examples in the remainder of this section play a part analogous to the "epistemic" examples of *Naming and Necessity*. They are all examples involving situations that are either plainly true or not a priori excludable as true in the actual world. Thus they apply even to dispositionalist theories that postulate that the equivalence between being red and looking red is not necessary but merely a priori true of the actual world.

Killer Intensities, Faint Intensities, and Jaundice

The surface of the sun is very hot. This is not a sophisticated result of science, but something that we believe on the basis of very modest inferences. On a Lockean dispositionalist theory, to be hot is to be disposed to produce a certain sensation of heat in normal humans under normal conditions, and to get hotter and hotter is to become disposed to produce it in higher and higher intensity. To be very hot is then to be disposed to produce a sensation of great heat in normal humans under normal conditions. And then, if the surface of the sun is very hot, the surface of the sun must produce a sensation of great heat in normal humans under normal conditions. But the surface of the sun does not produce any such sensation in humans, because any human would be disintegrated instantly if he or she were put in the position of feeling any such thing. Thus, whether the dispositionalist postulates that being near the surface of the sun is a normal or an abnormal condition, he must say that the surface of the sun is not very hot after all. (Recall the modified biconditional of Section 1.)

Similarly, there are very loud sounds, so loud that they produce deafness as soon as one is put in a position to hear them. The dispositionalist has a problem again here, for on his theory loudness is supposed to be a disposition to produce loud auditory sensations, and louder and louder sounds are those that produce more and more intense auditory sensations of loudness. His theory has the consequence that there aren't any deafening sounds.

By analogy with killer heat and deafening sound, Kripke notes that it is imaginable that there could be (and perhaps there are) killer or blinding shades of some color. Besides the dimension of hue, the perceived colors of objects vary along the dimensions of saturation and brightness. (Saturation is proportional to the strength of a given hue, with more saturated colors being more vivid. Brightness is proportional to the amount of light that the object seems to reflect, with lighter colors seeming closer to white.) One could well imagine that greater degrees of saturation of a color, or especially greater degrees of brightness, tended to kill us or to drive us blind. We might even see this effect coming as we saw the variation along the continua of hue strength or of apparently reflected light. The idea that an object is red but so very vividly red or so very bright red that we could never see it is far from unintelligible. The possibility of a color that does not produce sensations in us arises also as we consider other processes that give rise to a continuous variation in colors, for example the mixture of two dyes. It is imaginable, for example, that two dyes mixed in different proportions give rise to different shades of blue, but one shade of blue along the continuum is permanently missing, because people looking at objects of that shade get killed or are driven blind. These objects would not produce any sensory effects and so would not be red, or blue, or any color.[33]

The dispositionalist also has a problem in the case of very low sounds, so very low that most humans under most conditions don't hear them. There are all sorts of reasons to accept the existence of such sounds (some to be mentioned shortly), but the dispositionalist must reject it, given the equivalence between being very low and producing a sensation of being very low in normal humans under normal conditions. For most humans under most conditions just won't get any such sensation. Also, there arguably are colors that do not produce any differential sensation in most of us under most conditions. As we decrease the saturation of a certain red paint, putting more and more white into it, the paint will look more and more pink. But at some point it will look white to most of us in most conditions in spite of the fact that the color is not pure white. Here we would have grounds for calling the paint pink, even if it looks white. But the dispositionalist must reject this, if he is committed to the equivalence between being pink and looking pink to normal humans under normal conditions. The only premise required is that most humans are normal and most conditions under which we look at such a paint are normal, which seems even analytic.

A somewhat different kind of case imagined by Kripke, where we would also be inclined to say that some objects have a certain color but do not look

---

[33] Note that it is hard to see how the mere fact of listening to a deafening sound or looking at a killer red object could be declared abnormal conditions of observation – though even if this ad hoc declaration is made, these cases provide counterexamples to dispositionalism.

that color, is the following. On Berkeley's (wrong) conception of jaundice, its sufferers see everything yellow (in fact, it's their skin that becomes yellowish). Suppose Berkeleyan jaundice is produced by a very toxic substance. If a normal human is in direct contact with a bar of this substance and takes a look, it will waft onto his face and give him jaundice, making everything look yellow to him. (This is how one normally observes these jaundice-producing bars, or any ordinary object for that matter.) However, there might be good reasons for calling the bar itself red. For example, a color picture is taken of the scene, in which everything appears with its expected color, and the bar appears red; further, we also know that it was made with dyes that mix to produce red; we know through a measuring apparatus that it reflects mostly light of long wavelength, and so on. Perhaps the fact that every object looks yellow to the jaundice sufferer might give some grounds for calling this an abnormal condition. (In few circumstances does everything look yellow.) But we can further imagine that the effect of the substance is differential and it just affects the eyes in that only things near the substance, or even only the substance, looks yellow.

An interesting aspect of many of these examples and others devised by Kripke is what one would be inclined to say about them if we add the further supposition that there are exceptional people who appear not to be subject to the problem or appear to be much better than normal humans at detecting quality intensities and differences among them. People of this sort certainly exist who seem especially able to detect faint sounds and highly desaturated colors, for example. They are a minority, however, so they cannot constitute the class of normal humans that a dispositionalist mentions in his theory – the normal people must be a majority. Still, the intuitive view is that these people have a better perception of sound or color. Their judgments are respected, and we have reasons for respecting them, both sophisticated and crude. But according to a dispositionalist view, their judgments must be irrelevant. (Averill 1982 makes similar points.)

In all these cases, there is no special problem from the point of view of the Kripkean methodology described at the end of the last section. In the cases of heat, sound, and color, we have analogous prejudices to the effect that the heat intensities, sound properties, and color shades are not Lockean dispositional properties, but rather nonsubjective properties "out there." This is consistent with some of them not being detectable, and with some of them being detectable only by especially gifted perceivers, even if they are only a minority. The dispositionalist theory, on the other hand, is in tension with our intuitive judgments about the cases described.

The Analogy between Yellowness and Solidity

A case where the Kripkean methodology can be more substantively applied to explain our intuitions is provided by certain cases of color mixture. It is well known that in some cases an object that is perceived as yellow from a certain distance can in fact be seen to be composed of red and green parts (and no yellow part) when looked at from closer up. Examples are patches of some pointillist paintings, of television screens, and of real-life mountains.[34] This is very striking, because yellow seems to have no phenomenal connection to red or green.

Kripke emphasizes the close relation of these examples to analogous examples involving the notion of solidity. An object that has lots of gaps in it may look solid from a distance and gappy from closer up. The basic reaction to both kinds of examples is to think, with pressure from the dissectiveness prejudice and the "no gaps" prejudice and in the absence of pressures against them from the paradigms prejudices, that the apparently yellow object is in fact red and green, and the apparently solid object is in fact gappy. Both cases would be cases of illusion: there is so much mixing that we can't distinguish from a sufficiently long distance the red and the green parts (or the solid parts and the gaps), but the object is red and green (or gappy).

(Kripke noted that in some contexts of description of cases like these, we are primarily interested in appearances or phenomenal effects, and we speak as if things were as they appear. This happens when we are interested in aesthetic effects, for example. Thus, looking at a pointillist painting, we may speak of the contrast between the golden field and the blue sky, even if the field is seen not to be really golden on closer inspection. We also say things like "The lights were switched off and all went black." There is similar talk involving traditionally primary qualities. The Parthenon has pillars of unequal heights that appear of equal height, and we describe them as equal if we are primarily interested in the aesthetic effect. We also say things like "She walked toward the horizon until she was only a dot." The existence of these contexts does not invalidate the thought that the field is really a mosaic of red and green and the pillars of the Parthenon

---

[34] A related classical example is provided by things like blood, which looks red all over from a normal distance but looks red with transparent gaps under the microscope. (See, for example, Berkeley, *Dialogues* I; Armstrong [1969]; Hilbert [1987, chapter 2].) However, this is different from the examples in the text in that microscope observation is not a paradigmatic circumstance, while observation from close up certainly is.

are really of unequal height, which is the appropriate description in stricter contexts.)

The methodology hypothesized by Kripke gives a more sophisticated prediction in cases where there arise conflicts between the different prejudices. Think first of an imaginary case in which most ordinary paradigmatic solid objects had turned out to be composed of continuous matter without any gaps, but a few exceptional trick objects produced in the laboratory (and sometimes used by magicians) were composed of discrete molecules with very small gaps between them, undetectable with the naked eye. Both the objects made of continuous matter and the gappy objects would look solid. In this case, given that the gappy objects would be relatively few, we would be happy to say that they are not really solid, that they are cases of "fool's solid." This imaginary case is to be contrasted with what has turned out to be the real case according to current science, namely that all ordinary objects are gappy. In the real case, given that the "no gaps" prejudice has turned out to be in such a large-scale conflict with experience, the pressure from the paradigms prejudice is strong and may prevail, as we may not want to deny that paradigmatically solid objects are solid.

The case of yellow is analogous. If it had turned out to be the case that all or most ordinary yellow things were seen on closer examination to be composed of red and green parts, then the paradigms prejudice would perhaps have won, since we might not want to deny that paradigmatically yellow objects are yellow. However, it seems that most things that we call yellow are not composed of red and green parts. If this is true, then the existence of relatively few apparently yellow objects that are in fact composed of red and green parts does not create too much pressure for the dissectiveness principle. This principle can be retained, provided just that we are ready to call the exceptional objects cases of "fool's yellow."

What one would say about 'solid' and 'yellow' is thus similar to what one would say about 'gold' in analogous cases. In particular, the existence of a relatively small class of objects in the paradigmatic sample that fail to satisfy a certain general prejudice about the sample is only a motive for distinguishing between basic cases and exceptional, or "fool's" cases. Another similarity is that in all these cases, contingent facts of our history can affect what is regarded as paradigmatic and what is not. Thus, for example, patches in color television screens would presumably not be regarded as paradigmatic as things are now, but perhaps they would be so regarded if most people were permanently in front of television screens. Just as with the reference of 'Madagascar' in the proper name case (cf. Evans 1974), the paradigmatic sample that helps fix the reference of 'yellowness' may vary if the things that most people in the linguistic community are acquainted with vary.

Color Illusions

One prejudice about color not mentioned earlier is that color not only is a manifest property of the object, but also is not relative to its state of motion or rest with respect to an observer: if the object doesn't change its intrinsic properties, it will not change color merely because it starts moving with respect to the observer. But the so-called Benham disk, which contains only a black and white pattern, looks multicolored when it rotates at certain speeds. (The Benham and other disks that produce "subjective colors" are similar to the case of a fan that may appear solid, with no gaps, if it rotates fast enough.) Related illusions occur in cases where the object is stationary relative to the observer. The Butterfield television encoder creates the appearance of certain colors using a set of pulsated black and white signals. Even some stationary, nonpulsating black and white patterns create a color appearance if one stares at them for some time, apparently due to eye motions (see, for example, Hardin 1988, 72ff.). In all these cases, the objects appear to have certain colors to normal observers under what seem to be normal conditions, and yet they really stay black and white (so say the prejudices mentioned earlier). (Averill 1982 also uses similar examples against dispositionalism.)

Another relevant type of illusions are the so-called simultaneous contrast illusions. In these, colored patches of some material dyed with one and the same pigment are placed in the center of bigger patches dyed with a variety of other pigments. The perceived color of the smaller patches then varies, sometimes greatly, depending on the color of the bigger patch that surrounds them (see, for example, Hardin 1988, 49 and plate 2). We certainly have the prejudice that two patches dyed with the same pigment cannot be of different colors, and in particular that their color doesn't change with a change in their backgrounds. This implies that the smaller patches are of the same color, even if they look different against their backgrounds. It is hard to think how these cases could have been declared abnormal a priori. In fact, it is hard to see how they could be specified without restricting normal conditions excessively (simultaneous contrasts are ubiquitous), or without presupposing that background patches have a color independently of how they appear. Similar illusions occur in the domain of Locke's primary qualities. Take the well-known Müller-Lyer illusion, where two arrows of equal length look like they have different lengths because arrow-tails with different orientations are placed at their ends. The existence of this illusion could hardly have been predicted a priori, but it seems analogous in all relevant respects to the simultaneous contrast illusions. In both cases, our intuition is that there is a distinction between the real and the apparent quality even under normal conditions, contra dispositionalism.

5. REMARKS ON SOME RECENT DEFENSES OF LOCKEAN DISPOSITIONALISM

Unaltered, Unmasked, Standardly Mediated, and Relativized Dispositions

Johnston (1992) has proposed to weaken the right-hand side of dispositionalist biconditionals by, essentially, adding new conditions of an abstract nature to the antecedent of the counterfactual, conditions of which it may not be implausible to think as a priori required.[35] In particular, Johnston distinguishes three types of cases in which counterfactuals such as those featured in the right-hand side of typical dispositionalist biconditionals are true, but we are not inclined to take this as a sign that the corresponding postulated disposition has really manifested itself; and he proposes to modify the dispositionalist analysis by excluding those cases. In the first type of case, that of "mimicked dispositions," something extrinsic to the object and the normal conditions of observation is the cause of a color sensation, including possibly a type of sensation that would have been produced by the object if left alone. (For example: "There might have been a ray emitted from the center of green objects, a ray which acted directly on our visual cortices so that green objects always would look red to us" [1992, 231].) In the second type of case, that of "altered dispositions," there are extrinsic properties of the object that cause it to change intrinsically before conditions become normal, and these changes cause a color sensation that would not have been produced without them. (For example: the skin of "a shy but powerfully intuitive chameleon which in

---

[35] See Johnston (1992, 229–30) for his version of the apriority requirement. It must be mentioned that Johnston presents his defense of dispositionalism merely as a defense of the claim that it accommodates a greater number of common beliefs about color than realist views; for him, the set of all common beliefs about color is inconsistent. It must also be said that in more recent work (1998) he has distanced himself from dispositionalism, though on grounds different from those to be given here.

the dark was green but also would intuit when it was about to be put in a
viewing condition and would instantaneously blush bright red as a result"
[1992, 231].) In the third type of case, that of "masked dispositions,"
something extrinsic to the object and the normal conditions of observation is the cause of a color sensation that would not have been produced
by the object otherwise. (This is just a special case of the first case, and the
ray example is one of a masked disposition as well.) A proposal that takes
care of these cases is, then: "an object is green iff (it can be observed by
normal humans under normal conditions and there are intrinsic features
of it that, in normal humans, under normal conditions, and masking,
altering and mimicking aside, would produce sensations of green)" (cf.
Johnston 1992, 234; but this is not Johnston's final proposal).

All the counterexamples of Section 4 continue to work against this
proposal, except for one construal of the jaundice example.[36] In the
killer cases, there isn't even any masking, altered, or mimicked sensation
taking place; but more generally, in the killer and faint intensities cases,
there isn't anything extrinsic to the object and the normal conditions
of observation that is responsible for the absence of the appropriate
sensation. The same can be said of cases of color mixture: the red and
green field in the pointillist painting, say, produces a yellow sensation
without any masking interference from elements extrinsic to the object
or the normal conditions of observation. The Benham disk and related
illusions equally do not seem to involve the operation of any extrinsic
cause. The case of simultaneous contrast illusions may be prima facie less
clear, but it is also unaffected; it might be claimed that the background
patch is extrinsic to the smaller patch and masks its disposition to look
its real color, but the background patch as such is certainly not extrinsic
to the normal conditions of observation; in fact, simultaneous contrast
effects occur continuously in nearly all conditions of observation (only
observation with the help of a dark reduction screen – hardly a normal
condition – will avoid these effects completely). Finally, if the jaundice-
producing substance produces jaundice because some virus is attached to
it, then we may perhaps suppose that the virus is something extrinsic that
masks the disposition of the substance to look red: the substance is red,
but the proposed analysis of this color ascription is not false. However,
we still get a counterexample if we alternatively suppose that the yellow

---

[36] It may be useful to point this out, as some philosophers in conversation have told me
  that a proposal of this sort took care of the word-of-mouth version of Kripke's counterexamples that had reached them.

sensation is produced by some poisonous intrinsic chemical feature of the substance itself. (Note that the killer cases provide counterexamples to the "only if" direction of the biconditionals for the killer properties. The faint intensities, color mixture, color illusions, and "intrinsic" jaundice examples provide counterexamples both to the "only if" direction of the biconditionals for the real properties and to the "if" direction of the biconditionals for the apparent properties.)

Johnston's reaction to examples like the "intrinsic" version of jaundice is to introduce the further condition that "the processes which mediate the relevant dispositions to produce color appearances be among the processes which are standard or typical when it comes to seeing color" (Johnston 1992, 245). A dispositionalist account might incorporate this condition thus: "an object is yellow iff (it can be observed by normal humans under normal conditions through normal mediating processes and there are intrinsic features of it that, in normal humans, under normal conditions, through normal mediating processes, and masking, altering, and mimicking aside, would produce sensations of green)." The "intrinsic" version of jaundice is no longer a counterexample to the "if" direction of this biconditional for yellow, provided we count the process by which the jaundice bar produces the sensation of yellow as atypical; as Johnston would put it, this kind of dispositionalist need not count the bar as yellow. However, the "intrinsic" jaundice is still a counterexample to the "only if" direction of the biconditional for red: given that the bar cannot be observed through normal mediating processes, the biconditional implies that the bar is not red. Note also that the relevantly analogous biconditionals imply that the surface of the sun is not very hot, that there aren't any (inaudibly) loud or soft sounds, that no objects are killer blue, and so on, whether we count the corresponding processes as normal or not.

The new proposal also fails to take care of simultaneous contrast illusions. The requirement that dispositions be normally mediated disposes perhaps of the Benham disk and related counterexamples; as Johnston notes, the processes that mediate the illusory color sensations in these cases can be reasonably called atypical, for they are processes in which packets of different kinds of light come to the eye in very swift sequence from the same location, and this is unusual. But in the case of simultaneous contrast illusions, we cannot speak of an atypical mediating process. As noted earlier, simultaneous contrast effects are ubiquitous.

In order to deal with color mixture examples, Johnston considers approvingly the possibility of relativizing color ascriptions. The ground for this is that it seems reasonable to say that "for many or all of the things we take to be colored there are no standard perceivers nor standard viewing conditions," which suggests that "the best we can do [may be to] talk about the color relative to this kind of perceiver or that kind of viewing condition" (Johnston 1992, 230–1; later [1992, 248], he seems to envisage the possibility of relativizing color also to kinds of mediating processes). Applied to the mixture cases, this relativizing maneuver postulates that "the field in the pointillist painting *is* golden when viewed from two yards," not absolutely, and that an analysans of this ascription will always contain "when viewed from two yards" as a part of what is substituted for "under normal conditions." However, although it seems reasonable to say that viewing the pointillist painting from a distance of two yards and viewing it from much closer up are equally "normal" viewing conditions, this idea does not intuitively incline us, even when faced with the mixture examples, to relativize color ascriptions or an antecedently tempting dispositionalist account of them. Rather, we stick to color absolutism and we accept at most that, strictly speaking, the field *looks* golden when viewed from two yards.[37] As things are, we will simply say that the field is really red and green, perhaps because we implicitly accept an intuitive version of the dissectiveness prejudice.[38] Kripke's

[37] The use of relativization to try to avoid other Kripkean counterexamples seems even more difficult to motivate by appeal to intuitive claims about what is normal or not. There are no actual (and perhaps no possible) observers or conditions in which the surface of the sun produces suitable sensations of great heat, so it is certainly not on relativistic grounds that we speak of the surface of the sun as very hot. We intuitively think of the surface of the sun as very hot – and of the killer blue objects as killer blue – in an absolute sense, and on grounds quite independent of any additional speculation about possible conditions and observers in which they would produce suitable sensations. Relativization is also poorly endowed to deal with our intuitions about simultaneous contrast illusions. There is a clear intuitive sense in which the smaller patch has an absolute color property independent of changes in its background (especially if we choose the smaller patch so that by itself it reflects only one kind of unmixed light), but relativization to a background does not single out any such privileged sense.

[38] Kripke also notes that if most paradigmatic surfaces that look yellow were composed of red and green parts, we would perhaps not be so determined to say that the field is not golden. Suppose this became the case, perhaps because most colored objects viewed by humans ended up being patches of television screens. Then we would probably accept that the pointillist field is golden, and also that it *looks* golden when viewed from two yards and *looks* red and green when viewed from much closer up, and perhaps *also* that it *is* red and green. But not even in this case would we say, I think, that it *is* golden (but not red and green) when viewed from two yards and it *is* red and green (but not golden) when looked at from much closer up. (Of course we may talk this way in some occasions such as those noted by Kripke, in which we are primarily interested in aesthetic or related effects. It may be equally acceptable to say rhetorically that "the table is solid for the common man," even if we know that properly speaking it is not solid in an absolute sense.)

account explains these intuitions, and is thus preferable to a relativist dispositionalism as an account of our color concepts.

Color Similarities

A frequent argument against objectivist views of color, such as Kripke's view, is based on the observation that we intuitively accept similarity and dissimilarity claims about colors. For example, we naturally say that blue is more similar to green than it is to red, or that canary yellow is not as similar to the shades of blue as these are among themselves (an example of Johnston 1992, 236). However, the argument continues, it might turn out that science ends up concluding that the manifest property that causes sensations of canary yellow is as similar to the manifest properties that cause sensations of the shades of blue as these latter properties are among themselves; it might even discover that the manifest property of canary yellowness is more similar to some of the manifest blueness properties than these are among themselves.[39] These are certainly possibilities left open by realist accounts. But it would seem that claims such as the claim that canary yellow is not as similar to the shades of blue as they are among themselves are not open to scientific refutation.[40] In Johnston's words, "we take ourselves to know these principles just on the basis of visual experience and ordinary grasp of color language" (Johnston 1992, 237; for similar arguments see also Boghossian and Velleman 1991, 85ff., and Maund 1995, 146).

Johnston has claimed that this type of consideration strongly supports dispositionalism. The idea is that dispositionalism is not consistent with the possibility that canary yellow is not as similar to the blues as these are among themselves, because the disposition to produce sensations of canary yellow is not as similar to the dispositions to produce sensations of the shades of blue as these dispositions are among themselves.

---

[39] As Byrne (2003, 642, n.5) notes, similarity arguments assume, not implausibly, that "if [objectivism] about color is true, then any genuine respects of similarity between the colors will be evident at the level of the canonical [scientific] description of those properties." (Some kind of objectivist might propose that the sensation it produces is a way of epistemic access to the manifest property of yellowness, but this would be odd.)

[40] Gold (1999, 37ff.), makes an attempt to argue that science could in fact discover that canary yellow looks more similar to certain laboratory-produced appearances of yellowish shades of blue than the shades of blue in general look among themselves. If this is right, it's nevertheless unclear that the dispositionalist could not simply switch to less controversial examples, such as the judgment that blue resembles green more than red.

The dispositions to produce sensations of the shades of blue are similar among themselves because the sensations corresponding to the different shades of blue are similar among themselves. And the disposition to produce sensations of canary yellow is not comparably similar to these, just because sensations of yellow are not as similar to sensations of blue as these are among themselves. Since these principles about the similarity and dissimilarity of sensations are justified just on the basis of visual experience, dispositionalism is supported by our intuitive judgments of similarity and dissimilarity among the colors.[41]

There is no doubt that we do make intuitive claims of color similarity and dissimilarity, and that the apparent justification for these claims we make is visual experience. What is not so clear is that this supports dispositionalism in any way, for comparable similarity claims, also apparently justified on purely visual grounds, are naturally made about traditionally primary qualities. Think of the shape of an orange, which though roughly spherical is in fact highly irregular. It is nevertheless natural for us to say that the shapes of oranges are similar to that of a sphere, that the shape of a sphere is more similar to the shapes of oranges than it is to the shape of a certain highly compressed but regular ellipsoid. It is also natural to say that science could not refute these judgments made on purely visual grounds. How should these claims be viewed? By itself, the dissimilarity claim certainly does not incline us toward a dispositionalism about shape; uncontroversially, the stable intuitive view of shapes is that they are nondispositional properties. But the prima facie impression that the dissimilarity claim is not open to scientific refutation equally fails to support dispositionalism. After a moment's thought, it becomes clear that it is part of the stable common beliefs about shapes that the geometer can find similarities that are not justified on purely visual grounds. (At any rate, if this is not part of a thoroughly unsophisticated common conception of shape, it is at least part of a more sophisticated but still common conception. And it is certainly part of the dispositionalist's view that science can overturn intuitive judgments that the common folk make about

---

[41] Surely the manifest property of canary yellowness (if it exists) is not as similar to the manifest blueness properties as these are among themselves, in that that property produces sensations that are not as phenomenally similar to the sensations produced by the latter properties as these sensations are among themselves. But the existence of these properties and their effects is not justifiable merely on the basis of visual experience and ordinary grasp of color language. The existence of a disposition to produce the same effects is supposed to be so justifiable (Johnston 1992, 242). Although I find this latter claim dubious, it can be granted for the sake of argument.

the primary qualities purely on the basis of their sensory experience of them.) And in fact the geometer tells us that the ellipsoidal shape is genuinely more similar to the spherical shape than to the shapes of the oranges.[42] So it is clear after a moderate amount of reflection that, if the intuitive dissimilarity claim is meant as a claim about shape properties, then it is upset by science and does not receive an adequate ground from pure visual experience. This shows that natural claims of dissimilarity about sensible qualities, which are apparently justified on purely visual grounds, are made in cases where the stable intuitive view is that there is no temptation to think of them as supporting dispositionalism. Thus the argument from similarity cannot by itself support the thesis that color properties are dispositional.

This points to a unified explanation of similarity and dissimilarity claims as being in some nonliteral sense about appearances. As we saw, Kripke pointed out that it is common to find examples of claims that are not literally about appearances but are in some sense meant as claims about appearances – and that, we might add, are epistemically grounded only insofar as they are about appearances. As shown by the analogy with shape, it is very reasonable to take intuitive similarity and dissimilarity claims about the sensible properties quite generally as being in some sense about appearances. This explains the intuition that they are true: a sensation of a highly compressed ellipsoidal shape is not as similar to the sensations of sphericality or of the shapes of oranges as these latter sensations are among themselves (a highly compressed ellipsoidal shape does not look as similar to the orange shapes and spherical shapes as these look among themselves); a sensation of canary yellow is not as similar to the sensations of the shades of blue as these latter sensations are among themselves (canary yellow does not look as similar to the blues as these look among themselves). And it explains the impression that the literal claims are justified on purely visual grounds, for the corresponding judgments about appearances are justified on purely visual grounds, and could not be scientifically refuted. That the claims are typically meant as claims about appearances is also independently plausible, since the aspects of similarity and dissimilarity between sensible properties that we presumably care about in everyday contexts have to do with appearances.

---

[42] The analytical equation of the sphere bears an evident similarity to those of ellipsoids in general (the sphere is just a particular case of an ellipsoid). Any orange has a vastly more complicated shape.

Johnston (1992, 253) contemplates the reply that similarity claims are in some sense really about appearances. He objects that it implies that "vision tells us almost nothing about what canary yellow, teal, turquoise, sky blue are like.... On the other hand, vision can acquaint us with the natures of the color properties if these properties are dispositions to produce visual responses" (1992, 253). This is supposed to be an advantage because, according to Johnston, "our implicit cognitive values favor acquaintance with objects, people, places, and hence with their properties. If that is so then we have reason to want vision to be a mode of access to the natures of visible properties [such as the colors]" (1992, 255). Ultimately, thus, Johnston's similarity argument for dispositionalism relies on the additional premise that we have some intuition that vision acquaints us with the natures of the color properties. I have no such intuition, and I think that it's clear that several much more clearly intuitive ideas about color go against it.[43] It is surely part of the common view that there are all kinds of scientific truths about color shades that are not available just on the basis of visual perception.[44] (And it is part of the common view that science might discover tomorrow that Kripke's killer blue exists, although its existence and properties could not be known on the basis of pure visual experience.) Just as in the case of shape, once we note this momentarily forgotten intuition, we reach the stable view that if an intuitive dissimilarity claim is meant as a claim about color properties, then it may be upset by science and does not receive an adequate ground from pure visual experience. The natural view is then that the claim is not typically meant as about color properties, as we just argued.

Unrecognizable Conceptually Necessary Truths

Motivated especially by altered dispositions (see above), Wright (1988, 14, n.26; 1989, 193ff.; 1992, 117ff.) has proposed to withdraw biconditional analyses in favor of dispositionalist "provisoed biconditionals." An example is "For any perceiver S: if S were perceptually normal and x were presented to S under perceptually normal conditions, then (S would judge x to be green if and only if x was green)." Note that this kind of principle fails to assign the color green to Johnston's chameleon's

---

[43] So we should doubt that it is part of our common view of colors unless we want to follow Johnston in convicting this view of blatant inconsistency.

[44] See related remarks in Jackson (1996, 210f.).

skin in the dark, and in general fails to assign a color to an object while it's not being observed under normal conditions. Wright proposes that our concepts of the colors are only partially dispositional and that the color of objects not observed under normal conditions is determined by nondispositional characteristics (cf. 1992, 126f.). This is a weak form of dispositionalism. Still, it falls prey to Kripke's killer blue, faint colors, color mixture, and color illusion counterexamples, provided simply that we take the conditions of observation in them as normal.

Wright (2002, 426) has nevertheless suggested the possibility of including the requisite that "the surface be presented against a matt black background" in the list of conditions under which an object is green iff it produces an immediate perceptual judgment that it is green; in fact, among these conditions he includes also requirements such as that the object be "relatively stationary (i.e., stationary or slow-moving relative to you the observer)," and that the observer be "free of spots before the eyes, after-images, and so on" (2002, 426). Perhaps Wright would be ready to include also the conditions of observation that obtain in all known counterexamples to biconditional analyses. One among several objections to this move would be that there is a strong intuition that the resulting "provisoed biconditional" cannot possibly be a priori or conceptually necessary – as needed by Wright, who intends to sustain the primary/secondary quality distinction claiming that corresponding "provisoed biconditionals" about Locke's primary qualities are, if true, a posteriori so. But Wright has argued that no enrichment of the antecedent would inevitably take away the conceptual necessity of the "provisoed biconditional."

Wright's reason for this claim is an alleged parallel with Church's thesis, the hypothesis that the effectively calculable functions are the recursive ones:

> Effective calculability is an intuitive notion; general recursiveness is a mathematically precise one. The thesis is precisely an attempt to give a mathematically exact characterization of something pre-formal. In the nature of the case, it therefore admits of no conclusive formal proof. Yet, if it is true, it is true purely as a reflection of the character of the concepts involved.... Our concept of the variety of ways in which the redness of an object might in principle be masked by how it seems, or in which how it seems might be deceptive, ought to allow of correct circumscription, just as the concept of effective calculability ought. If we alight upon such a circumscription, it will certainly be too complicated to enable its truth to be recognizable immediately, just by the light cast by the analytic understanding, as it were; and there is no basis on which its truth might be recognized inferentially.

As with Church's thesis, its a priori correctness, if it is correct, will ultimately be supportable only defeasibly, by the failure of hard reflection to find it wanting. (Wright 2002, 427)

Of course Wright could not claim that the mere "failure of hard reflection to find it wanting" is sufficient to effect a distinction between a true dispositionalist "provisoed biconditional" for color and a true dispositionalist "provisoed biconditional" for shape, say. Suppose we have managed to formulate a "provisoed biconditional" for yellowness that after many years both hard reflection and experience have been unable to find wanting. Would this show that yellowness is a dispositional property, or that dispositionalism is a priori? Not at all. It is equally imaginable that we could manage to formulate a "provisoed biconditional" for sphericality that after many years both hard reflection and experience would be unable to find wanting. Wright's suggestion seems to be, rather, that the case of Church's thesis gives us grounds for thinking that some propositions that should be considered as conceptually necessary (if true) are unrecognizable as true, whether immediately or inferentially.[45] A suitable dispositionalist thesis, for all we know, might be one of these. This would provide a partial defense of dispositionalism.

A decisive problem here, however, is that, although it is in fact a popular view, or has been so until recently, there is actually nothing in the nature of the case that precludes a recognizably conclusive proof of Church's thesis. Surely no proof within standard mathematics can be given, because the concept of effective calculability is not a concept of standard mathematics. But if by a conclusive proof we just mean, as we certainly must in a philosophical context, a proof that uses only conclusive truths and rules (regardless of their subject), then there is no obstacle in principle to a conclusive proof of Church's thesis, just as there is no obstacle in principle to a conclusive proof of any a priori truth containing concepts from outside standard mathematics (such as 'one melon plus one melon equals two melons').[46] This spoils Wright's partial defense of dispositionalism. For Wright's basic idea is that we know that some propositions that should be considered as conceptually necessary cannot be conclusively

---

[45] Thus, if Wright assumes that conceptually necessary truths are a priori, he must be using "a priori" in some unusual sense on which conclusive knowability (by humans), or knowability tout court, is not a necessary condition of apriority. This by itself is no objection to Wright as long as he holds that "provisoed biconditionals" for the traditionally primary qualities are not a priori in his sense.

[46] Incidentally, Kripke has long noted in his classes on recursion theory that there is no obstacle in principle to a proof of Church's thesis.

recognized as true. But Church's thesis is certainly not an example, and it is unclear that one can be produced. Without an example (or a proof that it exists), we cannot say that there is no basis to think that the truth of a conceptually necessary "provisoed biconditional" might be conclusively recognized inferentially, as needed for Wright's defense to work. The default presumption is that there is no obstacle in principle to conclusive proofs of conceptually necessary truths.

In any case, nothing but a proof that the true dispositionalist "provisoed biconditional" would not be conclusively recognizable as true could give some comfort to the dispositionalist. Suppose we managed to prove that some other proposition is conceptually necessary but not conclusively recognizable as true. Then an appeal to this fact could be used also by a proponent of the thesis that shape properties are dispositional as a matter of conceptual necessity. He might claim that our impression that we cannot convince ourselves conclusively that they are true is explained by the possibility that the true dispositionalist "provisoed biconditional" about sphericality is one of the conceptually necessary truths that are not conclusively recognizable as true. This leaves us where we stood. Unless we are antecedently convinced that some dispositionalist "provisoed biconditional" about color is a conceptual truth, the most reasonable explanation of our impression that we could not conclusively convince ourselves that it is true is not that it might be unrecognizably true, but that it is not conceptually necessary.

References

Armstrong, D. M. (1961), *Perception and the Physical World*, London: Routledge and Kegan Paul.

(1968), *A Materialist Theory of the Mind*, London: Routledge and Kegan Paul.

(1969), "Colour Realism and the Argument from Microscopes," reprinted in Armstrong, *The Nature of Mind and Other Essays*, Ithaca, N.Y.: Cornell University Press, 1981, 104–19.

Averill, E. W. (1982), "The Primary-Secondary Quality Distinction," *Philosophical Review*, vol. 91, 343–61.

(1985), "Color and the Anthropocentric Problem," *Journal of Philosophy*, vol. 82, 281–304.

(1992), "The Relational Nature of Color," *Philosophical Review*, vol. 101, 551–88.

Berkeley, G. (1962), *The Principles of Human Knowledge and Three Dialogues between Hylas and Philonous*, ed. by G. J. Warnock, London: Collins.

Boghossian, P. and D. Velleman (1989), "Colour as a Secondary Quality," *Mind*, vol. 98, 81–103.

(1991), "Physicalist Theories of Color," *Philosophical Review*, vol. 100, 67–106.

Broackes, J. (1992), "The Autonomy of Colour," in D. Charles and K. Lennon (eds.), *Reduction, Explanation and Realism*, Oxford: Oxford University Press, 421–65.

Byrne, A. (2003), "Color and Similarity," *Philosophy and Phenomenological Research*, vol. 66, 641–65.

Byrne, A. and D. Hilbert (1997), "Colors and Reflectances," in A. Byrne and D. Hilbert (eds.), *Readings on Color, Vol. 1: The Philosophy of Color*, Cambridge: MIT Press, 263–88.

Eddington, A. S. (1928), *The Nature of the Physical World*, New York: Macmillan.

Evans, G. (1974), "The Causal Theory of Names," reprinted in G. Evans, *Collected Papers*, Oxford: Clarendon Press, 1–24.

——— (1980), "Things Without the Mind – A Commentary upon Chapter Two of Strawson's *Individuals*," reprinted in G. Evans, *Collected Papers*, Oxford: Clarendon Press, 1985, 249–90.

Feynman, R. P., R. B. Leighton, and M. Sands (1963), *The Feynman Lectures on Physics, Mainly Mechanics, Radiation and Heat, Volume I*, Reading, Mass.: Addison-Wesley.

Gold, I. (1999), "Dispositions and the Central Problem of Color," *Philosophical Studies*, vol. 93, 21–44.

Goodman, N. (1951), *The Structure of Appearance*, Cambridge: Harvard University Press.

——— (1955), *Fact, Fiction, and Forecast*, Cambridge: Harvard University Press.

Hardin, C. L. (1988), *Color for Philosophers: Unweaving the Rainbow*, Indianapolis: Hackett. Expanded edition: Indianapolis: Hackett, 1993.

Hilbert, D. (1987), *Color and Color Perception: A Study in Anthropocentric Realism*, Stanford, Calif.: CSLI.

Jackson, F. (1996), "The Primary Quality View of Color," *Philosophical Perspectives*, vol. 10, 199–219.

Johnston, M. (1992), "How to Speak of the Colors," *Philosophical Studies*, vol. 68, 221–63.

——— (1998), "Are Manifest Qualities Response-Dependent?" *The Monist*, vol. 81, 3–43.

Kripke, S. (1972), "Naming and Necessity", in D. Davidson and G. Harman (eds.), *Semantics of Natural Language*, Dordrecht: Reidel, 253–355, 763–9. Revised book edition with an added preface: *Naming and Necessity*, Cambridge: Harvard University Press, 1980. (References are to the book edition.)

Locke, J. (1975), *An Essay Concerning Human Understanding*, ed. by P. H. Nidditch, Oxford: Clarendon Press.

McDowell, J. (1985), "Values and Secondary Qualities," in T. Honderich (ed.), *Morality and Objectivity: A Tribute to J. L. Mackie*, London: Routledge and Kegan Paul, 110–29.

McGinn, C. (1983), *The Subjective View: Secondary Qualities and Indexical Thoughts*, Oxford: Clarendon Press.

——— (1996), "Another Look at Color," *Journal of Philosophy*, vol. 93, 537–53.

(1999), "Postscript to 'Another Look at Colour'", in McGinn, *Knowledge and Reality: Selected Essays*, Oxford: Clarendon Press, 313.

Mackie, J. L. (1976), *Problems from Locke*, Oxford: Clarendon Press.

Maund, J. B. (1995), *Colours: Their Nature and Representation*, Cambridge: Cambridge University Press.

Nagel, T. (1983), Review of McGinn (1983), *Times Literary Supplement*, November 18, 1983, 1283.

(1986), *The View from Nowhere*, Oxford: Oxford University Press.

Peacocke, C. (1984), "Colour Concepts and Colour Experience," *Synthese*, vol. 68, 365–82.

Shoemaker, S. (1986), Review of McGinn (1983), *Journal of Philosophy*, vol. 83, 407–13.

Smart, J. J. C. (1963), *Philosophy and Scientific Realism*, London: Routledge.

(1975), "On Some Criticisms of a Physicalist Theory of Colors," reprinted in A. Byrne and D. Hilbert (eds.), *Readings on Color, Vol. 1: The Philosophy of Color*, Cambridge: MIT Press, 1997, 1–10.

Smith, A. D. (1990), "Of Primary and Secondary Qualities," *Philosophical Review*, vol. 99, 221–54.

Stebbing, L. S. (1937), *Philosophy and the Physicists*, New York: Dover, 1958.

Stuart, M. (2003), "Locke's Colors," *Philosophical Review*, vol. 112, 57–96.

Wedgwood, R. (1998), "The Essence of Response-Dependence", in R. Casati and C. Tappolet (eds.), *European Review of Philosophy 3: Response-Dependence*, Stanford, Calif: CSLI, 31–54.

Wright, C. (1988), "Moral Values, Projection and Secondary Qualities," *Proceedings of the Aristotelian Society*, supp. vol. 62, 1–26.

(1989), "Wittgenstein's Rule-Following Considerations and the Central Project of Theoretical Linguistics," reprinted in Wright, *Rails to Infinity*, Cambridge: Harvard University Press, 2001, 170–213.

(1992), *Truth and Objectivity*, Cambridge: Harvard University Press.

(2002), "The Conceivability of Naturalism," in T. S. Gendler and J. Hawthorne (eds.), *Conceivability and Possibility*, Oxford: Oxford University Press, 401–39.

PART IV

PHILOSOPHY OF MIND AND PHILOSOPHICAL PSYCHOLOGY

13

Kripke and Cartesianism

Sydney Shoemaker

The metaphysical and semantical ideas Saul Kripke advanced in the early 1970s, in *Naming and Necessity* and "Identity and Necessity," have found wide acceptance among philosophers. But what is perhaps the most intriguing application he made of these ideas was in his discussion of the mind/body problem, where his arguments and conclusions are widely regarded as Cartesian in spirit; and here many fewer have been convinced. Those who accept the central ideas of his philosophy, but also accept materialist or physicalist views of the sort Kripke uses these ideas to attack, face the challenge of showing that these are not, as he forcefully argued, incompatible.

The central ideas in question include Kripke's view that the relation of identity holds necessarily when it holds at all, that identity statements in which the terms are "rigid designators" are necessarily true or necessarily false, and his view that there can be knowledge of necessary truths, the knowledge of identity statements being a case in point, that is a posteriori (empirical) rather than a priori. A rigid designator (such as a name) is a referring expression that is to be understood as referring to the same thing in statements about counterfactual situations, "other possible worlds," as it does in statements about the actual world. So, to use one of Kripke's examples, in the statement "Benjamin Franklin was the inventor of bifocals," the name "Benjamin Franklin" is a rigid designator while the definite description "the inventor of bifocals" is not. The inventor of bifocals could have been someone else (is someone else in some possible world), but Benjamin Franklin could not have been someone else. The statement "Benjamin Franklin was the inventor of bifocals" is contingent, because one of the designators in it is not rigid. But names are rigid designators, so an identity statement like "Mark Twain is Samuel Clemens," in

Thanks to Christopher Hill for comments on an earlier version of this paper.

which both terms are names, is necessarily true if true. Yet the knowledge
of such a statement will be empirical. That Hesperus (the evening star)
is identical with Phosphorus (the morning star), these being two names
for the planet Venus, was an empirical discovery, though the statement
"Hesperus is Phosphorus" expresses a necessarily true proposition. The
same is true of identity statements about kinds and properties, such as
"Water is H_2O" and "Heat is molecular motion," and our knowledge of
them. Empirical knowledge of necessary truths is not limited to knowledge of identity propositions; Kripke holds that statements about natural
kinds, such as "Gold is an element," can also be necessary a posteriori.

Materialist views about the mind are often expressed in identity
statements – persons (subjects of mental states) are held to be identical with material objects of certain kinds, and mental states are held to
be identical with physical (presumably neurological) states. At one time
(in the 1950s) it was widely held that there are "contingent identities"
between mental and physical entities; the identities were thought to be
contingent because they could be known only empirically. That view was
abandoned when Kripke argued persuasively for the view that identities
hold necessarily if they hold at all, and that there are necessary truths
that can be known only empirically. So proponents of identity theories
must hold that there are necessary identities between mental and physical entities. Kripke finds that view problematic, to say the least. To the
extent that he is a Cartesian, his Cartesianism consists largely, if not
entirely, in his rejection of such identities.

Kripke's discussion of this is in the third lecture of his *Naming and
Necessity* (*NN*) and the final part of his "Identity and Necessity" (IN). In
both places he presents three arguments for "Cartesian" conclusions.
One is an argument against the claim that a person is identical with his
or her body. Another is an argument against the claim that particular
("token") mental states and events are identical with particular physical
states and events. And another is an argument against the claim that
mental state types, for example, pain, are identical with physical event
types, for example, C-fiber stimulation. (In what follows, "C-fiber stimulation" stands in for any physical state or event that might be offered as a
candidate for being what pain is.) The general structure of all three arguments is the same. Intuitively it seems possible that a person could exist
without the particular object that is her body existing (and vice versa),
that a particular episode of pain could exist without a particular episode
of C-fiber stimulation existing (and vice versa), and that there should
be pains unaccompanied by C-fiber stimulation and C-fiber stimulation

unaccompanied by pain; and these possibilities seem incompatible with the identity claims under attack. Kripke says (*NN*, p. 144) that his primary concern is with the type-type identity claim, but he precedes his discussion of this with brief discussions of the others.

The first argument goes as follows. Let "Descartes" be the name (and rigid designator) of a person, and let "B" rigidly designate that person's body. If "Descartes = B" is true it must be necessarily true. But arguably, Descartes (or Descartes's mind) could exist without B existing. Also, B could exist without Descartes existing (and arguably does so when B is a corpse). So the identity statement cannot be necessarily true, and so cannot be true at all.

This argument is used more to illustrate Kripke's strategy than to support a Cartesian conclusion. Kripke makes it clear that one could reject the identity statement without endorsing any sort of Cartesian dualism. One could hold that a person's relation to his body is like that of a statue to a hunk of matter – that the person is "nothing over and above" the body, but not identical with it. And in a footnote to *NN* he says that the rejection of identity theories about mental states and events, for example, sensations like pain, does not support Cartesian dualism, and says that his own view that a person could not have originated in sperm and egg different from those that he or she in fact originated in "suggests a rejection of the Cartesian picture" (p. 155). He also says that "Descartes' notion seems to have been rendered dubious ever since Hume's critique of the notion of a Cartesian self."

So if Kripke supports any sort of dualism, it is property and event dualism rather than substance dualism. He never calls himself a dualist of any sort. But if property and event dualism is a consequence of the rejection of the view that mental states (token or type) are identical with physical states, his arguments seem to commit him to such a view.[1]

The argument against token-token identity goes as follows (see *NN*, pp. 146–7). Let "A" name a particular pain sensation and let "B" name the corresponding brain state. Prima facie it seems at least logically possible that B should have existed without A, and that A should have existed without B. If A is the same as B, the identity would have to be necessary, and these could not be possibilities. He considers a response to the first possibility (of B without A) that says that *being a pain* is merely

---

[1] It is controversial whether materialists are committed to either type-type identities or token-token identities of the sort Kripke discusses. For a denial that they are, see Boyd (1980).

a contingent property of A, and that therefore the possibility of B existing without there being pain does not imply the possibility of B existing
without A. He rejects this as completely implausible, on the grounds that
being a pain is a necessary property of every pain. He links the idea that
being a pain is a contingent property of pains with the idea, common to
functionalist views of the mind, that *being a pain* is to be analyzed in terms
of causal role. He says that he usually finds such analyses faulty on specific grounds independent of modal considerations. (This is one expression of Kripke's skepticism about functionalist and causal accounts of the
mental.) But at any rate, he finds it "self-evidently absurd" to take *being a
pain* as a contingent property of pains.[2]

With regard to the second possibility, of A without B, he stresses both
that A is essentially a pain and that B is essentially a brain state of a certain sort. Someone who asserts that A is identical with B must deny that
A could have occurred without there occurring a brain state of a certain
sort – a "quite specific configuration of molecules." So the token identity
theorist must explain away the intuition that "the correlative presence of
anything with mental properties is merely contingent to B, and the correlative presence of any specific physical properties is contingent to A."

I will return to token-token identities shortly. But first I will present the
argument that Kripke mainly focuses on, that against type-type identities, of the sort expressed by "Pain is identical with C-fiber stimulation."
Kripke takes it that "pain," understood as the name of a type of mental
state, and "C-fiber stimulation," understood as the name of a type of
physiological state, are both rigid designators. So the identity theorist is
committed to the view that there could not be a C-fiber stimulation that
was not a pain or a pain that was not a C-fiber stimulation. These consequences are "surprising and counterintuitive" (p. 149). As he says in IN,
"we can imagine the brain state occurring though there is no pain at all,"
and "one might imagine a creature being in pain, but not being in any
specified brain state at all, maybe not having a brain at all" (p. 161). If
these imagined cases are really possible, then no statement of the kind
"Pain is identical with C-fiber stimulation" can be a necessary truth, and
no such statement can be true.

Kripke goes on to consider whether the appearance that mental state
types and physical state types are always at best contingently connected

---

[2] It should be noted that functionalists and causal theorists are not committed to this contingency claim; it is open to them to hold that what is a pain necessarily has the causal
role that makes it a pain.

can be explained away – whether the appearance that there can be pain without C-fiber stimulation, or vice versa, can be explained away in a way analogous to that in which the appearance that there can be heat without molecular motion, or water without H_2O, can be explained away. But before we get to that, let us pause to consider the bearing of what has been argued so far on the mind/body problem.

Many materialists are functionalists, and think that mental states are "multiply realizable" in the physical. This means that pain, for example, might be realized in one way in us – in C-fiber stimulation, for example – and in some quite different way in some other species (David Lewis imagined Martians in whom pain is realized in the inflation of thousands of tiny cavities in the feet.[3]) Some hold that it might be true even within our species that pain might have different physical realizations in different creatures, or even in the same creature on different occasions. Usually the "realization" of a mental state in a physical state is thought to be a matter of the physical state occupying a causal role that is somehow definitive of the mental state. Kripke has made it clear that he has no sympathy with this sort of view – associated with functionalism, or causal theories of the mind – but he has not explicitly argued against it. At any rate, proponents of such a view will agree with Kripke that there are no true type-type identities of the form "Pain is identical with C-fiber stimulation." At best, they will say, C-fiber stimulation could be one of the realizers of pain, not something identical with it. But while such theorists could agree with Kripke that for any physical state type P there could be pain without P, they could not agree with him that for any physical state P, there could be P without pain. If indeed C-fiber stimulation is one of the realizers of pain, then while there can be pain without C-fiber stimulation (for it might have another of its possible realizations), there could not be C-fiber stimulation without pain. The realizers of a state must be sufficient for it. Since on this materialist view every mental state must be physically realized, for every mental state type there must be one or more physical state types whose instantiations are sufficient for the instantiation of that mental state type. If, as Kripke suggests, every physical state type is such that states of that type could occur without pain occurring, then this materialist view is false. So Kripke's claims are threatening to more than just the type-type identity theory. They are threatening to any view that says that mental states have mental realizers, or that the mental supervenes on the physical. And that means that they are threatening to materialism as such.

[3] See Lewis (1980).

A possible response to this is that functionalists are committed only to the claim that the instantiation of certain physical state types is *nomologically* sufficient for the instantiation of certain mental state types, and that this is compatible with its being *metaphysically* possible for such physical state types to be instantiated without the mental state types being instantiated. The idea is that this can happen in worlds in which the physical laws are different from what they are in the actual world, and not such as to give those physical states the causal features that in the actual world make them realizers of those mental states. But the functionalist must at least hold that the instantiation of these physical state types *together with the obtaining of the actual world physical laws* is metaphysically sufficient for the instantiation of the mental state types. Or to put it differently, that the instantiation of these physical state types, *and their being such as to play certain causal roles*, is metaphysically sufficient for the instantiation of the mental state types. And this view will be challenged if it can be held that there are possible worlds governed by these physical laws in which the physical states are instantiated without the mental states being instantiated – these would be worlds in which the physical laws are the same but the psychophysical laws are different. Some have held, on the basis of arguments similar to Kripke's, that the possible worlds include "zombie worlds" that are physically just like the actual world and are governed by the same physical laws but contain no conscious mental states whatever. I think Kripke would agree.

Let's return to the case of token-token identities. Many readers have found the possibility claims Kripke uses to question these less convincing than those he uses to question whether there are type-type identities. Suppose I am in pain and my C-fibers are stimulated. It is certainly plausible to say that one can imagine being in pain without having C-fibers stimulated, or having C-fibers stimulated without being in pain. It is less clear whether one can imagine *this* pain occurring without one's C-fibers being stimulated (or without one's even having C-fibers), and whether one can imagine *this* episode of C-fiber stimulation occurring unaccompanied by pain. Still, it would seem that if a token physical event is an episode of pain, there must be something about it that accounts for its being so, and on a physicalist view this would have to consist in its having some physical property or being of some physical type. Let's suppose that the only candidate for being what accounts for a certain physical event's being a pain is its being an episode of C-fiber stimulation. Then being an episode of C-fiber stimulation should be sufficient for being a pain. In that case, the possibility of C-fiber stimulation without pain would rule out any token identities between pains and C-fiber stimulations. And if this goes for C-fiber stimulation, it presumably goes for any other physical state type. If for any physical state type P it is possible for P to be instantiated unaccompanied by pain, then there can be no token-token identities between instances of pain and instances of physical types. Which is hardly surprising, given the earlier result that the claim that this is possible entails the falsity of materialism.

But Kripke does not think that the imaginability of X without Y in all cases establishes the possibility of X without Y and the nonidentity of X and Y. He could hardly think this given his insistence that while identity truths are necessary truths (when the designators involved are rigid), knowledge of these is typically empirical. When a statement is such that it can only be known empirically, it will always be possible for it to seem possible to someone that it is false. And so it is with the identity statements "Hesperus is Phosphorus," "Heat is molecular motion," and "Water is H_2O." Given that each of these is true, it cannot be really possible for any of them to be false. So it must be possible to explain away the seeming possibility of their being false. If we could in the same way explain away the seeming possibility of "Pain is C-fiber stimulation" being false, that is, of pain without C-fiber stimulation or vice versa, then Kripke's case against the type-type identity theory, and more generally his case against materialism, would collapse. So Kripke's next task is to show that we can't do this.

He focuses on the statement that heat is molecular motion, which he takes to be a truth established by science. He grants that it could seem to someone that it is possible that there should be heat without molecular motion. The general strategy for handling the apparent contingency of cases of necessary a posteriori truths is "to argue that although the statement itself is necessary, someone could, *qualitatively* speaking, be in the same epistemic situation as the original, and in such a situation a *qualitatively* analogous statement could be false" (*NN*, p. 150). He takes it that the reference of the term "heat" is fixed by the sort of sensation it typically causes. This is not to say that "heat" is synonymous with some such description as "that which produces this kind of sensation." Rather, the fact that heat produces such a sensation is a contingent fact about it that serves to determine the reference (or, as Kripke puts it, "fix the reference") of the word "heat" – oversimplifying, we might think of the word "heat" as introduced by saying "Heat is whatever property of things is (in the actual world) responsible for these sorts of sensations." According to Kripke, "When someone says, inaccurately, that heat might have turned

out not to be molecular motion, what is true in what he says is that someone could have sensed a phenomenon in the same way we feel heat, that
is, feel it by means of its production of the sensation we call 'the sensation of heat' (call it 'S')" (*NN*, p. 150). He imagines creatures who get
this sensation from something else, and perhaps rigidly designate what
causes it with the word "heat." But what they call "heat" would not be
what we call "heat"; it would not be heat. The seeming possibility of heat
without molecular motion is really the possibility of something other
than heat producing the phenomena that are for us indicators of heat.

Similarly, the seeming possibility of water not being H_2O is really the
possibility of a world (for example, Hilary Putnam's Twin Earth) where
the watery stuff – the stuff that looks and acts the way H_2O does – is not
H_2O.[4] And the seeming possibility that Hesperus is not Phosphorus is
really the possibility of a world in which the heavenly body that appears
at a certain time in the evening is not the same as the one that appears at
a certain time in the morning.

Kripke claims that this strategy cannot be used to explain away the
apparent possibility of pain without C-fiber stimulation, or vice versa. The
case is not analogous to the case of heat and molecular motion. It is possible for molecular motion not to be felt as heat and still be heat, but it is
not possible for C-fiber stimulation not to be felt as pain but still be pain.
It is possible for something to be felt as heat (produce the sensation of
heat) and not be heat, but it is not possible for something to be felt as
pain and not be pain – for what is felt as pain *is* pain. What accounts for
the seeming possibility of heat without molecular motion (or vice versa)
is that here there is an intermediary (the sensation of heat) between the
external phenomenon (heat) and the observer – an intermediary that in
principle can be there without the external phenomenon, and can fail to
be there when the external phenomenon is present. But there is no such
intermediary between pain and the observer. Whereas heat is "picked out
contingently by the fact that it affects us in such and such a way, we cannot
similarly say that we pick out pain contingently by the fact that it affects us
in such and such a way" (IN, p. 161). One can be in the epistemic situation
one is in when heat is present without heat being present, and one can be
in the epistemic situation one is in when heat is not present when heat is
present. But "to be in the same epistemic situation that would obtain if
one had a pain *is* to have a pain; to be in the same epistemic situation that
would obtain in the absence of pain *is* not to have a pain" (*NN*, p. 152).

---

[4] See Putnam (1975).

One assumption that appears to be operating here is what Crispin Wright calls the "Counter-Conceivability Principle."[5] This says that "if one has what at least *appears to be* a lucid conception of how it might be that not-P, then that should count as a good, albeit defeasible, ground for its not being necessary that P," and that this makes "*all* purportedly metaphysically necessary statements … hostage to what we can, to borrow Descartes' happy phrase, clearly and distinctly conceive" (Wright, p. 408). Also operating, apparently, is what Steven Yablo calls "Textbook Kripkeanism," which says that "The one and only way for E to be conceptually possible but not 'really' – metaphysically – possible is for something *else* to be really possible, namely E's presentation E*." Wright's principle says that the conceivability of E is a defeasible ground for its possibility, and Yablo's principle tells us that the only way to defeat this ground is to find a presentation of E, E*, such that the real possibility of E* is mistaken for the possibility of E.[6] Where E is the presence of heat, the "presentation" E* will be the production of the sensation of heat – the latter can be present without molecular motion, that is, heat, creating the illusion that E (heat) can be present without molecular motion. But there is no presentation of pain other than pain itself; so we can't explain the seeming possibility of pain without C-fiber stimulation by saying that what is really possible is not pain without C-fiber stimulation but the presentation of pain without C-fiber stimulation.

It should be noted that it is only if our imagining or conceiving is from a first-person point of view that pain has no presentation other than itself. When we are conceiving of other persons as being in pain, or not being in pain, one could say that the person's behavior and circumstances serve as presentations of pain, or its absence, that are only contingently related to it. But it seems sufficient for Kripke's purposes that there is one way of conceiving of pain, or its absence, such that there is no presentation of it other than the pain itself, or the absence of pain.

One response to Kripke's argument that is compatible with both the Counter-Conceivability Principle and with Textbook Kripkeanism rests on a point made by Richard Boyd, namely that while pain has, in the first-person case, no presentation other than itself, the same is not true of C-fiber stimulation.[7] A possibility that might be mistaken for the possibility of pain without C-fiber stimulation is that of pain occurring and

---

[5] Wright (2002).
[6] Wright and Yablo both reject the principles I have called by their names.
[7] Boyd (1980).

the brain monitor mistakenly indicating the absence of C-fiber stimulation; and a possibility that might be mistaken for the possibility of C-fiber stimulation without pain is that of the brain monitor mistakenly indicating C-fiber stimulation in a case where there is no pain. Crispin Wright, although he rejects Kripke's argument, finds this response implausible. For it to succeed, he thinks, the concept of C-fiber stimulation would have to be a "derivative natural kind concept," like that of water, rather than a "primary natural kind concept," like that of H_2O. But in fact it is the latter. The reference of such concepts "is fixed not by adverting to indicator properties, but directly in the light of the explicit content of the concepts themselves," and so the concepts "are thus associated with no analogues of the distinction between water and symptomatic counterparts of water, and thought experiments in which they figure cannot be faulted for insensitivity to such distinctions" (Wright, p. 417).

But many who are unconvinced by Kripke's argument reject Textbook Kripkeanism, and some reject the Counter-Conceivability principle. These theorists hold that we can explain the seeming possibility of pain without C-fiber stimulation and of C-fiber stimulation without pain without employing what Kripke takes to be the only available strategy for explaining away the apparent possibility of what are in fact impossible situations, namely the one he employs in the case of heat and molecular motion.

In a footnote to his well-known paper "What Is It Like to Be a Bat?" Thomas Nagel distinguishes three ways in which something can be represented in the imagining of it; it can be represented perceptually, sympathetically, or symbolically.[8] "To imagine something perceptually, we put ourselves in a state similar to that we would be in if we perceived it. To represent something sympathetically, we put ourselves in a conscious state resembling the thing itself" (Nagel, pp. 175–6). He suggests that what makes it seem possible that there should be pain in the absence of any given physical state, or that there should be any given physical state without pain, is that we imagine the pain or its absence sympathetically while imagining one's physical condition perceptually. And he says that this will make the relation between the states seem contingent even if it is necessary. This suggestion is developed further in papers by Christopher Hill and by Hill and Brian McLaughlin.[9] As Hill develops it, we get into trouble in using our imaginings or conceivings to arrive at modal conclusions (conclusions about the possibility of states of affairs) when the imagining or conceiving involves "splicing together" imaginings or

---

[8] Nagel (1979).
[9] See Hill (1997) and Hill and McLaughlin (1999).

conceivings of different kinds. This might involve, as in Nagel's discussion, splicing together a perceptual imagining and a sympathetic imagining, this resulting in an intuition that the objects of these different imaginings are separable. Or it might be a conception that is the result of combining two concepts that are not analytically related, and are such that one has no empirical reason for thinking that they are necessarily coextensive, this resulting in an intuition that the properties or kinds these concepts represent are separable. This can also happen when one of the concepts is a commonsense concept and the other is a theoretical concept. Hill says that such intuitions are the result of a psychological mechanism that we have good reason to think is unreliable. An example of its unreliability is the intuition on the part of the scientifically untutored that heat is separable from molecular motion. But the same mechanism is involved in producing the intuition that there can be pain without C-fiber stimulation, or vice versa; more generally, the intuition that pain is separable from any physical state that is a candidate for being identical with it. So these intuitions are not to be trusted.

Hill needn't be read as rejecting the Counter-Conceivability principle formulated by Wright. While it holds that the lucid conceivability of something is a good ground for holding it possible, that principle allows that this ground is "defeasible." And Hill could be read as accepting the principle but offering a view about what one of the defeaters is – namely, the imagining or conceiving being the result of the "splicing" psychological mechanism that is unreliable. But I think that Hill does reject Textbook Kripkeanism. It is not part of his suggestion that the mistaken modal intuitions resulting from this mechanism get *something* right, that is, that they reflect the metaphysical possibility of some state of affairs whose nature they misrepresent.

Crispin Wright has a different way of rejecting Kripke's argument. He assumes, with Kripke, that it is a necessary truth about a person that he was the child of certain parents. But he says that one can conceive of not being the child of what are in fact one's parents, and instead being the child of some other pair of people. This is conceiving of what is in fact impossible, and it does not seem that one can explain it along Kripkean lines. It is not a case of imagining someone else, whom one mistakes for oneself, being the child of those other people. If I imagine myself being the child of different parents, I do not identify myself by any set of features, so my conception cannot be charged with insensitivity to "the distinction between myself and a mere counterpart, a mere 'fool's self,' as it were, sharing the surface features by which I identify myself but differing in essence" (Wright, p. 436). Another case is that of a mathematician who conceives of finding counterexamples to Fermat's Last Theorem and finding mistakes in Andrew Wiles's proof of it – when in fact the proof is correct and the theorem is necessarily true. One certainly should not say that his conceivings "are insensitive to the distinction between finding counter-examples to Fermat's theorem and finding counter-examples to an *epistemic counterpart* of it" (p. 437). What we have in both these cases, Wright says, is insensitivity to the distinction "between genuinely conceiving of a scenario in which P fails to obtain and conceiving, rather, what it would be like if, *per impossibile*, P were found to be false" (p. 437). He remarks that for a large number of impossibilities, there are "determinate ways things would seem if they obtained." This would apply to the impossibility, supposing it to be such, of pain existing without C-fiber stimulation, or vice versa. So why should the conceivability of this not be like the mathematician's imagining himself refuting Fermat's Last Theorem, or someone's imagining finding that he has parents other than what in fact are his actual ones? Wright does not reject the Counter-Conceivability Principle, but holds that "it provides no practical controls at all on the ascription of necessity in cases where necessity would follow from truth – as is the situation of all potential necessities a posteriori" (p. 438).

David Papineau has the example of a woman who has picked up from her community the names "Cicero" and "Tully" but does not have any beliefs that distinguish their referents.[10] Although it is a necessary truth that Cicero is Tully, she might think it possible, and might even think it is true, that Cicero is not Tully. And this would not be a matter of there being some genuine possibility that she mistakenly takes to be the possibility that Cicero is not Tully.

Something frequently pointed out is that the *epistemic* possibility of something is compatible with its being *metaphysically* impossible. In Papineau's example it was epistemically possible for the woman, possible to the best of her knowledge, that Cicero is not Tully. Prior to learning of Wiles's proof, it was for the rest of us epistemically possible that Fermat's Last Theorem was false. Of course, something's being epistemically possible for one is compatible with one's realizing that it is either necessarily true or necessarily false; it isn't always true that when the truth of a proposition is epistemically possible for one that it is also epistemically possible for one that its logical status is that of being contingent – this wasn't true of Fermat's Last Theorem before it was proved. But if one doesn't realize that a proposition is such that it is either necessarily true or necessarily false, or doesn't have this fact in mind, its being epistemically possible for one is likely to lead one to think it is metaphysically possible that it is true, and that if true it is contingently true. When Wright says that for a large number of impossibilities, there are "determinate ways things would seem if they were true," he seems to be speaking of the ways things could seem such that imagining things seeming in one of those ways could make the corresponding impossibility epistemically possible for one. Speaking of having different parents from what he in fact has, he says "I can, it seems, lucidly imagine my finding all this out tomorrow" (p. 435). If he had any doubts about his actual parentage, and was ignorant of the essentiality of origins, this would make his having those other parents epistemically possible for him, and would lead to his having the belief that it is metaphysically possible.

So one response to Kripke's argument, one that would seem in line with what Wright says, is to say that what is directly shown by the imaginability of pain without C-fiber stimulation, or vice versa, is that these situations are, or can be, epistemically possible for us, that this does not imply that they are metaphysically possible, but that it can easily lead to the impression that they are. The idea is not that we first judge that something is epistemically possible and then conclude that it is metaphysically possible; anyone who is clear about what epistemic possibility is would realize that this would be a bad inference. It is rather that the fact that something is epistemically possible for one leads to the judgment "It's possible," which is true if taken as a statement of epistemic possibility but is mistakenly taken as a judgment of metaphysical possibility. The mistake is easy to make except when one is aware, as we normally are in the case of mathematical propositions, that the proposition in question is either a necessary truth or a necessary falsehood. Christopher Hill's account can be seen as describing a kind of circumstance in which the separability of A and B is epistemically possible for us without being metaphysically possible; this can happen when the ways A and B are imagined or conceived differ in the manner Hill described (for example, one is imagined perceptually and the other is imagined sympathetically). And Richard Boyd's account describes a way in which it could be epistemically possible for us that there is pain without C-fiber stimulation, or vice versa, compatibly with pain being identical with C-fiber stimulation. One imagines being in pain while having good perceptual evidence that there is no C-fiber stimulation going on. This could occur even if pain were identical with C-fiber stimulation, but only because the perceptual evidence could be due to misperception or instrument failure. Notice that this is not a case of imagining one genuine metaphysical possibility and mistaking it for another, analogous to Kripke's case of imagining a case in which something other than molecular motion is the standard cause of the sensation of heat, and mistaking the possibility of this for the possibility of heat without molecular motion. There being evidence of pain without C-fiber stimulation is undoubtedly metaphysically possible, but one does not mistake this possibility for the possibility of pain without C-fiber stimulation. No genuine possibility is mistaken for the latter possibility; it is simply that the epistemic possibility of this, stemming from the possibility (or seeming possibility) of there being such evidence, leads to the intuition that it is metaphysically possible, an intuition that is mistaken if in fact pain is C-fiber stimulation.

It might be objected to Papineau's Tully/Cicero example that there is a genuine possibility that the woman could mistakenly take to be the possibility that Cicero is not Tully, namely the possibility that two terms acquired in the way she acquired these should have different referents. But this is not an application of Textbook Kripkeanism. We would have an application of Textbook Kripkeanism if the woman associated different descriptions with the names "Cicero" and "Tully," and it was a genuine possibility that the descriptions be satisfied by different people; that would give us a "presentation" of the nonidentity proposition whose possibility might be mistaken for its possibility. In Papineau's example there is no such presentation. In any case, if we count the possibility of "Cicero" and "Tully" having different referents as a possibility that Papineau's woman might mistake for the possibility of Cicero not being Tully, it is unclear why we shouldn't count the possibility of "pain" and "C-fiber stimulation" having different referents as a possibility that we mistake for the possibility of pain not being C-fiber stimulation, when the latter seems to us a genuine possibility. To counter this, one would have to maintain that while what Papineau's woman knows about how she acquired the terms "Cicero" and "Tully" leaves it open whether they have the same referent, what we know about how we acquired the terms "pain" and "C-fiber stimulation" does not leave it open whether they have the same referent. And that is far from obvious.

Let's return to Kripke. He formulates his strategy for explaining the apparent contingency of certain cases of the necessary a posteriori as follows: "The strategy was to argue that although the statement itself is necessary, someone could, *qualitatively* speaking, be in the same epistemic situation as the original, and in such a situation a *qualitatively* analogous statement could be false" (*NN*, p. 150). This might be read as saying that while the statement, say that heat is molecular motion, is true and necessary, one might be in an epistemic situation that make its falsehood epistemically possible. But Kripke evidently means something slightly stronger – that in the qualitatively identical epistemic situation a metaphysical possible situation is presented to one, and one mistakes the possibility of it for the possibility of the falsity of the original statement. His claim is that this strategy fails in the case of "Pain is C-fiber stimulation" – when we imagine pain without C-fiber stimulation, we cannot be conceiving of some other possibility that we mistake for the possibility of pain without C-fiber stimulation. But one wonders why the explanation in terms of epistemic possibility is not enough; why must there be a genuine metaphysical possibility that is mistaken for the possibility of the situation imagined or conceived of? And if it is enough, why don't we have a way of reconciling the claim that pain is C-fiber stimulation with the imaginability or conceivability of pain without C-fiber stimulation, namely saying that the imaginability establishes only the epistemic possibility of pain without C-fiber stimulation, and that this is compatible with its metaphysical impossibility?

The view that conceiving of something that is metaphysically impossible requires there being a genuine metaphysical possibility one mistakes for the possibility of what one conceives is what Yablo calls Textbook Kripkeanism. Yablo explicitly refrains from claiming that Kripke himself endorses Textbook Kripkeanism. But as I have indicated, Kripke's argument seems to commit him to it. The one reason I can see for questioning whether he holds it is that in one or two places he leaves it open whether physical necessity is necessity "in the highest degree," that is, I take it, metaphysical necessity (see *NN*, p. 99). The view that physical necessity, or nomological necessity, is a special case of metaphysical necessity is one that others have defended.[11] For all we know, the laws of nature rule out the possibility of there being states of affairs other than molecular motion that standardly produce sensations of heat, of there being substances other than H_2O that are phenomenally indistinguishable from it, and of there being a substance other than gold that passes all of the layperson's and jeweller's tests for being gold. If the necessity of those laws is metaphysical necessity, these things are metaphysically impossible; and in that case, Textbook Kripkeanism is false. But it is not easy to see how Kripke could hold this, or even allow it as a possibility, while arguing as he does against psychophysical identities involving pain. For rejecting Textbook Kripkeanism seems to require rejecting the contrast Kripke draws between the seeming possibility of heat without molecular motion and the seeming possibility of pain without C-fiber stimulation (where,

---

[11] See Shoemaker (1980) and Swoyer (1982).

again, C-fiber stimulation stands in for any physical event type that is a candidate for being pain). And given that the former seeming possibility is not a genuine one, the lack of this contrast seems to leave it open that the latter seeming possibility is also not a genuine one.

The intuition that pain cannot be C-fiber stimulation, or any other physical state, has many sources, and most professed physicalists acknowledge its force. The mind/body problem will not be fully solved until we have an understanding of its sources sufficient either to vindicate the intuition or to convincingly explain it away. This state has not been achieved; but such progress as has been made towards achieving it is due in good part to the debate generated by Kripke's arguments.

References

Boyd, R. 1980. "Materialism without Reductionism: What Physicalism Does Not Entail." In N. Block, ed., *Readings in Philosophical Psychology*, vol. I. Cambridge: Harvard University Press.

Hill, C. 1997. "Imaginability, Conceivability, Possibility and the Mind-Body Problem," *Philosophical Studies*, 87, 61–85.

Hill, C. and McLaughlin, B. 1999. "There Are Fewer Things in Reality Than Are Dreamt of in Chalmers's Philosophy," *Philosophy and Phenomenological Research*, 64: 2, 445–54.

Kripke, S. 1980. *Naming and Necessity*. Cambridge: Harvard University Press.

    1971. "Identity and Necessity." In M. Munitz, ed., *Identity and Individuation*. New York: New York University Press.

Lewis, D. 1980. "Mad Pain and Martian Pain." In N. Block, ed., *Readings in Philosophical Psychology*, vol. I. Cambridge: Harvard University Press.

Nagel, T. 1979. "What Is It Like to Be a Bat?" In Nagel, *Mortal Questions*. Cambridge: Cambridge University Press.

Papineau, D. 2002. *Thinking About Consciousness*. Oxford: The Clarendon Press.

Putnam, H. 1975. "The Meaning of Meaning." In *Mind, Language, and Reality*. Cambridge: Cambridge University Press.

Shoemaker, S. 1980. "Causality and Properties." In P. van Inwagen, ed., *Time and Cause*. Dordrecht, Netherlands: D. Reidel Publishing Co.

Swoyer, C. 1982. "The Nature of Causal Laws," *Australasian Journal of Philosophy*, 60.

Yablo, S. 2000. "Textbook Kripkeanism and the Open Texture of Concepts," *Pacific Philosophical Quarterly*, 81, 98–122.

Wright, C. 2002. "The Conceivability of Naturalism." In T. Szabo Gendler and J. Hawhorne, eds., *Conceivability and Possibility*. Oxford: Clarendon Press.

14

Not Even Computing Machines Can Follow Rules

Kripke's Critique of Functionalism

Jeff Buechner

ABSTRACT

Saul Kripke's refutation of functionalism, unlike any previous attempts at a refutation, is a corollary of his work in *Wittgenstein: On Rules and Private Language*; in particular, it is a corollary of the arguments against dispositionalist (and extended dispositionalist) solutions to the meaning normativity paradox. Kripke's attack is, as he acknowledges, the weakest possible, since it focuses on what many take to be the strongest aspect of functionalism: that a physical computing machine embodies the abstract diagrams of a mathematical automaton. However, any physical computing machine imperfectly realizes those abstract diagrams, since physical machines may either break down or malfunction. Indeed, that they do so is something we know only if we assume that the physical computing machine computes the function that we take it to compute. If it does not compute that function, then what we take to be a breakdown might, in fact, be part of its normal conditions of operation. That is, it might be computing a different function and not undergoing a breakdown of any sort at all. Unless we idealize its behavior, it might compute any function at all. But how we idealize its behavior depends upon what function we take it to compute. In the absence of idealizing its behavior, we don't know what function it computes. But we can only idealize its behavior if we already know what function it computes.

If we know the intentions of the designer of the physical computing machine, then we know what function it computes. (Similarly, if we know the intentions of the user of a word or expression, such as 'plus', then we know that they mean the arithmetical function 'plus' when they use the word 'plus'. But there are no facts that determine that one's intention is to use the word 'plus' for the arithmetical function 'plus' when one uses the word 'plus'.) However, it is preposterous to think we can find the designer of human minds. For whose mind would count as the paradigm mind? Any such candidate would itself be subject to the problems Kripke raises for physical computing machines. In which case, functionalism is a vacuous theory of the human mind, since we can't know what functions it computes unless we already know what functions it computes.

Kripke observed that there is a deep connection between his arguments against functionalism and his arguments against dispositionalist solutions to his skeptical paradox. Alan Berger has observed a deeper connection, between the arguments against functionalism, the arguments against dispositionalist solutions to the skeptical paradox, and Kripke's arguments against the tenability of alternative logics.

INTRODUCTION

In footnote 24 in *Wittgenstein on Rules and Private Language*,[1] Saul Kripke provides several remarks that point in the direction of a full-scale attack upon functionalism, the important and still widely held doctrine in the philosophy of mind that provides an answer to the mind/body problem. He says he "hope[s] to elaborate on these remarks elsewhere."[2] Within two years of the publication of *Wittgenstein*, Kripke delivered several public lectures in which he delivered his refutation of functionalism, greatly amplifying the remarks made in footnote 24.[3] One of them – the Kirchberg-am-Wechsel lecture – has been transcribed (though it has never been published). Our purpose here is to give the reader a simple and detailed exposition of Kripke's refutation of functionalism.[4]

---

[1] Saul Kripke, *Wittgenstein on Rules and Private Language*, Cambridge: Harvard University Press, 1982. Footnote 24 is on pp. 35–7.

[2] *Wittgenstein*, p. 37.

[3] The Kirchberg-am-Wechsel lecture – entitled "Lessons on Functionalism and Automata" – took place on August 23, 1984, as an invited lecture at the International Wittgenstein Symposium. There are two transcriptions of this lecture. The second was made by Roderick Chisholm in September 1984. The two transcriptions are notated in the Kripke Archives as KR-M56 and KR-M57. (The Chisholm transcription is KR-M57.) There is also a tape recording in the Kripke Archives of the antifunctionalism lecture he gave at Duke University on April 1, 1984, the Patterson Lecture (notated as KR-T352).

[4] There is an important difference between the antifunctionalist lectures and the views expressed in *Wittgenstein*. In the latter, Kripke is expounding Wittgenstein's views and is not committed to holding any of them. That is not true of his antifunctionalist lectures. In these lectures he explicitly notes that he speaks in his own voice and that he believes what he says is true. In the Patterson lecture he remarks: "What I have to say is, I think, as far as it goes, true. It is inspired at least in part by thinking about Wittgenstein and reading him, but I don't profess to speak with his voice tonight, but rather with my own."

One source of the power and fascination of functionalism lies in our intuition, corroborated in our observations of actual computing machines, that it is easy for them to follow finite sets of finitary instructions. Indeed, that is what we take one essential feature of all classical computing machines to be: the ability to correctly follow finite sets of finitary instructions. The guiding idea of functionalism is that there is a level of description at which human minds have the same computational powers as computing machines. Conceiving of our mental capacities on the model of a computing machine is a natural and sound way both to stave off skepticism about the epistemic reliability of those capacities and to provide a scientific metaphysics for mental states. The computational mechanism underlying the mental actions of a human being could provide a clear account of what those actions consist in and how they work. As Jerry Fodor – functionalism's well-known advocate – has remarked, the computer model of the mind is the only one that gives us a plausible account of how human thinking preserves truth and of how natural languages can have combinatorial structure, enabling such features as systematicity and productivity.[5] The modern cognitive revolution in psychology arises out of conceiving of the mind as a computational device.

What makes Kripke's refutation of functionalism different from all of the other attempts in the literature to refute it is that he attacks functionalism at its strongest link, rather than at any of its weaker links. "My intention is to give the weakest attack possible, or rather, to put it differently, I intend to criticize functionalism on what I myself think is its strongest rather than its weakest link."[6]

The core idea of Kripke's refutation of functionalism is that functionalists fail to recognize a deep problem engendered by the distinction central to functionalism: namely, "the distinction between the abstract diagram of an abstract mathematical automaton, which can be realized by a physical machine in various ways, and the physical machines themselves that realize the diagram."[7] The deep problem is that the abstract diagrams of an abstract mathematical automaton are only imperfectly realized in physical computing machines (PCM). One cannot read off

---

[5] Jerry Fodor, *Representations: Philosophical Essays on the Foundations of Cognitive Science*, Cambridge: MIT Press, 1981. Fodor also criticizes machine functionalism. See *The Modularity of Mind*, Cambridge: MIT Press, 1983, and *The Mind Doesn't Work That Way*, Cambridge: MIT Press, 2000.

[6] KR-M56, p. 1.

[7] KR-M56, pp. 2–3.

the function computed by a PCM from its physical causal behavior. To do that, its physical behavior must be idealized. But the choice of an idealization depends upon what its designer intends it to compute. There are no physical facts that conclusively determine the function it computes. If we do not already know what function it computes, we will not know how to idealize its behavior. Its physical behavior cannot determine which function it computes. Thus, what function it computes is determined solely by the intentions of its designer. What is shocking and original about Kripke's refutation of functionalism is that it shows functionalism is an incorrect account of how both human minds and PCMs – such as your new Dell laptop – work.

Kripke is claiming that there is nothing intrinsic to human beings that determines that we are – if we conceive of ourselves as computers – instantiating a certain program or computing a certain function or following a certain rule. Different external observers can justifiably take one and the same human being to be computing different functions, instantiating different programs, and following different rules.

FUNCTIONALIST CONCEPTIONS OF THE MIND

Functionalism is an important doctrine in twentieth-century philosophy since it provides an answer to ancient questions about the human mind that are the bread and butter of philosophy. Pitched at a general level, they can be appreciated by the nonphilosopher: What makes a mind a mind? What is the nature of thinking? What is the nature of pain? In virtue of what are pains different from thoughts?

Functionalism makes a bold move: rather than looking at the physical realizations of mental properties, it focuses instead on what is common to all beings to whom mental properties are ascribed – namely, the causal roles (or causal functions) defining those mental properties. Taken as a theory of the metaphysical nature of the mind, functionalism abstracts away from the specifics of how minds are physically realized and takes the nature of the mind to consist in essential functional properties.

The literature distinguishes two broad types of functionalism: machine functionalism and causal-theoretical functionalism.[8] There are family resemblances between each broad type and there is substantial

---

[8] For a perspicuous discussion of machine and causal-theoretical functionalism, see Jaegwon Kim, *Philosophy of Mind*, Boulder, Colo.: Westview Press, 1996, pp. 73–124.

crosscutting among specific kinds of functionalism falling under the two broad types. Moreover, orthogonal to this distinction is a twofold distinction between analytic (or a priori) functionalism and scientific functionalism (or psychofunctionalism). The latter distinction corresponds to whether functional states are empirically verified to be true (scientific functionalism) or are true as a matter of definition (analytic functionalism). Most cognitive scientists eschew analytic functionalism, adopting instead scientific functionalism. It would be hard for a cognitive scientist to swallow, for example, the view that seeing the edges of objects is, by definition, computing the rate of change of the rate of change of light intensity arrays. From the standpoint of cognitive science, it appears absurd to say that a mental state is, by definition, a computational state.

Machine – or computational – functionalism is the view that human psychology can be represented by a computational model, such as a Turing machine or a probabilistic automaton.[9] Hilary Putnam first conceived of the idea that mental states could be characterized functionally in terms of a computing machine.[10] Causal-theoretical functionalism conceives of human psychology as a causal network in which input states, mental states, and output states are causally connected. Mental states (and mental kinds, such as pains) are distinguished from one another by the network of causal relations in which they are situated. For instance, the mental kind pain is individuated by its causes, effects, and relations with other mental states. Typically, folk psychology provides the theory of the set of causal connections and how each state is described.

In his lectures on functionalism, Kripke claims, without further elaboration, that every variety of functionalism is refuted by his argument.[11] The causal-theoretical functionalist does not conceive of the human mind as a computing machine, but rather as instantiating the states of commonsense "folk" psychology. Whatever level of abstraction causal-theoretical functionalists choose for their total psychological

9 Jerry Fodor, *The Mind Doesn't Work That Way* (and elsewhere), distinguishes "the functionalist program in metaphysics... the idea that mental properties have functional essences" from "the computational program in psychology" (p. 105 n. 4). Kripke's problem symmetrically undermines both programs.
10 Hilary Putnam, "Minds and Machines," "Brains and Behavior," and "The Mental Life of Some Machines," collected in *Mind, Language and Reality, Philosophical Papers*, vol. 2, Cambridge: Cambridge University Press, 1975. For an overview of functionalism, see Ned Block's introduction to Ned Block (ed.) *Readings in Philosophy of Psychology*, vol. 1, Cambridge: Harvard University Press, 1980, as well as his introduction to part three.
11 KR-M56, p. 2.

theory, they must employ the distinction between the abstract states of an abstract causal network and the purely physical states of the brain realizing that causal network. But that *is* the basic distinction that gives rise to Kripke's problem for functionalism. It does not matter whether the abstract causal connections in the abstract causal network constituting the total psychological theory of human beings can or cannot be modeled in a computational structure. Kripke's refutation of functionalism demands only that the functionalist posits a distinction between an abstract diagram and the physical object physically realizing it. Causal-theoretical and machine functionalists make that distinction. That is why Kripke's refutation of functionalism targets both of them.

ATTACKING FUNCTIONALISM ON ITS WEAKEST POINTS

Kripke's refutation of functionalism differs from all of the known critiques of it in the literature, which he collectively refers to as attacks on functionalism's weakest points. One well-known criticism he cites approvingly is that functionalists cannot account for the subjective character of experiences. Two different individuals might satisfy the same abstract causal diagram, but differ in the subjective character of their experiences. Another criticism is that it requires that a single psychological state be individuated in terms of the entire abstract causal diagram of the individual's total psychology. The state of being in pain will be a single node in the vast abstract network, but it is individuated in terms of the entire network. Change the network ever so slightly and the nature of the state of being in pain changes as well. For instance, when Jack is in pain and he believes that it is raining, he is in a different mental state than when he is in pain and he believes it is not raining. But surely the state of being in pain is the same regardless of one's beliefs about the weather. That is not to say that one's beliefs about the weather could not affect the quality of the pain state, nor even that they could not cause a pain state to come into existence. On the other hand, individuating a mental state in terms of the entire network of one's beliefs and desires leads to absurdity.

Other well-known criticisms of functionalism are that there are cognitive tasks that human beings can and that PCMs cannot do (such as establish the truth of a Gödel sentence), the labeling problem and the triviality problem (both discussed below), and the problem of precisely defining a psychological state computationally.

FINITE-STATE AUTOMATA, TURING MACHINES, AND COMPUTATIONAL MODELS OF COGNITION

An example of a human cognitive skill is the ability to add positive integers. On the machine functionalist view, humans who add two positive integers physically realize the abstract diagram of the addition function. Physical causal connections between distinct physical stages of a human being adding two positive integers are physical realizations of the transitions between computational states for addition defined by the abstract addition program. There are different computational models of computations.

One is the finite-state automaton, an abstract mathematical object defined over a finite set of internal states and an alphabet. An internal state specifies the overall condition of any of its components, and it changes state according to a transition function: given its current state and a symbol sequence from the alphabet, it transitions into its next state. The set of sequences of symbols recognized by a finite-state automaton is the language it recognizes. Mathematical problems are encoded as sentences in this language. Thus, we can characterize the set of mathematical problems solvable by a finite-state automaton by the language (or set of languages) it can recognize. The transition function for a finite-state automaton specifies everything there is to know about it. From this it does not follow that we know everything about the behavior of a PCM that physically realizes the abstract diagram of a finite-state automaton, since the physical realization may be imperfect. A virtue of machine functionalism defined over PCMs is that we have both a precisely defined reduction class for and a complete description of mental properties and events.

Finite-state automata cannot analyze anything more complex than simple linear patterns. They fail on the simple hierarchical parse trees of context-free languages. In the theory of grammar, Noam Chomsky proved in the 1950s that natural languages cannot be analyzed by finite-state automata because their grammars, minimally, have the structure of context-free languages. (Pumping lemmas provide mathematical proofs that there are languages that cannot be recognized by finite-state automata – and thus mathematical problems that cannot be solved by them.)

Turing machines are computational models that are much more powerful than finite-state automata. All partial recursive functions (which, if Church's thesis is true, exhaust the computable functions) can be computed by a universal Turing machine. It consists of an infinite tape divided into infinitely many sections on which symbols can be inscribed or erased and a reading device that scans a single section of the tape and then acts according to its state transition diagram. The reading head can erase the symbol currently on the section it is scanning (if there is a symbol), inscribe a new symbol (if there is now no symbol on the scanned section), or do nothing to that section of the tape. It then advances the tape either one section to the right or one section to the left.

Turing machines possess a (potentially) infinite amount, and finite-state automata a small, finite amount, of internal memory. An elementary result in computability theory shows there are simple arithmetical functions requiring either an unbounded amount of memory or an unbounded number of internal states in the computational model in which they are computed. This is not true of addition, but it is true of multiplication. Thus a finite-state automaton and a Turing machine can both add, but no finite-state automaton can multiply. Since finite-state automata have a very small amount of memory and a finite number of internal states, there will always be multiplication problems any given finite-state automaton cannot solve that a Turing machine, because it has unlimited memory capacity, can solve. So no finite-state automaton can abstractly realize the diagram of the multiplication function. However, it is unlikely the Turing machine model fits us, since it has infinitely many and we have only finitely many memory cells. If so, the computational model that best fits us is either a finite-state or a probabilistic finite-state automaton. But in that case we cannot multiply!

KRIPKE'S PROBLEM FOR FUNCTIONALISM

Pocket calculators cannot multiply, since they physically realize finite-state automata. Yet we unhesitatingly use them to multiply and don't question the results when we know they are functioning properly. Why do this if they cannot physically realize the multiplication function? PCMs suffer breakdowns, have finite lifetimes, and cannot accommodate infinitely many memory cells. The abstract diagrams of the functions they compute have no such limitations nor do they suffer breakdowns. If we look at their physical behavior, it will never match the abstract diagram of the functions they compute. We must idealize their physical behavior so that it properly aligns with the abstract diagrams that, in reality and without idealization, they imperfectly realize. The engineer who designed the pocket calculator knows finite-state automata cannot, and Turing machines can, multiply. But if its physical behavior is idealized so that it has infinitely many memory cells, it will realize an abstract Turing machine. We make such remarks as: "If the pocket-calculator had N more memory cells (or N more states), it would be able to compute such-and-such multiplication problems." Kripke's problem for functionalism is that what functions we or a PCM compute are relative to how we or a PCM is idealized and that how we or a PCM is idealized is relative to the intentions of our designer. Two different designers of the same PCM can idealize it differently. What it computes for one designer may differ from what it computes for the other designer, even though each designer idealizes the same physical object.

THE TRIVIALITY PROBLEM

There are two vexing problems for functionalism that are not Kripke's problem. The triviality argument against machine functionalism is surprisingly robust. Triviality arguments originated with Ian Hinckfuss, Hilary Putnam, and John Searle in the mid-1960s.[12] A triviality argument claims that any physical object computes any abstract function. These arguments are driven by the looseness of the definition of what it is for a physical system to physically realize an abstract computational state. Where there are insufficiently many constraints on what counts as a genuine physical realization of an abstract computational state, we can find computational states in any physical system.

How is the relation of physical realization, as in "physical object PO physically realizes abstract mathematical object MO," defined? A minimal requirement is that PO be interpreted so that it represents MO. If MO is a computational state in a sequence of computational states, we cannot do with just a structureless PO. It must be structured in terms of physical states that correspond to computational states. There is leeway as to how we can interpret the PO. Without empirical and a priori constraints on what counts as an interpretation, we are free to view "interpretation" as we please.

For instance, we can build it into the interpretation that PO represents function F. By specifying physical conditions PO always satisfies, we ensure that it enters into a succession of causally connected physical states that represent the succession of abstract computational stages in

---

[12] For a critical discussion of triviality arguments (especially Putnam's triviality theorem) and Searle's metaphysics of computation, see Jeff Buechner, *Gödel, Putnam, and Computational Functionalism*, Cambridge: MIT Press, 2007, chapters 4–6.

the computation of F. Suppose we take as PO a car key, which has the trivial physical property of being extended throughout the time interval [To,..., Tn]. We interpret the succession of physical states of the car key throughout [To,..., Tn] as the representations of the sequence of computational states in the computation of a value of F. In this way, your car key will compute a set of values of F while you are driving to work.

The triviality problem is not Kripke's problem for functionalism. To see this, assume the triviality problem has been solved. Select for a PCM a PO that satisfies the definition of an authentic physical realization relation with respect to a particular MO. But since the PO we use as a PCM only imperfectly realizes the abstract diagram of the MO it computes, we do not know which function it computes until we know the intentions of its designer.

THE LABELING PROBLEM

The labeling problem concerns how we label input, output, and internal states of either a PCM or a human being. How we label their input and output states determines the kinds of objects computed. There are blatant examples of this problem. John's output behavior consists of agonizing cries. Should we label this pain behavior or pleasure behavior? Kripke remarks in his Patterson lecture that we could label the states of a human being so that the person sees with their ears and hears with their eyes. This labeling would not destroy the isomorphism of the abstract functional diagram of that bizarre human being with the abstract functional diagram of a normal human being who hears with his ears and sees with his eyes.

The labeling problem is different from the triviality problem. It arises for physical systems performing genuine computations and for those performing trivial computations. Suppose that the labeling problem is solved. Even so, Kripke's problem for functionalism remains, since PCMs don't perfectly realize abstract state diagrams. It arises no matter how we label the input and output states of a PCM.

THE ROLES OF IDEALIZATION AND ABSTRACTION IN SPECIFYING FUNCTIONAL STATES

A PCM described at the physical level obeys the laws of physics. It is subject to breakdowns and has a finite lifetime (bounded from above by the heat death of the universe). When a PCM either malfunctions or goes out of existence, it ceases to realize the abstract state diagram of whatever F it computes. It is precisely because PCMs imperfectly realize their abstract state diagrams that in attributing functions or programs to them we must engage in both idealization and abstraction.[13] If we lived in a world in which (i) malfunctions of any kind cannot occur, (ii) PCMs last forever – a world without error of any kind, (iii) we knew this to be so, and (iv) we were immortal, then Kripke's problem for functionalism would not arise. However, if PCMs never malfunctioned, but lasted only a finite time, Kripke's problem would still arise, since there are infinitely many functions that are in accord with any finite segment of input and output behavior of any PCM.

We must idealize even to claim that a PCM is in error. If we do not already know that it computes F, we will not know whether a given output is an error. *If* it computes F, then if the output is not in the range of F, an error has been made. But *if* it computes G, and the output that is not in the range of F is in the range of G, an error has not been made. For any kind of error (relative to F) a PCM makes, there is some function G for which it is not an error, but a condition of normal operation. Similarly, we must idealize even to claim that a PCM is operating normally. If we do not already know that it computes F, we will not know whether a given output is an instance of normal functioning. *If* it computes F, then if the output is in the range of F, it is an instance of normal functioning. But *if* it computes G, and the output that is in the range of F is not in the range of G, then an error has been made and so the PCM is not functioning normally. And if there are functions whose range values agree with the range values of F for the observed outputs, we cannot determine if it computes F or one of the other functions. If we do not know it computes F, we cannot take outputs that belong to the range of F as evidence for it computing F and we cannot take outputs that do not belong to the range of F as evidence for it not computing F.

There are basic ways we can idealize a PCM. One idealization is that it does not break down. A second idealization is that it does not malfunction. A third idealization is that it has an infinite number of memory cells (or an infinite number of internal states). These idealizations are necessary if we want its physical behavior to physically realize the abstract diagrams of mathematical functions. Under one idealization it computes F, while under a different idealization it computes G. In the absence of an idealization, it is meaningless to assert that it intrinsically computes

[13] KR-M56, p. 13.

any function. Since idealizations are chosen by human beings, choice of a particular one only shows that the human being who chose it intends that it computes F.

All the idealizations we choose are false of actual PCMs. Those we choose will depend upon what we intend they compute. Can't we tell what they compute without idealizing their behavior and without idealizing that they compute F (in order to show they compute F), by showing conditionals about them are true? Consider (where the subscript 'I' means "idealized PCM" and the subscript 'A' means "actual PCM"):

(i) $Compute_I$ F → $Compute_A$ F

(ii) $Compute_A$ F → $Compute_I$ F

If these conditionals are true, we could read off the function a PCM computes from its physical behavior. But neither is true. Consider (i). If it is true that it computes F under idealization I, it may also be true that, considered *physically*, it computes G. For instance, it might malfunction. If it does and computes G, under its physical description it computes G. Since the abstract state diagrams are imperfectly realized in a PCM, what the actual PCM computes (without being idealized in any way) and what the idealized PCM computes are different. Consider (ii). Even if the PCM considered physically computes F, it can be false that it computes F when idealized. If it computes F only because it malfunctions (that is, it would not compute F if it did not malfunction), and the malfunction is idealized away, it will not compute F under the idealization.

What if a PCM never malfunctions? Can we read off its physical behavior the F it computes? No, we cannot. The reason why we cannot is that whether it operates normally is an idealization we make. Observing that it always operates normally depends upon that idealization. Thus to meaningfully say "That PCM never malfunctions" already supposes that an idealization has been made. If it computes F under the idealization, we can know both when it malfunctions and when it operates normally. Suppose it behaves, in the absence of an idealization as to what it computes, as though it is computing F. We cannot conclude that it *is* computing F nor can we conclude that it is not malfunctioning. If we had idealized it to compute G, then what is normal behavior for computing F is a malfunction in computing G. We cannot know when a PCM is malfunctioning or when it is behaving normally unless we idealize its behavior.

But surely one's pocket calculator adds independently of what anyone intends it to compute. If its designer disappeared from the face of the earth, it would still be true that it adds. Suppose everyone on earth disappears overnight and the following day rain falls on a pocket calculator and the pressure of the raindrops depresses its keys so as to add '2' and '2' to get the result '4'. Isn't it adding, even though there is no one to idealize its behavior?

Without anyone to idealize its physical behavior, it is unknown what function it is computing. It is only because we are situated in a social network in which we all agree what is being computed when we use pocket calculators that we take it for granted that they are, as an objective matter of fact, adding. However, there is no objective matter of fact what they calculate, independently of our intentions about what they calculate. Because (i) there is a gap between the actual physical behavior of a PCM and the abstract state diagram that it imperfectly realizes and (ii) the gap can be filled only by acknowledging the intentions of its designer, functionalism is an incorrect account of how any PCM works, since the intentions of its designer have been expunged in functionalist accounts of them.

That we have to idealize them even when we do not believe they malfunction is an important and cautionary moral. Its importance is that Kripke's problem arises even for PCMs that we are confident do not malfunction. It is cautionary because it is a warning that even what we take to be normal conditions of operation are relative to the intentions of the designer.

One idea the functionalist might use to undermine Kripke's problem is that malfunctions and normal conditions of operation can each be assigned to equivalence classes. If so, all PCMs will malfunction in similar ways and will function normally in similar ways. There is no need to appeal to the intentions of the designer of a particular PCM since malfunctions and normal conditions of operation are invariant from designer to designer.

But this response to Kripke's problem will not work. There is no finite bound on the distinct kinds of errors that any PCM might make because there are indefinitely many distinct physical processes that can result in it making an error. Assigning equivalence classes to all errors that output the number N categorizes the differences in causes of errors as the same. Outputting N because a microchip overheats and outputting N because of a conformational change in a molecule are not the same thing, even though each outputs N. One designer might take the hot microchip to be a malfunction, but the conformational change in the molecule to be normal. For each physical process a PCM undergoes that is an error relative to the intentions of one designer, there is another designer for whom it is not an error, but a normal condition of operation. Thus the error-inducing physical processes a PCM undergoes cannot be assigned to an equivalence class, since what is an error is not an intrinsic condition of it, but is relative to the intentions of its designers.

"THE FALSE CAN ALWAYS BE TURNED INTO THE TRUE BY INVOKING THE APPROPRIATE COUNTERFACTUAL"[14]

One functionalist response to Kripke's problem is to invoke counterfactuals to describe what a PCM would compute if it never malfunctions, lasts forever, and has infinitely many memory cells (or infinitely many internal states). These counterfactuals will provide us with the objective truth of the matter as to what it intrinsically computes, and that is independent of what anyone intends it computes.

The strategy of invoking counterfactuals to undermine Kripke's problem is irremediably defective. Suppose you see a paper bag and invoke the counterfactual: "If this paper bag had been filled with transistors [and more – the details are not needed here], it would compute the addition function." Yes, that is true. But it hardly shows that the paper bag intrinsically adds. The choice of an antecedent for the counterfactual about what functions a PCM computes depends upon how we idealize it and does not show what functions it intrinsically computes. A PCM does not intrinsically compute, since what it does compute is relative to the intentions of its designer.

The abstract causal state transition diagram is not the truth about the actual PCM, but is, rather, the truth about what would be the case if it were to behave in certain ways, although, in actuality, it does not. Given one set of designer intentions, one chooses a particular antecedent for the counterfactual, while given another set of designer intentions one chooses a different antecedent for the counterfactual. That the counterfactual comes out true in either case in no way uniquely determines the answer to the question of what F the PCM intrinsically computes.

We find in *Wittgenstein* a similar dismissal of counterfactuals. Adding ceteris paribus clauses to a dispositionalist account of what someone means when she uses the symbol '+' will not determine what she means. Kripke remarks: "But a disposition to make a mistake is simply a disposition to *give an answer other than the one that accords with the function I meant.* To presuppose this concept in the present discussion is of course blatantly

---

[14] The Patterson lecture (KR-T352 in the Kripke Archives).

circular."[15] This circularity arises in attempts to justify the claim that a PCM computes F by appealing to how we idealize it. The idealization we choose will depend upon the function we intend that it computes. That is why it is a fallacy of circularity to justify our claim that it computes F by appealing to the choice of an idealization for it. The idealization works only if we already know or we intend that it computes F.

In *Wittgenstein* Kripke argues that evaluating such counterfactuals may be indeterminate. He considers the case where his brain is stuffed with extra brain matter so he can compute the plus-function and not the quus-function. "How in the world can I tell what would happen if my brain were stuffed with extra brain matter, or if my life were prolonged by some magic elixir? Surely such speculation should be left to science fiction writers and futurologists.... The outcome really is obviously indeterminate, failing further specification of these magic mind-expanding processes; and even with such specifications, it is highly speculative."[16]

Some have argued that Kripke's claim that evaluation of such counterfactuals is highly indeterminate and speculative is false. Jerry Fodor, responding to the passage just quoted, writes: "Apparently Kripke assumes that we can't have reason to accept that a generalization defined for idealized conditions is lawful unless we can specify the counterfactuals which would be true if the idealized conditions were to obtain.... It is, however, hard to see why one should take this methodology seriously... if there are psychological laws that idealize to unbounded working memory... all we need to know is that, if we did have unbounded memory, then, ceteris paribus, we would be able to compute the value of m + n for arbitrary m and n. And *that* counterfactual *the theory itself tells us is true.*"[17]

I think Fodor misses the main point about the use of such counterfactuals to determine whether we are using the plus-function or the quus-function. If our theory is that we are using the plus-function, then the counterfactuals extending our capacities so that we compute the plus-function will agree with our theory. *But we want to know whether our theory is, in fact, true.* Do we, in fact, compute the plus-function? Kripke's point is that it is circular to determine that we compute the plus-function by first theorizing we do and then evaluating the appropriate counterfactuals under which we do in order to confirm the theory. If we already know our theory is true, then, of course, we know which are the appropriate

---

[15] *Wittgenstein*, p. 30.
[16] *Wittgenstein*, p. 27.
[17] Jerry Fodor, *A Theory of Content and Other Essays*, Cambridge: MIT Press, 1990, in the essay "A Theory of Content II," pp. 94–5.

counterfactuals for it and that the theory itself tells us they are true. It is false to say, as Fodor does, that Kripke claims we can't accept a generalization as lawful in the absence of specifying all the counterfactuals which would be true under idealized conditions. It is not Kripke's claim that we can't accept a generalization as being lawful in the absence of specifying the appropriate counterfactuals, but rather that it is circular reasoning to use those counterfactuals to demonstrate that we indeed have a genuine law.

That determining the truth of these counterfactuals is highly speculative is an additional problem in addition to the fundamental problem that using them to determine the F that we compute commits the fallacy of circular reasoning. Even if that problem were dissolved, the circularity problem for using counterfactuals to determine the F a PCM computes remains. It is the circularity problem that renders defective any attempt by the functionalist to appeal to counterfactuals to determine what F it computes. Even if one could evaluate such counterfactuals determinately and without speculation of any kind, it would be pointless to appeal to them to determine the F it computes.

THE FALLACY OF SOPHOMORIC RELATIVISM AND WHY FUNCTIONALISM MUST COMMIT IT

No cognitive scientist would want to say (or would want to be told) that the computations the human mind engages in depend upon the intentions of a designer. Can the dependency upon the intentions of the designer of a PCM be eliminated? If so, both functionalism and cognitive science escape Kripke's problem. To give the view that the dependency can be eliminated a run for its money, we need an account of the structure of relativity statements and how the relativity in relativity statements is eliminated.

Relativity statements are incomplete on their surface. For instance, vague words are incomplete on the surface, since the comparison class that would eliminate the vagueness does not explicitly accompany them. When we say "Frederick is fat," the comparison class that objectively determines who satisfies the property of being fat is implicit. Specify the comparison class and "Frederick is fat" ceases to be vague. We obtain a statement that is not relative to anything at all and that has an objective truth value. If people who are fat for the height of six feet weigh more than 230 pounds and Frederick is six feet tall and weighs 240 pounds, the statement 'Frederick is fat' is objectively true.

Kripke invites us to consider what it means for a predicate to be relative. If a predicate is relative, then it will have the superficial form of the predicate schema

$$P(x_1, x_2, x_3, \ldots, x_n).$$

The true form of the predicate schema for relativity statements is different from this, for it will have "hidden places" that do not explicitly appear in the predicate. We can emend the predicate schema to explicitly reflect these hidden places:

$$P(x_1, x_2, x_3, \ldots, x_n, y_1, y_2, y_3, \ldots, y_m)$$

where the y variables are the hidden places. The values of the x variables will depend upon the values of the y variables. Once all of the values of the x and y variables have been given, we have a predicate that is not relative to anything. If P denotes the predicate 'fat', then the y variables will specify the relevant properties of the comparison class used to determine who is fat. The important point is that once the hidden places have been filled in, the predicate is no longer relative to anything at all.

If it is either in principle impossible or infeasible to explicitly specify all of the hidden places, we are left with a sentence that is still relative to something. We do not yet know what it means, since we do not yet have all of the hidden places explicitly spelled out. Suppose that one hidden place itself depends upon another hidden place, ad infinitum. We then have an endless regress. Kripke calls any kind of relativity statement for which it is in principle impossible to specify all of the hidden places because the relativity theory requires us to fill in hidden places ad infinitum vulnerable to "sophomoric relativism." If a relativity statement succumbs to sophomoric relativism, then we will never know what the original relativity statement (with the superficial surface form) means.

Consider the relativity predicate COMPUTE(PCM, F). Although some of us may be under the illusion that this is an objective predicate not relative to anything, Kripke's problem for functionalism reveals to us that it is a relativity predicate. Let us conjecture the actual form of the predicate is $R(PCM, F, PG, C_1, C_2)$, where PG is the program that the PCM uses to compute F and C_1 and C_2 are the correspondence rules that determine, respectively, how we should interpret the input, output, and internal states of the PCM (thus solving the labeling problem) and how we should constrain the physical states of the PCM so that they are genuine physical realizations of computational states (thus solving the triviality problem).

The predicate COMPUTE(PCM, F) is a relativity predicate because that a PCM computes F is relative to the intentions of its designer. Two different designers might take it to compute different functions. For designer1, it computes F, while for designer2, it computes G. Designer1 will specify the program and correspondence rules it uses to compute F, while designer2 will specify the program and correspondence rules it uses to compute G. The predicate COMPUTE(PCM, F, PG, C_1, C_2,) is relative to the intentions of its designer. So we will need to specify that. There must be an additional hidden parameter for the intentions of its designer. The actual form of the predicate is:

$$\text{COMPUTE}(\text{PCM, F, PG, } C_1, C_2, D).$$

Even though this is an objective predicate not relative to anything at all, it shows that what F the PCM computes is relative to the intentions of its designer, D. The *predicate* has been derelativized, but the relative relation between what F the PCM computes and the intentions of its designer remains. Knowing the values of PCM, F, PG, C_1, C_2, and D, we can objectively evaluate the predicate P and determine the truth value of a sentence in which it figures – provided that all other sentential elements can be properly evaluated for truth.

A human mind *is* a PCM according to machine – or computational – functionalism. Which set of abstract functions does the human mind so described compute? We have already seen that all PCMs compute abstract functions only relative to a certain parameter, namely, the intentions of the designer of the PCM, since the physical causal history of any given PCM imperfectly realizes the abstract diagram of the function that it computes. Similarly, when we wish to say what functions the human mind conceived of as a PCM computes, we utter a relativity statement. The F that we, conceived of as a PCM, compute is relative to the intentions of a designer. Can this relativity to the intentions of a designer be eliminated?

Let's step back to look at the situation. We have a human being H_1 whose mental life is described from the point of view of machine functionalism. We have the relativity predicate $CC(H_1, F)$, where 'CC' stands for the predicate 'cognitively compute', for which we must specify and fill in its hidden parameters. We have another human being, H_2, who attributes to H_1 a distinct computational structure. So we have the predicate

(i) $CC(H_1, F, PG, C_1, C_2, H_2)$.

This predicate is obtained from the original relativity predicate by specifying and filling in the hidden parameters. Doing that results in a predicate that is no longer relative to anything (even though the relative relation of H1 to H2 remains). But according to functionalism, H2 also has a computational structure. So there is a predicate that characterizes her computational structure. It is

(ii) CC(H2, F, PG, C1, C2, H3).

From this it follows that (i) has not been derelativized. To derelativize (i) we need to substitute (ii) for H2 in (i) to get:

(iii) CC(H1, F, PG, C1, C2, CC(H2, F, PG, C1, C2, H3))

However, this predicate is not derelativized because according to functionalism, H3 has a computational structure, so there is a predicate that characterizes it. It is:

(iv) CC(H3, F, PG, C1, C2, H4).

Substituting (iv) for H3 in (iii) we get:

(v) CC(H1, F, PG, C1, C2, CC(H2, F, PG, C1, C2, CC(H3, F, PG, C1, C2, H4)))

This predicate is not derelativized, because according to functionalism, H4 has a computational structure. Since any Hi will be a human being who, according to functionalism, has a computational structure, it is easy to see that we will never arrive at a predicate for the computational structure of H1 (nor for any Hi) that is fully derelativized. Rather, the predicate has hidden places that depend endlessly on other hidden places. The relativity statement expressed by the predicate succumbs to sophomoric relativism.

Machine functionalism is vulnerable to sophomoric relativism. Can this vulnerability be ameliorated (or even eliminated) if human intentions are replaced by impersonal intentions embedded in Nature? Suppose the designer of human beings is Nature. We cannot appeal to Nature to derelativize a relativity statement by positing its intentions, for it does not have intentions. Suppose we attribute to Nature a telos. Then we will need to appeal to the notion of a telos in Nature to provide a metaphysics of human minds. The telos is simply a brute fact that makes it the case that we compute F and not some other function and thus our metaphysics is saddled with special brute facts.

Perhaps we can do better. Since human evolution is governed by Darwinian laws, we can appeal to evolutionary processes in determining the programs human minds instantiate. The problem is that this appeal will not specify a unique program we instantiate. For any program we conjecture we instantiate, there are infinitely many alternative programs, computing different functions, that all have survival value identical to that of the conjectured program. That is clear, since the finitely many data points we as machines compute when we instantiate some program are what was computed by what survived, and there are infinitely many different programs, computing different functions, which all agree on that finite set of data points.

It is thus not possible to eliminate the relativity of what function a PCM computes to the intentions of its designer, and so Kripke's problem for functionalism remains. The problem rules out *any* scientific study of the mind that envisions it as an information-processing device, which is the core idea underlying cognitive science.

STABLER'S OBJECTIONS TO KRIPKE'S ANTIFUNCTIONALIST ARGUMENT

Perhaps the only extended discussion in the literature of Kripke's refutation of functionalism is a paper by Edward P. Stabler.[18] The basic idea that underlies Stabler's attempt to answer Kripke's problem for functionalism is that when a PCM computes a function, a unique set of physical conditions obtain. For each function, there is a unique set of physical conditions that occurs when a PCM computes it. Knowledge of those physical conditions allows one to reliably read off the function the PCM computes.

Stabler provides an example that is stripped of any complexity that might obscure his exposition of how his basic idea works. He envisages a simple computing device – a single wire connecting an input and an output. This device computes the identity function. When N distinct voltage impulses are input to this PCM, it outputs N distinct voltage impulses. Stabler assumes, for the sake of the argument, that there is a legitimate correspondence relation mapping physical conditions into mathematical objects, such as positive integers. He thus sidesteps the triviality problem.

If the positive integer N is input to the wire as N voltage impulses, it will output the positive integer N as N voltage impulses. The physical condition that underlies this computation is that the wire conducts electrical impulses between the input and output terminals. Appealing to physical laws establishes that this physical condition will (ceteris paribus)

---

[18] Stabler, "Kripke on Functionalism and Finite Automata," *Synthese*, vol. 70 (1987), pp. 1–22. Stabler heard Kripke speak at York University, Toronto, in December 1983. There is a recording, but no transcription, of that talk in the Kripke Archives.

occur – that N electrical pulses will be transmitted from the input terminal to the output terminal of the wire when it is engineered in the proper way.

Stabler's key definition is:

A PCM computes the function F if, and only if, "there is an interpretation function IN which maps a set of finite sequences of physical 'input' states of the system onto the domain of F, and an interpretation function Out which maps a set of finite sequences of physical 'output' states onto the range of F, such that physical laws guarantee that (in certain circumstances C, and *if the system satisfied conditions of normal operation N for long enough*), if the system went successively through the states of an input sequence i, it would go successively through the states of the corresponding output sequence f where Out(f) = F(In(i))."[19]

Since there is little chance that the physical conditions that are necessary for computing the identity function will occur for temporal intervals of arbitrary size – breakdowns will happen – we must appeal to a counterfactual about what would have happened had the device not suffered a breakdown. The counterfactual is straightforward: if the physical conditions necessary for computing the identity function continued to obtain, the device would have computed the identity function.[20]

Stabler aptly calls the physical conditions that obtain when a PCM computes F the "conditions of normal operation."[21] He claims that to verify that a PCM computes F, we do not have to know the intentions of its designer, nor do we have to show that the PCM must satisfy some set of normative conditions, nor must we already know that it computes F. To verify that it computes F, we ascertain that the normal conditions of operation for it to compute occur. That is, we ascertain that the appropriate physical conditions for computing F actually occur.

For Stabler the proper form in which to express a computational claim that a PCM computes a function is not

(i)   PCM computes function F

but rather

(ii) Given interpretation I, circumstances C, and normal conditions of operation N, PCM computes function F.

[19] Stabler, "Kripke on Functionalism and Finite Automata," p. 11.
[20] Note that the phrase "physical conditions" in the antecedent of the counterfactual needs to be replaced with the actual physical conditions necessary for computing the identity function.
[21] Stabler, "Kripke on Functionalism and Finite Automata," p. 8.

When a PCM suffers a breakdown, (ii) remains true, even though (i) becomes false. And (ii) remains true because a PCM that suffers a breakdown will not fall within its scope, since N and/or C will fail to obtain. The virtue of Stabler's proposal is that it appears to define what it is for a PCM to compute F in terms of purely physical conditions. Kripke's problem for functionalism is that what F a PCM computes cannot be read off from a description of its purely physical conditions of operation. For Kripke, it is only the intentions of the designer of PCM that can couple its physical description to the abstract diagram of the F it computes.

It is easy to see that Stabler's account of when a PCM computes F requires that C, I, and N yield F and no other function G. If two or more functions satisfied the same physical description, we would still have Kripke's problem. Suppose that the physical description in terms of C, I, and N is satisfied by one and only one F. Then C, I, and N are necessary and sufficient for F. They are criterial for the presence of F. Thus all we need do – and this is what I take it Stabler's proposal recommends – is to register their presence when we wish to determine that a PCM computes F.

Stabler's wire device for computing the identity function provides a good case in point to test the recommendation. Any wire that satisfies C, I, and N computes the identity function. If we deny this, then we also deny the basic principles of electromagnetism – the laws that explain how our household electrical devices properly function. That the wire computer computes the identity function does not depend upon the intentions of its designer. If so, then Kripke's problem has been dissolved.

Let's now consider the wire computer from the point of view of its designer. To design it, he or she must know that the wire will conduct electrical impulses from one end to the other end and that there are physical laws which explain how this happens. Without that knowledge, the designer will have no guarantee that the wire does what he or she intends it to do – compute the identity function. The designer also needs to know that the wire would compute the identity function if it did not malfunction. That is, that C, I, and N would continue to obtain if the wire did not malfunction. However, in declaring that the wire would satisfy C, I, and N if it did not malfunction, we are idealizing its physical behavior according to our intention that it computes the identity function. Another designer with different intentions about what F the wire computes would idealize its physical behavior in another way. The problem with Stabler's proposal for defining the conditions under which a PCM computes F in terms of physical conditions is that appealing to what it would compute if it did not malfunction," is an idealization that is different from a mere description of the physical conditions it satisfies.

The idealization is voiced in the counterfactual: if the wire did not malfunction, then it would compute the identity function. But the choice of the appropriate counterfactual will vary from designer to designer. How might it happen that two different designers design the same wire but with different intentions? How could it compute anything but the identity function? Recall that the wire will, with virtual certainty, malfunction at some point in its history. We will need to appeal to the appropriate counterfactual in making our claim that it computes the identity function. If we do not know the intentions of its designer, we do not know whether he or she has designed a wire for which the appropriate counterfactual is the one we have cited – for which the wire computes the identity function, or some other counterfactual for which the wire computes a different function. Each counterfactual is a way of idealizing the actual physical behavior of the wire. Different idealizations of the wire's physical behavior reflect different views as to which F it computes. Specifying a particular counterfactual is equivalent to specifying the intentions of the wire's designer.

If we already know the wire computes the identity function, then we will know which counterfactual to employ to describe how we idealize its physical behavior. We can read off the F the wire computes from the counterfactual we choose for it, since that counterfactual presupposes that the wire computes F. What we cannot do is define the function that it computes in terms that advert to such counterfactuals, since if we do we are smuggling into the description of the wire's physical behavior the intentions of its designer. If we lived in a universe in which wires never malfunctioned and lasted infinitely long (and we knew this), Stabler's proposal would define how a wire computes F without appealing to the intentions of a designer, since the description of the physical conditions C and N would not need to advert to counterfactuals about what the wire would have done had it not malfunctioned.

Stabler's counterfactual "if the system had continued to satisfy the conditions of normal operation for long enough, it would have computed arbitrary values of the identity function,"[22] is defective, since the phrase "conditions of normal operation" is a surrogate for the function that is computed. Thus the emended counterfactual reads: "If the

---

[22] Stabler, "Kripke on Functionalism and Finite Automata," p. 9; italics are in the original.

system had computed the identity function for long enough, then it would have computed arbitrary values of the identity function." This is certainly true. Indeed, it is a tautology. But it cannot provide an answer to the problem of how to describe the idealization of a PCM purely in terms of its physical behavior and without bringing in the intentions of its designer.

It is circular to attempt to define the F a PCM computes in terms of its physical behavior, since an appeal must be made to the intentions of its designer via the counterfactuals that we want to be true of it when it malfunctions or operates normally. But the intentions of the designer are that it computes F. Thus the description of C, I, and N do not determine the F a PCM computes. Rather, they must advert to the F a PCM computes in order to imply that it computes F. Stabler's proposal is mired in circularity.

Stabler's proposal for avoiding Kripke's problem for functionalism succumbs to a dilemma: if we know the F a PCM computes, then we must antecedently have known the intentions of its designer. If we do not know the F it computes, then we must appeal to the intentions of its designer. Although Stabler's use of physical conditions appears prima facie to avoid adverting to the intentions of a designer, we have seen that the counterfactuals extending the physical behavior of the PCM through periods of malfunctioning must advert to such intentions. And so there is an ineliminable appeal to the intentions of the designer of a PCM in Stabler's account of how a PCM avoids Kripke's problem. Since Kripke's problem *is* that there is such an ineliminable appeal in functional accounts of what F a PCM computes, it is easy to see Stabler's proposal does not evade it.

THE FALLACY IN FUNCTIONALISM

We close with Kripke's statement of the fallacy he has uncovered in functionalism:

> The fallacy in the literature is simply this: they [the functionalists] take the physical object. Then they switch to an abstract causal program that it only approximately realizes and then they imagine me as if I were a physical object uniquely related to this program and actually instantiating it even though the first part, the unique relation, is explicitly admitted to be false. One can then easily read off from the program that I am multiplying.[23]

---

[23] The Patterson lecture (KR-T352 in the Kripke Archives).

Michael Dummett commits this fallacy in his well-known remark: "A machine can follow this rule; whence does a human being gain a freedom of choice in this matter which a machine does not possess?"[24] We have seen that we can never read off from the physical causal connections between the physical stages of a PCM the F that it computes. Functionalism is not only a false theory of how human minds work; it is also a false theory of how computing machines work. That a PCM or a human mind computes a function, instantiates a program, or follows a rule is relative to the intentions of its human designers. For both machines and humans as machines, there is an ineliminable element of choice as to what they compute. Two different designers will take the same PCM or the same human mind to be computing entirely different functions. That this is so is a consequence of Kripke's deep problem for functionalism.

[24] M. A. E. Dummett, "Wittgenstein's Philosophy of Mathematics," *The Philosophical Review*, vol. 68 (1959), pp. 324–48, at p. 331.

Index